# THE WORLD ON A PLATE

## 40 CUISINES, 100 RECIPES, AND THE STORIES BEHIND THEM

# MINA HOLLAND

PENGUIN BOOKS

PENGUIN BOOKS
Published by the Penguin Group
Penguin Group (USA) LLC
375 Hudson Street
New York, New York 10014

USA | Canada | UK | Ireland | Australia | New Zealand | India | South Africa | China
penguin.com
A Penguin Random House Company

First published as *The Edible Atlas* in Great Britain by Canongate Books Ltd 2014
Published as *The World on a Plate* in Penguin Books 2015

LIBRARY OF CONGRESS CATALOGING-IN-PUBLICATION DATA
Holland, Mina.
The world on a plate : 40 cuisines, 100 recipes, and
the stories behind them / Mina Holland.
pages cm
ISBN 978-0-14-312765-9
1. International cooking.   2. Food—History.   3. Food habits.   I. Title.
TX725.A1H5674 2015
641.59—dc23     2014042524

Printed in the United States of America
10  9  8  7  6  5  4  3  2  1

Set in Clavo Book and Granby
Designed by Rafaela Romaya
Symbols by Peter Adlington

• FOR MY GRANDMOTHERS •

# CONTENTS

# • THE MIDDLE EAST •

# • ASIA •

# • AFRICA •

# • THE AMERICAS •

○ Denotes Map/Diagram

# • THE WORLD ON A PLATE •

# INTRODUCTION

It is not just the great works of mankind that make a culture.
It is the daily things, like what people eat and how they serve it.
• LAURIE COLWIN, *Home Cooking* •

WHEN WE EAT, we travel.

Think back to your last trip. Which are the memories that stand out? If you're anything like me, meals will be in the forefront of your mind when you reminisce about travels past. Tortilla, golden and oozing, on a lazy Sunday in Madrid; piping hot *shakshuka* for breakfast in Tel Aviv; oysters shucked and sucked from their shells on Whitstable shingle. My memories of the things I saw in each of those places have acquired a hazy, sepia quality with the passing of time. But those dishes I remember in Technicolor.

As Proust noted on eating a *petit madeleine** with his tea, food escorts us back in time and shapes our memory. The distinct flavors, ingredients and cooking techniques that we experience in other spaces and times are also a gateway to the culture in question. What we ate in a certain place is as important, if not more so, than the other things we did there—visits to galleries and museums, walks, tours—because food quite literally gives us a taste of everyday life.

Whenever I go abroad my focus is on finding the food most typical of wherever I am, and the best examples of it. Food typifies everything that is different about another culture and gives the most authentic insight into how people live. Everyone has to eat, and food is a common language.

The late, great American novelist and home cook Laurie Colwin put everyday food alongside "the great works of mankind" in making a culture. I

• • • •

*Writers love referencing the Proustian moment—the point in *Remembrance of Things Past* at which young Marcel realizes the power of taste to invoke the past—perhaps because it somehow vindicates food, makes it a real "thing" recognized in literature, not just a sentimental fancy. Here's the quote in full: "Whence could it have come to me, this all-powerful joy? I sensed that it was connected with the taste of the tea and the cake, but that it infinitely transcended those savors . . . the whole of Combray and its surroundings, taking shape and solidity, sprang into being, town and gardens alike, from my cup of tea." Marcel Proust, *Swann's Way*.

have to agree. A baguette, the beloved French bread stick, is the canvas for infinite combinations of quintessential Gallic flavors (from cheese to charcuterie and more). It is steeped in history[*] and can arguably tell you more about French culture than Monet's lilies. Moroccan food expert Paula Wolfert, a beatnik of the 1960s who flitted from Paris to Tangier with the likes of Paul Bowles and Jack Kerouac, also relates to Colwin's words. "Food is a way of seeing people," she once said to me—such a simple statement, but so true. Unlike guidebooks and bus tours, food provides a grassroots view of populations as they live and breathe. When we eat from the plate of another culture, we grow to understand—mouthful by mouthful—what it is about.

Eating from different cultures is not just a way of seeing people: it can train a different lens on the food itself, too. I started eating meat again a few years ago after twelve years of being a (fish-eating) vegetarian. But while I was happy to try all sorts of cuts and organs, lamb still troubled me. I've loathed the fatty, cloying scent of roasting lamb since I was a child, an aversion that had become almost pathological. When I met Lebanese cook Anissa Helou for the first time, I casually slipped my antipathy for lamb into the conversation. Her jaw dropped. She told me this was impossible, that I couldn't write a book about the world's food without a taste for lamb. A few months later I was at her Shoreditch apartment eating raw lamb *kibbeh* (see page 170) and *devouring* it. Her delicately balanced homemade *sabe' bharat* (seven spice mix) didn't so much mask as complement the strong flavor of raw meat, which we ate with white *tabbouleh*. I might not like British roast lamb, the smell of which wafted around my grandparents' kitchen on many a Sunday, but it turns out I love raw lamb prepared in a Levantine kitchen. Persian *ghormeh sabzi* (lamb stew with herbs and kidney beans, see page 187) was also a revelation. Ingredients take on different guises in other cuisines, and this can transform our perception of them.

In recent years food has assumed a status analogous to film, literature and music in popular culture, expressing the tastes of society in the moment. Food manifests the zeitgeist. There are now global trends in food. In cosmopolitan cities from London to New York, Tokyo to Melbourne, crowds flock to no-reservations restaurants that serve sharing plates against a backdrop of distressed décor, or to street-food hawkers selling gourmet junk food and twee baked goods. Today's most famous food professionals—from the multi-Michelin-starred René Redzepi

• • • •

[*]One almost certainly apocryphal account has it that the baguette was developed during the Napoleonic Wars and was designed to fit down soldiers' trousers in order to economize on backpack space. In fact, long thin loaves have been a feature of French cuisine for hundreds of years, but the now standard baguette probably dates from the early twentieth century.

to neo-Middle Eastern pastry chef Yotam Ottolenghi and TV cook Nigella Lawson—are another facet to celebrity culture. They prize creativity in the kitchen, drawing on many different culinary and cultural influences to make dishes that are unique to them, for which society's food lovers have a serious appetite.

Amidst this enthusiasm for food and the growing fascination with culinary trends (which seem to change as frequently as the biannual fashion calendar), there are gaps in our knowledge about "pedigree" cuisines. Self-proclaimed "foodies" may know who David Chang[*] is, proudly order offal dishes in restaurants or champion raw milk over pasteurized alternatives, but can they pinpoint what actually makes a national or regional cuisine? How do you define the food of, say, Lebanon or Iran? What distinguishes these cuisines from one another? What are the principle tastes, techniques of cooking and signature dishes from each? In short, what and why do people eat as they do in different parts of the world?

Taking you on a journey around forty world cuisines, my aim is to demystify their essential features and enable you to bring dishes from each of them to life. Remember: when we eat, we travel. Treat this book as your passport to visit any of these places and sample their delicacies—all from your very own kitchen.

## • WHAT IS A CUISINE? •

AMERICAN ACADEMIC-CUM-FARMER Wendell Berry once said that "eating is an agricultural act," drawing attention to the fact that what we eat in a given place reflects the terrain and climate where local produce lives and grows. But this is an oversimplification, taking only geography into consideration.

In fact, a cuisine is the edible lovechild of both geography and history. Invasions, imperialism and immigration solder the influence of people's movement onto the landscape, creating cuisines that are unique to the place but, by definition, hybrid—like that of Sicily, where the Greeks, Romans, Normans, Arabs, Spanish, French and, most recently, Italians have all had their moment of governance. Today, Sicilian dishes express both the peoples that have inhabited the island and the rich Mediterranean produce available there.

••••

[*]The Korean-American chef and owner of the Momofuku restaurant group. Chang has two Michelin stars to his name and is also the coeditor of Lucky Peach. Each issue of the zeitgeisty food quarterly takes a theme like "Ramen," "American Food" and "Before and After the Apocalypse."

I have learned that no cuisine is "pedigree"; they are all mongrels, as hybrid as your average hound in the pound. Even those with the most distinctive national and regional character are the result of different human traditions being fused with physical geography and its produce.* Some cuisines are much younger than others—those of the New World, for example—but our knowledge of the more recent history in which they were formed proves a fascinating lesson in how a cuisine develops.

For example, we're going to travel to California (see page 297) not only because I have what might fairly be described as an overtly sentimental attachment to the place, but also because I believe that it has changed the way we look at food. Much of the food revolution that has taken place in recent years can be traced back to the Golden State and its distinctive approach to fusing its various inherited cooking traditions. They are the building blocks of something wholly new—derivative yet authentic.

I like to think of cuisines as stews—they often have the same or similar components as one another, but produce wildly different results. Consider how different Indian and Moroccan foods are, despite many fundamental similarities: clay-pot cooking, stewing and, most significantly, the specific spices they have in common: cumin, turmeric, cinnamon and infinite blends of these and others. As you'll see on the Spice Route map on pages 154–55, the interplay between terrain and people—geography and history—gives each cuisine I explore in this book a unique chemistry and individual magic.

## • HOW THIS BOOK WORKS •

ESTABLISHING AN EXHAUSTIVE DNA of forty world cuisines would be no mean feat. This book is intended to be an entry point only, a go-to guide for anyone with a fledgling curiosity about the building blocks that make up some of the world's key cuisines. It covers flavors and ingredients—which spices are used, whether oil or butter (or no fat at all) is favored—as well as how things are cooked and served. I've highlighted key features of each cuisine in the Pantry Lists, your essential shopping list for each cuisine we visit on our journey. I've also given you a few really typical recipes from each

• • • •

*There is, however, an important difference between this—the gradual fusion of geography and history to form a cuisine—and self-conscious "fusion food" created by a particular chef in the present day.

place. If you're keen to know more, turn to the Further Reading section on page 349 for suggested books on individual cuisines, by experts.

The Pantry Lists are not intended to be definitive catalogues, more an indication of the kinds of things you might want to have in stock (in addition to the Kitchen Essentials—see page 7) when you cook from a particular tradition. They include ingredients that struck me as unique or localized to certain places—such as Sichuan peppers from the Sichuan province of China, dried limes in Iran or *pimentón* in Spain—and, I hope, will inspire you to read the chapter in question before embarking on your culinary voyage. Assume that, most of the time, the Pantry Lists won't include the ingredients I've put on the Kitchen Essentials list unless I want to stress the prevalence of one in a certain place—chickpeas in the Mediterranean, for example, or tahini paste in the Levant and Israel. No matter how important they are to a cuisine, the likes of extra virgin olive oil and garlic don't feature on Pantry Lists: they are staples to be found in every well-stocked kitchen, no matter which cuisine you are tackling.

I've always taken a pretty relaxed approach to following recipes. They can be enormously useful in helping us to bring a dish to life, but too many of us are shackled by the idea that a recipe is a set of rules, which is a recipe for disaster. My advice would be to do what feels right. Put in more salt or avoid the fresh coriander if that's what appeals to your tastes, sear the steak or fry the omelette for a couple of minutes more or less if you're so inclined. No one knows your palate and cooking equipment like you do, so exercise some creative license.

Following the same logic, if you really want to make one of these recipes but can't find a certain ingredient or don't have a piece of equipment, don't let that put you off. Just try substituting the closest possible thing. Not everyone has access to a metropolitan array of ethnic shops selling niche ingredients or owns a tagine pot, and I firmly believe that you can embody authentic flavors without following a recipe to the letter.

You'll find a list of my Kitchen Essentials on page 7—these are the equipment and ingredients I prefer never to be without in my own kitchen. A list like this will obviously differ from one person to another and you may find that mine doesn't reflect how you like to eat, but in my experience the things I have included enable me to whip up something tasty from a number of different culinary canons without too much difficulty.

Though in part a reference book, *The World on a Plate* is also deeply personal, showcasing my own culinary interests and experiences. It reflects where I've been, the people I have spoken to, and what I like to eat. I've chosen just forty of countless world cuisines so there are of course gaps, but I've included those I consider particularly formative in our contemporary eating habits.

(One particular revelation was the extent to which Persian cuisine—the ancient cooking traditions of the country known today as Iran—has influenced so many of the major cuisines we know and love: Indian, Turkish, Levantine, Mediterranean. You'll see that Persian influences keep cropping up over the course of this book.) For three European countries (France, Spain and Italy), China, India and the United States, I have included more than one region. They seemed to me too established and too regionally nuanced to justify grouping their various culinary enclaves together.

I want this book to be as comfortable by your bedside as it is by your stovetop—as much a book to be read as to cook from. My job as a food journalist affords me the opportunity to meet some incredibly talented chefs, food experts and writers, from whom I've taken inspiration and practical tips in equal measure. In each chapter, you'll encounter an authority about the cuisine in question. They are too numerous to name here, but all have been generous with their time, knowledge and cooking. (I have been well fed while writing this book.)

I hope you enjoy reading and cooking from *The World on a Plate* and that, with its help, you feel inspired to set off on some international journeys from your kitchen, reminisce about places already visited or enthuse about travels to come.

*Bon voyage* and *bon appétit*!

# KITCHEN ESSENTIALS

## • EQUIPMENT •

WHEN I SAY "essentials," I really mean it. I've read plenty of cookbooks that assume you have a mandolin, a Kitchenaid, even a *sous vide*, all of which have their place—but I wouldn't class any of them as essential. You won't need anything too specialist for most of the recipes featured in these pages. Remember, this is home-cooked food of the world and should require only the most rudimentary accoutrements of a working home kitchen.

I'm of the opinion that too much cooking apparatus confuses things, and personally I avoid using anything that endangers my fingers with an electronic blade or leads to a lot of tedious washing up. That said, a blender, for example, is definitely a useful piece of equipment if you want to make dips, sauces, soups and so on, and therefore makes it onto my list.

My favorite list of essential kitchen equipment is "The Low-Tech Person's *Batterie de Cuisine*" in Laurie Colwin's *Home Cooking*. (If you like reading about food as much as you like cooking it, and if you like your food writing wry, dry and sometimes a little cutting, then you need to acquire this book.) I'd echo most of Colwin's recommendations, although in many instances she suggests having two of things (spatulas, even soup pots), which aren't always entirely essential in my view, particularly if you have a partner/roommate/parent/other minion who is willing to wash up as you cook.

So here is a short list of what I consider to be necessary to make any of the recipes I've featured in this book, and indeed for you to freestyle from any of the cuisines I have covered. The corkscrew and radio are obviously optional, but if you're anything like me . . .

**LARGE NONSTICK FRYING PAN** • It doesn't need to be expensive. I bought my favorite for less than twenty dollars in the supermarket.

**SAUCEPANS** • A heavy-bottomed Le Creuset-style one that can also go in the oven and a light, medium-sized one (again, of the affordable supermarket kind). It does help here to have two on hand.

**WOK** • An essential accessory in the student kitchen circa 1998, but still very useful for blasting stir-fry ingredients quickly and effectively so that they cook without losing their crunch and goodness.

**DEEP BAKING DISH/ROASTING PAN**

**CASSEROLE DISH**

**PRESSURE COOKER** • Arguably not an essential, but really useful if you get into the habit of making stews, or just to soften ingredients in a fraction of the time. Pressure cookers generally require less water and, because they are cooked for a shorter period, ingredients are kept tender (meat), crunchier (vegetables) and full of nutrients (compared to regular boiling). They are relatively cheap to buy.

**COLANDER**

**BIG MIXING BOWL** • Glass, metal, plastic, doesn't matter, but having a couple is always handy.

**GOOD-QUALITY SHARP KNIFE**

**LONG FORK/PRONG**

**STURDY CHOPPING BOARD** • "Sturdy" is important here. Nothing worse than the board sliding around while you work (which is also dangerous when knives are involved, of course). Invest in a solid, heavy wooden board if possible.

**FOOD PROCESSOR OR BLENDER**

**MORTAR AND PESTLE** • A heavy-bottomed one (mine is made of granite). I've learned that there's nothing like grinding your own spices for a Neanderthal thrill.

**FINE GRATER**

**PEELER**

**WOODEN SPOON**

**SPATULA** • It never fails to delight me how good these are at clearing *every last drop* of mixture from a bowl.

**SERVING PLATES/BOWLS** • My favorite way of serving, and eating, is from big bowls or platters. I find this is a really easy way of making food look beautiful, no matter how underwhelming it might look before you serve it. Hummus, for example, can look pretty beige when you've just blended it. But transfer to a pretty ceramic bowl, drizzle on some good, extra virgin olive oil and a dusting of *za'atar* (see page 168) and it'll look lovely.

**1-QUART MEASURING CUP**

**KITCHEN SCALES**

**WHISK** • An electric one is nice to have but not strictly speaking essential.

**LARGE, FINE SIEVE**

**CAKE PAN**

**SPRINGFORM PAN**

**RANGE OF TUPPERWARE** • Not just for housewives of the 1970s. Very useful if you want to make stuff to use or serve later, and for leftovers.

**PLASTIC WRAP AND PARCHMENT PAPER**

**CORKSCREW**

**KITCHEN RADIO**

# • INGREDIENTS •

THIS IS A list of all the ingredients I try to keep in stock so I can depart the UK whenever the fancy takes me—my edible vehicles, if you like. I find that having these on hand guarantees being able to whip up something interesting, international and authentic at the drop of a hat, from a curry with coconut milk to pasta sauce or Levantine dip.

As ever, this is a personal list based on the food I like to eat. For example, I rarely use meat when cooking only for myself or one other person unless I have planned it in advance. If you are of a more carnivorous ilk than I, I recommend keeping some chorizo and/or pancetta in the fridge to add to things like pasta sauces or soups. You might also want to keep some kind of minced meat in the freezer—beef or pork for meatballs, pasta sauces or easy East-Asian dishes. A little plea: try to use organic meat where possible. It tastes so much better—not to mention being better for you, and for the world.

I'd recommend growing your own herbs. It's much more ecological than buying them ready-picked in supermarkets and herbs in those plastic packages turn bad very quickly. But even more than this, growing your own is a rewarding, low-maintenance way of producing your own ingredients—and ingredients that can transform a dish, at that. Just buy a window box and fill it with thyme, mint, parsley and basil to start. All they need is good exposure to sunlight and regular watering. And while we're on the subject, you can assume that all herbs specified in the recipes are fresh unless it says otherwise.

**FRESH** • onions (white or red) • scallions • garlic • ginger • lemons • limes • eggplant • zucchini • spinach • tomatoes • fresh herbs: parsley, coriander, basil, mint, thyme • good loaf of bread

**FRIDGE** • unsalted butter • eggs • milk • Greek yogurt • Parmesan cheese • tahini paste • preserved lemons

**FREEZER** • peas • bread crumbs • chopped parsley • pita bread

**CUPBOARD** • dried pasta and noodles • basmati rice • dried couscous • all-purpose flour • granulated sugar • baking powder • cocoa powder • vanilla extract • dark chocolate • good-quality extra virgin olive oil • sesame oil • balsamic vinegar—again, good quality: they can really vary • white wine vinegar • soy sauce • fish sauce • canned tomatoes • tomato purée • canned chickpeas • canned coconut milk • dried chili flakes • dried spices: cinnamon, cumin, fennel seed, *pimentón,* ground coriander, caraway seed, garam masala, whole cloves • dried herbs: tarragon, oregano, rosemary • black pepper • Maldon sea salt • dried orange lentils • canned anchovies • jar of capers • canned olives • honey • Marmite*

• • • •

*Okay, this one is optional. You won't find it in this book, but my cupboard is literally *never* without it, so I can't exclude it here. Butter, Marmite and black pepper over pasta is still my solution to an empty fridge . . . and a hangover.

EUR

# OPE

# THE GRAPE VINE

...

Like me, grapes are keen travelers. They have toured the world in search of optimal conditions in which to grow. If you drink a lot of wine, you'll know that many of the grape varietals grow all over the world, but with very different characteristics in their resulting wines. A Syrah from the French Rhône Valley is an altogether different beast from one from South Australia, for example. I've included this map to show France's influence on international gastronomy from a different angle. It demonstrates where the key French grapes have traveled to in the New World, and their defining qualities are explained on the facing page.

**WESTERN UNITED STATES**
Chardonnay
Merlot
Cabernet Sauvignon
Pinot Noir

**CHILE**
Merlot
Cabernet Sauvignon
Sauvignon Blanc
Carménère

**ARGENTINA**
Malbec
Cabernet Sauvignon

**LOIRE VALLEY**
Sauvignon Blanc
Chenin Blanc

**BURGUNDY**
Pinot Noir
Chardonnay

**RHÔNE VALLEY**
Shiraz (Syrah)
Grenache

**BORDEAUX**
Carménère
Merlot
Cabernet Sauvignon
Malbec

**FRANCE**

**SOUTH AFRICA**
Chenin Blanc
Pinotage (hybrid grape)

**AUSTRALIA**
Shiraz (Syrah)
Cabernet Sauvignon
Merlot
Chardonnay

**NEW ZEALAND**
Sauvignon Blanc
Pinot Noir

# • THE BORDEAUX GRAPES •

**BORDEAUX**

Bordeaux is most famous for grapes like Cabernet Sauvignon (high tannin, high acidity) and Merlot (fleshier, fruitier). These are primarily grown on the left and right banks of the Gironde estuary respectively and are often blended to make famous wines like Médoc, Saint Emilion and celebrated châteaux wines like Margaux. These grapes have traveled extensively, thriving in the abundance of sunlight and temperature extremes in parts of the New World like the United States, Argentina, Chile and Australia. In these locations they make for "bigger" (fuller bodied with more tannin, which is indicated by the dry sensation a red wine leaves on your palate) wines than their more reserved French counterparts. Malbec is traditionally a Bordeaux grape too, and is still grown around Cahors. It is, however, better suited to the terroirs of Argentina, which has become internationally celebrated for the "big" Malbecs that its high altitude and temperature extremes produce.

# • THE LOIRE GRAPES •

**LOIRE VALLEY**

Internationally, the Loire Valley is best known for its refined, high-acid white wine varietals such as Sauvignon Blanc (think Sancerre and Pouilly-Fumé) and the Chenin Blanc of Vouvray. Sauvignon Blanc finds its most popular New World expression in New Zealand, where the vines of areas like Marlborough Estate produce distinctive, kiwi-flavored (pure coincidence!), almost grassy white wines. Chile, Argentina and the United States produce more rounded Sauvignon Blancs than either the French originals or New Zealand. Very often a grape variety becomes so strongly associated with New World wines that its French origins are overlooked. A case in point is the slightly fizzy, high-alcohol whites of Vouvray, which are made from Chenin Blanc, a grape that has made its name as the emblematic white wine of South Africa.

# • THE BURGUNDY GRAPES •

Wines from the Bourgogne are often regarded as the most premium in the world, with the likes of Puligny-Montrachet and Chablis whites and Gevrey-Chambertin and Nuits-Saint-Georges for reds. Burgundy white wines are made from the Chardonnay grape. Chardonnay still elicits mixed feelings among some people, who associate it with cheaply produced New World wines, like those of the Californian Central Valley or Australian boxed wine. (I grew up with my parents' mantra "ABC"—"Anything But Chardonnay," due to less favorable associations with the grape during the 1990s.) Chardonnay is actually a very versatile grape that makes for New World wines of varied quality, ranging from entry level to high-end on the West Coast and in South America, Australia and South Africa. Pinot Noir is one of the lighter red varietals, which produces wines as suited to fish and vegetarian meals as they are to meat. It can have mushroomy, almost gamy notes and has been grown with success in the New World, particularly on the West Coast (in places like the Napa Valley and Oregon), New Zealand and in South Africa, which has also developed a Pinot Noir/Cinsault hybrid grape called Pinotage.

# • THE RHÔNE GRAPES •

The Rhône Valley is most famous for the production of Syrah and Grenache grapes. It is a vast area which, though referred to collectively as "The Rhône Valley," actually splits more accurately into two: the northern and southern Rhône. The northern Rhône is best known for pure Syrah wines like Crozes-Hermitage and Saint Joseph, while the south is better known for Grenache blends Côtes du Rhône and, at the high end, Châteauneuf-du-Pape. Syrahs are known for their smoky notes, black fruit and peppery flavor and have been grown very successfully (and famously) in the Australian valleys such as Barossa and McLaren Vale, where they are referred to as Shiraz and make for some seriously big red wines. Grenache thrives in hot climates and can also be found widely in Spain, where it is known as Garnacha.

# • THE IMPACT OF PHYLLOXERA •

In the nineteenth century an invidious vine pest known as phylloxera, and similar to an aphid, devastated European vineyards. An estimated figure of between two thirds and nine tenths of vineyards were destroyed, and many areas of France were hit particularly hard. The insect was probably brought to Britain by a group of botanists who had been collecting specimens in America, where the bug is native (making American vines more resistant than European ones). From there it spread slowly across the continent. Some varietals were all but wiped out in their native lands. Specimens of Bordeaux vines like Malbec and Carménère had already been taken to the New World, providing these varietals with long-term protection. Today they thrive in Argentina and Chile respectively—almost the signature grapes of each—but are comparatively rare back in France. Malbec production in Bordeaux is small, while Carménère is considered the region's "lost grape." Argentine Malbec is renowned for its violet, vanilla and smoked notes while similarly smoky Carménère is known for its blackcurrant character.

# FRANCE

The French . . . bring to their consideration of the table the same
appreciation, respect, intelligence and lively interest that they have
for the other arts, for painting, for literature and for the theatre.
• ALICE B. TOKLAS, *The Alice B. Toklas Cook Book* •

THE FRENCH HAVE long seen food as high art. They were perhaps the first to adopt the notion that a dish could, like a painting or a novel, be a masterpiece in its own right.* And while the rest of Europe has gradually come around to such ideas, haute cuisine is still championed and most classically executed by our Gallic neighbors.

But the wonderful thing about French food is that, for all its pomp and circumstance, Michelin-star† culture is by no means the only thing that matters. The French take great pride in their food at every level of production and consumption, with some of the most distinguished raw materials in the world. From rustic pâté and wine to crusty, soft, white bread, perhaps dunked in a vibrant pot-au-feu (a casserole of boiled beef cuts and vegetables, dubbed "soul food for socialists" by Anthony Bourdain); or boeuf bourguignon (the Burgundy stew of beef and vegetables in a sauce of bay leaves, juniper and Pinot Noir), French food culture is one that celebrates great ingredients as much as their plated results.

Look at a good road map of France and it will quickly dawn on you just how many of the world's celebrated ingredients are French. Numerous towns and villages that have shared their names with a local food product pepper the roads, running like veins through the body of France: Dijon, Camembert, Pithiviers, Cognac . . . the French have gastronomy in their blood, they

• • • •

* Marcel Proust, arguably France's greatest writer, is, after all, inextricably associated in the popular imagination with a cake—see page 1.

† The Michelin brothers, founders of the Michelin tire company, produced the first Michelin Guide to restaurants in 1900 in an attempt to encourage enthusiasm for motoring out to eat at their recommendations. In 1926 they launched the star grading system, now the highest and most internationally recognized clue to a restaurant's credentials.

just *get* it. I think it's fair to say that on average they have a superior level of knowledge about gastronomy, one that's often noticeably lacking elsewhere. For instance, working in restaurant service has an altogether different cachet. Staff are expected to be highly knowledgeable about food and wine in order to answer the more probing questions of patrons. What is the chef's technique for making the béarnaise sauce? Why is one vintage of Côte-Rôtie better than another? And so on.

It was French chef and writer Auguste Escoffier[*] who said, "If it had been an Italian who codified the world of cuisine, it would be thought of as Italian." Though culinary trends come and go, French cuisine remains the benchmark for other culinary cultures and is endowed with a sense of timelessness. For chefs in the making, a classical training is grounded in French cuisine—its techniques, equipment, flavor and ingredient pairings, the attitude to wine—to which cooks can then add their own flair or, equally, apply to another cuisine. Learn to cook French, and the world is your oyster. Or should I say *huître*?

Arguably, the emergence of Modernist cuisine—think the developments in Spain and Scandinavia (El Bulli and Noma respectively)—wouldn't have happened without French cuisine paving the way. Mastering the (simple, yet deceptively tricky) technique to make the likes of sauces and roux as well as presenting their culinary creations immaculately, France set the bar—a precedent on which subsequent culinary developments have been able to build. Coinciding with the decline of the aristocracy, this was the point at which French food became "codified" (to borrow Escoffier's term), following a surge of restaurant openings by former private chefs. French cuisine as we know it, then, with its heavy sauces and immaculate presentation, developed as a result of shifts in the French class system. Restaurant culture became, and still is, integral to the advancement of French cuisine, allowing people other than the very privileged to buy into culinary advancements that had previously belonged in a noble, exclusive setting.

For a long time French food enjoyed a golden age of international veneration from cooks and eaters alike. In the past twenty years or so, innovations elsewhere—Ferran Adrià's maverick creations at the now closed El Bulli in Spain, for example—mean that French food has been relegated by some for being unexciting. But for me, this misses the point. Innovation doesn't really sit at the heart of French food culture. Technique is key—precise quantities

• • • •

[*] Auguste Escoffier (1846–1935) is the French chef credited as possibly the most important figure in developing modern French cuisine. *Le Guide Culinaire*, published in 1906, is his best-known work— a recipe and reference book that remains a first port of call for chefs across the world to this day.

and timings—as is having the correct, well-sourced ingredients and beautiful presentation. The ability of the French to repeat this formula time and again is, indeed, an art.

I have covered just four of the French regions, each with culinary offerings reflecting their climate and cultural mix. Normandy, where the landscape and produce are in many ways similar to those of the south of England, where orchards bloom and cream-colored cattle graze; the Loire Valley, one of France's cooler wine-producing areas, which blooms with wonderful fruit, vegetables and river fish; Rhône-Alpes, the center of French charcuterie and home to the food capital of Lyon; and Provence, where flavors of the French Mediterranean collide in dishes that taste of the sunshine.

# NORMANDY

It was an opening up of the soul and spirit for me.
• JULIA CHILD •

IN AN INTERVIEW with the *New York Times*, Julia Child[*] described her first meal in Rouen, Normandy, thus. She ate oysters and *sole meunière* and drank fine wine, experiencing the freshness and accessibility of just-caught seafood and the heady rush of eating great food in its homeland. Normandy might be just across the English Channel but there is nevertheless a noticeable shift in attitude around food when you arrive there. This "opening up" that Child experienced is a food ecstasy born of a place to which food is absolutely central. You have entered France. Food is life, and life is food. *Bienvenue.*

There's not a huge amount of technique, or even necessarily cooking, attached to re-creating an authentic Norman meal. This isn't the case with other areas of France, so Normandy is the perfect first stop on the home cook's journey, allowing you to sample authentic French food without too much effort. This is the cuisine of which the best picnics are made: home to some of the world's finest butter, most famous cheese, most delicious cider and, as everywhere in France, exemplary bread. Normandy draws attention to the fundamental simplicity of good food, the elemental composition of a satisfying meal, and puts the spotlight on the skill of producers rather than chefs. Normandy could be said to have less of a "cuisine" than other regions in France, simply because ingredients are often left to speak for themselves, in their natural state. The elements of Norman food derive from the rolling greenery of the Pays d'Auge, where the *vaches des lunettes* ("cows with spectacles"—named for the markings around their eyes) graze, and where razor clams and whelks wash up onto the brooding gray beaches beloved of the Impressionists.

• • • •

[*]Julia Child was an American cook, author and TV personality who is credited with bringing French food to the United States via the publication in 1961 of her seminal book *Mastering the Art of French Cooking*. In 2009, Meryl Streep played the eccentric and difficult Child in the movie *Julie and Julia*, about a blogger's challenge to cook all the recipes from *Mastering the Art of French Cooking* in a year.

As France's dairy capital, Normandy is—quite literally—*la crème de la crème*. Cheeses are usually named after their hometowns—Pont l'Evêque, Livarot and, of course, Camembert (a surprisingly tiny village with only a church, a museum and a soundtrack of "moos")—and are memorable for their chunky rinds and pungency, pairing brilliantly with local dry cider. Camembert was developed during the French Revolution by one Marie Harel, a Norman farmer and local cheese maker who sheltered one of the priests taking refuge in the countryside. The priest in question happened to be from Brie. The story goes that he shared with Harel the secret to making brie-style cheese, and the rest is history. It fast became the most popular cheese in France, iconic in its round wooden boxes, which, along with a spray of penicillium to preserve it, enabled the cheese to travel.[*] Half a million boxes were purportedly shipped to the trenches each week during World War I.

Great butter naturally paves the way for consummate pastry. In Normandy, puff pastry is used to make the beloved tarte tatin and *douillons*, in which pastry turnovers hug a filling of caramelized apple or pear; sweet crust features in a range of fruit-based tarts (see the recipe on page 25 for my mum's Norman-inspired apple tart) and brioche, which can be found all over France, reaches an apogee of deliciousness.

Orchards boasting crops of apples ripening on gnarled old trees create a patchwork of greens across Normandy. Apples can be loosely divided into two camps—those for eating and those for cider or Calvados production. Normandy cider is dry—or it can be, if dry is your thing. I love the smokiness of oak aged brut ciders made in the town of Calvados, and also Calvados itself—the apple brandy for which the region is celebrated. This is widely used in cookery, as in flambéed *tarte aux pommes*, or sipped as a digestif. If you prefer a lighter, sweeter aperitif you could try *pommeau*—an apple liquor made by most of the little local cider and Calvados producers, which you'll fall upon in practically every Norman village.

Third in Normandy's triptych of great produce is its seafood. *Moules* (mussels) are ubiquitous, caught fresh daily and served *à la marinière* with bright yellow crispy *frites*. Turbot is the region's most prized fish, but sea bass, sole, monkfish and skate are also common and eaten widely. They are served simply, with mashed potatoes and fennel, for example, with a

• • • •

[*]Camembert varies massively—go to the Camembert museum and included in price of entry is the chance to taste three cheeses of varying maturity—but what all types have in common is their round wooden box with characterful (and collectible) branding on the top. Livarot is a more acquired taste than crowd-pleasing Camembert or Pont L'Evêque (which comes in a distinctive square mold), which has an almost crunchy golden rind.

*meunière*\* sauce like Julia Child's sole or, in the case of oysters, in their natural state. For me, local oysters epitomize the richness of Norman food in its purest form. They were longer and creamier than any I had tried before. It's not surprising that the Normans are purists about serving them—a small squeeze of lemon juice to enhance, but not disguise, the salty flavor. Wash them down with a glass of Loire Valley Muscadet, and feel your soul and spirit open up—just like Julia Child's.

**PANTRY LIST** • apples • freshly churned butter • cream • cheeses (Camembert, Pont l'Evêque, Livarot) • shellfish (oysters, mussels, clams, winkles, whelks) • fish (turbot, sole, monkfish, skate) • brut cider • homemade pastry

• • •

# • BAKED CAMEMBERT •

I almost didn't include this "recipe" for fear of patronizing you, but seeing as a) Camembert is quintessentially Norman; b) I make this all the time and c) it's bloody delicious, I soon talked myself into it. You can use a range of "toppings" for the cheese or none at all, depending on your preferences. The Calvados-soaked version I've given below is the most dramatic, and clearly nods to Norman soil but, unlike alternatives such as drizzling some honey and scattering dried thyme over the cheese just before placing it in the oven, it does need to be prepared in advance.

### • SERVES 1–2 PIGS OR 4–6 PIGLETS •

1 x 9-oz round of Camembert, in its box
2 tbsp Calvados
1 sprig rosemary, leaves only
sea salt and freshly ground black pepper
French bread and crudités, to serve

• • • •

\* *Meunière* sauce, or "miller's wife sauce," for fish is so called because it involves coating the fish in flour before frying it in brown butter or deep-frying it in oil, then seasoning with lemon and parsley.

**1** • Remove the lid from the Camembert box, unwrap the cheese and discard the wrapping before returning the cheese to the box. Pierce the top of the cheese with a fork and carefully spoon the Calvados all over it, followed by the rosemary and seasoning.

**2** • Allow to marinate at room temperature for up to eight hours (if you can marinate in the morning before you wish to serve it, that's ideal), or for as long as you can short of that.

**3** • Preheat the oven to 350°F and bake for 10–20 minutes. I like it super gooey in the center, so you can break through the white rind into a molten explosion of boozy cheese.

# • APPLE TART NORMANDE •

My mum is an infinitely superior baker to me and excels at dishes in which fruit, pastry and frangipane get jiggy. This tart lasts a good few days in the fridge and bridges that long, lonely stretch of time between breakfast and lunch very well indeed. Try sifting a small amount of confectioners' sugar over the top and serving with some crème fraiche (and a shot of Calvados?).

### • SERVES 8 •

FOR THE SHORTCRUST PASTRY
1¼ cups all-purpose flour, plus extra for dusting
2 tbsp superfine sugar
7 tbsp cold unsalted butter, cubed
1 egg yolk
1 tbsp cold water
1 tsp vanilla extract
pinch salt

FOR THE FRANGIPANE
½ cup (1 stick) unsalted butter, softened
9 tbsp superfine sugar
1 medium egg, beaten
1 egg yolk
1 tbsp Calvados
2 tbsp all-purpose flour
1 cup ground almonds

3 medium apples, peeled, cored and thinly sliced
2 tbsp apricot jam for glazing (optional)

**1** • To make the pastry, sift the flour into a mixing bowl and stir in the sugar. Lightly rub the cubes of butter into the flour using your fingertips, until the mixture resembles fine bread crumbs.

**2** • In the center of the mixture make a well and add the egg yolk, water, vanilla and salt. Combine to make a smooth dough and gather together into a ball. Cover with plastic wrap and refrigerate for at least 30 minutes.

**3** • To make the frangipane, cream the butter and sugar together in a bowl and then add the egg and egg yolk separately. Mix in the Calvados. In a separate bowl, stir the flour into the ground almonds and then add to the batter mixture.

**4** • Roll the pastry out onto a floured surface into a 10-inch circle about ⅛ inch thick. Lift into a 9- or 10-inch springform pan and then press down into the bottom of the pan and up the sides. Chill once again for 10–20 minutes.

**5** • Preheat the oven to 400°F. Place a baking sheet in the oven while it heats up.

**6** • Spoon the frangipane into the chilled pastry base and distribute it evenly. Arrange the apples in an overlapping spiral pattern, starting from the outside first.

**7** • Place the tart on the heated baking sheet and bake for 15 minutes. Reduce the heat to 350°F and bake for another 15–20 minutes.

**8** • To make the glaze, combine the apricot jam with a little water and then heat gently until runny. Remove the tart from the oven and brush all over with the glaze. Allow to cool in the springform pan for 5–10 minutes before turning out.

# LOIRE VALLEY

They were wonderful days for us, days that I wished would last forever,
swimming in the Loire or catching crayfish in the shallows, exploring the woods,
making ourselves sick with cherries or plums or green gooseberries, fighting,
sniping at one another with potato rifles and decorating the Standing Stones
with the spoils of our adventuring.
• JOANNE HARRIS, *Five Quarters of the Orange* •

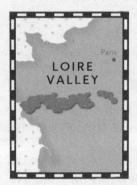

DURING THE SUMMER of 2012 I spent five days cycling through the Loire Valley with a friend. Our ride began in Tours and ended in Angers, and we pedaled from one famed wine region to the next—the Touraine, Chinon, Saumur Champigny, Anjou. We didn't make it to Sancerre or Muscadet, but you get the picture: this area of three hundred square miles along the Loire River is internationally celebrated for great wine and known for its distinctive expressions of Sauvignon Blanc, the unique Chenin Blancs of Vouvray and for mastering the notoriously difficult Cabernet Franc grape. I didn't know much about the food scene in the Loire before I went, but—on the basis that such good wine would surely be matched by great food—I wasn't surprised to find culinary prowess that equaled its viticulture.

Respect for local wine is key to cooking in the Loire kitchen. Food and wine are almost yin and yang, designed for one another, and many of the sauces with which meat and fish are eaten contain wine produced nearby. The emblematic beurre blanc, for which you'll find a recipe at the end of this chapter, is an obvious example.[*] To borrow Fernande Garvin's words from *The Art of French Cooking*,[†] "Wine makes a symphony of a good meal."

Abbeys, châteaux, convents and pastel farmhouses punctuate the landscape and stud the banks of the Loire. This delicate balance of nature and the

••••

[*] Cooking with wine is common across France, of course, with the likes of *boeuf bourguignon* and *boeuf en daube* in Burgundy and Provence respectively.

[†] Published in 1965, *The Art of French Cooking* is a delightful paperback filled with classic French dishes like Coq au Vin and Croque Monsieur—simple, elegant dishes which impress without being too fussy.

man-made encapsulates something effortless about rural France: quaintness erring on the right side of twee. Fruit trees from which fairy-tale red apples and ripe plums dangle are commonplace, as are fields of sunflowers standing at attention like ranks of smiling soldiers. With more sun than Normandy farther north, fruits like apples and pears are sweeter here, and farmed for food rather than drink. We cycled past patchworks of allotments boasting a glorious stench of onions, green and white beans, carrots and leeks, mushrooms and asparagus, pumpkins and *primeurs* (early season baby vegetables).

The Loire River is extensive, stretching from its source in the Rhône-Alpes (see page 33) and traveling alongside Burgundy before taking a sharp left toward the Atlantic Ocean. The Loire Valley region is surrounded by very varied, mineral-rich soils as well as different microclimates. Both food and wine take on an ultra-local character here as a result; each city has its own food speciality and the attributes of local wines change dramatically from one village to another. Two-wheeled travel was the ideal way to experience this, enabling us to make regular stops to taste local wines, charcuterie and pastries.

The three *rilles* are the region's signature meat dishes and make a mean accompaniment to a local dry white wine: *rillettes*, a pork-based paste from the Tours and Saumur areas; *rillons*, cubes of belly pork preserved in fat, from Touraine; and *rillauds*, slow-roasted chunks of belly pork from Anjou. As we will see once we get to the Rhône-Alpes, French cuisine has long championed the use of offal and offcuts of meat. In the United States and the UK this might be thought of in terms of chef Fergus Henderson's concept of "nose to tail eating," but in France eating the whole animal isn't a concept, it is common practice. Typical of the Loire and western France is pig's head soup, a recipe for which appears in the 1929 book *Les Belles Recettes des Provinces Françaises* ("Beautiful Recipes from the French Provinces"), contributed by one Madame Meunier from L'Oie in La Vendée, just south of the Loire. She instructs us to boil a salted pig's head for just under three hours with kale, stale bread, peppercorns and garlic before serving the broth over more bread and eating the head separately (with cabbage that has been cooked in cream). This is the kind of food still eaten in Loire villages. In some countries, using the whole animal might be a tradition to which we have returned, but in France it is one that they never lost.

The Loire felt to me like a landscape of storybooks and fairy tales, with knights on colorfully decorated steeds, damsels with plaited hair and courtship in the mazes of the immaculate châteaux gardens. I imagine medieval huntsmen returning from the forests to châteaux kitchens bearing spoils of deer and wild boar, which chefs would prepare with wild mushrooms and sauces *a la crème*. The good table wine and hearty meals you find in the region today are part of a long tradition.

As well as the abundance of the forests, the river itself is brimming with food: freshwater fish such as pike, trout, salmon and eel. They are delicious in dark soups or stews like *matelotte d'anguille*—eel stew, rich in local red wine, cognac and shallots—or more simply served with a beurre blanc. This is a classic sauce of the Loire Valley, prepared by reducing butter with shallots, vinegar and Muscadet, a simple dry white wine native to the zone surrounding the city of Nantes (and made from the Melon de Bourgogne grape).

Goat cheese from the Loire is iconic and a good example of local food produced to complement the region's wine. Pyramid-shaped, ash-dusted and made with raw goat's milk, Valençay is perhaps the most famous, but Chabichou du Poitou, Crottin de Chavignol and Pouligny-Saint-Pierre (all from the Berry region between the Cher and Indre Rivers) are also well-known. Most local wines would accompany these beautifully, but I had a particularly ecstatic experience with a chilled Saint-Nicolas-de-Bourgueil and some Valençay.

Desserts, patisserie and sweets put the vibrant fruits of the Loire Valley to good use and inspire Joanne Harris in *Five Quarters of the Orange.*[*] French staples like *chausson aux pommes* (apple turnover, one of which my mother would buy me every Saturday on her unlikely baguette run in Streatham, where I grew up), and tarts filled with *crème patissière* and crowned with strawberries, line shop windows alongside local favorites like tarte tatin. This tart of caramelized apples turned upside down on pastry is said to have originated at the Hotel Tatin in Lamotte-Beuvron, a town between the Loire and the Cher. Meanwhile, Angers is known for its plum cake, *pâté aux prunes*, which is not unlike a *tarte aux quetsches*[†] and the city of Tours produces a nougat with almonds, cherries, apricots and candied orange. The local *moelleux* or *doux* Vouvray, sweetened by noble rot,[‡] would make a beguiling partner for either one of these—if you're indulging in dessert.

Stock up on freshwater fish, some ripe vegetables, Muscadet and the wherewithal to whip up a beurre blanc on your first kitchen trip to the Loire Valley, and imagine yourself riverside: your bike propped on its side, the breeze in your face, booze on your breath, surrounded by wildflowers . . . and the stench of onions. Just the right side of twee, indeed.

• • • •

[*]The third in her food trilogy, in which the main characters are all named after fruits or fruity products—Framboise, Cassis and so on.

[†] *Tarte aux quetsches* is a plum tart considered to be a speciality of Alsace.

[‡]Noble rot, otherwise known as Botrytis, is a gray fungus that grows on ripe grapes which is actively encouraged by winemakers to produce sweeter wines like Sauternes.

**PANTRY LIST** • freshwater fish (pike, trout, salmon, eel) • local charcuterie (rillons, rillettes, rillauds) • local cheese (Valençay, Chabichou du Poitou, Crottin de Chavignol, Pouligny-Saint-Pierre) • fruits (apples, pears, plums, strawberries) • vegetables (shallots, carrots) • good butter • homemade pastry

• • •

# • SALMON AND BEURRE BLANC •

In theory a beurre blanc is simple. In practice it is a little harder, but making one is a skill well worth honing. It's the typical sauce of the Loire region and perfect served with river fish such as salmon. You'd be mad not to use a (good-value) Loire Valley wine to do the region justice. Muscadet almost always comes at a decent price, is usually tasty and/or inoffensive (depending on your views on Muscadet—I love it), and isn't wasted on cooking.

## • SERVES 4 •

2 shallots, finely chopped
1 ½ tbsp flat-leaf parsley, chopped
4 salmon fillets (5 oz each)
juice of ½ lemon
sea salt and freshly ground black pepper

FOR THE BEURRE BLANC
1 shallot, chopped
½ cup white wine, preferably a Loire Valley one
    such as Muscadet
1 ½ tsp white wine vinegar
1 ½ tsp flat-leaf parsley, chopped
½ cup (1 stick) unsalted butter, cubed
sea salt and freshly ground black pepper

**1** • Preheat the oven to 400°F.
**2** • Line a casserole dish with foil and lay a bed of shallots and parsley across it, then place the salmon fillets on top. Squeeze the lemon juice and sprinkle the seasoning over the fish, then put another sheet of foil over the fillets, securely.

**3** • Bake the fish in the oven for 20–25 minutes, until it just starts to flake.

**4** • Meanwhile, make your beurre blanc. Put the shallot, white wine, vinegar and parsley together in a pan and bring to the boil, then reduce to a simmer over a medium heat. Allow to simmer until the sauce has dramatically reduced in volume (it will thicken, too) to about 2 tablespoons of liquid. Turn the heat to very low and whisk in the butter, a little at a time. Season with salt and pepper.

**5** • Strain the sauce through a fine sieve into a heatproof bowl. Discard the shallot, parsley and seasoning sediment and then place the bowl with the liquid into another bowl half-filled with boiling water to keep the sauce warm until you are ready to serve.

**6** • Place the salmon, shallots and parsley on plates. Spoon the beurre blanc over the fish and serve with boiled new potatoes or rice.

# • UPSIDE-DOWN PLUM CAKE •

I was determined to pay tribute to the garden fruits of the Loire Valley and especially the plums, since I am an ardent lover of plums in all forms: fresh from the tree, in jams, compotes, puddings and, best of all, my mother's pièce de résistance, the plum shuttle, in which she sandwiches tart prunes and almond frangipane between two pieces of puff pastry and bakes it in an egg wash. The typical pastry of Angers (the end point on my Loire Valley cycle trip) is known as *pâté aux prunes*, a similar plum and pastry arrangement. I felt the apple tart *Normande* would suffice for French pastry, however, so have instead taken inspiration from Angers and included this fantastic plum cake recipe from Eric Lanlard's book, *Home Bake. Merci beaucoup*, Eric!

## • SERVES 8 •

14 tbsp unsalted butter, plus extra for greasing
1 cup superfine sugar
5 medium eggs
1 ⅓ cups self-rising flour
10½–14 oz fresh plums, stoned and halved
1–2 tbsp light brown sugar
sprinkling of mixed spice
2⅓ tbsp golden syrup*

• • • •

*If you can't find golden syrup (quintessenitially English and available online and in specialty stores), then try using two parts corn syrup and one part molasses, or equal parts honey and corn or maple syrup. Neither is quite the same as the real deal, but either will suffice for this recipe.

**1** • Preheat the oven to 350°F. Grease a shallow 9-inch springform pan with the extra butter, and then line it with parchment paper.

**2** • In a large bowl, cream the butter and sugar together until light and fluffy. Whisk in the eggs, one at a time, until well combined. Sift in the flour, then fold it in gently.

**3** • Put the plums in a roasting dish and sprinkle with the light brown sugar and mixed spice. Bake in the oven for about 15 minutes or until the fruit is soft and sweet. Drain off the excess juice.

**4** • Place the roasted plums in the base of your prepared springform pan. Add the golden syrup, then spoon the cake mixture on top. Bake in the oven for an hour or until the cake is cooked through. Allow to cool in the pan, then remove. Flip the sponge onto a serving dish, so the fruit and syrup are visible.

# RHÔNE-ALPES

In a dining establishment in Lyon, you can eat pig fat fried in pig fat, a pig's brain
dressed in a porky vinaigrette, a salad made with creamy pig lard, a chicken
cooked inside a sealed pig's bladder, a pig's digestive tract filled up with pig's
blood and cooked like a custard, nuggets of a pig's belly mixed with cold vinegary
lentils, a piggy intestine blown up like a balloon and stuffed thickly with a handful of piggy intestines, and a sausage roasted in a brioche (an elevated version
of a "pig in a blanket"). For these and other reasons, Lyon, for 76 years, has been
recognised as the gastronomic capital of France and the world.
The world is a big place.
• BILL BUFORD, *Observer Food Monthly* •

MUCH OF THE French food we are exploring concen-
trates on the masterful manipulation of raw materials,
or indeed the raw materials themselves. As Bill Buford[*]
notes, these take on a particularly carnivorous character in this nook of southeast France, which is encircled
by five other French regions including Provence (see
page 40) and Burgundy, as well as Switzerland and Italy
to the east. Welcome to the Rhône-Alpes, home to Lyon,
France's second-largest city and charcuterie capital.

The region of Rhône-Alpes is a confluence, most
literally, of two rivers: the Rhône and the Saône, but it is also where many of
France's agricultural and culinary kingdoms meet, giving the region a wide
range of ingredients on which to draw. In *French Country Cooking*, the Roux
brothers[†] cite Charolais cattle, Auvergne lamb, trout from the Alps and dairy
from Bugey and Dauphine as among the riches of the area, to which I would
add the white truffles from Tricastin and Drôme (a vast majority of the French
truffle harvest), as well as produce from Provence to the south (think seafood

••••

[*]Buford liked it so much in Lyon that he moved his family there and took on an apprenticeship in
a boulangerie, an experience he recounts in his book, *Heat*.

[†]Michel and Albert Roux set up Mayfair's legendary French restaurant Le Gavroche in 1967 and
are uncle and father respectively to the restaurant's current chef patron (and star of *MasterChef*),
Michel Roux Jr.

and endless herbs) and Burgundy to the north (Dijon mustard, Epoisses cheese and fine wines).

Lyon typifies France in all its rustic glory, in all its perfected coarseness, in all the polished simplicity of cheese and charcuterie, bread and wine eaten off a crumby gingham cloth. This is the food I remember over Michelin-starred meals. It is usually delicious, very often gruesome and always real. Local food like some of the charcuterie outlined by Bill Buford above is often enjoyed in *bouchons*, typical Lyonnais taverns. Meat products including *rosette* (pork salami), andouille (smoked sausage with garlic, wine and onions), andouillette (fried sausage of small intestine stuffed with tripe), boiled sausage with potatoes, and *Jésus de Lyon* (the fat, knobbly hard sausage not dissimilar to the *rosette* or andouille but with meat chopped more coarsely) are all central to the *bouchon* experience. Quenelles are another favorite, small oval dumplings of minced fish or meat bound by egg yolk and bread crumbs, then poached. In Lyon these are typically made of pike sourced from the Rhône and served in a white sauce not unlike a béchamel, making for comfort food of the freshest, most local sort.

The Lyonnais and people of the Rhône-Alpes at large take great pride in local food, much of which has achieved AOC status.[*] This includes the chickens from Bresse (*poulet de Bresse*)—often described as the Dom Perignon champagne or Beluga caviar of the hen world—which are almost an emblem of the *Tricolor* flag with their white feathers, red crown and blue feet. Many chefs say this is the most tender poultry out there.

AOC wine and cheese go hand in hand in the Rhône Valley. Syrahs such as Crozes-Hermitage and blends such as Côtes du Rhône (which use grapes such as Carignan, Mourvèdre and Grenache blended with Syrah) are world famous. The region also produces some beautifully crisp Viognier for blending. Mixed breed cattle such as Abondance, Tarine, and Montbéliarde graze the luscious pastures. Given the prominence of foraged items such as chestnuts (from Ardèche) and hazelnuts and walnuts (from Grenoble) in the cuisine of the Rhône-Alpes, it comes as little surprise that the grasses produce a consistently nutty flavor in cheese made from cow's milk, regardless of the texture. Cheeses like Vacherin, Reblochon and Raclette are some of the well-loved results.

Raclette—from *racler* meaning "to scrape"— is a hard, dark yellow cheese of-

• • • •

[*] AOC stands for *Appellation d'Origine Contrôlée*, a government-awarded certification granting products from certain geographical areas protection. This means that sparkling wine producers from outside Champagne can't call their wines champagne, nor can any chickens reared outside the Bresse AOC be termed "Bresse."

ten served melted over boiled potatoes and eaten with charcuterie and pickles (the perfect antidote to a cold day spent on the Alps) while Reblochon's name derives from the verb *reblocher*, "to squeeze a cow's udder again," and harks back to the Middle Ages when farmers were taxed on their milk yields. They would avoid milking each cow of every last drop until the landowner had measured their yields. Reblochon—the cheese of the re-milked cows, was made from the second milking. This was also the cheese known as *fromage de dévotion*, the cheese offered to Carthusian monks by farmers after their land had been blessed. Vacherin, that wonderful, stinky cheese mess sold in wooden rounds, also originates in the Rhône-Alpes (although there is a Swiss version, too).

Cheeses are fashioned into a rich array of dishes such as *gratin Savoyard*, native to Savoie (an eastern area of the Rhône-Alpes), which is cooked in meat stock with fresh hard cheese (often Swiss cheese, like Gruyère, from just over the border—see recipe on page 38). Cheese fondue also expresses the slightly more Germanic tendencies of the Rhône-Alpes cuisine. Fondue, which is said to have originated in Switzerland but is also popular in Austria, is a specialty in and around Savoie and Lyon. The local variety might contain a mix of melted Comté, Emmental, Vacherin or Beaufort. Bread spiked with long forks is dipped into a big bowl of hot melted cheese shared between eaters.

Speak to someone who has spent an extended period in Lyon and they'll probably say they gained weight—and that's hardly surprising. Add sweet goods to all this cheese, meat, cream and wine and the calories keep on coming. There's *Viennoiserie*, pastry and patisserie products that, as the name suggests, originally came from Vienna, but which have been perfected by the French—*brioche aux pralines*, *pain au chocolat*. The chestnuts of the Ardèche are made into *crème des marrons* for use in cakes, tarts and pastries or are glazed with sugar syrup (to make *marrons glacés*), sometimes used in puddings such as a Mont Blanc (chestnuts and whipped cream). There's France's best white nougat from Montélimar,[*] and then there's brioche. Brioche is one of those foods that straddles savory and sweet to make a versatile canvas for fruit, cream and the likes of *cocon de Lyon*—little pastry parcels with sweet almond cream—but equally for meat and cheese. This confirms my suspicion that, in the Rhône-Alpes, you're never far from some meat. It's a great place to be piggy, but perhaps not to be a pig.

• • • •

[*] Nougat is thought to have come into France with the Greeks and examples of it can be found across the Mediterranean and Middle East, from Spanish *turron* to *gaz* in Iran. The nougat of Montélimar is a purer sort, however, made with just honey, eggs, sugar and almonds.

PANTRY LIST • charcuterie (andouille, andouillette) • good-quality chicken (if you can't get an AOC poulet de Bresse, then, no matter, just get the best organic chicken you can find, preferably from an independent butcher) • quenelles • cheese (Vacherin, Reblochon, Raclette) • butter • olive oil • brioche • nougat • marrons glacés • crème des marrons • wine (Syrah, Viognier)

• • •

# • GREEN SALAD WITH VINAIGRETTE •

*Alors!* So this dish is hardly unique to the Rhône-Alpes, but given the proliferation of porky products in the region, this simple salad would be a respite from meat-eating and the perfect side to accompany quenelles or andouille with good French bread. Few things beat a really well-executed green salad doused in garlicky dressing, and I fear I'd be shortchanging you if I didn't provide instructions on how to make an authentic French vinaigrette, one that will linger on your breath for the rest of the day after eating it. This is very similar to my grandmother's version, except I have swapped in Dijon mustard (infinitely superior to all other mustards, in my view) for the dry Colman's that Granny used (she was ever faithful to Norfolk, where Colman's is made). Dijon mustard also marks this dressing as local to southeastern France, if not to the Rhône-Alpes, then just a short distance north in Bourgogne. The salad can be as basic or elaborate as you want. I prefer to go for garden vegetables, avoiding the radicchio and frilly lettuces of farther south in Italy. Round lettuce or lamb's lettuce is lovely and soft. Sliced radishes, grated carrot and chopped chives make nice additions.

## • SERVES 3–4 •

4 tbsp extra virgin olive oil
1 tbsp white wine vinegar
1 heaping tsp Dijon mustard
juice of ½ lemon
2 garlic cloves, very finely chopped
big pinch sea salt and freshly ground black pepper
salad leaves of your choice

**1** • Simply put all the ingredients other than the salad leaves into a jam jar and shake vigorously. The vinaigrette matures well, so make in advance for an even better dressing.

**2** • Douse your salad in vinaigrette just before serving. (Don't do this bit in advance or you'll be left with soggy lettuce.)

# • A NOT-QUITE-CASSOULET •

I created this simple recipe that showcases andouille, the smoked sausage of the Rhône-Alpes, but without using duck, as in a regular cassoulet. (Expensive + greasy + cute = duck just isn't my favorite meat to cook with.) It combines the other basics of the classic dish—navy beans, bacon lardons, lots of garlic and bay leaves—into a stew that's crying out to be washed down with one of the region's Syrah or Syrah/Grenache blends.

## • SERVES 6 •

14 oz dried navy beans (or cannellini),
    soaked overnight
7 oz pork shoulder, diced
7 oz bacon or pancetta, diced into lardons
2 bay leaves
2–3 tbsp olive oil
1 stick celery, coarsely chopped
1 onion, coarsely chopped
1 carrot, coarsely chopped
6 garlic cloves, finely chopped
1 bouquet garni (two stems each of thyme
    and rosemary, tied together)
10½ oz andouille, cut into ½-inch slices (if you
    can't find andouille, use another smoked
    sausage such as chorizo)
juice of ½ lemon
2 whole cloves
sea salt and freshly ground black pepper

TO SERVE
¾ cup fresh bread crumbs, toasted
3 tbps flat-leaf parsley, coarsely chopped
drizzle of extra virgin olive oil

**1** • Preheat the oven to 285°F.

**2** • Drain the beans of their liquid and put them in a large saucepan, covered with water. Add the pork shoulder, bacon lardons and bay leaves, bring to the boil and simmer together for 15–20 minutes over medium heat. Then drain the mixture, keeping back about 1 cup of the cooking liquid, skimmed of any foam.

**3** • Heat the olive oil in a large frying pan over medium heat and fry the celery, onion, carrot and garlic for 5 minutes or until the onions start to turn translucent. Do not let the garlic burn.

**4** • Add the bouquet garni, andouille and the mixture of beans and other meats. Put the reserved cup of cooking water over them, plus more water to cover, then add the lemon juice and cloves and bring to a boil.

**5** • Transfer to a casserole dish and cover with foil or a lid, then place in the oven for 2½ hours. Fish out the bay leaves, cloves and the bouquet garni and season to taste. Serve spooned into bowls with a scattering of toasted bread crumbs, parsley and drizzle of olive oil.

# • GRATIN SAVOYARD •

This indulgent potato dish makes a great side dish for many of the pork products for which the Rhône-Alpes is best known, as well as roast dinners. It's even delicious on its own with some green salad. It is native to the Savoie region (hence its name) and for true authenticity Beaufort cheese is used, though given that this isn't exactly ubiquitous, most people make it with Gruyère. I prefer to use chicken stock and always add the nutmeg, which builds in a delicate layer of warming spice.

## • SERVES 4 •

2¼ lb potatoes (preferably waxy, but any suited to
    boiling will work), peeled and sliced into ⅛-inch disks
1 garlic clove
3 tbsp unsalted butter
5 oz Gruyère cheese, grated (about 1¼ cups)
½ tsp ground nutmeg (optional)

sea salt and freshly ground black pepper
⅔ cup beef or chicken stock

**1** • Preheat the oven to 425°F.

**2** • Crush the garlic with the back of a spoon to release the flavor and rub it all over a wide ovenproof dish. Then grease the dish with one third of the butter. Place half of the potato slices in a layer in the bottom.

**3** • In a bowl, mix together the cheese, nutmeg, salt and pepper. Sprinkle half of this over the potatoes. Take another third of the butter and break it into little bits. Dot these over the potatoes and cheese, then layer the rest of the potatoes on top, followed by the rest of the cheese and the final third of the butter. Pour the stock into the dish.

**4** • This last stage is optional, but if you're a garlic freak like me, I recommend slicing whatever's left of the clove super finely and sprinkling it over the top. Bake the gratin in the oven for 30–40 minutes and allow to stand for 5 minutes before serving.

# PROVENCE

*It went beyond the gastronomic frontiers of anything we had ever experienced . . . We ate the green salad with knuckles of bread fried in garlic and olive oil, we ate the plump round crottins of goat's cheese, we ate the almond and cream gateau that the daughter of the house had prepared. That night, we ate for England.*
• PETER MAYLE, *A Year in Provence* •

THE CUISINE OF Provence has been canonized by writers and brought to life as much with words as with flavors. It might just be me, but the very word "Provençal" seems somehow to glisten on the page, calling to mind a sapphire blue sea, green and red salads gleaming in olive oil and dreamlike imaginings of the Riviera as conjured by writers like F. Scott Fitzgerald. In her introduction to *A Book of Mediterranean Food*, the great Elizabeth David lists just some of the features of the Mediterranean culinary tradition of which Provence is no small part: ". . . the saffron, the garlic, the pungent local wines; the aromatic perfume of rosemary, wild marjoram and basil drying in the kitchens." Ingredients make up a bright palette, and on the Provençal table, are used to create a masterpiece.[*]

The French writer and filmmaker Alain Robbe-Grillet recalls his friend the literary theorist Roland Barthes musing, "In a restaurant it is the menu that people enjoy consuming—not the dishes, but their description."[†] The words, the bright names of ingredients, the voluptuous-sounding dishes are

••••

[*] La Colombe d'Or hotel and restaurant in the village of Saint-Paul de Vence (just inland from the Côte d'Azur) is testimony to Provence's history of attracting artists, writers and other creatives like a magnet. It is a relic of fading Bohemianism, with works by Picasso, Miró and Calder hanging casually on its weather-beaten walls—all these artists stayed there and paid their way in art. Little has changed at La Colombe d'Or over the decades, and certainly not the menu of staple Provençale dishes: bouillabaisse, *boeuf en daube* (see below), *fricassée de volaille* (chicken breast with a creamy morel sauce and perfect rice)—not to mention raw Provençale food at its best: bright orange melons, *crevettes* (prawns), and giant radishes, artichokes and tomatoes served as crudités with *anchoïade* (see page 44).

[†] From *Why I Love Barthes* by Alain Robbe-Grillet.

all part of the experience of the food—perhaps in no cuisine more than the Provençal. Elizabeth David, writing shortly after World War II when rationing was still in force, took this idea to prose, verbally awakening the imaginations of British cooks to a canon of dishes involving not powdered egg or Spam, but hefty glugs of olive oil, hunks of butter, garlic, aromatic herbs and strong salty flavors from both land and sea.

On a more tangible level, Provençal cuisine shows us what food can be when great produce is available. Ingredients are a combination of those we have on home soil but better, riper—tomatoes, herbs, fresh fish—and those that only a Mediterranean climate can produce—such as capers, anchovies, olives. This cuisine prizes simple, well-loved flavor combinations and the mastery of technique, of getting the meat, the shellfish, the vegetables, the sauces perfectly *au point*. As we well know, only practice makes perfect. I hope I can introduce you to the skills so that you can at least start practicing.

First things first, always keep a few Provençal staples in the kitchen: canned anchovies and olives, jarred capers, good olive oil and a flat-leaf parsley plant neither break the bank nor take much upkeep, and when coarsely chopped and mixed together make a good tapenade. This is wonderful to dunk vegetables or bread into with drinks before a meal, complements cheese beautifully or can accompany chicken. Another super simple but very typical thing to try is combining butter with olive oil, lemon juice, capers and parsley to make a classic multipurpose sauce for fish such as mackerel and bream.

Herbs are not used in Provence in the same volume as they are in eastern Mediterranean and Middle Eastern cooking but they are essential: parsley, thyme, marjoram, oregano, tarragon, basil, dill and bay leaf—all of which grow happily inside or out in the United States. Provençal cuisine involves a kind of orchestral collaboration among ingredients. If garlic is the conductor, then wine and oil are on the cello and double bass, proteins like meat or fish are on violin and herbs provide percussion with the power to transform a dish entirely.

As a description, *à la provençale* usually refers to something (typically meat or fish) cooked in olive oil, garlic and parsley—the three essential Provençal ingredients. Among Elizabeth David's favorite dishes that follow this formula are partridges, crayfish, scallops, frog's legs, mushrooms, leeks, tomatoes . . . It works with almost anything and many other typical Provençal dishes such as bouillabaisse* or bourride, another regional fish soup, are simple embellishments of this underlying trinity of ingredients.

• • • •

*This uses several, varying types of fish and crustacean, along with onions, tomatoes, thyme, fennel, bay leaf and orange peel.

Fennel is an important vegetable in Provence, partly because it can be an addition to the orchestra or take a solo part. And it can also, of course, operate as an herb—either in seed form or as the wispy fronds that garnish salads and meats with the taste of grassy licorice. One classic local dish is *grillade au fenouil*—a meaty white fish such as sea bass or red mullet buttered and grilled with fennel and then coated in lit Armagnac, which sets the fennel on fire. In its raw form, fennel might be eaten as a crudité along with a host of other local vegetables—radishes, sweet red onions, cucumber, artichoke, celery and tomatoes. These could be dipped into an *anchoïade*, a cold sauce of blended anchovies, garlic and olive oil, to punctuate the palate before a meal. *Anchoïade* is a simple Provençal dip that's easily executed at home—give it a go with my recipe.

Provence's classic beef dish, for which I've also included a recipe, is *boeuf en daube à la Niçoise*: cutlets of beef slow-cooked for twelve hours in a rich stock with olives, whole oranges, garlic, bay leaves and juniper berries. *Gigot à la provençale* (a regional leg of lamb dish involving bread crumbs, garlic, parsley and thyme) is very typical, as is a cassoulet of mutton, pork or sometimes chicken cooked with white navy beans. Similar to Spanish and Portuguese *cocido* stews, this is an example of what is trendily termed "peasant food" (regardless of whether it's *actually* what peasants ate), and a meal that can be dressed up or down. Either the *gigot* or the *boeuf en daube* would be a wonderful centerpiece for a summer Sunday lunch. Start it cooking early in the morning or even the night before, and once all the ingredients are in you can just leave it on a low heat (giving it the occasional stir) until serving, with plain rice.

Using familiar ingredients and uncomplicated methods, a trip to Provence from your own kitchen isn't such a schlep. Equip yourself with the basic ingredients and the pantry staples suggested below, and you're all set to go. As on any trip, good reading is essential and Elizabeth David will provide that extra bit of inspiration, or magic, to bring a veritable symphony to your table.

**PANTRY LIST** • fennel • tomatoes • red wine (for true southern French character look for wines from the Pays d'Oc such as Grenache, Carignan and some Syrahs) • aromatic herbs (parsley, oregano, thyme, marjoram, tarragon, basil, dill, bay leaves) • spices (cinnamon, clove, juniper)

# • TAPENADE •

Ironically, given that I've always thought of tapenade as a dish that celebrates olives, its name comes from the local Provençal dialect word for capers (*tapenas*). This recipe was created by my uncle Justin, a wine buff with a vested interest in nibbles to accompany a great tipple. Some inspiration, courtesy of Justin, on what to drink with it: "When it comes to French wine, I prefer the good stuff, which is not right with this. So I would probably go for Côtes de Gascogne—something rustic and feisty enough to be a good foil for the tapenade. You certainly wouldn't waste a bottle of Pouilly, Montrachet, etc., on it. How about Louis Latour Pinot Noir? Awesome." Indeed. I'm quite fussy about olives—try not to use canned (although they will suffice) and definitely don't use delicious Kalamata (too Greek!). My preference would be the gorgeous, rich, wrinkled, stoned black olives you find on deli counters.

## • SERVES 10 AS AN APPETIZER •

4 oz good-quality black olives, stoned

1 x 2-oz can good-quality anchovies in olive oil, drained
 and coarsely chopped

2 whole chilies, de-seeded and chopped

2 garlic cloves, coarsely chopped

1 heaping tbsp capers

1½ tbsp flat-leaf parsley, chopped

1½ tbsp chives, chopped

2 tbsp extra virgin olive oil

1–2 tbsp crème fraiche (depending on how fiery your
 chilies are)

**1** • Throw all the ingredients in a food processor and combine until puréed. Transfer to a bowl, cover and refrigerate. The cold accentuates the "bite," according to my uncle Justin, so leave it in the fridge (preferably overnight) until you're ready to serve with some slices of your very best French bread or fresh vegetable crudités.

# • ANCHOÏADE •

For something so yummy, *anchoïade* is singularly unbeautiful. But that certainly changes once it's in your mouth. The most important thing is that you want to achieve a smooth sauce (either with a food processor or a mortar and pestle )—otherwise you'll end up with something resembling a tapenade or *bagna cauda*.

## • SERVES 6 AS AN APPETIZER •

1 x 2-oz can good-quality anchovies in olive oil,
    drained and coarsely chopped
2 garlic cloves, coarsely chopped
1 tsp red wine vinegar
freshly ground black pepper
⅔ cup extra virgin olive oil
toast, coarsely chopped flat-leaf parsley and
    crudités to serve

**1** • Blend the anchovies, garlic, vinegar and pepper in a food processor until they become a smooth paste. Alternatively, you could grind the ingredients together in a deep mortar and pestle, though it will be much harder work.

**2** • Once you're happy with the consistency of your paste you can start to add the olive oil—very, very gradually. Pour it into the mixture, with the motor running, in a fine and steady stream. You should be left with a thick sauce. If you're doing it by hand, add the oil gradually, beating between each addition of oil.

**3** • Serve on toast (topped with parsley to prettify) or with crudités, and try washing the whole lot down with a chilled Provençal rosé.

# • BOEUF EN DAUBE •

In Virginia Woolf's novel *To the Lighthouse*, this Provençal stew of braised beef in red wine is the maid's "masterpiece" over which she slaves for three days, "a confusion of savoury brown and yellow meats" made from a family recipe. The first time I made it, I simmered my own beef stock from bones. This took eight long hours and, although the resulting broth was outstanding, if you're pushed for time you can use a decent chicken stock. Just make sure you buy quality beef and give it the time it needs on the cooktop. I wouldn't bother forking out on expensive wine for this—a good value Côte de Rhône or something from the Pays d'Oc will do nicely. My method of marinating the beef in herbs, garlic and wine overnight before cooking isn't used by everyone, but I like to impart as much flavor as possible to the meat. I think this dish is best served with rice, although mashed potatoes and buttered pasta work well, too.

### • SERVES 4–6 •

2 tsp juniper berries
2 tsp black peppercorns
6 garlic cloves
big pinch sea salt
2¼ lb beef chuck (or any braising steak), trimmed
    and cut into 2-inch pieces
2 tbsp olive oil
3 sprigs thyme
1 tbsp flat-leaf parsley
3 sprigs rosemary
1 bottle red wine
2–3 tbsp all-purpose flour
¼ cup (½ stick) butter
2 yellow or white onions, or 6 shallots, coarsely chopped
2 carrots, coarsely chopped
3 celery sticks, coarsely chopped
2 plum tomatoes, coarsely chopped
7 oz diced bacon (pancetta or lardons)
2 bay leaves
2 cups beef or chicken stock
2 handfuls button mushrooms, cut in half if big
freshly grated nutmeg
sea salt and freshly ground black pepper
flat-leaf parsley to serve, chopped

**1 •** Grind the juniper berries, black peppercorns, 3 cloves of the garlic and the sea salt in a mortar and pestle and rub the mixture into the chunks of beef with the olive oil.

**2 •** Make a bouquet garni (a little fastened bundle of herbs) with the thyme, parsley and rosemary and place in a deep bowl with the seasoned beef. Pour enough red wine over the mixture to cover and leave in the fridge overnight, covered.

**3** • Remove the beef with a slotted spoon and coat each piece in flour. Heat 3½ tbsp of the butter in a heavy-bottomed flameproof and ovenproof pan (a Le Creuset number or similar is ideal for this) and brown the meat for 4–5 minutes or so, in batches if necessary. Remove and set aside.

**4** • Sauté the onion, carrots, celery, tomatoes and bacon in the residual butter over low heat for about 15 minutes until soft, then crush the remaining 3 garlic cloves and add with the bay leaves for another 2 minutes.

**5** • Add the seasoned meat and juices back to the pan. Pour on the marinade in which it sat overnight, the bouquet garni, the remainder of the bottle of wine and the stock. Simmer on the lowest heat possible for an hour.

**6** • Preheat the oven to 350°F.

**7** • Sauté the mushrooms in the remaining 2 tsp butter for 5 minutes. Set aside until you remove the casserole from the heat and then fold them in. Cover the casserole with foil and transfer to the oven for 2 hours before checking the meat to gauge how cooked it is—it should give way between your thumb and forefinger. The stew should be thick, so give it another 20–30 minutes in the oven uncovered if your sauce is too liquid.

**8** • Before serving, remove the bouquet garni and bay leaves, grate in a little nutmeg, season with salt and pepper and sprinkle with some fresh parsley.

# SPAIN

As one who appreciated the tragic side of eating, it seemed to him that anything other than fruit for dessert implied a reprehensible frivolity, and cakes in particular ended up annihilating the flavour of quiet sadness that must be allowed to linger at the end of a great culinary performance.
• MANUEL VÁZQUEZ MONTALBÁN, *The Angst-Ridden Executive* •

GROWING UP IN southeast London and being called Ximena* wasn't always straightforward. My classmates had an array of pronunciations for my old-fashioned Castilian name, the least enjoyable being "eczema." Wanting to avoid any association between their daughter and a skin complaint, my parents shortened it to Mina but, when I grew up and started to see the world, Ximena really came into its own. Over time, as my love affair with Spain, Spanish and the Hispanic diaspora has blossomed, I've grown to love my given name.

I find Spain intoxicating, and not just because my name is so identified with it. There is something more-ish (and, as we will discover, Moorish) about this culture that always leaves you wanting. From the food, I love the salt and the fat; from the language, the poeticism uttered in a nasal drawl. I love the gamut of Spanish music, from folksy flamenco guitars to saccharine Latin pop. I love the people's boundless energy blended with a *sin prisas* ("no rush") approach to life. And at home, I love their *mi casa es tu casa* attitude—Spanish doors are always open.

Spain has a hugely varied landscape and vast cultural inheritance, both reflected in its food. I've tried to give you a taste for the distinct character of four mainland regions, all with their own qualities to offer hungry travelers: rebellious and artsy Catalonia; Andalucía, of cold soups and Moorish architecture; the independent-spirited, gastronomic north; and the plateau

• • • •

*For the record, I'm not Spanish, but I kind of wish I was. It took my mum and dad three weeks and several books of baby names to agree on a name for me. In such circumstances, you might think that parents arguing over their newborn's name would settle on something easy, inoffensive—Jane maybe, or possibly Lucy. But no, I'm Ximena, the name of my mother's equally English great-aunt.

of central Spain that surrounds my beloved Madrid. When cooking Spanish food, you often only need one good, deep pot. The technique for dishes like *tortilla de patatas* can seem simple, sometimes even slapdash, but you'll find there is a knack. Try Javi's Tortilla recipe on page 67.

Maria José Sevilla, Spanish food expert and manager of food and wines at the Spanish Trade Commission in London, says that "Spanish cuisine was given two gifts: the Moors and the Roman Empire." To this I would add a third: the New World. While, as Sevilla said, the Islamic and Christian traditions are the founding pillars of Spanish cuisine, from the sixteenth century onward ingredients like potatoes, peppers, tomatoes and corn were brought in from the Americas and braided into Spanish cuisine. Without these, many of the typically Spanish dishes we know and love today would not exist.

Following the Expulsion of the *Moriscos* (Spaniards descended from Muslim Moors who had been forced to convert to Christianity) between 1609 and 1614, the agricultural territories of the central and southern Spanish Meseta[*] regions became latifundios—vast expanses of farmland owned by the Crown or awarded to nobility. A large landless class worked on the latifundios, which led to a striking dichotomy between rich and poor. In the north of the country, the pattern of land ownership was the reverse—*minifundios* were a hotchpotch of small farms owned predominantly by poor farmers. The food produced and eaten by the different social groups depended on the respective system within which they were operating, as well as their social class.

Spain is still no stranger to stark social dichotomies. Rachel McCormack, an expert in Spanish cuisine, notes: "In Andalucía, for example, you're either a person of status—a *señorito*—or a poor peasant. Ideas about hierarchy have been perpetuated over the centuries and still reign strong today." In the middle years of the twentieth century, when other European countries were consolidating their democratic systems, many of which had been developing for hundreds of years, Spain swapped the remnants of the old feudalism for fascism. The Franco regime ruled from 1939 to 1975, stunting Spain's cultural development on the world stage. When we think about Spain and Spanish food, it is worth remembering that it was only released from the straitjacket of a Fascist government within the last forty years. These days the division in Spanish cuisine is not so much about latifundios versus *minifundios* as the creations of the modernist culinary superstars concentrated around Barcelona, the Basque Country and Madrid, versus the food (such as *cocidos* and tapas) that the majority of people all over the country actually eat.

● ● ● ●

[*]The Meseta is the central Spanish plateau.

I feel passionate about demonstrating the depth and breadth of Spanish cuisine, about showing that there's more to it than some ham with fried potatoes or an omelette swimming in oil. Like Nieves Barragán Mohacho, head chef at London's Fino and Barrafina Spanish restaurants, I want to quash—once and for all—the clichés around it being greasy and bland. "I try to cook like Grandma used to," Nieves told me. "Nobody does that anymore. For me, eating well is a spoon in one hand and bread in the other. That is the essence of Spain." If you've ever been suspicious of Spanish food, hopefully I can win you round—as I was won round to my name.

# PIMENTÓN

• • •

*Pimentón* is the smoked paprika flavor that is often seen to define Spanish food. People are more likely to recognize it as a flavor than as an ingredient. London-based chef, food writer and restaurateur José Pizarro told me he'd been accused of feeding vegetarians chorizo in the past, when in fact what they could taste was a sprinkle of *pimentón* in a meat-free dish. It is a fine, deep red powder that is often dusted over dishes like *pulpo a la Gallega* just before serving, leaving little red flecks over the boiled octopus and potatoes. *Pimentón* is also a key ingredient of many national dishes like *cocido* stews and chorizo, where it is responsible for the red color and strong, smoky notes. *Pimentón* is made in both Murcia and Extremadura (in the south) by drying out capsicum peppers in industrial chambers before being milled to make the smoky dust. Capsicum peppers first came into Spain with Christopher Columbus in the sixteenth century, who returned from his New World adventures with a handful of ingredients including the potatoes and tomatoes that would change Spanish food irreversibly. *Pimentón* comes in different varieties from sweet through to spicy, though always with smoky notes; this smokiness is particularly intense in *pimentón de la Vera*, the Extremaduran DOC (denomination of origin).

This is a must-have pantry ingredient if you're interested in making Spanish food—it is prevalent all across Spain with the exception of Catalonia (see page 51). My cupboard is never without a *pimentón*, either to sprinkle over a Spanish creation or to embellish simple soups, ham or cheese with some smoky oomph.

• • •

# CATALONIA

Their attitude towards food, like that of the rest of the stall-holders in the market,
was deeply serious; it was not something they had learned, or been told about;
it was in their blood, it was in their eyes when they turned to you...'
• COLM TÓIBÍN, *Homage to Barcelona* •

THE CATALANS HAVE an independent spirit and a strong sense of self. This cascades into almost every facet of life in Catalonia, from the language (a striking blend of Castilian Spanish, French and Italian) to art and architecture of dizzying originality* and, naturally, food. In the quote above, Colm Tóibín alludes to the merchants' intrinsic knowledge of local food (in this case duck) at Barcelona's Boqueria market—an edible clue to the Catalans' fierce pride in all things native to their region. There's nothing quack about their knowledge of local duck...

On a political level, Catalan separatism dates back as far as the seventeenth century and remains alive and well today.[†] This separatist sensibility has inevitably permeated into food culture. Though there are similarities with other Spanish cuisines, particularly Central and Andalucían, there are also significant departures from the quintessentially Castilian food of central Spain (see page 63). For instance, *pimentón—the* Spanish condiment spice, found peppered over countless dishes— is absent from Catalan cuisine, which means its dishes tend to be more subtle. Without this dominating flavor, which is as strong as its bright red color suggests, the palate picks up other

••••

*Catalonia's most famous architectural riches are perhaps Gaudí's buildings such as the Sagrada Familia church in Barcelona while, in terms of art, the work of Salvador Dalí and Joan Miró display some of the unique work of Catalan creatives.

†Successive treaties between France and Spain saw Catalonia passed between the two countries and its identity molded to wherever it belonged at a given time, inevitably creating a place that stood apart from both nation-states. Catalan nationalism emerged from this and intensified with the arrival of the Franco regime (1939–1975), which saw a crackdown on the use of the Catalan language in an official capacity and a resulting determination on the part of the Catalans to uphold their cultural individuality.

things. Take the *butifarra* cured sausage typical of Catalonia in which spices like cinnamon and nutmeg come through, as well as the taste of the pork itself. *Butifarra* is eaten across Catalonia, most typically with white beans[*] and onions but sometimes on its own or in *escudella i carn d'olla*, or *escudella* for short, a meat soup served over two courses.

A favorite at Christmas and a restorative meal for cold winter months, the *escudella* combines spiced meatballs (called *pilotes*), *butifarra*, bones and any offcuts of meat you may have, all cooked in a stock with seasonal vegetables such as carrots and cabbage. The stock is then drained off and boiled with pasta to make a broth for a first course. Next, the meat and the vegetables are eaten separately. It's a simple, economic way to serve a meal with a civilized structure out of a one-pot technique.

Catalan cuisine resembles that of Provence in its use of a dried mountain-herb mix including thyme, rosemary, bay leaf and laurel, and in some dishes. *Samafaina*, for example, a slow-cooked reduction of onions, garlic, eggplants, zucchini and bell peppers, is almost identical to the Provençale ratatouille.

The base for almost every Catalan dish is a *sofregit*, the regional equivalent of the better-known Castilian Spanish *sofrito*. Essentially, this is a soft and sweet foundation upon which to add other ingredients (see pages 74–75). The *sofregit* is fundamental to the Catalan kitchen, composed of wilted white onions simmered with double quantities of tomatoes and olive oil over a low heat. Catalan cooks will always have it on hand, perhaps prepared in advance and ready for whenever a recipe calls for it. So many Catalan dishes start with a *sofregit*, so get yours going on the cooktop, pronto. In fact, there's no reason why you can't make a batch and freeze it, ready for when you fancy a brief kitchen sojourn in Catalonia.

Sauces are integral to Catalan food, the perfect complement to local ingredients like fish and seafood. *Romesco*, originally from the fisherman's quarter of Tarragona, is a versatile roasted pepper sauce lending sweet Mediterranean flavors to fish (for which it was purportedly designed) and meat dishes. Combining ground almonds, hazelnuts and bread crumbs with roasted peppers and *sofregit*, *romesco* is a dense and delicious condiment. The same goes for *picada*, a paste of ground nuts, bread crumbs, chocolate, parsley and saffron used to thicken and finish stews. The *picada*, described by American writer and expert on the cuisine of Catalonia Colman Andrews as one of the "bookends" of Catalan cuisine (alongside the *sofregit*), echoes both the nutti-

••••

[*] The Catalans favor white and broad beans over chickpeas, both served in salads or in dishes like the *cocidos* of central Spain.

ness and the sweet and savory qualities you might find in Mexican dishes like moles (see pages 313–14; 316–17).* While *romesco* is definitely a condiment with visible presence on a plate, *picada* works more as a seasoning before serving.

Another very basic and versatile Catalan sauce is *alioli*, an emulsion of garlic and olive oil that's eaten alongside game, white meat or fish. Whether or not to make the (nontraditional) addition of eggs to *alioli* inspires heated debate in Catalonia. Whipping up oil and garlic alone into a thick, white sauce is a difficult art made easier by adding egg yolks, but this changes the sauce to something more closely resembling mayonnaise. (As if mayonnaise isn't already difficult enough!)

Just a stone's throw from Spain's "market garden" of Navarra (see pages 58–61), the rich range of fruit and vegetables in Catalonia means medieval and Moorish influences are expressed differently here from in drier Andalucia. (Think dishes such as duck with pears, peaches stuffed with mince, pears stuffed with beef, pork, onion, cinnamon and chocolate.) The verdant environment makes for wonderful vegetables: as we have seen, onions and tomatoes are crucial to this cuisine. One of the most typical Catalan dishes for me is *pa amb tomàquet* (literally "bread with tomato"), lightly toasted crusty bread onto which a little garlic is rubbed, oil drizzled and a whole tomato squeezed and emptied from its skin into a kind of light red mush. The importance of this dish to Catalan identity is put beautifully by Colman Andrews in his seminal book on Catalan cuisine. "*Pa amb tomàquet* arouses great nostalgic passion, great Proustian stirrings of sensuous recollection. It is Catalan comfort food, almost the very bread and butter (as it were) of Catalan cultural identity."†

Eggplants, peppers and zucchini are also key to Catalan cooking—once again mirroring Provençale cuisine. *Escalivada*, a mixture of steamed and softened strips of pepper and eggplant, is a typically Catalan accompaniment to meat (I've come across *butifarra* sausages in which the meat is mixed with a fine *escalivada* for sweetness). Catalans also combine eggplant with the likes of honey, raisins and pine nuts, which, reminiscent of Morocco (see page 283), hints at their Moorish culinary inheritance.

• • • •

*Chocolate might seem a bizarre addition to a savory dish, but it enriches sauces like these with an earthy bitterness and thickened texture, creating dishes of wonderful complexity. Why not try it in your kitchen sometime, either with something as simple as a tomato-based pasta sauce or to jazz up a red meat or game dish.

†I used to blog about foods inspired by the novels I read. After reading Carmen Laforet's *Nada*, the famous Catalan existential novel set in Barcelona, I made *pa amb tomàquet*. It was the first dish that sprang to mind when I thought of Catalonia, the image of lightly reddened, slightly soggy salty bread inseparable from my own memories of that city.

Garum, the flavoring made from fermented fish paste prevalent in the cuisine of Lazio (see page 86), was introduced by the Romans and still features in Catalan cuisine today, though it has been adapted into an anchovy and olive dip. Anchovies are widely eaten in various forms: deep-fried *per picar* ("to pick at") or along with vegetables like eggplants. The widespread use of salt cod (*bacallà*—see page 83) is also a product of ancient eating habits. It is served in various forms: with *samafaina*, in fritters or as a purée alongside vegetables. Though Catalonia has a wealth of seafood, preserved products like *bacallà* would have been a fallback on days when the catch was bad or perhaps during Lent, when the consumption of meat (but not fish) was prohibited.

Catalonia has a number of fish stews that bring together some of the hallmarks of the region's food. *Suquet* is perhaps the best-known example, a classic fisherman's stew of monkfish, halibut and bass heated in a stock of *sofregit* and *picada*, which is eaten all over Catalonia. Catalan food expert Rachel McCormack has contributed a fantastic recipe, which I urge you to try when you have easy access to fresh, meaty white fish.

Tossa de Mar, about a hundred miles north of Barcelona, has its own highly localized and simple fish and potato stew, which is often eaten with *alioli*. The *sarsuela* is altogether more elaborate. It calls for lobster, prawns, squid, clams and the most decadent varieties of fish available to you—sole, maybe—all cooked together in a *sofregit* base, a spice mixture (allspice, cinnamon, bay leaves) and rum. If *sarsuela* is the RuPaul of Catalan dishes—over the top—then I say embrace it. Catalonia's all about celebrating difference, after all.

**PANTRY LIST** • fresh fish (monkfish, halibut, anchovy) • salt cod • *butifarra* sausage • eggs • aromatic herbs (parsley, oregano, thyme, marjoram, tarragon, basil, dill, bay leaves) • white beans • honey • raisins • pine nuts • the *sofregit* ingredients: tomato, onion and olive oil

• • •

# • CATALAN FISH STEW •

Typically bookended with a *sofregit* at the beginning and a *picada* at the end of the cooking process, this fantastic fish stew—fortified with (preferably local) white wine—is a proud example of Catalan cuisine. Rachel McCormack reminds us that measurements here are approximate—this is more a way of cooking than a dish that relies on precise technique or quantities. If you can't find *guindilla* peppers, you could substitute small green chili peppers.

## • SERVES 4 •

1 large onion, finely diced
5 tbsp olive oil
3 garlic cloves, finely chopped
2 guindilla peppers, deseeded and chopped
5 tomatoes, skinned and chopped
½ cup all-purpose flour for coating
sea salt and freshly ground black pepper
1⅔ lb skinless and boneless white fish (preferably
    monkfish, haddock, cod, or bass but
    any fish would do)
9 oz waxy potatoes, peeled and thinly sliced
2 cups fish stock
¾ cup dry white wine
7 oz raw shelled king prawns
11 oz raw cleaned mussels in shells
⅔ cup ground almonds
2 tbsp flat-leaf parsley, chopped

**1 •** Sauté the onions in 2 tablespoons of the olive oil in a saucepan for 10 minutes. Add the garlic and sauté for another 3–4 minutes or until almost transparent. Add the guindilla peppers and tomatoes, reduce the heat to low and cook, uncovered, for 30 minutes.

**2 •** Place the flour in a shallow bowl and season it lightly. Heat another 2 tablespoons of the olive oil over high heat in a large frying pan (one with a lid). Flour the pieces of fish and fry them quickly, in batches if necessary, for 2–3 minutes, turning them frequently. Remove and set aside.

**3 •** Add the sliced potatoes to the frying pan with the remaining tablespoon of olive oil and let them sauté for 7 minutes. Add the tomato sauce, ½ cup of the fish stock and the white wine and let the potatoes cook for 15–20 minutes, until they're tender. Add the fried fish, the prawns and then the mussels and the rest of the stock and cook, covered this time, for about 5 minutes, until the fish is cooked and all the mussels have opened. Stir in the ground almonds and the parsley and test for seasoning just before serving.

## • HAZELNUT SOUP WITH HAZELNUT CROCANTI AND ICE CREAM •

This recipe for a delicious hazelnut "soup," another from Catalan food expert Rachel McCormack, was inspired by a dish she ate at Morros restaurant in Torredembarra, a town in the Tarragona region of Catalonia known for its prolific hazelnut production.

### • SERVES 6 •

1 pound blanched hazelnuts
1¼ cups superfine sugar
⅓ cup salted butter
3 oz heavy cream
3⅓ cups water
2 cups vanilla ice cream

**1** • Toast the hazelnuts in a large frying pan over medium-high heat for 5 minutes, shaking the pan regularly so the nuts brown evenly. Remove from the heat and allow to cool completely.
**2** • Preheat the oven to 350°F.
**3** • To make the crocanti, put one fifth of the cooled toasted hazelnuts in a food processor and process for about 1 minute, until they are finely ground. Place the ground hazelnuts, ½ cup of the sugar, the butter and cream in a saucepan over medium heat, stirring constantly, until the butter has melted and all the ingredients have combined.
**4** • Line a large baking sheet with a silicone sheet or some nonstick parchment paper and spread the hazelnut mixture on it thinly. Bake for 10–12 minutes in the oven, until lightly golden, watching carefully so it doesn't burn—the crocanti will melt further and spread on the tray. Remove and allow to cool and harden.
**5** • To make the soup put the remaining whole toasted hazelnuts, the remaining sugar and the water in a food processor and process for about 1 minute, until the ha-

zelnuts are very finely ground. Strain through a fine sieve, pushing through as much of the liquid as possible and discarding the leftover nuts. Place the strained soup in a jar, cover and refrigerate for at least 4 hours, or preferably overnight.

**6** • To serve, place a ball of ice cream in a bowl and pour the hazelnut soup over it. Break the crocanti up into large pieces and scatter over the soup.

# NORTHERN SPAIN

*It is autumn in Galicia and the rain is falling silently and slowly on the gentle green land. Sometimes pine-covered hills emerge from hazy, slumbering clouds.*
• FEDERICO GARCÍA LORCA, *Sketches of Spain* •

THE NORTH OF Spain, from Aragon in the east to the western pocket of Galicia tucked in above Portugal, is an agricultural and culinary dreamscape. Tiny farmsteads, the former *minifundios*, cover the stunningly varied northern terrain—from lush green pastures to forests heavily populated with game, and from gorse-carpeted, snow-peaked mountains to what is arguably Europe's richest coastline. Each region of northern Spain has its own set of raw ingredients, dishes and gastronomic identity: La Rioja, famous across the world for its distinctive Tempranillo blend red wines, Navarra, known as Spain's "market garden," and the popular *pintxo* (northern-style tapas) culture of Pais Vasco (the Basque Country).

Yet despite the rich landscape, produce and cuisine in the Spanish North, I can't help but feel it's better known for other things: Santiago de Compostela in Galicia, the destination for thousands of Catholic pilgrims who trek to the tomb of Saint James each year; or Pamplona in Navarre, where every July the Running of the Bulls—the festival known as San Fermin—descends to its cobbled streets; or for regional languages (in Pais Vasco and Galicia) and political tensions.[*]

In recent decades, Pais Vasco (and by default, northern Spain as a whole) has become famous for *la nueva cocina*, Spain's answer to nouvelle cuisine. Situated so close to neighboring France, French haute cuisine has inevitably had a bearing on the high-end cuisine of the Spanish Basque country. But in the mid-1970s the first seeds of something uniquely Spanish were sewn, drawing on local ingredients, classical French and modernist techniques. Today the su-

• • • •

[*] Separatist movements hold substantial sway in northern Spain, particularly around the Basque country, where a unique language and independent sensibility exist. The best-known separatist group is ETA, *Euskadi Ta Askatasuna*, which translates to "Basque Homeland and Freedom."

perstars of Basque haute cuisine—restaurants like Arzak, Mugaritz, Elkano—understandably get a lot of press, but often eclipse the profile of Basque home-cooking, which is fantastic in its own right. Though *nueva cocina* is a product of northern Spain, it is of course not representative of what most people eat on a daily basis.

The temperate climate of the north of Spain favors apples, pears, peaches and cherries rather than the citrus fruits of the south of the country; white beans are more common than chickpeas; and artichokes, asparagus and peas are grown rather than almonds and pistachios. The variety of olives changes, too. Up here, groves of Arbequina olives thrive on the chalky soils surrounding the river Ebro, and cope well with the temperature extremes from one season to the next.[*]

In *The Food of Spain*, Claudia Roden describes northern Spanish food as "seafood and milk puddings," while others call it Spain's "cheese and apple country." Expanses of pasture offer a rich source of nourishment to cattle, and convert to high-quality milk. The prevalence of dairy—butter, cream—and the French influence on northern cuisines (particularly Basque cuisine) mean that creamy sauces are more frequently found here than elsewhere in Spain. Foods we would normally associate with France, like quiches and béchamel sauces, are not uncommon. The "milk puddings" to which Roden refers include *natillas* (incredibly delicious Spanish custards), *arroz con leche* (rice pudding), *leche frita* (fried custard) and cooked eggy flans not unlike *crema Catalana*. The perennial practice of bullfighting reminds us how important cattle are in the Spanish north. Cows are raised both for beef and dairy. According to chef José Pizarro, this is the best beef in Spain, with cuts like *chuleton* (Txuleton in Basque, or "rib-eye steak" in English), which pair beautifully with local cider.

Cheese of all varieties is a big deal in northern Spain, not least in the Asturias, the northern coastal region sandwiched between Galicia and Cantabria, known in Spanish as *El Pais de los Quesos* or "the Land of Cheese." Defined by their rusticity, cheeses are aged in bat-inhabited caves nestled into the Picos de Europa[†] mountain range. *Cabrales* is the best-known, a blue cow's cheese made from unpasteurized milk and aged for several months. Coarse, crumbly and pungent, it pairs beautifully with the region's ciders.[‡] Others include *treviso*

• • • •

[*] In arid Andalucia, olive varieties like the Picual grow better.

[†] Spanning Asturias, Cantabria, Castilla-Leon.

[‡] Wine from northwestern Spain is particularly à la mode right now. The gorgeously dry Albarino grape does very well in Galicia, with its minerally soils and extremes in climate. Until recently, wine was more the strength of the northeast—La Rioja being the most famous example—and the northwest focused more on home-brewed ciders and local ales.

from Cantabria (another, slightly lighter, blue cow's cheese) and, from Galicia, *tetilla*. The name means "little breast" and the cheese comes shaped in small peaks resembling just that—complete with tips like nipples. Toward the Basque country and farther east in Navarra, hard sheep's cheeses are more common. Smoky, unpasteurized *Idiazabal* and *Itxas Egi* are both infused with the taste of sweet herbs and clover, again reflecting the pastures on which the animals graze.

Seafood is emblematic in Galicia; the scallop shell for example, so often found washed up on Galician shores, has become symbolic of the Santiago pilgrimage. From hake (*merluza*), octopus (*pulpo*) and clams (*tellinas*) to lesser known *quisquillas* (baby prawns, which wriggle fresh on a bed of ice at Barrafina) and obscure *percebes*[*] (known in English as goose barnacles), the northern Spanish coastline is replete with outstanding seafood. For me, the most exciting dish in the whole of Spain—and one of my favorite of all foods—is *pulpo a la Gallega* (literally, "Galician octopus"), octopus boiled several times and served simply with boiled potatoes and a dusting of *pimentón*.

Lorca wrote of "Galicia's eternal drizzle," which equally applies to Asturias and Cantabria. Produce local to these regions is hardy and wild, suited to unpredictable weather and cooler temperatures. Apples are rife and are used in the production of local ciders as well as desserts like sweet apple pies (*empanadas de manzana*). Potatoes, white beans, maize chestnuts and walnuts are just some of the local ingredients now used to complement meat and seafood, but which probably made up the core diet of peasants over the centuries.

Historically, there was crippling poverty in Galicia. In *A Hospice in Galicia*, Lorca describes the hospice inmates, "rachitic, emaciated children," as smelling "of poorly seasoned food and extreme poverty." Roden is fascinating on this subject and says of nineteenth-century Galicia that "the only way out of poverty was emigration." For this reason, local dishes such as boiled octopus, *pimientos de Padrón*,[†] meat empanadas (see page 343) and even potato and white bean stews are found in the places to which Galicians fled—all over Spain and the Hispanic New World.

• • • •

[*] These are found almost exclusively along the Galician *Costa da Morte*, or "Coast of Death" (so called because it was the scene of so many shipwrecks), and are perilously hand-harvested each winter for Christmas spreads. With long, bark-colored stems leading into beak-like tips, *percebes* are sucked from their shells and, in the words of Nieves Barragán Mohacho, are like "having a sip of the sea."

[†] *Pimientos de Padrón* are small green capsicum peppers native to the Galician town of Padrón. They are usually sautéed with olive oil and salt, and are utterly addictive—particularly when accompanied by a glass of Albarino (Galician white wine).

Moving eastward, plentiful green vegetables, mushrooms and even white truffles become more common. Cuisine is increasingly enriched by the French tradition, wines of Rioja and the courtly history of Aragon and Navarra, which together make for delicious sauces to accompany dark meats like *chuletillas* (suckling lamb chops with a milky flesh texture) and game like rabbit. Delicious sauces, indeed, but as Cervantes observed in *Don Quixote*, "Hunger is the best sauce in the world." And he was right. You'd best be hungry when you embark on this voyage—there's a lot of delicious ground to cover.

**PANTRY LIST** • seafood (*percebes*, octopus, langoustine, razor clams, squid) • cheese (Cabrales, Treviso, Tetilla) • white beans • chestnuts • walnuts • wine grapes like Albarino (Galicia), Tempranillo and Tempranillo blends (Rioja)

• • •

# • PADRÓN PEPPERS •

Here we have the easiest recipe in this book. Effortless, delicious and quintessentially Galician, these little green peppers may look like chilies but are for the most part harmless, with a sweetness complemented by crunchy sea salt and good olive oil. Roughly one in ten, however, is spiked with a burst of heat. Eating them becomes Russian roulette for the greedy.

### • SERVES AS MANY AS YOU LIKE •

1–2 tbsp extra virgin olive oil
as many Padrón peppers as you like
big pinch sea salt

**1** • Pour the olive oil into a heavy frying pan, set over medium-high heat and let it get hot. Stand back.
**2** • Tip the peppers into the pan (again, keep it at arm's length) and let them fry, slightly blackening and blistering over the heat. Keep shaking the pan to move them around.
**3** • When the peppers are blistered and charred on all sides, take them off the heat and arrange on a plate. They will start to deflate slightly. Sprinkle with a good pinch of salt and serve hot.

# • GARLIC PRAWNS AND ASPARAGUS •

This dish is found all over Spain but perhaps sits most comfortably in this section, combining as it does the gorgeous vegetables of Spain's temperate "market garden" regions such as Navarra with the exemplary seafood of the northern coast. This recipe is from José Pizarro, who says that the key to this dish is the use of raw prawns, which ensures they don't become overcooked. Good-quality olive oil is also essential, as is an appetite for intense quantities of lightly cooked garlic! You may want to add some citrus punch with a squeeze of lemon to serve. *Buen provecho*!

## • SERVES 4 AS A STARTER •

6 asparagus spears
20 large raw prawns, shelled
6 tbsp extra virgin olive oil
10 garlic cloves, finely chopped
1 dried chili, crumbled
1½ tbsp flat-leaf parsley, chopped
big pinch sea salt flakes
lemons for serving

**1 •** Wash and dry the asparagus spears and snap off the woody ends. Cut on the diagonal into lengths that match the size of the prawns. Blanch in boiling salted water for a minute. Drain and dry on paper towel.

**2 •** Heat the olive oil in a large frying pan over a high heat and add the chopped garlic. Stir and add the prawns and asparagus before the garlic colors. Cook for about a minute. The prawns will start to turn pink. Turn them over, add the chili and cook for another minute, until the prawns are completely pink all over.

**3 •** Stir in the parsley, scatter over some salt flakes, add a squeeze of lemon juice and eat immediately with lots of bread to mop up the glorious juices.

# CENTRAL SPAIN

His habitual diet consisted of a stew, more beef than mutton,
of hash most nights, boiled bones on Saturdays, lentils on Fridays,
and a young pigeon as a Sunday treat.
• MIGUEL DE CERVANTES, *Don Quixote* •

AS YOU LEAVE Madrid on the train, a graying crinoline of the city suburb blends into a vast stretch of farmland on the horizon, where little happens save for the wind grazing the crops. Life is simple across most of Spain's Meseta (plateau), belying the sense of license you find in Madrid—where the political pulse and hedonistic heartbeat of Spain beat strongest.

Countless writers have evoked the big-skied bleakness of this countryside—stiflingly hot in summer, biting cold in winter—not to mention films like Bigas Luna's *Jamón Jamón*, in which a 1990s-washed Penélope Cruz is but a dot on the massive, dry, rolling horizon. The odd wooden bull—giant, painted black—crowns the occasional hill and reminds you of your Spanish whereabouts as the nondescript yellow landscape flashes past.

Central Spanish cuisine is noticeably less varied than elsewhere in the country. Seized from the Moors in 1492, this is a vast area that was governed by a small elite until relatively recently, limiting the scope of different foods available to the majority of people. Meat has traditionally been a luxury. Carnivorous delicacies include *cochinillo* (suckling pig), game (squab, quail, partridge, rabbit and wild boar, which sometimes congregate in a stew to be eaten alongside local flatbread made with chickpea flour) or baby lamb. Nevertheless, some of the products that most define Spanish flavors, such as *pimentón* (see page 50) and saffron, have their origins in central Spain. It is also a cuisine in which the lingering influence of the Moors and the Jews is clearly visible.

Though it is the largest city in Spain, Madrid is a small, compact place. The population of its metropolitan area (about 6.5 million) is roughly double that of the city center, which you can walk across in half an hour. In 2009, I lived just north of Fuencarral by Bilbao metro station, which I was virtually able to ignore, preferring to walk down through the bohemian nook of Malasaña to reach the center. My route took me along busy Gran Via, past the sad faces of girls waiting for business on Calle Montera, and the throbbing Plaza del Sol, where people protest and visitors flock. Beyond that: Plaza Santa Ana, where street artists woo tourists; the big galleries of Huertas; ever-sunny Retiro park and La Latina, where on Sunday the city's tapas culture comes out in full swing.

Small in size but endowed with a sense of endless possibility (I was frustrated only by an inability to find good hummus and my bra size), Madrid is a special place. Even amidst the din of noisy Spaniards and tourists, of boozy nights and traffic, you can find peace. And although I ended up making my own hummus (no hardship, really), Madrid boasts some of the best food in Spain. There is a huge appetite for Spanish regional cuisines, which is reflected on a Sunday amble down Calle de Cava Baja in La Latina. This little street becomes (unofficially) pedestrianized on a Sunday afternoon, when the tourists and locals alike hop between bars specializing in anything from Canarian to Galician and Andalucían to Catalan cuisines.

You might expect that being so far inland would compromise the quality of its seafood. But the capital arguably has the best fish market in all of Spain, Mercado de San Miguel, where old faithfuls like *gambas* (prawns) and *trucha* (trout) convene with the more regional specialties like *percebes* (goose barnacles) and *pulpo* (octopus) of Galicia.

For all the great food that assembles there, however, Madrid doesn't have a lot to call its own. *Cocido Madrileño* is the exception: a slow-cooked stew using chickpeas, potatoes, several types of meat and sausage including chorizo, morcilla (blood sausage), pork leg, beef brisket, *jamón serrano* and sometimes chicken. The dish is said to have originated with the Spanish Sephardic Jews and bears similarities to *adafina*, a slow-cooked stew for the Jewish Sabbath.[*] Jewish influences are everywhere in central and southern Spanish cuisine— from the use of chickpeas and eggplants to generous lashings of garlic and almonds, or honey in desserts. The food native to Madrid is similar to that found out on the Meseta: stews made with pulses and offcuts of meat, bread, Manchego sheep's cheese and *jamón*. Dishes from central Spain are guaranteed to please the lover of one-pot dishes: rustic flavors congregate in simple, warming *cocidos* or soups (as in Portugal, see page 76). If you understand the

• • • •

[*] After the Spanish Inquisition, around forty thousand Jews converted to Christianity and, eager to appear integrated, began to eat pork—hence its starring role in *cocido Madrileño* and the departure from a traditional *adafina* recipe.

fundamental base ingredients—*pimentón*, garlic and salt—then these dishes are easy to replicate at home, or can simply be used as inspiration for meals cooked in a Spanish style.

Claudia Roden aptly subtitles her chapter on central Spain with "bread and chickpeas"—two foodstuffs eaten across central Spanish society, from peasants to princes. The Meseta, with its light, dry soil and long hot summers, is suited to the growth of grains like wheat and barley and pulses like chickpeas (*garbanzos*) and lentils (*lentejas*). Chickpeas are a good canvas for other flavors: chorizo or offcuts of meat, *pimentón* in soups and *cocidos*. These are cheap, nutritious and perennially sustaining complete meals.*

*Migas*, bread crumbs sautéed in olive oil, make a simple but filling accompaniment to all sorts of food and can be seasoned with chorizo, bacon, garlic, *pimentón* and vegetables such as bell peppers. A classic poor man's dish— the food of the transhumant ranchers who traveled the Meseta with their herds—*migas* are found across Spain and the dish has recently undergone a kind of gentrification, finding its way onto restaurant menus. *Torrijas*, or "Spanish French toast" (bread fried with cinnamon, cardamom and citrus zest), is most often enjoyed around Easter week. Simple but satisfying, it is foods like *migas*, *torrijas* and *cocidos* that give central Spanish cuisine what chef José Pizarro describes as its "comfort food" qualities.

José, of London restaurants José and Pizarro, comes from Extremadura in the southwest of central Spain. He says that while the region's traditionally ascetic qualities and its immense poverty are reflected in its food, local flavors are in fact amplified by this simplicity. "Spanish food, particularly that of Extremadura and Castilla-Leon, is all about letting the ingredients speak for themselves." Nowhere is this truer than in Extremadura, where some of the country's best ham and cheese are produced, the result of the nutritious diet of acorns and wild herbs in the *dehesa*,† on which pigs and sheep graze.

Central Spain is famous all over the world for its ham, aged for between one and a half and four years, which comes in several forms from *jamón serrano* (younger, lighter, pinker ham which is cured at high altitudes all over Spain) to *jamón Ibérico* (made from the meat of acorn-fed black-hooved pigs, it is darker and richer than its serrano cousin and, in my opinion, is best

• • • •

*There's also an abundance of lentils and various types of bean, which are similarly useful for stews and soups, carrying small amounts of cheaper meat for rich flavors.

†The *dehesa* is a grassland ecosystem unique to the central Iberian peninsula and is populated by oak trees, wild herbs, game, mushrooms, sheep and pigs. It is extensive in Extremadura, where black-footed pigs (*pata negra*) feast on acorns, making for intense, nutty ham that lasts long enough to be eaten year-round.

enjoyed on its own). The longer it is aged, the more of a delicacy it is. Killed between December and March, every morsel of pig is used—blood, intestines and bones all go toward stocks and sausages such as morcilla (like the British black pudding). A combination of *Ibérico* ham and barbecued chicken seduced me to the wiles of omnivorism. Be mindful, vegetarians.

**PANTRY LIST** • *pimentón* • coriander, bay leaves, thyme and parsley • *Ibérico* ham • Manchego cheese • tomatoes • chickpeas • beans • lentils • almonds • chorizo • morcilla

• • •

# • ZUCCHINI CREAM •

This almost embarrassingly easy soup, the recipe for which comes from my friend Javi, can be whipped up very quickly as a starter before supper, or makes a good hearty lunch year-round. Use Manchego cheese if you want to be authentic, though cheddar also works perfectly well.

### • SERVES 4 AS STARTER OR 2 AS A MAIN WITH BREAD •

2 large zucchini (about 1⅛ lb), sliced thickly
1 leek, cut into chunks
1 large potato, peeled and cut into chunks
2 oz hard cheese, chopped or grated (about ½ cup)
1⅓ tbsp butter
⅔ cup milk
extra virgin olive oil
salt to taste

**1** • Place the zucchini, leek and potato in a large pan and just cover them with water. Be careful not to add too much—2 cups should do it. Bring to a simmer over medium heat and cook for 20–25 minutes, until the potatoes are tender.
**2** • Remove from the heat and while the mixture is still hot, add the cheese, butter, milk and a large tablespoon of extra virgin olive oil. Blend to a creamy consistency and season with salt to taste before serving right away.

# • TORTILLA •

The best tortilla, in my opinion, is one with dark, almost caramelized potatoes and onion, with a gooey center of not-quite-cooked egg. This is just how they cook it at Juana La Loca (a restaurant named for a "crazy girl" called Juana) in Madrid's La Latina. My friend Javi taught me how to make the perfect tortilla. His technique is maverick, freestyle and involves a lot of expletives but, having made tortilla with him more times than I can remember, this recipe is a pretty good guide.

## • SERVES 4 •

2 cups sunflower oil
2¼ lb waxy potatoes (red ones such as Desiree
    work well), peeled, halved then sliced thickly
1 white onion, finely sliced
6 medium eggs
½ tsp salt
olive oil for frying

**1** • Heat the sunflower oil in a deep-sided pan for 5–10 minutes over medium-high heat. Drop the potatoes and onion in the oil and cook until they start to brown (but not burn). You are essentially "boiling" the potatoes and onion in oil, which should be gently bubbling. Keep moving the mixture to prevent it sticking. This will take 30–40 minutes. Drain off the oil and retain for the next time you want to whip up a tortilla (you can use it two or three times).
**2** • In a large bowl, beat together the eggs and the salt. Then stir in the drained potatoes and onions, making sure they become coated in the egg. Mash the ingredients a little, but make sure it's all still nice and lumpy.
**3** • Heat a large tablespoon of olive oil in a frying pan until it starts to smoke. Raise the heat to high and pour in the mixture. After 30 seconds or so, reduce the heat to medium to low. Cook until the tortilla starts to come away from the sides of the pan slightly and is golden in color when you peek underneath—3–5 minutes. Now it is time to turn.
**4** • Take a big plate and slide the tortilla onto it without tipping it—the cooked side of the tortilla should be against the plate. Now turn the plate back into the pan so that the uncooked side hits the heat. Cook for a minute or so. Then put back onto the plate and serve.

# ANDALUCÍA

We talked of manly things, of horses and knives and ropes, and crops and watering and hunting and wine. Maria brought dishes of pepper and meat to the table. Pedro loaded my plate with the choicest pieces. Then he helped himself while Maria crouched beside him and picked at pieces from his plate.

• CHRIS STEWART, *Driving over Lemons* •

THE ANDALUCÍAN LANDSCAPE is a treasure trove of natural beauty and ingredients—olive groves and terraces of garlic, almonds and pomegranates, oranges and, naturally, lemons, to name just a few. The scenery shines off the pages of (writer, farmer and founding member of the pop band Genesis) Chris Stewart's memoir. This is an enchanted land of nuts, fruit, vegetables and happy livestock maturing in the golden sunlight. And that's before you consider all that humanity has contributed to the landscape: Granada's Alhambra, the Caliphate in Cordoba and orange-lined avenues in Seville.

These opulent surroundings are paired with a stripped back cuisine. Andalucíans have a no-frills approach to food—but when the raw materials are this good, who needs thrills? "Peasant food" is undoubtedly an overused expression in our age of glorifying authentic home-cooked fare, but much Andalucían food is the genuine article: a cuisine born both of the land and the necessity to feed a large workforce.[*] Sustaining and practical, it was designed to complement the blistering summers and bright sunshine, and drew on ingredients that were immediately available. This simple and affordable food was, over time, seamlessly integrated into the canon of Andalucían cooking as a whole and hasn't been eaten by the peasant class exclusively for quite some time.

Examples include the famous trio of refreshing Andalucían soups: gazpacho (cold tomato soup from Seville), *salmorejo* (the equivalent from Cordoba, though often more elaborately garnished with eggs) and *ajo blanco* (garlic

••••

[*] The latifundios created a culture in which a tiny privileged minority were responsible for massive stretches of agricultural land and a substantial peasant labor force to work it (see page 48).

soup). Another is *papas a lo pobre* (literally, "poor man's potatoes"). Stewart describes a farmer whipping up some poor man's papas before him: frying two big cups of olive oil with a couple of onions, a whole, unpeeled head of garlic, coarsely chopped potatoes, whole green and red bell peppers, a fistful of olives, a dozen pickled chili peppers, thyme and lavender.

Seville, located on the Guadalquivir River in the southwest of Spain, was the first stop for goods arriving from the New World (see "Sugar and Spice and All Things Nice," pages 154–57). This means it would have been the point of entry for ingredients like potatoes, tomatoes and chili peppers, chocolate and vanilla, all of which are seamlessly integrated into Spanish and European cuisines today. Essential by-products of these ingredients such as *pimentón* and "old favorite" Spanish dishes like *patatas bravas*[*] as well as the *sofrito*[†] base for so many dishes, have all been enabled by goods that first came into Europe via Andalucía.

Andalucían cuisine combines many of the qualities you see in central Spanish food—the ham, the *pimentón*, the chickpeas—and Catalonia, with its fish and seafood, often deep-fried and enjoyed with Catalan sauces such as *romesco* and *alioli*. Claudia Roden goes so far as to say, "Andalucíans are the world's best at frying fish and seafood," and she may well be right. I can remember eating *buñuelos de bacalao* (salt cod deep-fried in a crisp batter) and fried prawns on a back street just off the Constitution Square in Malaga, thinking that, sitting there, shaded from the sun with a *caña* (little glass of beer) and a ripe tomato salad, life wasn't going to get much better.

While central Spain and Catalonia are flecked with residual Moorish influences to varying degrees, Andalucía remains Moorish by definition. The region's name provides a direct semantic link to Al-Andalus, the Moorish Iberian kingdom that occupied most of Spain and Portugal for over seven hundred years.[‡] Here the Muslim (and later Berber) invaders found terrain suited to their native ingredients such as olives, nuts and citrus, and brought with them their fondness for meat cooked with fruit, eggplants and honey and pastries with almonds and spices. With Spain's southernmost point of Tarifa just twenty-three miles from the Moroccan city of Tangier, Andalucía is, to this

• • • •

[*] *Patatas bravas* are deep-fried cubes of boiled potato accompanied by a spicy tomato sauce, which sometimes has a consistency not dissimilar to mayonnaise.

[†] Sliced onions and tomatoes slow fried in olive oil—the base for countless Andalucían, and Mediterranean, dishes. Turn to the *sofrito* chart on pages 74–75 for more information.

[‡] The kingdom of Al-Andalus varied in size over this period, during which wars with Christian kingdoms saw parts of the territory taken and then restored to the Moors. The name describes parts of the Iberian peninsula ruled by Muslims between 711 and 1492.

day, the Spanish gateway to North Africa. Moorish culinary inspiration didn't end when the Moors were expelled—it continues to shape the Andalucian cuisine of today. Think deep-fried cheese drizzled with honey, salt-baked fish in a cinnamon and pepper sauce, almond tart and even the beloved paella, whose main ingredients of rice and saffron are integral to the Moorish kitchen. Roden says that "no other region had so captured the allure of the old Muslim presence," a statement as applicable to Andalucian cuisine as to its architecture. This allure was in turn taken to the New World and can be seen in the tiling, courtyards and churches of colonial settlements in Latin America.

Andalucia is the home of sherry, the sweet fortified wine of Jerez, near Cadiz, and the surrounding region. Almost overnight, the perception of sherry has changed from "Granny's Christmas tipple" to a sophisticated alternative to wine. The wine lists of London's numerous (and highly successful) Spanish restaurants are now flooded with sherries; there are even dedicated sherry bars. And with the blossoming popularity of mixed drinks that combine spirits with wine, sherry also has a burgeoning presence on cocktail lists in bars and restaurants alike. It comes in various forms, from light and dry Fino and Amontillado through to darker, also dry Oloroso and dark, sweet Palo Cortado and Pedro Ximenez (try pouring some of the last over vanilla ice cream—delicious). Lesser known, perhaps because many people find them rather cloying, are the Moscatel equivalents from Malaga. These are also dark, incredibly sweet and, at 17 to 18 percent alcohol, very strong. Sipping Moscatel while idly picking at almonds in the midday sun isn't always a good idea. Trust me, I've tried.

If your next kitchen destination is Andalucia, be a little bit creative. You could try Nieves's or José's recipes, or you could imagine fusing the Spanish and Moorish culinary traditions and see what you come up with. This might take the form of a paella, which is relatively easy to freestyle. Play with your spices and quantities of them—cinnamon, cumin, saffron, *pimentón*—and make sure you have some typical Mediterranean ingredients like oranges, honey, dried fruit and nuts in stock. I'd suggest cooking with a glass of chilled Manzanilla sherry on hand, some smoked almonds to nibble and, if you're feeling cheesy, an immersive sound track of the Gipsy Kings.

**PANTRY LIST** • pomegranates • citrus fruit • tomatoes • spices (saffron, cinnamon, cumin) • eggs • herbs (parsley, lavender) • seafood • salt cod • sherry (Manzanilla, Fino, Oloroso, Amontillado, Pedro Ximenez)

# • GAZPACHO •

As I write this, London is scorching and gazpacho is the edible dream. For this very reason, the southern Spanish eat (or drink?) gallons of this tomato, vegetable and olive oil emulsion throughout their hot summers. José Pizarro, who contributed this recipe from his book, *Seasonal Spanish Food*, says that his family always has a jug of gazpacho in the fridge: it's the perfect light, cooling meal during 104-degree summers. Happily, it's also very easy to make. Just make sure you add the oil slowly and disperse it evenly through the other ingredients. The ham and melon are optional here, but oh so delicious. Good-quality ingredients are absolutely essential; as José says, "there is nowhere to hide." Buy the best ingredients you can find and you'll want to eat this year-round— scorching or otherwise. I do.

## • SERVES 4 •

2¼ pounds very ripe tomatoes
2 scallions, sliced
¼ small cucumber
½ garlic clove
1 tbsp sherry vinegar, to taste (Pedro Ximenez
    vinegar if you can get it)
3–5 tbsp extra virgin olive oil
sea salt and freshly ground black pepper
1½ oz cured ham, preferably *Ibérico*, diced (optional)
1½ oz sweet (very ripe) cantaloupe melon, diced (optional)

**1** • Simply put all the vegetables and the vinegar into a food processor. Then, with the motor running, slowly add the oil through the top. If the soup is too thick, add a little water to thin it out. Chill for 4 hours. Just before serving, add salt and pepper and adjust the vinegar balance if necessary. Garnish with the diced ham and melon.

# • SALT COD FRITTERS
# WITH TARTARE SAUCE •

Said to originate with the Moriscos (people descended from those Spanish Muslims who were forced to convert to Christianity in the fifteenth century), these
fishy fried dough balls display true Andalucían character: a penchant for deep-
frying fish and a nod toward the historic kingdom of Al-Andalus. Don't be put off
by the number of ingredients listed below—half are for the optional (but wonderful) tartare sauce. Also, though a deep fryer always helps, it is not essential here.
Just get the vegetable oil really hot in a deep saucepan. This is one of Nieves
Barragán Mohacho's spectacular recipes. You're learning from the best.

## • SERVES 4–6 AS A TAPA •

FOR THE FRITTERS
1 lb salt cod
1⅓ cups whole milk
2¼ cups water
7 tbsp unsalted butter, cubed
1¼ cups all-purpose flour
4 medium eggs
2 garlic cloves, very finely chopped
2½ tbsp flat-leaf parsley, chopped
juice of 1 lemon
salt and pepper
4 cups vegetable oil for deep-frying

FOR THE TARTARE SAUCE
2 egg yolks
2 tsp Dijon mustard
½ cup light olive oil
½ cup vegetable oil
1 shallot, finely chopped
1 oz capers, drained and chopped
1 oz cocktail gherkins, drained and chopped
juice of ½ lemon
1 hard-boiled egg, finely chopped
1½ tbsp flat-leaf parsley, finely chopped

**1** • Soak the salt cod in a bowl of cold water and refrigerate for 24 hours, refreshing the water at least three times. Drain, then pat dry with paper towels and cut into 1-inch cubes.

**2** • Place in a wide, deep saucepan and cover with the milk and 1¼ cups water. Slowly bring to the boil, then remove the pieces of cod from the pan with a slotted spoon. Allow to cool a little and then gently break up the cubes and remove any bones or skin.

**3** • In a different, medium-sized saucepan, heat 1 cup water and the butter together until the butter has melted. Bring to the boil and then remove from the heat. Immediately add the flour and whisk until smooth. Return the saucepan to the cooktop and place over a very low heat for 10 minutes, stirring frequently. When cooked remove from the heat and allow to cool for 10 minutes. Next, beat in the eggs one at a time. Add the salt cod pieces along with the garlic, parsley and lemon juice. Mix together and season. Transfer the mixture to a bowl and allow to cool, then cover and refrigerate for at least 2 hours.

**4** • To make the tartare sauce, whisk the egg yolks and mustard together in a bowl. Mix the oils in a separate bowl and gradually drizzle into the egg yolks, whisking continuously to form an emulsion with a thick mayonnaise-like consistency. When the oil is fully incorporated, add the shallot, capers and gherkins. Add the lemon juice and mix well, and finally stir in the chopped hard-boiled egg and parsley and season with salt and pepper. Refrigerate until needed.

**5** • When ready to cook the fritters, remove the mixture from the fridge and form into 1¼- to 1½-inch balls using a pair of spoons or your hands, whatever's easier. Heat the vegetable oil to 350°F in a deep fryer or a large, deep pan. Fry the *buñuelos* in small batches for 3–4 minutes or until golden brown and crisp, turning occasionally with a slotted spoon as they cook. Remove from the oil, drain on paper towels, season with salt and pepper and serve immediately with the tartare sauce.

# FRIED FOUNDATIONS

...

A *sofrito* is a lightly fried base for a dish, often a stew or soup, and is common across many cuisines—albeit with different ingredients (and different spellings). The word derives from the Spanish verb *sofreir* meaning "to fry lightly," although in France it is called a mirepoix (after the eighteenth-century aristocrat of Languedoc who employed the cook that created it) and in the Creole and Cajun cuisines of the American South it is known as the "holy trinity" of ingredients.

Ingredients differ according to the *terroirs* and food culture of the cuisine in question. These fried mixtures provide the founding flavors of a typical dish—the sweetness of onion, the spice from some chili, for example—and are often made in advance of cooking the dish for which they are intended. In Catalonia, for example, the *sofregit* of white onion, tomato and olive oil will be slowly sautéed and refrigerated so it is ready for use whenever called for (see page 52). Some of the most important regional variants have been illustrated for you opposite. Remember: as with any product of the kitchen, there are no hard and fast rules and many cooks will freestyle their *sofrito*. This is a rough guide to how these foundations for cooking are executed in different countries and regions.

| CUISINE | INGREDIENTS |
| --- | --- |
| FRANCE | celery + onion + carrot |
| SPAIN | onion + tomato + garlic + bell pepper |
| ITALY | garlic + onion + celery |
| PORTUGAL | onion + garlic |
| CREOLE & CAJUN | bell pepper + celery + onion |
| CARIBBEAN | onion + scotch bonnet + bell pepper |
| WEST AFRICA | tomato + pepper + onion |

# PORTUGAL

*The journey is never over . . . You have to see what you've missed the first time, see again what you already saw, see in the springtime what you saw in the summer, in daylight what you saw at night, see the sun shining where you saw the rain falling, see the crops growing, the fruits ripen, the stone which has moved, the shadow that was not there before.*

• JOSÉ SARAMAGO, *Journey to Portugal* •

NO TRIP IS ever the same twice, said the Nobel Prize–winning Portuguese writer José Saramago, for there are too many variables affecting the nature of travel: the seasons, the people, your own interests, tastes and perceptions. I've been to my favorite places many times (after all, it's familiarity that cements them as favorites, surely?), from the woods on Streatham Common to the north Norfolk coast, from the middle of Retiro park in Madrid to the top of Berkeley's Campanile tower. Each time the trip has been different, molded by who I was with, what we ate, the time of year, my mood.

In this respect, cookery is just like travel: food cannot be cloned. It would be nigh-on impossible to reproduce a dish exactly, since food is subject to the quality and provenance of ingredients, the preferences of its creator on a given day, the water, heat and equipment available. What we *can* do, however, when we cook a favorite meal, is reignite our memories of other places and times, transporting ourselves back to the past via flavors and textures.

Nuno Mendes is well versed in these kinds of Proustian journeys. A self-described "food adventurer," the chef patron of London's Viajante restaurant left his native Portugal for the United States to receive his formal education in cooking because "every restaurant in Portugal was a 'mamapap' kind of joint. I needed to leave in order to develop my own style." Having since cemented a very particular style of nouvelle cuisine as his own at Viajante—think, set crab milk with foraged beach herbs—Nuno exudes love when he remembers the dishes with which he grew up. He draws on them in the restaurant but more often makes dishes like *acorda Alentejana* soup (see his recipe, Salt Cod Broth, on page 80) at home. Talking about this rustic soup—a simple blend of *bacalhau** stock, coriander, garlic, olive oil and soaked bread all topped with a poached egg—Nuno remembers his grandmother's friend Maria Luisa, whom he spent many hours watching as she worked in her Alentejo kitchen. She also made a devastating tomato soup in a similar vein, with an egg poached into a rustic chicken stock with tomatoes, onions, garlic, bay leaf and mint. Just talking about this food lets him revisit not only the happy meal times but also the sparse desert, rolling hills and peasant soups of childhood summers spent in the Alentejo.

Alentejo produces many of the basic components of Portuguese cuisine— the flavors, the ingredients, the spirit. On the one hand, this is communal food rooted in the spirit of sharing (a trait that Portugal clearly passed on to its colonial territories—see the Brazilian *paneladas* on pages 334–36). On the other, Alentejo is a landscape ripe for solitary reflection, "a space where you imagine yourself sitting, reading and understanding the seasons," as Nuno puts it. The terrain is similar to that of Andalucía, with sparse desert and rolling hills—something of a no-man's-land. Situated right next to the Spanish pork-raising region of Extremadura, it's no surprise that this is also a hot spot for acorn-fed black-hooved pigs as well as olive groves. Hams and olives provide the basis of the region's cuisine, along with wood-fired local breads. These typically come in two forms, one larger than the other, and are highly salted with a grainy base, thick smoky crusts and airy insides. Bread is eaten with most meals in Portugal and in Alentejo it is a key ingredient in local soups.

True to the ethos of sharing dishes, stews are also ubiquitous in Portugal, where they are called *cozidos*. Portuguese cookery capitalizes on the wealth of pork the country has to offer. One classic dish is *cozido à Portuguesa*, which combines beef, chicken, garlic sausage, *chouriço* and root vegetables such as potatoes, turnips and carrots. Other examples of meaty treats include *feijoada*, a pork and bean stew which has traveled far and wide with the imperial Portuguese (see Brazil, page 333), and *leitão* (suckling pig cooked over charcoal).

Meat is a particularly strong feature of northern Portuguese cuisine and dishes made with chicken, beef, lamb and pork make hearty accompaniments to the region's famous wines. Rice is also a key ingredient in the north. The two collaborate in a pair of rather pungent-sounding dishes known as

• • • •

*Bacalhau*, Portuguese for "cod," particularly in its dried and salted incarnation, is a staple ingredient in Portuguese (and Spanish) cookery. It is actually native to Scandinavia, from where it was traditionally imported, but is now produced in Portugal itself. It can be used either as a seasoning or the basis for dishes.

*arroz de cabidela* (chicken's blood) and *arroz de sarrabulho* (pig's blood), in which the rice stews in the animal's blood.

It's common to fry up whole cuts of meat such as pork loins, sometimes after marinating them in a paprika paste known as *massa de pimentão*. But the most fascinating Portuguese pork offering has got to be *carne de vinha d'Alhos*, a traditional slow-cooked dish made with fennel, cumin, cinnamon and red wine, served with fried bread, oranges and parsley. This is the dish that inspired the Goan vindaloo, the intensely spicy south Indian curry made by marinating meat in vinegar, sugar, spices and hot chili overnight. Clearly, the dish mutated substantially in India to become the scorching hot curry we know today.

Much of Portugal is surrounded by coastline. Lisbon is the only European capital where the sun sets over the sea (good pub quiz fact!), so make sure to order some grilled sardines or fried shrimp turnovers if you find yourself there. Fish and seafood are an important component of the national cuisine, either fried or grilled simply, in dishes like *amêijoas à bulhão pato* (soft-shell clams with garlic and coriander) or embellished into a maritime *cozido*. Examples include *caldeirada* (combining a medley of oily and white fish with potatoes, tomatoes and onions) or *cataplana*, a dish named after the steel and copper *papillote*[*] in which it is cooked in the oven. A typical *cataplana* might mix *chouriço*, shrimps, scallops and clams to showcase the Portuguese way with seafood and pork. The airtight metal shell intensifies the flavors as they cook in the oven, leaving the contents supremely tender.

Both Alentejo and the Algarve are strong on uniting seafood and meat. The *cataplana* is one example and *carne de porco Alentejana* another, using pork fillet alongside clams, potatoes, *pimentão*, white wine, coriander and orange. Elsewhere, although the Azores has largely inherited its cuisine from the Portuguese mainland, an unusual technique of slow-cooking stews in the ground over twelve to fifteen hours is occasionally used. The islands' volcanic heat is utilized to bind the aromas of meat, blood, garlic, sausage, offcuts and cabbage into the powerfully flavored *cozido das furnas*.

The Algarve, in the south, is rich in almonds, figs and oranges. Almonds in particular are a major feature of southern Portugal, which is the birthplace of the almond liquor Armaguinha. Marzipan, introduced by the Moors,

••••

[*] To cook food, often fish, *en papillote* involves encasing it in something—traditionally parchment paper—and baking it. Subjecting covered fish to this treatment gently steams it, leaving the fish tender and infused with flavors from accompanying ingredients. The *cataplana* dish features two clam-shell-shaped metal halves hinged together, which conduct heat to steam the fish.

is also much used in desserts. The flavors in many Portuguese desserts wouldn't be out of place in North Africa or the Middle East, with their sweet combinations of dried fruits, nuts and citrus.

The basis for most Portuguese desserts, however, is egg yolk and sugar—from *toucinho do céu*, for which I've included a recipe below, to *sonhos* (doughnuts); from *papos de anjo* (or "convent cakes"—a simple Portuguese crème caramel), via *trouxas de ovos* (also traditionally from convents in the Caldos da Rainha region: the custard cools in sheets which are then rolled into bite-sized chunks) to the classic *pastéis de nata* (those gorgeous plush mini-custard tarts from the Lisbon port of Belém). In the aftermath of the Liberal Revolution of 1820, the monks and nuns of the ancient monastery of Belém were expelled from their home. The story has it that, in an attempt to survive, the monastery (which was next to a sugar refinery) started to sell these little custard tarts, which quickly earned a name for themselves. The recipe is said to have changed little in nearly two hundred years and, for me, one of the best things about visiting Lisbon is a mid-afternoon (or late night . . . oh, go on then, even an early morning) *pastel de Belém*, washed down with *ginjinha*, the Morello cherry liqueur typical of the city. Standing on Lisbon's cobbled streets clutching two such bastions of Portuguese gastronomy feels like an experience untainted by modern developments in cuisine—these are time-old recipes and traditions that have lasted.

While other cuisines of western Europe such as the French and Spanish are famed as much for haute cuisine as home cooking, Portuguese "peasant food" still dominates its culinary positioning: stews, soups and bread-based dishes that celebrate native produce. The good news is that this makes Portuguese food especially achievable at home, in your kitchen. Though it might take a little practice, you could soon be making soups like those of Maria Luisa, which Nuno Mendes still remembers, before you know it.

PANTRY LIST • *bacalhau* • chili • *chouriço* • pork and chicken cuts • sardines • prawns • potatoes • coriander and mint • cinnamon • cumin • saffron • turmeric • almonds • chickpeas • desserts made with eggs and sugar

• • •

# • SALT COD BROTH •

Serve this concoction of mashed bread, salt cod, eggs and coriander in a terracotta bowl and it almost looks like the Portuguese flag. Green-flecked and with the poached egg yolk bursting on top of the bread and broth, it is the epitome of Portuguese peasant food and has even the most avant garde of chefs, Nuno Mendes (this recipe's creator), cross-eyed with wonder. Use good eggs, preferably brown, or better still eggs fresh from the hen, for bright orange yolks and a fuller flavor; good-quality bread is also key.

## • SERVES 4 •

3 garlic cloves, bitter middle bits removed
1½ tbsp coriander, separated into stems and leaves and chopped
big pinch sea salt
6 tbsp extra virgin olive oil
3½ oz salt cod soaked in cold water for 24 hours
   (refrigerate, and change water three times)
4 eggs
1 tbsp white wine vinegar
8 thick slices of good-quality crusty white bread
   (not sourdough)
sea salt and freshly ground pepper

**1** • With a mortar and pestle , crush 2 cloves of the garlic, the coriander stems and sea salt to taste. Grind into a fine paste. Then add 4 tablespoons of the olive oil and blend together. It should be very fragrant.

**2** • Bring the salt cod to a boil in 4 cups of water and simmer for 15 minutes.

**3** • Add the paste to the salt cod. Cook for another 5 minutes over medium heat.

**4** • Poach the eggs separately in a pan of simmering water with the white wine vinegar for 3 minutes.

**5** • Lightly grill or toast the bread and rub the remaining garlic clove onto each slice along with the remaining 2 tablespoons of olive oil and some of the chopped coriander leaves.

**6** • Line the bottom of four deep soup bowls with the bread. Strain the broth into a pitcher, discarding the cod, garlic and coriander stems, then pour over the bread.

**7** • Place a poached egg on top of each bowl, sprinkle the remaining coriander leaves over the top, season with salt and pepper and serve immediately.

# • ALMOND CAKE •

Rich in almonds, eggs (particularly egg yolks) and orange zest, this cake epitomizes Portuguese sweets. Its name (*toucinho do céu*) literally means "bacon from heaven" because it was originally made with pork lard. This recipe yields a sponge cake that is beautifully moist and you only need a little to experience satiation! Ground almonds replace flour here, and the sheer quantity of sugar, egg yolk and almond flavoring (I can highly recommend the Amaretto option) make for a cake as suited to snacking as a full-on dessert. Try eating it with a little yogurt or crème fraiche.

## • SERVES 8 •

¼ cup (½ stick) unsalted butter, at room temperature, plus
more for greasing the cake pan
all-purpose flour for dusting the cake pan
¾ cup water
1¾ cups superfine sugar
pinch salt
1¾ cups ground almonds
2 eggs
5 egg yolks
1 tsp almond extract (or Amaretto)
zest of ½ orange
confectioners' sugar to dust

**1** • Preheat the oven to 300°F. Grease a 10-inch round or 8-inch square cake pan with butter and dust flour onto it. Place a piece of parchment paper over the bottom.

**2** • In a saucepan set over medium heat, boil the water with the sugar and salt. Add the ground almonds as soon as it is boiling. Reduce the heat to low-medium and keep stirring the mixture for 5–6 minutes, until it becomes a soft, thick almond paste.

**3** • Cut lumps of the butter into the mixture and fold in as it melts.

**4 •** In a bowl, lightly beat together the eggs and egg yolks. Stir in the almond mixture, then add the almond extract (or Amaretto) and orange zest and stir to combine thoroughly. Pour the batter into the prepared cake pan and bake in the oven for 40–50 minutes, or until the cake is firm and golden brown on top.

**5 •** Allow to cool inside the pan, then remove the parchment paper from the bottom of the cake, sprinkle with some confectioners' sugar and serve.

# SALT COD

· · ·

Salt cod—or *bacalhau*—is made with Atlantic cod (and, more recently, other varieties of white fish such as pollock and whiting). The fish is gutted and laid flat, then salted and dried to create a crispy shell that preserves the product for a couple of years, making it both a practical and an economical source of protein. Salt cod needs to be soaked and boiled to rehydrate it before cooking.

Although salt cod is most commonly associated with the cuisine of Portugal, it is in fact native to North Atlantic countries like Norway, Iceland and parts of Canada. *Bacalhau* is so important in Portuguese cuisine, however, where it has thousands of uses including fritters (*bolinhos*), *bacalhau à Minhota* (salt cod fried with potatoes, onions and paprika, from the northern region of Minho), and *bacalhau à Gomes de Sá* (a casserole of potatoes, eggs, olives and salt cod) that it seems remiss not to include it here. It also plays an important role in other cuisines of the Mediterranean including that of Spain (see Nieves's recipe for *buñuelos de bacalao* on page 72) and areas of Italy such as Veneto, where it is known as *baccalà*.*

Salt cod has been an important point of trade between the Old and New Worlds. While many of the ingredients which are now integral to European cuisines originated in the New World—from rice to spice, chilies, potatoes and tomatoes—on the flip side, European salt cod has become essential to cuisines of West Africa and the Americas, for dishes eaten perennially and ubiquitously (like ackee and saltfish—see page 312). It features heavily in the cuisines of former Portuguese colonies like Brazil, the Philippines, Macau and Goa.

· · ·

* Russell Norman purportedly gave Florence Knight her job as head chef at his acclaimed London restaurant Polpetto on the basis of her ability to make the famously tricky Venetian dish, *baccalà mantecato*—salt cod poached with milk, onions and bay leaf, then whipped into a mousse.

# ITALY

To make time to eat as Italians still do is to share in their inexhaustible gift
for making art out of life.
• MARCELLA HAZAN, *The Essentials of Classic Italian Cooking* •

THE MOTHER FIGURE reigns supreme in the Italian kitchen. For centuries the cuisine has been developed, upheld and perpetuated by matriarchs, mamas and grandmothers. Food in Italy is almost synonymous with family. Bowls of pasta are drizzled in love and sprinkled with nurture—can you blame the stereotypical Italian mummy's boys who stay living at home well into their thirties? Home cooks have traditionally held the keys to the very best Italian fare.

Jacob Kenedy, owner of London restaurant Bocca di Lupo, talks of Italy's "*Nonna* Problem" in reference to the hegemonic status of mothers in the kitchen. Italian food has long experienced an unhappy tension between its domestic roots and the opportunity to become more glamorous or high-end. True Italian food can seem too fundamentally rustic, too often the product of a moment at the stove, too much the result of a cook's passing fancies or what's in the pantry to be groomed into the stuff of Michelin guides. Those who have made eating Italian food a more upscale dining experience in London—Giorgio Locatelli, Jacob Kenedy, Francesco Mazzei—have honored the simplicity of authentic Italian cooking: the regions, the seasons, the mother figures, in elegant restaurants that have a strong concept of what they want to deliver. For Kenedy at Bocca di Lupo this means modestly sized dishes intended for sharing, giving diners the opportunity to try specialities from regions all over Italy. Francesco Mazzei (see Calabria, page 100) even described the cuisine at his restaurant, L'Anima, as "Mama's cooking with chef hats."

Italian cuisine plays tricks on the nonnative cook. Let me give you an example. We all know that a lot of Italian food is simple. But I spent *years* in pursuit of the perfect tomato sauce for pasta. To this day, spaghetti with *pomodoro* sauce is my favorite comfort food; I eat it at home and I eat it in restaurants, much to the bewilderment of various companions. *Order something a bit more interesting! You can make that at home!* But, you see, I couldn't. Not with the same depth, the same richness or sweetness or wickedness that's masked as remedial goodness. *Why* couldn't I get it right? I tried everything—with and without garlic; with sliced onions, chopped onions and no onions at all; fennel seeds, better-quality olive oil, milk (advocated by Nigella Lawson), cream (recommended by Martha Stewart), oregano, sugar—the works.

Then I discovered the late Italian American cook and writer Marcella Hazan, credited for having brought the secrets of Italian cuisine to English-speaking kitchens with books like *The Essentials of Italian Cooking*. Hazan's instruction was to empty a can of tomatoes into a saucepan with two halves of an onion facedown and a generous chunk of butter, all of which must be covered and left to simmer on the smallest flicker of flames for forty-five minutes. About twenty minutes in, I could smell what was happening. I'd done it. I was making the perfect *pomodoro* sauce with *four ingredients* (salt is added at the end). After all that, it was simply butter, the sweetness of onion and a long slow cooking time that made those tomatoes shine.

Italian food is also very diverse, however, which I wanted to illustrate in these chapters. I may not have covered all of the most high-profile Italian food regions—Naples, Tuscany and Piedmont are noticeably absent—but I've tried to give you an interesting cross section of Italian cooking styles: from the Moorish "fusion" cuisines of Calabria and Sicily, to the Slavic undertones of Veneto and select areas of quintessential Italian food in between, such as Emilia-Romagna and Lazio.

I don't know about you, but Italian ingredients are absolutely integral to my daily diet. (Have you ever been asked which cuisine you'd choose if you had to eat just one for the rest of your life? In my experience, pretty much everyone says Italian.) It seems unbelievable to me now that, when my parents were growing up, pasta and Parmesan cheese were novelties, butter was favored over olive oil and my mother didn't try a pizza until well into her twenties. Italian food is so achievable at home, from the perspectives of both cost and practicality. I've never been without a bag of dried pasta and a bottle of extra virgin olive oil in the cupboard; they are my classic fall-back ingredients. But as well as this practically daily Italian habit, we also have chefs producing high-end, innovative Italian cuisine so that it never becomes boring. The great thing about Italian food is its scope—it is multilayered and offers almost infinite possibilities for travel from your kitchen.

Given the popularity of brilliantly executed home-cooked food these days, not to mention the romance of family recipes shrouded in secrecy, the *Nonna* Problem isn't such a bad one to have. The recipes I've included in this journey into the Italian kitchen aren't hugely technical, but executing them well is reliant on fresh ingredients of fantastic quality and, less tangibly, respect for food's ability to sit at the heart of family life. If you have both of these, you're en route to cooking like an Italian Mama, or even a *Nonna*. So, *andiamo*.

# LAZIO

Rome—the city of visible history, where the past of a whole
hemisphere seems moving in funeral procession with strange ancestral
images and trophies gathered from afar.
• GEORGE ELIOT, *Middlemarch* •

YOU MIGHT EXPECT food in the Italian region that
Rome calls its home to be good—outstanding, even.
And it is. You might expect dishes to showcase the "visible
history" George Eliot described. And they do. But
for me, the best thing about the food of Lazio is its
unprepossessing quality; this is food with humility. Despite
a reputation for high culture and cosmopolitanism,
the Roman cuisine of Lazio still feels like a
hidden gem.

Beautiful everyday food abounds across Lazio. Jacob
Kenedy, chef patron of Bocca di Lupo in London, says that this is something
of which the Romans are well aware. "Not many people have tried to
make Lazio's cuisine fancy, as it often is elsewhere in Italy. The food isn't homogenized,
it's kept its roots, and the Romans are extremely proud of this."
The flavors are gutsy—clean, concise and bold—and there's an earthiness to
the cooking here that belies Rome's status as a capital city.

Nevertheless, there's versatility to the food in Lazio, owing to its geographical
position. You'll find all the usual Italian fare (pizza and pasta—both with
regional character, as you'd expect); great bread to rival that of the south (I
had the best sandwich of my life at the now legendary bakery Forno Campo
de' Fiori, made from light local flatbread and filled with pecorino and arugula);
vibrant garden vegetables like bitter greens; iconic cheeses, and heavy
meats like those you might find farther north in Piedmont. Every region's
food inevitably travels to Rome as people visit or migrate to the big city. "Lazio
sits in an uncomfortable middle ground—resented by both the north and
south in a country where there is a general north/south divide," says Kenedy.
Yet far from plagiarizing cuisine from elsewhere, or getting lost in the blur
of its "in-between-ness," Roman food has a strong character and a proud his-

tory. It's almost like the "old money" of cuisines—the culinary equivalent, perhaps, of an aristocrat driving a battered Volvo in torn slacks.

Ancient Roman influences remain strong and can be found in the richness of flavors as well as use of ingredients like garum, the fermented fish sauce made from red or gray mullet, or mackerel. This was *the* imperial Roman seasoning that added salt and umami to everything—much like fish sauce in Asia—and remains in use today, a condiment as common as ketchup for Americans.

In most Roman dishes flavors are few but amplified to the max, and there's a knack to balancing them. This can be seen in their approach to vegetables: produce such as the beautiful Romanesco broccoli—almost half broccoli/half cauliflower—is boiled until completely soft and then seasoned with the clean, strong flavors of lemon, garlic and chili. *Pasta cacio e pepe*, a classic pasta dish of the region, also emphasizes a delicate equilibrium of flavors. It is quite simply a combination of rigatoni (the classic Roman pasta shape—fat, serrated tubes suited to catching sauce en route from plate to mouth), pecorino Romano cheese and pepper. Its individual components may be cheap, pungent and farmyard, but together they make for something simple yet sophisticated.

Citrus, garlic and salt are the most important seasonings in Lazio, and the use of herbs is usually limited to bay leaves and rosemary. As is the case everywhere in Italy, the quality of fresh produce is key. In food markets like those of Trionfale and Piazza Vittorio, shoppers peruse stalls stacked high with pyramids of locally sourced pale zucchini, artichokes and *puntarelle*, the Medusa of the chicory family with its feathery bright green spears that grow upward from a central white root. *Puntarelle* is notoriously hard to grow outside of Italy, and pairs beautifully with *bagna cauda*, an anchovy and garlic dressing (for which I've included a recipe, with seared radicchio, in the Veneto chapter on page 112).

A particularly fertile part of Lazio lies just south of Rome: the Pontine Marshes. A malarial swamp until the middle of the last century, when Mussolini drained it for canals,[*] the marshes provide a lush and silty growing ground for fruits and vegetables. There's also the volcanic lake of Bracciano around which wild sweet-fruited plants such as peas, plums, apples, raspberries and strawberries blossom. When flawlessly ripe and accompanied with lemon and chili, these strawberries make for a simple balanced dessert.

• • • •

[*] "The Battle of the Swamps" started in 1922 as an effort to drain the Pontine Marshes and cultivate crops on this fertile land. The final canal was named after Mussolini.

Pecorino Romano is the famous local sheep's milk cheese, salty and used in much the same way as Parmesan: grated into or over pastas, rustic pizzas, sauces such as pesto and, traditionally, with fava beans. Mozzarella also starts to get good in Lazio, and improves the closer you get to Campagna.* Both pecorino and mozzarella are used on Roman pizza, which is thinner at the edge (and thickens toward the center) than its Neapolitan counterpart. In keeping with the mood of much Lazian food, pizza here comes with simple toppings—with plain tomato sauce, for example, or pizza *bianca* (without tomato sauce) with zucchini flowers and sausage.

Pasta is a major feature of Roman cuisine. *Bucatini* (like thicker spaghetti, with a hole running through the center), spaghettini (thin spaghetti), and short pastas like *tortilloni*, *ditali* and *ditalini* are all mainstays in Lazio's pasta dishes, along with good old chunky rigatoni. Pasta features in soups such as *pasta e fagioli* or *pasta e ceci*, the famous thick soups of *ditalini* (short macaroni) and beans or chickpeas. Both contain finely chopped onion and garlic as well as celery and carrots. This is true peasant food—cheap, nutritious and using ingredients that grow everywhere and are easily stored. If you really wanted to prepare a speedy version you could use canned beans, making the road to Rome both a quick and straightforward one from your kitchen. Rachel Roddy, the author of fantastic Roman food blog *Rachel Eats* and of a cookbook, has contributed her delicious recipe for *pasta e ceci*, included at the end of the section.

Other Roman pasta sauces include the classic carbonara, a carefully arranged combination of *guanciale*† (unsmoked Italian bacon) or pancetta, eggs, butter, cheese and black pepper with rigatoni or spaghetti. Freshness is key with carbonara and I urge you to dig out a good recipe (try Jacob Kenedy's in *The Geometry of Pasta*) and make it at home—you'll find it is a different beast from generic restaurant versions or, worse still, the stuff of supermarkets, which curdles so easily. Rigatoni might also be eaten with tomato sauce and *pajata*, in a dish that fuses the Roman penchant for pasta and heavy-duty meat eating. *Pajata* is not for the fainthearted; resembling a cheese sausage, this is an unweaned calf's intestine filled with milk chyme (its mother's milk, undigested). Believe it.

The Romans leave little to the imagination when it comes to eating meat

••••

*The next region down from Lazio on Italy's western shore and home to the world's best buffalo mozzarella.

†*Guancia*, or pig jowl, is emblematic here and the correct bacon for Roman carbonara, setting it apart from carbonara dishes found elsewhere in Italy—which would use the more generic pancetta.

and often indulge in its pleasures with minimal seasoning. *Abbacchio alla Romana* is a typical example: young lamb with garlic, anchovy and salt. At the other end of the spectrum are offal dishes such as *trippa alla Romana*, which features tripe cooked with tomatoes, white wine, pecorino, bay leaves and *mentuccia* (wild mint). This and more can be found in the Testaccio district just south of Rome, Lazio's slaughterhouse capital until 1975. Testaccio remains a center for butchery, with a highly localized cuisine prizing offcuts of meat, or "the fifth quarter."* These include *testarelle* (head, usually roasted), *milza* (spleen, often stewed or grilled), *coda* (tail, in stews and pasta sauces), and *coratella* (heart, lungs and esophagus, commonly eaten with purple artichokes).

Rome's long-established but traditionally poor Jewish community, ghettoized with a wall around them in the *rione* Sant'Angelo neighborhood (still termed "the Ghetto") until 1888, were some of the customers for these inexpensive "fifth quarter" meat cuts. Dishes such as *coda di bue* (stewed oxtails) or *pagliata con pomodoro* (pieces of veal intestine stewed in tomato sauce) showcase their use of offal. The emblematic Jewish-Roman offal dish, though, is perhaps fried brains or lamb innards with *carciofi* (artichokes), another hallmark of Ghetto cuisine that come served in several guises, either complementing meat or on their own, deep-fried, in *carciofi alla giudia* (Jewish-style artichokes). Seasoned only with salt and a little pepper, eating deep-fried artichoke feels like an obscene adventure, an act of unclothing your food. Start by peeling away the crisp, caramel-colored outer petals—almost thistly in texture—working inward to reveal the tender white heart. Jacob Kenedy's well-loved recipe for Jewish artichokes is shared here, so have your deep fryer at the ready.

Deep-frying doesn't stop at artichokes in the Ghetto: fritto misto, zucchini blossoms and *baccalà* are all favorite beneficiaries of the technique. Lastly—and as I write this I am eating a piece of challah (sweet bread of the Jewish Sabbath) bought in Golders Green—bakeries are a major feature of the Roman Ghetto. One in particular, Boccione Limentani on Via di Portico Ottavia, is an institution and serves all sorts of delicious things such as shortcrust pies stuffed with ricotta, *treccia* (a Friday treat of plaited pastry with cherries and sugar) and honey *pizzarelle* (unleavened fritters made with matzo meal, raisins and honey) for Passover.

• • • •

*The "fifth quarter" (or *quinto quarto*) refers to the meat not given to the nobility, clergy, bourgeoisie and army (the destinations for the first four quarters, the more premium cuts) in the nineteenth century. This was offal, essentially, destined for those at the lowest societal rung who, out of necessity, developed a rich local cuisine based on these undesirable cuts.

Roman-Jewish cuisine stands apart yet blends in with the city's broader culinary traditions all at once. It has been said that Ghetto food doesn't so much adhere to Jewish culinary traditions as take inspiration from them,[*] as well as from Ancient Roman cuisine—the Jews predate Christianity's arrival in the city, after all.

George Eliot called Rome "the city of visible history," and she was right—the plates, platters and pans of Roman kitchens display a rich and varied history. The same goes for Lazio as a whole; the region is Italy's interface between north and south and accommodates the cosmopolitanism of its capital city with its rural nooks, sporting their own micro-cuisines. Lazio's cooking always offers new territory to explore, whether it's a simple and nourishing *pasta e ceci* soup or whole fried artichokes, recipes for both of which are included in the following pages.

Whether I'm in Rome or simply visiting from my kitchen, I'm quite happy to do as the Romans do. Although I might give the *pajata* a miss.

PANTRY LIST • anchovy • pecorino Romano • artichokes • ricotta • offal • pancetta • bay leaf • wild mint • chickpeas • beans • pasta (rigatoni, bucatini) • basil • mozzarella • peas • broccoli • chicory

• • •

# • PASTA AND CHICKPEA SOUP •

On her blog, *Rachel Eats*, Rachel Roddy calls *pasta e ceci* "the Steve Buscemi of soups, a bit of a legend, oh so low-key if you take him for granted, but love him so much more than all the fancy pants hogging the limelight." *Pasta e ceci* is low-key: pasta and chickpeas, fortified by a sweet *soffritto* of onion, celery and carrot, good olive oil, some Parmesan, a little rosemary. A photograph of this dish might as well sit alongside a definition of "comfort food" in the dictionary—a comfort based not on indulgence (it's far too economical for that), but on nurture. The difference, if you like, between spoiling yourself with a boozy night out and going

• • • •

[*] Not all restaurants are strictly kosher, for example, and there are plenteous overlaps with standard Roman fare, such as *pasta e ceci* or *pasta e fagioli*.

back to the family home for a roast. In fact, this is family fare in Rome. Roddy describes the scent of simmering chickpeas all over her Testacchio neighborhood on Fridays, when *pasta e ceci* is traditionally eaten as a starter before *baccalà*, to see in the weekend. It was bean and pasta concoctions such as *pasta e ceci* or its cousin *pasta e fagioli* (made with borlotti or cannellini beans) that sustained me through a winter of book writing. Made with pantry staples, these are cheap, quick and honest dishes that nurtured my solitary stomach.

### • SERVES 8 AS A STARTER OR 6 AS A MAIN •

6 tbsp extra virgin olive oil
1 medium carrot, finely diced
1 stalk of celery, finely diced
1 white onion, finely diced
2 tbsp tomato purée
1 sprig rosemary
1½ cups dried chickpeas soaked overnight then
    simmered for 2 hours until tender,
    or 2 x 14-oz cans of cooked chickpeas
Parmesan rind
salt and freshly ground black pepper
8 oz small dried tubular pasta
    (macaroni or rigatoni works well)

**1** • In a deep saucepan warm the olive oil over medium heat, then add the carrots, celery and a pinch of salt. Sauté, stirring and turning them regularly, until they are very soft and golden, which should take about 15 minutes.

**2** • Add the tomato purée and rosemary, stir and then add two thirds of the cooked chickpeas. Stir again and then cover everything with 6 cups of water (use the cooked chickpea water if you have it). Add the Parmesan rind. Bring to the boil, reduce the heat and allow to simmer gently for about 20 minutes.

**3** • Remove the Parmesan rind and rosemary and purée everything in the blender to create a smooth soup.

**4** • Stir in the rest of the cooked chickpeas and season to taste. Bring the soup back to a boil and add the pasta. Keep stirring regularly while the pasta cooks—it should take 10–15 minutes—to keep it from sticking.

**5** • Once the pasta is cooked but still firm, take the pan off the heat. Allow it to sit for 5 minutes before stirring and serving with a tablespoon of your best olive oil.

# • FRIED WHOLE ARTICHOKES •

My friend Sophie was haunted by artichokes as a teenager. Reluctantly channeling Damien Hirst at our art teacher's insistence, she dropped an artichoke into a fish tank and drew it, beautifully, in pastels under duress—and eventually titled it "Art-I-Choke." Sophie subsequently lived in Italy and, more specifically, spent a good deal of time eating deep-fried artichokes in Rome. The delicate-petaled vegetable was transformed from hated muse to beloved foodstuff. With just three ingredients, these *carciofi alla guidia* demand a mastery of technique. Be meticulous. Choose the biggest artichokes you can find (2–3 inches across, with tightly closed leaves) and prepare them thoroughly before cooking. Begin by trimming the tough, dark parts of the leaves (which should fall off "like pencil sharpenings," according to Jacob Kenedy whose recipe this is), the stem, and the tip of the sharpened artichoke. It should look like a "pale rosebud." Wash very thoroughly, then plunge the cleaned artichokes into water acidulated with lemon juice to prevent discoloration.

## • SERVES 4 AS A STARTER •

8 artichokes
juice of 1–2 lemons
about 8 cups sunflower oil
salt

**1** • Clean and prep the artichokes (see above) and keep them in water acidulated with the lemon juice until you are ready to cook them.

**2** • Drain the artichokes well—blot them dry with a cloth—season generously with salt and deep-fry slowly in sunflower oil at least 2 inches deep at 265–285°F (this is about 8 cups of oil in an 8-inch pan) for about 15 minutes, until completely tender when tested with a toothpick to the heart, but not falling apart. Remove from the oil and allow to cool.

**3** • When you are ready to eat, reheat the artichoke oil until almost smoking (375°F). This is the hottest temperature it can safely be—great for flash-frying. Open the artichokes out into flowers by inserting your thumb in the middle and gently working the leaves out flat like an open chrysanthemum. Fry them upside-down in the oil (lower them in gently to keep them from turning over) for a few minutes until the leaves turn an autumnal brown. Drain the artichokes well. As the oil may get trapped between the leaves, it is best to shake the artichokes as you lift them from the pan with a pair of tongs, then to blot upside-down on paper towels. Sprinkle with salt and eat immediately.

# • THE ULTIMATE TOMATO SAUCE •

There are few things I would rather eat than this glorious, rounded red gloop thrown over pasta. Here is my version of Marcella Hazan's revelatory three-ingredient tomato sauce. Some people discard the onions once they have delivered their sweetness to the tomatoes, but I like to eat them, too—the layers of soft white flesh are a nice accompaniment to the pasta.

## • SERVES 4 •

2 yellow or white onions, halved
2 x 14-oz cans plum tomatoes
5 tbsp unsalted butter
salt to taste
14 oz dried pasta (I prefer spaghetti or
    linguine, but any kind will do)
freshly ground black pepper and grated
    Parmesan to serve

**1** • It is this easy. Lay the onions cut-side down in a big saucepan. Pour the tomatoes over the top, throw in the butter, cover, and cook over low heat for 45 minutes. Stir occasionally, blending in the melted butter and gently crushing the whole tomatoes to a pulp.
**2** • Cook your pasta according to the instructions on the package, making sure you don't overcook. Drain and return to the pan.
**3** • Add salt to the sauce to taste, pour over the pasta and mix well. Spoon into four wide bowls, dividing the onions equally, sprinkle with black pepper and Parmesan and serve.

# EMILIA-ROMAGNA

In Romagna, well-to-do families and peasants slaughter pigs at home,
which is an occasion to make merry and for the children to romp.
• PELLEGRINO ARTUSI, *Exciting Food for Southern Types* •

EMILIA-ROMAGNA IS a little bit like the Normandy of Italy—replete with wonderful produce that is exported and enjoyed all over the world, but without the same breadth of cuisine to be found in other regions of Italy. Many of the best-known Italian ingredients hail from Emilia-Romagna, yet we know strikingly little about this profitable nook of Italy tucked among Veneto, Lombardy and Tuscany. There's something a bit grim about the making merry and romping around the pig slaughter to which Artusi alludes. But this isn't a question of bloodthirstiness, it's the hallowed tradition that yields Parma ham.

Cutting across almost the entire width of Italy, Emilia-Romagna is a buffer zone between the Alpine north and Mediterranean south. It only just falls short of linking Italy's Adriatic coast in the east with the Ligurian Sea in the west, and has an area of over eighty-five hundred square miles, nearly half of which is plain (the rest is hills, mountains and Adriatic coastline).

Agriculture and food production are a big deal—very developed, industrialized and making significant contributions to a high gross domestic product per capita. Given its size, the number of famously beautiful cities (such as Bologna and Ravenna), and the proliferation of good food, it's surprising that Emilia-Romagna isn't more of a household name—like Tuscany or Sicily. Perhaps it's because, as names go, it's a bit of a mouthful. Whatever the reason, both familiar ingredients and delicious mouthfuls of a different kind abound here. *Prosciutto di Parma*, mortadella, Parmesan and balsamic vinegar all originate in Emilia-Romagna and can be counted as some of the world's most famous Italian ingredients. The region is also very strong on pasta; some of Italy's most exported shapes come from here: think tagliatelle, tortellini and lasagne.

But in terms of dishes, it's only really a few key pasta-based ones for which Emilia-Romagna is known. The production of great ingredients outweighs more "crafted" cuisine and, historically, it was probably this abundance of farmland that made it less of a tourist destination (unlike its neighbor, glamorous Tuscany). Emilia-Romagna's produce is stellar and you will almost certainly have heard of places like Modena, Bologna and Parma, from whence these ingredients came.

Prosciutto[*] is a generic term for Italian dry-cure ham, like Spanish Serrano, but Parma—Emilia-Romagna's appellation—is particularly famous. Parma is given a distinctive flavor by the unique diet on which the region's pigs are fed: chestnuts and whey. Although northern Italian pigs reared in the Apennine foothills are commonly fed chestnuts,[†] the addition of liquid whey drained from Parmesan cheese curds makes for a protein-rich and inimitably salty flavor in Parma ham. Mortadella is another local salumi product: round, light pink and flecked with white fat dapples and green peppercorns. I hemmed and hawed about going vegetarian for several years as a child and every time I felt ready to take the big leap, mortadella winked at me from behind the deli counter.

The region is also great for cheese, most notably Parmesan (or Parmigiano Reggiano to give it its Italian name). I remember too well that sicky readygrated stuff showered on pasta shapes when I was growing up. It was only on my first trip to Italy in my early teens that I discovered cutting chunks of Parmesan from a fresh block and eating it neat rather than as a condiment to pasta. I have never looked back. To me, there are few pleasures to rival a hunk of Parmesan with a glass of red wine, but its uses of course stretch way beyond its purest form. Pasta provides a stage on which Parmesan can wave its jazz hands.

A cheaper alternative also comes from Emilia-Romagna—Grana Padano, from the town of Piacenza. I regularly use Grana Padano as a substitute for Parmesan—it has a similar salty punch and crystally texture, but you can generally tell the difference on sight. Softer, smother and younger, Grana Padano lacks the maturity and sophistication of Parmesan (which, in block form, has a beautiful gnarled quality, like a worn old man photographed in black and white).

Balsamic vinegar, the sweet dark vinegar of Emilia-Romagna, has become an essential for salad dressings and bread dunking. I also love to add the tiniest drop to my tomato sauces for a satisfying jolt of acid sweetness. Balsamic is not your average vinegar. The clue is in its name—derived from "balsam"

• • • •

*This in turn comes in two broad varieties: prosciutto crudo (dry cure) and prosciutto cotto (cooked).

†Whereas in Spain and Portugal they feed on acorns and the wild herbs of the dehesa (see page 65).

in Latin, which implies a remedial quality to the substance. It is made from the concentrated reduction of Trebbiano white grapes and aged for upward of twelve years. Like Parma ham and Parmesan, with which it often goes hand in hand on antipasto plates, it has the refinement of äge.

Italians are very particular about the right pasta shape to accompany particular sauces.[*] Perhaps the biggest affront to an Emilia-Romagnan would be the notion of "spaghetti Bolognese." Where do I start? Bologna's classic *ragu* is traditionally eaten with tagliatelle (strips of pasta as long as spaghetti but about 3/16 inch wide) and is actually orange in color, not red. Importantly, Bolgonese is a *ragu* and not a sauce. It coats the pasta but it is dry not sloppy, made with morsels of meat such as pork, veal or possibly beef—and plenty of oil. The oil coats the pasta in intense flavors: bay leaves, wine, a hint of pancetta and essence of *soffritto* (the base for all *ragu*, made from very finely chopped onion, celery and carrots). This is hearty home food, but quite different from the common meat sauce that we know and love. Jacob Kenedy's fantastic recipe is included here and I urge you to give it a whirl—it may well be unrecognizable to you as "Bolognese" but you won't look back.

All the pastas of Emilia-Romagna are made with a traditional recipe of the region, known as *sfoglia*. Made simply from egg and flour and hand rolled until paper-thin and feather-light, the name means "to thumb through." If you look at a piece of tortellini, it starts to make sense; the filled pasta (which usually contains pork, Parma ham and Parmesan cheese) looks as though it has been shaped around a thumb into a delicately crafted dumpling. Simpler shapes like tagliatelle and even flat lasagne sheets are made with the *sfoglia* recipe, too. Thumbs through and thumbs up.

The most famous viticultural product of Emilia-Romagna could be seen to undermine its culinary greatness. Lambrusco, sweet sparkling red wine, is an altogether different beast in Italy and made in varying degrees of flavor, from sweet to dry. There are definitely wines I'd pick over Lambrusco— Barolo and Sardinian Cannonau spring to mind—but any Italian wine will pair effortlessly with Emilia-Romagnan food. Easy to prepare and with impressive results, this is the kind of food of which superlative drinks gatherings and grown-up picnics are made: good bread, great ham, wonderful cheese and matchless balsamic vinegar for lazy but delicious picking.

• • • •

[*] For more on this see Caz Hildebrand and Jacob Kenedy's excellent book *The Geometry of Pasta*.

**PANTRY LIST** • Parma ham • mortadella • Parmesan • balsamic vinegar • minced beef • pasta (tagliatelle, tortellini) • bay leaf • Lambrusco

• • •

# • EMILIA-ROMAGNA INSPIRED SALAD •

This salad brings together some of Emilia-Romagna's most celebrated ingredients. It's the stuff of which great summer lunches are made—perfect with good bread for mopping up and good wine for washing down.

### • SERVES 4 •

6 tbsp balsamic vinegar di Modena
2 tbsp brown sugar
8 slices Parma ham
4 fresh figs, quartered
handful whole almonds
freshly ground black pepper

**1** • First, make a balsamic glaze by setting a small saucepan over medium heat with the vinegar and sugar mixed together. Bring to the boil, stirring constantly, and then simmer over low heat for 15 minutes, making sure the sugar is dissolved. Set aside.
**2** • Arrange the Parma ham, figs and almonds (which you could decide to toast briefly first—up to you) on a plate and then, channeling Jackson Pollock, drizzle the balsamic glaze all over, in zigzags. Grind some black pepper over the plate and serve.

# • TAGLIATELLE BOLOGNESE •

Banish all associations with the spag bol you used to eat for lunch at school. As Jacob Kenedy, who contributed this recipe from his wonderful book *The Geometry of Pasta*, says, "It is orange, not red; it is more oil- than water-based, it is delicate, aromatic, creamy and subtle." Because it's from the ingredient capital of Italy, make sure you invest in good ingredients and do Emilia-Romagna proud. And don't—just don't—use spaghetti. Tagliatelle is the authentic pasta for Bolognese *ragu*.

## • SERVES 8 •

7 tbsp unsalted butter, plus more for serving
¼ cup extra virgin olive oil
1 carrot, diced
2 sticks celery, diced
1 medium onion, chopped
4 garlic cloves, sliced
4 oz pancetta (not smoked), cut in strips
salt
1¼ lb minced pork
1¼ lb minced veal (or beef)
4 oz chicken livers, finely chopped (optional)
1½ cups white wine
2⅔ cups whole milk
1x 14-oz can chopped tomatoes
1 cup beef or chicken stock (optional, otherwise
    an additional 1 cup milk)
freshly ground black pepper
28 oz dried, or 2¼ lb fresh, tagliatelle
¼ cup Parmesan, grated, for serving

**1** • In a large frying pan, melt the butter in the olive oil over medium heat. Add the carrot, celery, onion, garlic and pancetta along with a good pinch of salt and sauté for 10–15 minutes, until softened.
**2** • Raise the heat to high and add the meat in four or five additions, allowing time for any water to evaporate, stirring and breaking up any lumps with a spoon. Wait until the pan starts to splutter slightly, then reduce the heat to medium and sauté, stirring occasionally, until the meat has browned—15–20 minutes.
**3** • Deglaze the pan with the wine, then transfer to a saucepan along with the milk, tomatoes and stock as well as a good grinding of pepper and more salt to taste. Cook at a very gentle simmer, uncovered, for about 4 hours, until the sauce is thick, more oil- than water-based (add a little stock or water if it dries too much or too quickly).

When ready, the liquor will be as thick as heavy cream and, stirred up, the whole should be somewhat porridgy. Adjust the seasoning one last time.

**4** • Cook the pasta according to the package instructions. Drain when marginally undercooked, then add to the sauce to finish cooking for about 20 seconds, with a couple of pats of butter. Serve with grated Parmesan on top.

# CALABRIA

A traveller in Calabria has to surmount a large number of tortuous routes,
as though following the unpredictable path of a labyrinth. Broken by those
torrents with their steep descents, Calabria not only differs from zone to zone,
but is hushed with brusque metamorphoses, in the landscape, in the climate,
in the ethnic composition of its inhabitants.
• GUIDO PIOVENE, *Journey Through Italy* •

CALABRIA IS ITALY'S culinary wallflower, reminiscent of the protagonist in a '90s teen drama—arrestingly pretty beneath bad hair and glasses—and with an idiosyncratic potential that's beginning to be recognized. Situated in the toe of boot-shaped Italy, she is a region out on a limb, isolated from her peers. She has striking physical features—windswept on the sea, chiseled in the mountains, voluptuous with greenery—and the imperfections of craggy scrubland only enhance her beauty. This huge variety of terrain produces ingredients that translate into a spectrum of tastes unique in Italy.

Calabria is a wilderness and, as such, a haven for wild food sources ranging from game to seafood and fungi to citrus. This diversity of wildlife is a direct result of both the very varied geography and the resulting challenge to large-scale farming. Hot days and cool nights, not to mention a combination of mineral-rich and rocky sea soils, make for unique yields.

Calabria's cuisine is more similar to that of Sicily than any other (see page 105). The ethnic mix is one of western European and Moorish, expressed in the names of foods such as *n'duja* and *'ncantarata* as well as *'Ndrangheta*, the Calabrian mafia. Despite less international prominence than its Sicilian equivalent, *'Ndragheta* is still one of Calabria's few claims to fame.

Sandwiched between sea and mountains, far away from the bright lights of Naples or Palermo, the closest cities, Calabrese culture is very much alive but remains insular and hasn't been much exported. Its cuisine is similarly self-contained with an even greater focus on family, friends and regional self-sufficiency than elsewhere in Italy, where the possibilities inherent in the commodification of food dawned a long time ago. You'll have heard of Neapolitan pizza, Venetian risottos or Bolognese sauce, for instance, or famous Italian ingredients such as Parmesan cheese and balsamic vinegar, but perhaps not *n'duja* sausage, Tropea onions or some of the Calabrese recipes we'll explore here. You're in for a treat.

Chef Francesco Mazzei, a Calabrian native himself, now runs a southern Italian restaurant called L'Anima in London and is devoted to elevating the profile of Calabria abroad. *L'anima* means "the soul" in Italian, and for Francesco it expresses the close-knit, earthy way of life in his homeland. It's about family, producing your own ingredients, inherited cooking traditions—that brand of "Mama's cooking with chef hats on," to which I alluded earlier. Mazzei employs recipes passed down in the Calabrese genes, and food rituals such as preparing lunch together as a family every Sunday morning.

Calabria is the only region in Italy where spicy food is widespread. Francesco describes his father pulling antioxidant-rich *capsichina* chili peppers direct from the plant and eating them raw. *Capsichina* seeds are often used to add heat to food, most famously to *n'duja*—the Calabrese spicy sausage—and spicy *N'cantarata* sauce, made with paprika and honey. From the southern town of Spilinga, *n'duja* is Calabria's answer to salami, but piquant, pliable, and easily spread on bread or added to pasta sauces. (It is one of those ingredients quickly making its way onto cosmopolitan menus, a spicier alternative to chorizo that marries beautifully with seafood such as scallops, as you will discover.) Other spicy Calabrian dishes include *morzeddu*, a fiery lamb offal stew served as a sharing dish, and Calabrese *ragu*—made not with mince (as you might expect in Bologna) but with big chunks of meat such as lamb or pork—and a lot of chili. Like any Italian region, Calabria has its own native pasta shape—long twisted pieces known as *filei*, with which the robust *ragu* is served.

Few realize the gamut of meat and seafood available in Calabria, which ranges from goat and game to swordfish, scallops, lobster and tuna. In fact, the region's geography makes it an authentic purveyor of "surf and turf." Meat and fish are regularly served together, most famously in the antipasto *marimonte*, a pile of seafood, salamis and pickles often dished up at weddings and other big occasions. Scallops accompanied by *n'duja* and salsa verde is another popular example.

Perhaps the most exciting aspect of Calabrese cuisine is its range of wild and rare native flavors. It is one of the few places in the world where the bergamot orange, a delicately aromatic citrus fruit used in Earl Grey tea and some perfumes, grows in the wild. In Calabrian cookery, bergamot is infused into local olive oil or adds refreshing, complex citrus notes to dishes such as cuttlefish salad, simple grilled pork chops or sweet pastries.

Calabria is home to the world's only licorice museum, located in the town of Amarelli where a family business has been manufacturing products from the famous local licorice root since the mid-eighteenth century. As well as sweets, Calabrian licorice can be found in liqueurs or added to marinades for game, combining particularly well with deer.

Wild oregano is ubiquitous and thrown into many a dish, either as a key flavor or a pungent garnish to salads and meat dishes, one of which is *tiella*. This is a meat cake using layers of sliced *lisetta* potatoes (a particularly yellow and starchy variety), pork fat, pecorino, oregano, thyme and cep mushrooms foraged in the Sila mountains. Mushrooms flourish all over the forests and mountains of Calabria and can be picked until as late in the year as December. (Farther north in Italy, where the climate is cooler, the regular growing season is roughly April to October, but Calabria offers warmth, humidity and rain in abundance to happy mushrooms.) With Calabrian white mushrooms (*porcini bianco*), Francesco makes a basic salad—they need little embellishment—slicing and dressing them only with extra virgin olive oil and some lemon juice. Simple pleasures.

The Calabrese love sauces, condiments and marinades, the base for which is usually local olive oil. Francesco proudly told me not only that 36 percent of Italian olive oil is Calabrian, but that he uses nothing but his grandmother's own oil at L'Anima. It is a deep, dark extra virgin olive oil unlike anything you can get on supermarket shelves. Sauces and marinades are often embellished with *garum*, which Francesco calls "the ketchup of the Romans," a fish condiment made by crushing and fermenting the innards, livers and heads of blue fish like anchovies, sardines and mackerel. It adds salt and umami (see page 258). It can also be used as a dipping sauce with a kick.

At the end of our conversation, Francesco proudly sent me away with L'Anima's sweet chili jam, red onion marmalade and pecorino[*] cream. These condiments really showcase Calabria's native ingredients, in particular *capischina* and onions local to the Tropea municipality of Calabria. Intensely purple-red and extremely sweet, Tropea onions are a Calabrian staple famous all over Italy and can even be used to make gelato. In a similar vein, balsamic vinegar ice cream works brilliantly, the strong natural sweetness of the vinegar making for a surprising and tantalizing combination of tastes,

• • • •

[*] As in much of southern Italy, pecorino—the nutty, hard sheep's cheese—is the cheese of choice, often spiced with pepper or chili seeds or made into a cream, which is fantastic on bread.

cementing my impression that Calabria has, indeed, got an idiosyncratic potential that's beginning to be recognized. Just like the girl in that '90s teen drama.

**PANTRY LIST** • bergamot • licorice • Tropea onions • garum • *n'duja* • *capischina* seeds • seafood (lobster, tuna, swordfish, cuttlefish) • *baccalà* • lisetta potatoes • porcini mushrooms • truffle • asparagus • artichokes • pecorino

• • •

# • SCALLOPS WITH N'DUJA •

This dish from Francesco Mazzei showcases Calabria in all its glory: surf and turf with a local edge, provided by the *n'duja* spicy sausage that's unique to the region. No wonder it's in the "toe" of Italy—it's certainly got a kick!

### • SERVES 4 •

FOR THE TOPPING
2½ oz *n'duja*, outer casing removed
2 oz pecorino
1 garlic clove, coarsely chopped
2½ tbsp basil, chopped
2½ tbsp flat-leaf parsley, chopped
juice of ¼ lemon
sea salt and freshly ground black pepper

1 tbsp extra virgin olive oil
12 raw scallops with roe

**1** • Preheat the oven to 375°F.

**2** • In a mortar and pestle mash all the topping ingredients until nice and creamy.

**3** • Heat the olive oil in a frying pan and quickly sear the scallops over high heat for 1–2 minutes on each side. When ready, allow to cool a little.

**4** • Spread the *n'duja* paste on top of each scallop and bake in the oven for 4–5 minutes. Serve while very hot.

# • SPICY CHICKEN CALABRESE •

This is a classic example of Calabrese "Mama Cooking," a combination of chicken thighs, *n'duja*, mountain herbs and chili. This recipe is one of Francesco Mazzei's family-style specialties and can be rustled up in a mere half hour.

### • SERVES 4 •

8 chicken thighs, skin on
all-purpose flour, seasoned, for dusting
1 tbsp extra virgin olive oil
1 shallot, finely chopped
3½ oz *n'duja*
6 bell peppers (2 red, 2 green, 2 yellow), deseeded and diced
6 tbsp tomato purée
1⅓ cups chicken stock
1 heaping tsp marjoram, chopped (try oregano if you
    can't find marjoram)
1 heaping tsp chives, chopped
1 heaping tsp flat-leaf parsley, chopped
1 large red chili, deseeded and finely chopped
sea salt and freshly ground black pepper

**1** • Preheat the oven to 375°F.
**2** • Coat the chicken thighs lightly in the seasoned flour. Heat the olive oil in a large frying pan over medium heat, and brown (in batches if necessary) the chicken well on all sides until golden. This should take 5–6 minutes on each side.
**3** • In an ovenproof pan, fry the shallots and *n'duja* for a few minutes, stirring to soften the *n'duja* until it begins to melt and combine with the shallots. Add the diced peppers, passata and the chicken stock and bring to the boil. Then add the chicken, herbs and chili. Check the seasoning before baking in the oven for 20–30 minutes until the chicken is cooked through.
**4** • Serve hot with olive oil mashed potatoes.

# SICILY

For over twenty-five centuries we've been bearing the weight of superb
and heterogeneous civilizations, all from outside, none made by ourselves,
none that we could call our own. This violence of landscape, this cruelty of
climate, this continual tension in everything, and even these monuments
of the past, magnificent yet incomprehensible because not built by us and yet
standing round us like lovely mute ghosts . . . all these things have formed
our character, which is thus conditioned by events outside our control as
well as by a terrifying insularity of mind.

• GIUSEPPE TOMASI DI LAMPEDUSA, *The Leopard* •

SICILY IS A disoriented island. It is dizzy with inspiration, having had a multitude of international rulers
over hundreds upon thousands of years of changing
hands. Sicily was the baton passed in a three-thousand-
year relay race toward European dominance—taken
first by the Greeks, then the Romans, the Arabs, the
Normans, the Spanish and the French. Of course,
these days Sicily is part of the boot-shaped country.
She returned to the Italians when Garibaldi launched
his unification movement, beginning with the con-
quest of Sicily in 1860. But she retains an affinity to so many Mediterranean
countries as to render her almost without any affinity at all.

Giuseppe Tomasi di Lampedusa sounds in *The Leopard* like a man torn
between a sense of belonging to his homeland and a violent alienation from
its cultural monuments. His is the opposite of Goethe's hyperbolic assertion
that "To have seen Italy without having seen Sicily is to not have seen Italy at
all, for Sicily is the clue to everything." Closer to Tunisia and Greece than it
is to the north of the country, this is not the generic Italy of gingham table-
cloths and breadsticks. But it is, genuinely, perhaps more than anywhere, the
authentic Mediterranean.

The cuisine of Sicily is founded in the ingredients offered by the land and
the sea but displays countless variations derived from the island's constantly
changing culture. Fertile terrain and the warm surrounding seas provide a
rich palette of flavors and raw materials with which to cook. Sicilian food has

been equally determined by its seasonal ingredients, from zucchini flowers in spring to pickled olives in autumn, and by the perennial presence of brilliant citrus fruits.

"The Greeks found that if they dropped a seed, it would grow," says Giorgio Locatelli, a northern Italian and longtime lover of Sicily who fell for the island of baked pasta and meaty fish. Every year for the last seventeen, Locatelli has spent a month in Sicily, gradually learning its history, ingredients, dishes and idiosyncrasies. For him it is not only the "Garden of Europe"; its landscape and cuisine are incomparable to anywhere else in Italy—or the world, for that matter. He says that all over the island—from capital city Palermo to the most secluded rural nooks—you can find a mixture of foodstuffs that elsewhere would only be available in a big metropolis. Figs, olives and grapes (and therefore wine) brought by the Greeks; the durum wheat planted by Ancient Romans, which still defines the bread of Sicily, as well as lamb, kid and pork; stuffed eggplants, recalling the Arabs; North African couscous; and pasta, glorious pasta, which screams Italy. All this "determines a diet that is very particular, very Sicily-specific," says Locatelli.

These influences often collide in pasta dishes. I've included a brilliantly simple Sicilian pasta recipe below, in which *gemelli* (meaning "twins"—two strands of pasta twisted together, similar in size to *fusilli*) are coated in a glorious oily concoction of raisins, pine nuts, toasted bread crumbs and capers.

Sicily is a big island, almost double the size of the mainland province of Calabria just under two miles away over the sea, and unsurprisingly has lots of regional products. Varied *salumi* (the plural of salami) toward the center; the pistachios of Bronte in the northeast; the ancient rice paddies by the Verdura River;[*] *arancini*, originally from Palermo, now all of Sicily's beloved cheese-stuffed, deep-fried rice balls; the black bread of western Castelvetrano; couscous from the southwestern port of Mazara del Varo; Ribera Vanilla Oranges (with DOP status) from the south, and all the wild flora surrounding Mount Etna, Europe's largest active volcano, including six different types of sage. Every town or village seems to have its own shape of pasta, its own

• • • •

*The Arabs brought rice to Sicily in around the ninth century AD, where it both flourished and quickly became intrinsic to the cuisine, with the likes of *arancini* rice balls. After unification in the early nineteenth century, though, rice was no longer cultivated in Sicily, apparently because the prime minister, Camillo Benso, wanted to minimize competition for rice farmers in his native Piemonte. It had to be imported to meet local demand. This situation was made even worse by Mussolini's order to drain the rice paddies to make way for new home building (as he more famously did to the Pontine Marshes in Lazio). Only now is rice starting to be grown again in Sicily, using a half-dry system (always wet, never flooded) to mitigate the drained land. *Arancini* are on their way to becoming 100 percent Sicilian again.

unique way of baking bread. Sicily remains a land of patchwork, localized cuisine.

Some ingredients are ubiquitous. Though they change regionally, bread and pasta are omnipresent, made with hard durum wheat and semolina flour rather than the soft flour from farther north in Italy, where egg pasta dominates. Chickpeas, usually only found along the coast of mainland Italy, occur naturally all over the island and are a staple ingredient in soups and salads. Called *ceci* in Italian, they are also a key player in Moorish-influenced dishes like couscous and *panelle*, a delicious street-food snack of chickpea and polenta fritters.

Though beef can now easily be found in Sicilian supermarkets, the island isn't a traditional beef-producing area. Grazing cows demand substantial grassland (to which the prolific, and high-quality, beef production of Argentina bears testament [p. 341]), which Sicily's size and hot climate don't allow for. Modest bovine production, however, made way for sheep and goat products. More specifically, it made way for ricotta, which Locatelli has termed "the Mother of Sicilian cuisine." Made from sheep's milk, *ricotta di pecora* is a specialty and enjoyed in various forms: pure and sloppy, slathered onto bread; mixed with lemon juice and grated Parmesan blended with pasta and black pepper;[*] on gnocchi or lasagnes; or, very typically, in desserts paired with chocolate and candied fruits. The best known of these is cannoli, or "little tubes": circles of sweet pastry folded into cylinders and fried, then stuffed with ricotta, ice cream, fruit, jam, nuts or chocolate. Cannoli have become archetypal symbols of Sicily to rival the mafiosi's guns. As Peter Clemenza says to Rocco in the 1972 movie *The Godfather*, "Leave the gun, take the cannoli." The godfather of all desserts, indeed.

The large warm-water fish, such as albacore, swordfish and tuna, that collect around the Sicilian coast, make for chunky steaks. The waters off the northeastern town of Messina have particularly good swordfish. From mid-spring to mid-autumn they are caught by harpoon and devoured freshly grilled or baked with simple sauces like *salmoriglio*, the ingredients of which—olive oil, lemon, parsley, oregano and some garlic—reflect the Sicilian *terroirs*. A little more complex but no less quintessentially Mediterranean, a *ghiotta* salsa combines capers (which flourish all over Sicilian scrubland) with olives, tomatoes, onions

• • • •

*One of the pasta dishes for which Sicily is known is the *timballo*, or baked pasta with eggplant, which has a tendency to dry out. Never fear this when fresh ricotta is at hand: its scrambled curds coat the pasta in creamy loveliness, leaving a pool of residual whey for mopping.

and pine nuts.* Sicilian tuna makes for steaks of such intense burgundy color that they glisten almost blue. *The Silver Spoon* cookbook† offers a recipe for tuna with honey, potatoes and pine nuts, again recalling Moorish influences. These are particularly strong in the southwest of the island, around Mazara del Varo and Sciacca, where Locatelli buys his fish. Down here, Tunisian sailors tend to their boats and there are wonderful Tunisian restaurants. Swordfish and tuna are just two examples of Sicily's wealth of seafood; octopus, lobster, prawns and sardines are also top quality, and there are anchovies by the bucketful.

A multitude of green vegetables and herbs that we would consider premium goods grow all over Sicily. Artichokes, chicory, caper berries and fennel are inexpensive, not to mention the omnipresent tomatoes, broccoli, eggplants and zucchini. The cuisine is rich in herbs, too; parsley is the most important, followed by mountain oregano (which, Locatelli tells me, is deeply fragrant and has a scent midway between oregano and thyme), mint, wild fennel and, to a lesser extent, basil. Caponata, a popular antipasti dish of wild vegetables and herbs softened in olive oil, wine vinegar and seasoning, brings all this fresh greenery together.

Sicily is a land of citrus plenty, giving the Spanish city of Seville a run for its money when it comes to the cultivation of oranges. It is said that blood oranges originate on the island because of Mount Etna, whose volcanic temperature vacillations change the color of the fruits' flesh. Mandarins also grow in abundance, as do lemons, pomegranates and, not insignificantly, grapes.

Sicilian wine has both the sunlight and the spotlight shining on it at the moment, with grapes like *Nero d'Avola* giving it unprecedented fame across the wine-drinking world. It's not that grape cultivation is new, but that the local product has only recently started to be bottled on the island, and thereby gain international recognition. Previously, Sicilian wine was shipped out by the tank load to elsewhere in Italy, making up for any deficit in more recognized regions' harvests. To quote Locatelli again, "Growers are taking charge of their own destiny" by making drinkers realize that these deep, round, smooth wines—carrying all the benefits of sun, sugar and plenty of tannin—are as much an expression of Sicily as an *arancini* ball, or a cannoli dessert. They are all products of that land of "magnificent yet incomprehensible beauty" depicted in *The Leopard*.

● ● ● ●

* It's worth noting that chili is also used in Sicily, often as an addition to sauces such as those mentioned here. It's not found to the extent that it is in Calabria, but much, much more than anywhere else in the country.

† First published in 1950, *The Silver Spoon* is the most popular cookbook in Italy and is a wonderful compendium of hundreds of typical regional Italian dishes. If you're interested in Italian food, I'd urge you to invest in a copy, which will afford little kitchen journeys all over Italy.

**PANTRY LIST** • almonds • swordfish • tuna • pecorino • ricotta • raisins • capers • pasta (gemelli) • mint • wild fennel • chicory • parsley • olives • pine nuts • chickpeas

• • •

# • GEMELLI WITH SARDINES, RAISINS AND PINE NUTS •

This is a classic Sicilian pasta dish and can be found all over the island. It's also a great recipe to call on should you need to whip up something with pantry staples, an injection of exotic flavors from the far-flung climes of your kitchen cabinet. You can, of course, exclude some of the ingredients depending on what you have in stock and the tastes of those for whom you're cooking, which will make for varying degrees of potency. I find that a lot of people (or those I seem to cook for, anyway) don't like anchovies or capers (fools!), for example.

### • SERVES 4 •

14 oz dried gemelli or fusilli pasta (2–4 tbsp of pasta
    water retained)
1 ⅓ cups fresh bread crumbs
2 oz pine nuts
4 tbsp extra virgin olive oil
2 garlic cloves, finely sliced
1 tsp fennel seeds
3 anchovies, coarsely chopped
2 x 3½-oz cans boneless sardines, drained and coarsely
    chopped
½ cup raisins
3 tbsp capers
¾ cup white wine such as a Vermentino
zest of ½ lemon and a squeeze of juice
1½ tbsp mint, chopped
1½ tbsp flat-leaf parsley, chopped
sea salt and freshly ground black pepper

**1** • Cook the pasta according to the package instructions in salted water until al dente.

**2** • Meanwhile, toast the bread crumbs and pine nuts over medium heat in a small frying pan for 5–6 minutes, stirring constantly. Set aside.

**3** • Heat the olive oil in a deep frying pan on medium heat and add the garlic and fennel seeds. Cook for about a minute, moving them around constantly—this is just to release the flavors and to soften the seeds a little—you don't want the garlic to acquire too much color. Add the anchovies, sardines, raisins, capers, white wine and lemon zest and allow to simmer for 2–3 minutes.

**4** • Once the pasta is cooked, drain, reserving 2–4 tablespoons of the cooking water and add the water to the sauce (the quantity depends on how thick you like your pasta sauces). Add the pasta to the sauce and stir in the toasted bread crumbs, pine nuts and herbs and season with salt and pepper to taste.

# • SWORDFISH MESSINA-STYLE •

Glorious meaty swordfish cooked with olives, white wine and anchovies—all produce ultra local to Messina, Sicily's third-largest city and the island's closest point to the Italian mainland. This is an archetypal Sicilian dish that sings of the central Mediterranean, one for sunny days, to be made with a good catch. Make sure you have excellent bread on hand to mop up the juices. Many thanks to Giorgio Locatelli for the recipe.

## • SERVES 4 •

10 whole black olives in brine
1–2 tbsp extra virgin olive oil
4 x 5-oz swordfish steaks
sea salt and freshly ground black pepper
2 scallions, chopped
2 garlic cloves, finely chopped
1 oz capers, rinsed and well drained
pinch dried chili flakes
4 anchovy fillets in oil
$\frac{3}{8}$ cup white wine
1 x 14-oz can chopped tomatoes
6 tbsp tomato passata
1½ tbsp flat-leaf parsley, chopped, to serve
1 garlic clove, finely chopped, to serve

**1 •** Make three or four cuts in each olive from end to end, then cut each segment away from the stone as carefully as you can.

**2 •** Heat the olive oil in a pan, then put in the swordfish, season and seal on both sides—about 2 minutes on each side. Lift out and set aside. Add the scallions, garlic, capers, olives, chili and anchovy fillets to the pan, and cook gently until the anchovies "melt" into the oil and the onion is translucent.

**3 •** Add the white wine and simmer to evaporate the alcohol, then add the chopped tomatoes and passata. Mix well, cover and cook for 30 minutes over very low heat, adding the swordfish for the last 10–12 minutes or until just cooked through. Serve sprinkled with the parsley and garlic.

# • PEACHES IN WHITE WINE •

These "drunken" peaches make a great summer dessert and are quickly whipped up. The sweetness of the fruit seeps into the wine while the alcohol from good Italian grog is absorbed into peach flesh. Spiked with a hint of cinnamon, sugar and fresh mint, this is fruit salad (indeed, you can add other fruit such as cherries, melon and strawberries) with an edge. Do you dare to eat the peach? Yes, you most definitely do.

## • SERVES 4 •

4 peaches, stoned and halved
1 bottle white wine (I use good value, tasty Italians
    such as Vermentino or Soave)
1 tsp ground cinnamon
2 tsp sugar
mint leaves, chopped, to serve
vanilla ice cream to serve (optional)

**1 •** Cut each peach half into two or three slices and lay two halves' worth in a pretty glass, one glass per person.

**2 •** In individual bowls, submerge a portion of peaches in wine, enough to cover them. Add enough wine for each portion of peaches. Mix the cinnamon and sugar thoroughly into the wine.

**3 •** Drench the peaches in the wine mixture, cover, and refrigerate for at least 3 hours (the longer the better).

**4 •** Top with the fresh mint before serving, with ice cream if you're feeling especially indulgent.

# VENETO

*There was a hateful sultriness in the narrow streets. The air was so heavy that all the manifold smells wafted out of houses, shops, and cook-shops—smells of oil, perfumery, and so forth hung low, like exhalations, not dissipating . . .*

• THOMAS MANN, *Death in Venice* •

MANY HAVE BEEN seduced by the intensity of Venice over the centuries, not least writers. They tell of budding love, burning lust, madness and corruption against a backdrop of crumbling classical architecture and the waft of canal stench—from Shakespeare's *The Merchant of Venice* to the poetry of Byron, the works of Henry James, John Ruskin and Thomas Mann.

There is a heady decrepitude about Venice that gets under your skin. Like many, Thomas Mann fell for the city's shabbiness, which gives the Floating City an ethereal quality "unchanged from ballad times." It is a liveable museum, gradually rotting into one-day oblivion as sea levels rise. I can't think of any other place in Europe where reeking brown waters would be embraced with such romantic gusto.

The Veneto region of Italy sits in the country's northeast, its northernmost tip touching Austria and its coastline facing out onto the west coast of Croatia. It lies at the interface between eastern and western Europe. There's a fantastic culinary palette (for those of keen palate), but you've got to dig deep—particularly in the capital city. On the surface Venice is a poor food destination. Crowds of tourists find floppy cannelloni and sad pizza on every street corner, food that would be pronounced unrecognizable by Venetian natives. In Venice I have occasionally had that sorry feeling that I could eat better pizza, superior risotto, tastier pasta in London.

But there is far more to discover. Across the region and city, dotted inconspicuously around the "narrow streets" described by Thomas Mann, are *bàcari* bars. These are unique to the area, serving *ciccheti* (Venetian tapas such as a bite-sized piece of polenta with meat or seafood atop) alongside a little glass of wine, known as an *ombra* ("shadow"). And if these characterful names aren't enough, the *bàcari* are often packed with locals conversing loudly in the Veneto dialect.*

*Ciccheti* are not the only distinctive thing about Venetian food, of course, but as with most Italian cuisines, there is great emphasis on communal time spent eating and drinking, for which the *bàcari* culture is a platform. And, like much Italian food, Veneto's is deceptively simple, relying on a wealth of excellent local goods. The secret to the region's culinary character is often in combining these to optimal effect.

Pasta cedes some ground to other carbohydrate base ingredients in Veneto, in particular white polenta and a local type of risotto rice called *Vialone Nano* from the Po Valley, a lighter and longer grain than the more common *Arborio*. Despite its lesser importance, there is a local variety of pasta largely made from buckwheat flour and in a shape known as *bigoli*, long, fat, wormlike noodles. As we will see later in the chapter, this particularity stems from the region's proximity to central and eastern Europe, with which it is engaged in a subtle culinary interchange of flavors and ingredients.

Russell Norman, who runs London's Polpo restaurant group, says that the crucial difference between northern and southern Italian cookery is in the choice of fat base. Set back from the Mediterranean basin, northern Italy wasn't on the immediate trade route for Middle Eastern and North African wares such as olive trees. Instead of olive oil, Venetians and other northerners such as the Milanese historically used clarified butter, a seemingly small difference that makes for some significant variation in cuisines. The use of clarified butter, for example, accounts for Veneto's creamy risottos with their soup-like consistency. *Risi e bisi* (which translates to rice and peas, and also contains mint) is a local favorite that, from the fifteenth century onward, was made to honor Saint Mark's Day.†

Brassicas (leafy greens like cabbage and mustard) and bitter leaves are staple vegetables in Veneto, with several cabbages (Savoy, kale and green and red) used for dishes like *cavolo verza* soup (containing beans and Savoy cabbage), and sautéed green cabbage Vincentian style, with pancetta, garlic and vegetable broth. Every town seems to have its own radicchio. *Treviso tardivo* is perhaps the most famous, a curly-ended regional variant of the bitter, bright purple leaf that looks rather like vegetable octopuses. No coincidence, then, that Russell Norman (whose restaurant's name, Polpo, means "octopus"

• • • •

*The dialect, Veneto, bears similarities to Italian; it also resembles the Istriot tongue of nearby Croatia.

†Saint Mark is Venice's patron saint and he is celebrated on April 25 each year.

in Italian) says the Treviso radicchio is "almost a symbol" for Venice. We usually associate radicchio with salads, where it provides an acrid edge, but in Venice the brassica is also commonly cooked, beer-battered and deep-fried, or simply seasoned with lots of olive oil and grilled or baked (a great taste combination with strong meats, like game or good sausages).[*]

The third in a trinity of gorgeous purple vegetables, artichokes are another seasonal favorite in Venice. One local variety available at the Rialto market is known as *castraure* ("castrated") because they are cut at the stem. Artichokes can be braised and simply dressed with lemon juice and some extra virgin olive oil, but they can also be stuffed (bread crumbs, pecorino cheese, parsley), or added to creamy, lemony risottos.

Other popular vegetables include autumnal pumpkins and squash, the principal ingredient of *risotto di zucca*—a comforting, sweet and orange-ocher dish that beautifully epitomizes its season. Peas are also eaten in abundance, as is fennel—both fresh and in seed form for flavoring. Russell Norman recommends slicing the fresh vegetable and eating it with a little olive oil, lemon juice and some toasted hazelnuts. Bright garden herbs like basil, parsley and mint are the order of the day in Venetian cookery.

Venice served as the interface between east and west during the fifteenth century,[†] receiving all the spice riches that entered Europe from the Silk Road, which extended across the whole of Asia and through the Middle East and Africa. Ironically, the foul-smelling canals of Venice are reminders of its historic wealth. Gondolas were used to unload the newly arrived goods from the Byzantine Empire and farther afield. The use of exotic spices such as cardamom, clove, saffron and cinnamon in contemporary Venetian cuisine is a clue to this history of Spice Route trade.

Visit the Rialto market and you're sure to be reminded of Venice's trade history. Though her economy these days rests more on tourism and less on trading produce, Venice remains a hub for food merchants to deal their wares. Rialto is now split into several food-specific areas—*Spezializi* for spices, for example, *Naranzeria* for oranges and the covered *Pescheria* for fish. This is the freshest, most authentic place to buy local fish, evidenced by Russell's story of asking Luca, who runs the iconic Venetian seafood restaurant Alle Testieri, why on earth he wasn't open for half the weekend. "How

• • • •

[*] I sometimes dress cooked radicchio or red chicory (a closely related local product) with a *bagna cauda*, a Piedmontese garlicky anchovy butter, which seeps into the tightly pressed leaves. See page 116 for my recipe.

[†] Along with Genoa, the capital of Liguria on the other side of northern Italy.

can we possibly open on Sundays and Mondays? The market isn't open!" For days such as these, *baccalà* is always at hand—a Venetian pantry staple—perhaps rehydrated and creamed into *baccalà mantecato*, a mousse of fish with garlic, olive oil and bay leaf. This can be eaten on bread or with slices of polenta.

All sorts of local fish catches are available at Rialto; the preparation of each one showcases a different Veneto flavor or technique. With the cachet of two short seasons each year, soft-shell crab is very popular, either in a fritto misto or as the deep-fried crown to a salad with lemon juice. Then there are gó fish, the ugly little swimmers that can be found in the mud of the Venetian lagoon. They form the principal flavor in *risotto Buranello* (named after Venice's brightly colored island neighbor, a fishing village called Burano). There are clams galore—carpet shell, razor and more—which are best served simply grilled or cooked in ginger. Anchovies are used for the region's favorite pasta dish, *bigoli in salsa*, comprising buck- or wholewheat spaghetti, anchovies, onion and parsley.

The proximity of central Europe to Veneto explains the many culinary overlaps between Italy and other countries that, initially, seem so very different. Strudel, which I more readily associate with Austria and Germany, is eaten in the Dolomite mountains, and Venetians have a penchant for the bittersweet, reveling in strong pickly flavors like those that are common in central and eastern Europe[*] (see page 118). Classic Venetian dishes like *fegato alla Veneziana* are loaded with echoes of Slavic cuisine—finely sliced liver is sweetened with sliced onions, which, to look at, are reminiscent of sauerkraut. Vinegar or sage is frequently added for extra weight and pickly notes. Duck liver is also popular, and most classically put to work with pasta and sage in a dish called *bigoli con l'anatra*.

These flavors, and dishes such as sardines in *saor*[†] or the *agrodolce*[‡] sauce, typify the regional fascination with bittersweet foods. Given Venice's murky beauty, its simultaneous rotting and romance, bittersweet flavors seem aptly to represent the fading splendor of the city, perhaps even the region as a whole. Don't you agree, Thomas Mann?

••••

[*]On the other hand, you can see how noodle-style carbs such as spätzle came about in places like Hungary, given that the world's pasta capital isn't very far to the west at all.

[†]Sweet-and-sour sardines, typical of Venice. The fish are dredged in flour and fried, then served with a concoction of fried onions cooked in vinegar, saffron, cloves, bay leaves, sultanas and pine nuts.

[‡]Found all over Italy, this is a sweet-and-sour sauce made primarily with sugar and vinegar, often with the addition of fruit and vegetables. It pairs well with pepperoni, fish and, well, most things.

**PANTRY LIST** • risotto rice (particularly Arborio) • radicchio • chicory • *baccalà* • anchovy • sardines • pumpkin • artichoke • fennel • peas • fragrant garden herbs (parsley, mint, basil) • select spices (saffron, cardamom, cinnamon) • buckwheat pasta

• • •

# • RADICCHIO WITH BAGNA CAUDA •

*Bagna cauda* is a buttery, garlicky, anchovy sauce actually thought to be native to Piedmont. Nevertheless, it is eaten widely across northern Italy and, given the proliferation of anchovies and radicchio, this dish showcases some typically Venetian flavors and ingredients. It makes a nice starter or addition to a summery spread of salads and cold cuts. Try experimenting with chicory in place of the radicchio.

### • SERVES 4 AS A SIDE •

6 tbsp extra virgin olive oil plus a tablespoon for frying
3–4 heads radicchio, quartered
1 x 2-oz can anchovies and their oil
4 garlic cloves, finely chopped
7 tbsp unsalted butter, cubed

**1 •** In a large frying pan heat a tablespoon of olive oil over medium to high heat and add the quarters of radicchio. Turn every so often to make sure it is evenly cooked. It should take 5–7 minutes for it to soften and start to brown.
**2 •** In a separate pan, make the *bagna cauda*. Heat the 6 tbsp olive oil over medium heat, add the anchovies and garlic and cook for 1–2 minutes, stirring constantly, until the anchovies break up and dissolve into the sauce. Add the butter and allow it to melt.
**3 •** Arrange the radicchio on a plate, cut sides facing up, and spoon the *bagna cauda* over the top. Serve immediately.

# • PEA RISOTTO •

There are two "rice and peas" recipes in this book, of very different ilks. In Venice, this pea risotto was traditionally enjoyed on the feast day of Saint Mark, the city's patron saint, which is celebrated on April 25. Known as *risi e bisi* in Italian, it is more soupy than your average risotto, flavored simply with ample butter and pungent Parmesan, or made meatier with prosciutto pieces and chicken stock. Both the key ingredients are symbolic: the rice of abundance and the peas of springtime. If you're a fan of pea and mint together, you could add mint to the garnish or do away with the parsley all together.

## • SERVES 4–6 •

7 oz podded peas (pods reserved)
4¼ cups good-quality vegetable or chicken stock
7 tbsp unsalted butter
2 white onions or 4 shallots, finely chopped
4 oz diced dry ham such as prosciutto (optional)
7 oz Arborio rice
generous grating Parmesan
sea salt and freshly ground black pepper
flat-leaf parsley or mint to serve, chopped

**1** • Pod the peas and set them aside. Bring the stock to boil in a large saucepan, add the pods and simmer until soft. Remove the pods and purée in a blender (depending on how smooth the resulting purée is, you may want to strain it through a sieve to remove any woody stalks) before returning to the stock. The resulting liquid should resemble a pea soup. Set aside.

**2** • Melt the butter in a large frying pan and sauté the onions or shallots over medium heat. After about a minute, add the ham (if using), and continue to sauté for 8–10 minutes, until the onions become translucent and start to turn golden.

**3** • Add the rice and podded peas, coating them in the buttery, oniony mixture. Then gradually stir in your green stock mixture until it is thoroughly absorbed into the rice—this should take 10–15 minutes. The rice should be cooked al dente. If the grains are still granular, add a little more water.

**4** • Fold in the Parmesan, season with sea salt (if necessary) and black pepper and sprinkle with parsley or mint to serve.

# EASTERN EUROPE

Food, for her, is not *food*. It is terror, dignity, gratitude, vengeance, joyfulness, humiliation, religion, history and, of course, love. As if the fruits she always offered us were picked from the destroyed branches of our family tree.

• JONATHAN SAFRAN FOER, *Eating Animals* * •

FOR WRITER JONATHAN Safran Foer's Polish grandmother, meals were endowed not only with history, but with a sense of good fortune that food was on the table at all. Foer describes his grandmother fleeing the Holocaust, hiding potatoes in her trousers and taking refuge with a Russian farmer who offered her a meal of pork. Despite her immense hunger, she refused on the grounds that it was not permitted under kosher law.

The Ashkenazi Jewish diaspora—that is to say the Jews whose forebears originated in central and eastern Europe and of which Foer's grandmother was one—attach enormous importance to the traditions and belief systems surrounding food, many of which continue to be observed today. As Foer writes, "Thursday we baked bread, and *challah* and rolls, and they lasted the whole week. Friday we had pancakes. Shabbat we always had a chicken, and soup with noodles."

Sometimes Ashkenazi Jewish food can seem inextricable from that of central and eastern Europe. This is probably because the mass exodus made by European Jews ahead of and following the Holocaust enabled their cuisine to spread organically. Goulash and borscht,† to name just two well-known Slavic dishes, have thus been popularized in the Jewish name. It strikes me that although the quotes from Foer undoubtedly typify the eastern-European

• • • •

* *Eating Animals* charts the reasons behind Foer's decision to stop eating meat, which I have to admit resonated with me. But it is his exploration of his Ashkenazi Jewish upbringing that I found even more poignant.

†Two iconic soup or stew-based dishes from central and eastern Europe. Goulash is a stew of meat, noodles and vegetables seasoned with caraway and paprika. Borscht is beetroot soup. I have included recipes for both.

Jewish experience, the emphasis on gratitude, history and love is common across eastern European cultures, infusing their attitudes to food.

I've grouped together central and eastern European countries—those enclosed by the Black, Baltic and Adriatic Seas, east of Germany and Austria and west of Russia—somewhat crudely, on the basis of strong similarities among their cuisines. These countries' shared history of Communism has been a force for both good and bad in the kitchen, limiting the availability of ingredients while also preserving traditions from the onslaught of culinary modernization. Bulgarian chef and food writer Silvena Rowe notes, "Few good things came out of the isolation that Communism brought, but undoubtedly one benefit that we can now reap is that the foundations of the national cuisines were never adulterated by the changes in culinary fashions that swept across Europe during those years." She is, of course, right—and this is why "Eastern Bloc" food can taste somewhat alien. Rich new flavors and unexpected combinations arrest your palate. Like anything you try for the first time, eating really good Slavic food is an experience heightened by novelty. It seemed wrong to look at a single cuisine, so we're going to take a journey around Hungary, Poland and the Czech Republic and look at some of their common culinary traits.

Though collectively these cuisines were not "adulterated by culinary fashions," there was nevertheless mixing among the individual national cuisines. Culinary miscegenation among former "Eastern Bloc" countries led to regionally owned dishes like goulash, which, though native to Hungary, has been adopted as a local dish elsewhere, in countries like the Czech Republic. Other quintessentially "Eastern Bloc" fare includes soup, stews, dumplings that all use root vegetables (beets, carrots, spuds), meat (think lots of it and sparing little of the animal), pickles, grains, fruit, nuts and spices like paprika, caraway and dill. Intense flavors rule.

Central and eastern Europe offer a clear link between the cooking traditions of Scandinavia (see page 135) and Germany (see page 127) with those of the Middle East (see page 152–53). Flavors such as sour cream, dill, pickled fish, caraway and paprika meet the classic sweet-and-sour combinations of the Persian[*] and Arab worlds. In *Feasts*, her book about central and eastern European sharing foods, Silvena Rowe shares recipes such as pomegranate, pumpkin and lamb stew and duck with almond and pomegranate sauce, making me think

• • • •

[*]For example, Persian recipes such as *khoresht-e-mast*, which combines chicken with yogurt, orange and barberries (page 186) or Syrian dishes such as cherry kebabs.

of some of the dishes taken to southern Spain by the Moors, and which are still cooked there today. *Bigos*, the Polish national dish, a stew of beef, pork, sausage, sauerkraut, mushrooms, apples and prunes, also shares some of these traits. Equally, however, dishes like *papricas*, a famous Hungarian stew made from lean meat, paprika, tomatoes, peppers and sour cream, has a more Germanic, or at least less Mediterranean, feel to it. Located between two perhaps better-known culinary traditions—Scandinavian and Middle Eastern—eastern European dishes like *papricas* and *bigos* are edible expressions of their geography.

Centuries of poverty and then the arrival of Communism have defined the development of these cuisines, made up of simple ingredients but packing a punch in terms of flavor. Soups and stews are fundamental—cheap and easy one-pot nutrition in which a little meat or fat can go a long way. One classic example is borscht. I first discovered this truly wonderful beet soup as a nine-year-old when my friend Emilia Brunicki's Polish grandmother made it for us. I remember walking into her chintzy hallway in south London, where the aroma of beets, meat stock and slow-cooked goodness enveloped me. We were too young for vodka, but now I can imagine how well the two would pair, cocooning your body with heat and fuel for a long, cold night. When Granny Brunicka wasn't cooking borscht, she made the most delicious chicken soup with vermicelli noodles. It was unlike any chicken dish I'd eaten before, and I can remember devouring its difference—the carrots, cooked for hours until sweet and soft, the tiny flakes of brown chicken meat, that sense of coddled satiation afterward.

I've since learned that my young self's sense of the restorative, nurturing qualities of Granny Brunicka's soups was no coincidence. Chicken soup is affectionately known as "Jewish penicillin" and has become the typical Shabbat (Saturday Sabbath) meal for many Jews, especially those of Ashkenazi background. Every family seems to have its own version, but it is always golden brown, clear and with gorgeous globules of fat floating on its surface. Carrots and celery are usually in there and, often, *kneidlach*, or matzo balls, little dumplings made from matzo-meal flour, eggs and fat. People flock to the 2nd Avenue Deli in New York, a restaurant founded by Polish immigrants in the 1950s, for their authentic chicken soup and their cookbook contains no fewer than six chicken soup recipes!

In central and eastern Europe, soups range from the most rudimentary of peasant food (and here, "peasant food" really is the appropriate term, not a trendy moniker for "hearty" hot dishes) such as *soup mit nisht* ("soup with nothing," a potato and cabbage-based broth) to standard tomato or mushroom, through to sour rye, sour cucumber, tripe and chilled fruit soups, using blueberries or wild strawberries.

Stews are equally popular, thicker and meatier than the soups of the region. Goulash is generally acknowledged as Hungarian, which it is, but many of the surrounding countries have their own versions. My Czech friend Klara Cecmanova sometimes puts cumin and frankfurter-style sausage into hers but the dish more typically combines beef with onion, garlic, caraway, tomatoes and vegetables such as peppers and potatoes. This is a heavy meal designed to enable Hungarian farmers and shepherds to withstand cold weather. What these stews have in common, in addition to being affordable and substantial, is their ability to be "kept going," Easily extended with a little added water, it is said that they can stay good for up to a week.[*] Regional egg pasta, known as spätzle—rather heavier than Italian alternatives and resembling giant macaroni—is often eaten with stews, as are rye bread and mashed potato.

Dumplings are commonly eaten, sometimes as a side dish, sometimes as a main course, across eastern Europe. They can be egg-based (like Hungarian *galuska*) or potato-based (like Polish pierogi) and are served plain to accompany stews or with more elaborate fillings such as cream cheese, mushrooms, sauerkraut or chicken liver.

Cured fish is often used as an agent of sweet and sour. Pickled herrings, haddock, gravlax and even caviar are familiar features, often made into intricate snacks with rye bread and sour cream, or served breaded and fried for main courses. Fresh fish is equally good as a canvas for other sweet-and-sour flavors, complementing the likes of salted cucumber and zingy vinegar, lemon and dill.

Quickly cultivated and full of vitamin C and beta-carotene, cabbage is another fundamental ingredient across the center and east of Europe. Sauerkraut is a staple in the north—from Germany as far east as the Ukraine—and is used in numerous stews and soups and to fill dumplings. Most famously, however, *goblaki* are stuffed Polish cabbage leaves containing mince, sausage meat, rice and herbs—another testament to the region's culinary intricacies that avoid great expense.

Eastern Europe has an excellent reputation for beer—the Czech Republic produces particularly good pale lagers of the pilsner type, such as the internationally available Budvar and Staropramen—while vodka is a mainstay of Polish culture. It can be made with potatoes, rye or wheat (a point of contention, that last one) and, cheaply produced from widely available crops, one

••••

[*] According to Silvena Rowe, goulash was historically stored in a sheep's stomach to preserve it—perhaps not the most appetizing method of keeping food fresh, but at least it's resourceful.

can imagine it serving a purpose during the cold winters, another comforting mainstay alongside the stews, soups and delicious desserts.

The common constituents of east- and central-European desserts are sponge cake, soft pastry, nuts and seeds and wild fruits. Cake rolls filled with jam or poppyseeds, strudel, crêpe-like pancakes (*palacsinta*) with jam, and—my favorite—*bàbovka*, a ring-shaped cake from the Czech Republic. My family's Czech friend Petra Rychnovska lived with us during my teens and to this day remains the closest thing I have to a sister. When her mother visited, she'd come laden with boxes of foil-wrapped strudel and a *bàbovka*, a beautiful crown of dense, moist, marbled sponge cake made by Granny Rychnovska back in Prague. We'd spend the ensuing days eating these goodies at every (but every) meal and though Pet's mum couldn't speak any English, the knowing smiles shared across the table transcended language. The *bàbovka* spoke for us and united us all over two things: love of food and love of her daughter.

PANTRY LIST • hot paprika • caraway • bay leaf • dill • juniper • black pepper • marjoram • oregano • chives • sour cream • beets • cabbage • noodles (vermicelli for soups, spätzle for stew accompaniments) • matzo meal for dumplings • cured and pickled fish • poppyseed cakes

• • •

# • BORSCHT •

My friend Emilia's late Polish grandmother, Halina Brunicka, used to make this soup regularly—and I was lucky enough to eat it. When I asked Emilia if she would be happy to share it, however, she told me that it had all been in Granny B's head, made each week from memory. So, here you have the results of a Brunicki family brainstorm, during which they tried to remember each step and measurement as faithfully as possible. Although we'll never make it quite like Granny B did, I'm honored to include the nearest thing possible—her granddaughter's rendition. Dress borscht up with a dollop of sour cream or a splash of light cream and some dill for dinner parties, or enjoy it in its purest form on a cold Sunday evening. If you can't get beef on the bone from a butcher, beef cubes would do just as well. It can be made vegetarian if necessary by omitting the beef shank and replacing the beef stock with the same volume of vegetable bouillon.

6 cups good-quality stock (Granny B used beef)
1 beef shank (about 1⅔ lb on the bone)
1 white or yellow onion, quartered
6 large beets, half of them grated, half chopped
3 carrots, coarsely chopped
1 potato, peeled and cubed
5 mushrooms, sliced
½ small head cabbage, shredded
1 tsp allspice
1 tsp sugar
1–2 bay leaves
juice of ¼ lemon (more to taste if needed)
¼ cup vodka (optional)
sea salt to taste

TO SERVE
pierogi or cheese straws
crème fraiche
handful dill, chopped

**1** • In a large casserole dish, bring the beef stock, beef shank and onion to a boil, then reduce the heat and simmer for 1½–2 hours. Remove from the heat, allow the broth to cool and remove all the meat from the beef shank, discarding the bone, fat and sinew.

**2** • Several hours later, once the fat has cooled sufficiently to allow its removal, skim from the top of your broth and add the beets, carrots, potato and mushrooms. Bring to a boil, then reduce the heat again and simmer for 30 minutes.

**3** • Add the cabbage, allspice, sugar, bay leaves and lemon juice and cook until the cabbage is tender, 20–30 minutes. Add the vodka if using. It works well if you let the borscht sit overnight, allowing the flavors to bind and mature. Simply bring to a boil again before serving.

**4** • Some people like to strain the soup so that it is just a broth. I prefer to have the bits of beef, beets and mushroom for texture—whatever you prefer. Serve hot with pierogi or cheese straws, a dollop of crème fraiche and a garnish of chopped dill.

# • CHICKEN SOUP •

Chicken soup is *the* answer to colds and flu (remember Jewish penicillin). In fact, it's worth making and freezing a batch so there's a portion at the ready throughout the winter. In Ashkenazi Jewish communities, chicken broth is traditionally eaten with *kneidlach,* or matzo balls (dumplings made with matzo flour and chicken fat), particularly during Passover. This simple chicken soup leaves out the *kneidlach* and makes an excellent meal of leftovers, recycling the carcass from a chicken roast to make a different meal altogether. It's a Monday staple in my house following Sunday roasts and takes an easy, "one pot and leave it" approach. You could also try adding some fresh sage or thyme to make it more aromatic.

### • SERVES 4 •

3½ tbsp unsalted butter
1 white or yellow onion, coarsely chopped
1–2 large leeks, coarsely sliced
2–3 celery sticks, coarsely sliced
3–4 carrots, coarsely chopped
6 garlic cloves, 3 of them finely sliced and 3 of them unpeeled and whole
1 whole chicken carcass, complete with roasting juices
6⅓ cups good-quality chicken stock
1 bay leaf
small handful black peppercorns
sea salt
2 oz vermicelli noodles
flat-leaf parsley, coarsely chopped, to serve
freshly ground black pepper

**1** • Heat the butter in a large frying pan and sweat the onion, leeks, celery and carrots over low heat for 3–4 minutes. Add all the garlic and sweat for another minute.
**2** • Next, put the chicken carcass and any trimmings—bits of skin, bones, the juices or gravy in which it cooked—in with the *sofrito,* cover with the chicken stock and add the bay leaf and peppercorns. Season with salt.
**3** • Simmer over low heat for about an hour. When you're just ready to eat, strain the soup to remove the chicken carcass, bay leaf, garlic cloves (retain these—see below) and peppercorns and return the soup to the pan.

**4** • Break the vermicelli into smaller pieces and cook until al dente. Before serving I like to peel the whole garlic cloves, push them through a fine sieve into the soup and give it a good stir.

**5** • Serve the soup crowned with freshly chopped parsley and some freshly ground black pepper.

# • BÀBOVKA •

I would eat this morning, noon and night if I had the metabolism to withstand it. Thanks to the fabulous Klara Cecmanova (who definitely does have the metabolism to withstand regular *bàbovka* consumption) for her recipe. Klara is quick to stress the importance of Czech flour, which can be found in some Polish shops or online, but if you can't find it, you can substitute all-purpose flour. You can buy ready-made vanilla sugar in some supermarkets, but it's easy enough to make your own and a good thing to have in your pantry. Simply place 2–3 used and deseeded vanilla pods in a jar with 2½–5 cups of superfine sugar and allow to infuse for a week or so. Alternatively you can substitute the vanilla sugar with 1½ tbsp superfine sugar and 2–3 drops of vanilla essence. You will need a ring-shaped cake pan. Personally, I think *bàbovka* is best plain, but if you fancy jazzing it up a little, try adding a tablespoon of rum, some lemon juice, chocolate chips or dried fruit.

### • SERVES 10–12 •

14 tbsp unsalted butter, at room temperature,
    plus extra for greasing
1⅛ cups Czech flour (polohrube mouky) or all-purpose flour,
    plus extra for dusting the cake pan
1⅓ cups confectioners' sugar
1½ tbsp vanilla sugar (see above)
4 medium eggs, separated
½ tsp baking powder
2 tbsp cocoa powder
confectioners' sugar to dust

**1** • Preheat the oven to 350°F. Butter a 9½- to 10-inch ring-shaped cake pan, sprinkle a little flour around the sides and shake out the excess.

**2** • In a large bowl, cream the butter with approximately two thirds of the confectioners' sugar and the vanilla sugar. Slowly beat in the egg yolks and blend thoroughly. Add half the flour and the baking powder and beat well, then stir in the rest of the confectioners' sugar and the flour. Don't mix too much from hereon or your mixture will become too sticky.

**3** • In a separate bowl, beat the egg whites until they form peaks, then gently fold these into the mixture. Be careful not to overmix. The mixture should fall off a spoon in lumps, not drip. Halve the mixture and separate into two bowls. Sift the cocoa into one half and mix well. Keep the other half white.

**4** • Spoon the light and dark mixtures into the cake pan in layers, running a fork through the middle in a swirling motion to create a marble effect. The pan should be two thirds full.

**5** • Bake in the oven for 30–40 minutes or until a knife inserted into the center comes out clean. Allow to stand for 10 minutes before turning out of the pan and sifting some confectioners' sugar over the top to serve.

# GERMANY

Happy is it, indeed, for me that my heart is capable of feeling the same simple
and innocent pleasure as the peasant whose table is covered with food of his own
rearing, and who not only enjoys his meal, but remembers with delight the happy
days and sunny mornings when he planted it, the soft evenings when he watered
it, and the pleasure he experienced in watching its daily growth.
• JOHANN WOLFGANG VON GOETHE, *The Sorrows of Young Werther* •

TO MANY OF us, German food belongs with wooden
toys and accordion music at the Christmas markets
that grace our town squares each winter. When I was a
student living in Leeds, a group of us would hurry to
the Millennium Square for *glühwein* and *bratwurst* and
revel in the idea of the northern European Christmas —
all dark nights, deep snow, handicrafts and hearty
food. It was magical, but more because it was a cher-
ished Christmas tradition than a remarkable eating
experience. And while I am undoubtedly informed
by my own preferences and prejudices, I doubt many would hail hot dogs as
a gastronomic breakthrough.

Yes, if any cuisine is lacking in glamour, it's probably Germany's. Sausages and soured cabbage, rye bread and plain hard cheeses typify the international perception of German food as heavy. Food like this has served a
valuable purpose, of course, sustaining a population of manual laborers as
the country rapidly industrialized over the last two centuries.

A few years ago, some friends and I decided to cycle from London to Berlin in eleven days. A mad undertaking but we did it, in no small part thanks
to sustaining meat and potato stews rich in caraway and juniper, or gamy
sausage served with sauerkraut, all washed down with a malty evening
beer. These traditional dishes are still served in restaurants across Germany
but, though delicious when well executed, are hardly conducive to modern
notions of balanced nutrition (i.e., low in carbohydrate and fat). But despite
being unfashionable, German food can be both a delicious and a fascinating
expression of the land and history.

This is the country of Black Forest cake and Hansel and Gretel, the Brothers

Grimm siblings lost in a forest of dangerous edible temptations—"milk and pancakes, with sugar, apples, and nuts" and a wicked witch's house "built of bread and covered with cakes . . . the windows of clear sugar." Many of the foods we most associate with German cuisine, such as wild mushrooms and beets, freshly picked apples or pumpkin and sunflower seeds, feel as though they must have been foraged, sourced from the forest or newly uprooted from the soil. Seeds and grains, from wheat and oats to rye and pumpernickel, are crucial to the vast assortment of German breads and pretzels of different colors and concentrations of flavor.

For centuries, the land we know today as Germany was part of the block of central Europe known as the Holy Roman Empire, which (roughly) stretched across modern-day Austria, Germany, Burgundy in France, Italy, and much of eastern Europe (known then as Bohemia). As my father delights in saying, it is arguable whether it was "Holy," "Roman" or indeed an "Empire," and when it crumbled at the end of the Thirty Years War in 1648, Germany was divided into numerous states including Prussia, Bavaria and Saxony. These were subsequently unified into the German Empire in 1871.

That nutshell of a history lesson underpins two points. First, that Germany is in fact a relatively new arrival, as European countries go, and its culinary identity is arguably still being shaped. Secondly, it's hardly surprising that many of the foods we consider to be German are in fact Austrian—Wiener schnitzel* (by definition from Vienna), apple strudel and Sacher torte (Austrian chocolate cake) to name just a few. The fact that there is only a subtle distinction between "German" and "Germanic" is an important one.

Traditional cuisine in Germany has changed very little over the past few decades.† It would be shortsighted not to wonder whether events of the mid-twentieth century are still determining the evolution of native cuisine. While the food landscapes of America and Great Britain became commercialized and Mediterranean Europe carried on as it always had—rich in the natural produce of warmer climes, each village with its artisan bakery, the Arab, Jewish and Christian cooking traditions all playing their part—Germany's domestic policy took a nationalistic focus, shunning outside influences. In 1945, with the end of the war and fall of Nazism, the

• • • •

*Wiener schnitzel is a breaded, deep-fried thin piece of meat. Traditionally it is made with veal but is more commonly found made from pork, a cheaper alternative.

†At the other end of the spectrum, meticulous German chefs mimicking French and Spanish techniques in the name of "Modern European Cuisine" abound in big cities and expensive hotels.

international powers placed restrictions on German production to thwart the rise of further militarism. Combined with a relatively low ethnic mix, this meant that German cuisine evolved relatively little in the twentieth century.

The division of Germany into East and West in 1949 brought about some broad differences between the two food cultures. West Germany stayed truer to its roots and, since it contained the whole of the country's southern area (including the city of Frankfurt, capital city of sausages), championed the likes of wurst. Meanwhile, the East was inevitably influenced by neighboring countries such as Poland and Russia, inheriting their fondness for salt, pickles and herbs such as dill (see page 119). *Solyanka* (a thick Russian soup with a meat, fish or vegetable base, plenty of brine, cucumbers, cabbage and sour cream) was very popular in East Germany and neatly expresses the region's palette of ingredients.

Whatever the limitations on German cuisine in recent history, the range of foods available now is steadily increasing. The Turkish population of four million people, for example, forms the biggest ethnic minority in Germany today. I've eaten fantastic kebabs in Kreutzberg, Berlin's bohemian hot spot, where Turkish restaurants and food trucks offer an altogether healthier take on fast food than native wurst and oily onions.

There's also a lively green movement in Germany.* Seasonal vegetable produce—like cabbage (sauerkraut, in green and red colors) and asparagus (the white, typically German, variety called *spargel*)—is readily available. People are more likely to use smaller, more specialized shops and most towns have a weekly farmers' market. Grocery shopping on your bicycle, with fresh bread and vegetables in the front basket, is common in Germany. On my last visit I got the impression that this is a healthier nation than the much-loved bratwurst might suggest.

Herbs and spices deliver gusto to German food, but not heat. Caraway, chive, dill, parsley and thyme all pack in flavor and prepare the palate for intensification as you head farther east into Poland, Russia and eastern Europe. Chili is a rarity and, like garlic, came to Germany with immigrant communities such as the Italians and Turks. Heat is instead delivered in the form of mustard and horseradish, both of which can take a lead role in sauces for meat or river fish (like trout) or can be used as a condiment. They are often interchangeable and both complement the heavy meats and pickle flavors

• • • •

*This is largely driven by the Öko Institut, or the Institute of Applied Ecology, the private body dedicated to green living, renewable energies and biodiversity.

frequently found in Germanic and Slavic cuisines. The "three Cs"—cardamom, cinnamon and clove—the spices which combine well with sweet flavors, are commonly found in German desserts and sweets such as the spice cookies similar to those you can find in Scandinavia (see page 135), gingerbread and fruit tortes.

Last but not least, wurst refers to sausages both hot and cold. There are more than fifteen hundred varieties in Germany. They seem to be eaten at every meal, from cold cuts with cheese and bread at breakfast to hot dogs or alongside sauerkraut or potato salad for meals later on. *Bockwurst* and *wollwurst* (veal and pork combinations, the latter fried after boiling); *knackwurst* (short, and made from pork and garlic), *landjager* (beef and pork jerky, seasoned and dried), *frankfurters* and blood sausage, white sausage (*weisswurst*, predominantly veal meat, from Bavaria), are just a few of the best-known. American journalist H. L. Mencken can fill in the gaps with his wonderful description of the myriad wurst: "They run in size from little fellows so small and pale and fragile that it seems a crime to eat them to vast and formidable pieces that look like shells for heavy artillery. And they run in flavour from the most delicate to the most raucous, and in texture from that of feathers caught in a cobweb to that of linoleum, and in shape from straight cylinders to lovely kinks and curlycues."

For me, German meals are best devoured when I'm really hungry, when just home after a hellish commute on a cold winter's night, or when I've taken a lot of exercise—all washed down with a pint. In fact, beer is one of the more respected culinary products to emerge from Germany. Though we are most familiar with the big shots in German lager production such as Bitburger, Becks, Erdinger and Paulaner, when I cycled to Berlin every township we passed through seemed to have its own signature brew, ranging from white wheat beers to pale, amber and malty and hoppy dark beers. German wine, on the other hand, hasn't quite the reputation that German beer has earned itself. When I was growing up I was subtly indoctrinated by my parents to veer away from the slim wine bottles that indicated cloying sweet Rieslings and Gewürztraminers. In my experience, however (albeit experience built up in the last decade), Germany produces some fantastically delicate, high-quality wines such as the limey Rieslings of the Mosel Valley. Be aware, though, that German wine classification is a sometimes confusing business. The term *Prädikat*, for example, indicates that a wine is of superior quality, as well as its degree of sweetness. You may be familiar with labels such as *Spätlese* ("late harvest") and *Eiswein* ("ice wine"), just two of a possible six different classifications. I recommend reading *Drink Me!* by Matt Walls for more information. Then we mustn't forget schnapps—the strong, sweet, grain- or fruit-based spirits that originated in Germany.

Although it wouldn't be my cuisine of choice if I were stranded on a desert island, I think the German kitchen can offer fantastic accompaniments to the food we already eat regularly. For example, I often cook a couple of the two cabbage recipes below as part of a roast dinner. The red cabbage is my grandmother's specialty and (unsurprisingly) pairs well with sausage and mashed potatoes, while the Savoy cabbage with caraway seed is one of my aunt Mary's staples—we eat it with the turkey every Christmas. Pick and choose in small amounts from the German kitchen and, rather than overpowering you with weight, it will enhance your everyday meals with vigorous flavors. Below you'll find recipes for some of the best and the wurst of German food . . . (Sorry, I couldn't resist.)

**PANTRY LIST** • cabbage (red and white) • sausages • potatoes • wild mushrooms • rye and pumpernickel breads • mustard • horseradish • caraway • chives • thyme • juniper berries • star anise • cardamom • cinnamon and clove for desserts

• • •

# • SAVOY CABBAGE AND CARAWAY SEED •

I feel strongly that cabbage is an underrated vegetable. I love it, as do the Germans, and if you try one (or all) of the following three recipes you'll see why. This dish is as integral to my Christmas table as sprouts, but it is also a great vegetable to accompany meat (particularly chicken and other poultry, or sausage and mashed potatoes) year-round.

### • SERVES 4–6 AS A SIDE •

3½ tbsp unsalted butter
1 white or yellow onion, finely chopped

2 tsp caraway seeds
1 Savoy cabbage (around 1¾–2¼ lb),
    cored and shredded
sea salt and freshly ground black pepper

**1** • Melt the butter in a large saucepan over medium heat, add the onion and caraway seeds and sauté for 5 minutes, stirring frequently. Add the cabbage and sauté for another 2–3 minutes.
**2** • Add ¾ cup water and cover. Simmer for 5 minutes, then remove the lid and move the mixture around some more. You want the flavor of the seeds to be evenly distributed and for the cabbage to wilt without losing its crunch entirely. You may need a little more water depending on the volume of cabbage. Season with salt and pepper before serving.

## • BRAISED RED CABBAGE •

My maternal grandmother wasn't the most committed of cooks, but she was an expert at this. When my mum and uncles were kids they ate it with roast pheasant—farmer's children—but it is enjoyed across Germany alongside many types of meat, sausages, dumplings and mashed potatoes.

### • SERVES 4–6 AS A SIDE •

1 tbsp olive oil
1 onion, finely chopped
¾ cup red wine
1 red apple, cored and finely diced
1 medium head red cabbage,
    cored and shredded
4 tbsp red wine vinegar
2 tbsp sugar
1 cup vegetable stock
sea salt and freshly ground black
    pepper to taste

**1** • In a frying pan, heat the olive oil over medium heat and sauté the onions for 10 minutes until translucent.

**2** • Add half the red wine, half the apple, half the shredded cabbage, half the red wine vinegar and half the sugar and stir thoroughly. Repeat with the other half of the ingredients.

**3** • Cover with the stock and simmer for 30 minutes or so, stirring occasionally, until the cabbage is cooked. Season to taste—you may feel you want more acidity or more sweetness. If so, add more red wine vinegar or sugar accordingly.

# • SAUERKRAUT •

Sauerkraut, or "sour cabbage," is exactly what it says on the can except that, unlike the red cabbage recipe above, its sourness comes not from vinegar but from fermentation. This is, if you like, Germany's answer to kimchi (see pages 250–54). It's not to everyone's taste; it can be overpowering and I think it needs strong meat to balance it out. But game, beef, sausages—you name it, it goes.

## • SERVES 4–6 AS A SIDE •

1 head cabbage of your choice,
    cored and shredded
4 tbsp table salt
6 cracked juniper berries

**1** • In a bowl, mix the cabbage and the salt, making sure that the cabbage is well coated. Knead the mixture: this will extract moisture from the cabbage, the moisture in which it will ferment. Add the juniper berries.

**2** • Transfer it to a large pot and lay a wet cloth (a dish towel is perfect) over the top. Cover with a plate and put a weight on top. This will compress the mixture and force brine out of the cabbage.

**3** • Put the pot somewhere warm and dry (but not too warm, as this could compromise the flavor) for about a month. Press the weighted plate down into the pot every day to extract as much moisture from the cabbage as possible.

**4** • A month later, when you want to eat the sauerkraut, bring it to the boil in a small saucepan over a medium heat and spoon into sterilized jars or straight onto plates.

# • BEERY BRATWURST WITH SAUERKRAUT •

Here are the instructions for an edible German cliché—sausage, beer, sauerkraut—and an opportunity to use your recipe for the latter. You can get hold of authentic bratwurst online, if not in good supermarkets (depending on your whereabouts).

## • SERVES 6 •

6 bratwurst
4 cups German beer (such as Erdinger or Paulaner)
unsalted butter
6 good-quality white rolls
6 handfuls sauerkraut (see page 133)
mustard (I like whole-grain)

**1** • Prick each sausage with a fork several times, then put them in a saucepan, cover with the beer and bring to the boil. Cover, reduce the heat and simmer for 15–20 minutes, until the sausages are no longer pink.
**2** • Turn on your grill. Remove the sausages from the pan (and discard the beer) and grill for a few minutes on each side until they are golden brown.
**3** • Butter your rolls and throw a sausage, a handful of sauerkraut and a heaping teaspoon of mustard into each. Devour.

# SCANDINAVIA

Always rise
to an early meal,
but eat your fill before a feast.
If you're hungry
you have no time
to talk at the table.
• *The Hávamál*[*] •

DENMARK, SWEDEN, NORWAY and Finland—the cluster of connected Scandinavian countries sitting like an open sandwich among the North Sea, Germany, Russia and the Baltic—were until recently something of an enigma to the rest of the world, loosely associated in many people's minds only with minimalist design and Danish pastries. The food of the region, in reality, draws on an array of influences as well as a rich choice of native ingredients that echo the pine forests, cold coastline, long winters and dark nights. In fact, Scandinavia is of late the flavor of the month—both literally and metaphorically.

Yes, the world is experiencing something of a Nordic epiphany, of which food is only a part. Nordic Noir has flooded popular culture with depictions that are as eerie as they are compelling. Writers such as Norway's Jo Nesbø or Sweden's Stieg Larsson, and TV shows such as Denmark's *The Killing* and *Borgen* have captivated readers and viewers alike and—ironically for such a dark genre—helped shed some light on Scandinavia.

Scandinavian food—known in the past for soggy pastry, cheap bacon and Ikea meatballs—is now emerging from the darkness with its clean, colorful flavors. Delicacies salted, pickled and cured, whole-grain breads and hearty meats, tart fruits, hefty dairy and spices in baking: all have been under-exposed and narrowly appreciated until now. Danish superstar chef René Redzepi has undoubtedly played a key role in attracting epicurean eyes to Scandinavia with

• • • •

[*]The *Hávamál* is an epic Viking poem dating back to sometime between the ninth and thirteenth centuries. Its content is largely gnomic wisdom in the form of proverbs.

his restaurant Noma, voted the best in the world in the 2010, 2011 and 2012 San Pellegrino Restaurant Awards. He uses many native and sometimes unheard-of Scandinavian ingredients, but his cuisine is a Modernist fusion—a sort of Nordic version of what Ferran Adrià did at El Bulli.

The revival of interest in home baking in Britain has probably also been a factor in the collective discovery of Scandinavian food, since this is an area in which the countries of the region excel. Scandinavian baked goods have injected novelty into our understanding of cakes and bread, and that in turn has led to a deeper appreciation of these cuisines, with their smorgasbords, salted and smoked meats, cured fish, pickles and slaw-style salads. Scandinavia's baked goods make use of imported nuts and spices, dairy products and reams of sour fruit. I love the idea of *fika*, a convivial Swedish tradition based on sharing baked goods with coffee. Though *fika* itself belongs to the Swedes, a love of bread, cakes and baking binds all the Nordic cultures. There are the dark, intensely savory breads that combine so beautifully with fish, meat and cheese, and form the basis of the famed Scandinavian open sandwich. Cakes, cookies and the beloved cinnamon bun are also ubiquitous, though while berry-clad pastries might be more common in Finland, nutty sponge cakes like almond-topped *tosca* are popular in Norway and Sweden. Baking on the west coast of Norway is particularly idiosyncratic, with strong Jewish influences that reflect trading with Germany.

As you move east across Scandinavia, flavors shift subtly. Danish food has some strong Germanic qualities (think lots of pork and herbs such as sage), while on the other side, in Finland, Russian tastes enter the equation: an increased use of rich, earthy flavors like caraway seed, dill, beets, game and, of course, vodka—robust food and strong liquor to keep out the cold. Swedish and Norwegian cuisines are in many ways indistinguishable, the differences coming down to *terroirs*—the foraging of Sweden's plenteous wild mushrooms, for example, or the greater use of seafood in Norway.

Across the board, Scandinavians make breads both rustic and fibrous with local grains such as rye, oats, spelt and linseed. There's also a widespread love of pickles and preserves, which are eaten with most meals and are often made from highly local produce such as foraged cloudberries (a Norwegian obsession apparently, and like a sour, musky orange raspberry) or the more common lingonberry,[*] which Norwegian cook and food writer Signe Johansen describes as "the cranberry of Scandinavia."

• • • •

[*]Lingonberries are produced by evergreen shrubs that grow in forests across Scandinavia. Not dissimilar from cranberries but smaller and packed with juice, they have a tart flavor and make a jam that is often enjoyed with rich red meats such as beef, liver and game.

Fish such as trout, cod, sardines and salmon play a starring role in these cuisines and would have seen the population through long winters when little else was available. The historical necessity of curing fish has become the heart and soul of Scandinavian cooking. Pickled herring and gravlax (cured salmon flavored with dill*—see recipe below) are found all over Scandinavia, while Norway is the original home of the much-traveled *bacalhau* (see page 83). Salted dried cod† formed the basis of the Norwegian economy for hundreds of years and comes in a couple of guises: *lettsaltet torsk* (lightly salted cod) and *klippfisk* (wind- and air-dried salted cod).

There is a kind of Viking pragmatism to the quote from the *Hávamál* at the beginning of this chapter, a no-nonsense proverb for the hungry warrior. It is perhaps this kind of practicality—the way food responds to the land and connects to the lifestyle of its people—that has bolstered the popularity of Scandinavian cuisine in recent years. This is food that resonates strikingly well with a modern approach to a healthy, balanced diet without compromising on flavor or character. Nourishing grains and seasonal meat complemented by ultra local condiments and freshly caught fish mean that protein and fiber are prized highly. It's also a cuisine that has stayed true to a sustainable local and seasonal ethos, curing ingredients like cod and herrings to compensate for times of scarcity. In light of all this, is it any wonder that Scandinavian food is coming out of the dark?

**PANTRY LIST** • spices (allspice, nutmeg, cinnamon, cardamom) • dill • salmon • herring • salt cod • venison • whole-grain breads (rye and pumpernickel) • cabbage (red and white) • pickled cucumbers • beets • canned and preserved fruits (cherries, plums, apricots, lingonberries)

• • •

• • • •

*Although the use of herbs is not widespread, dill is an integral flavor to the Nordic table. Signe Johansen describes it as "the garlic of the north."

†*Bacalhau* appears more famously in Portuguese, Spanish and Italian cuisines but is native to Scandinavia, particularly to Norway, although it is now produced in countries such as Portugal and China, too.

# • GRAVLAX •

Before I started eating meat again, salmon fillet was the default meal served to me at dinner parties and in restaurants (this predates the rise of the sea bass). I got bored with salmon. Very bored with it. Gravlax saved me from this fishy fatigue, quite literally curing salmon of its blandness and dressing it up in a delicately spiced, sweet and dill-infused outfit of deliciousness. Try this typically Scandinavian recipe to serve as a starter or on little bite-sized morsels of sourdough for canapés, and witness the humble salmon transformed. (Just be aware that it takes a couple of days for the fish to marinate in the fridge, so prepare ahead of time.)

## • SERVES 10–15 AS PART OF A SMORGASBORD •

1 side of whole salmon, deboned
and cut into 2 fillets
1 tbsp white peppercorns
2 tbsp coriander seeds
6 tbsp demerara sugar
⅓ cup rock salt
9 tbsp dill

FOR THE DILL SAUCE
4½ tbsp dill
3 tbsp vegetable oil
3 tbsp white wine
3 tbsp demerara sugar
3 tbsp French mustard
sea salt

**1 •** Check the salmon for bones, then place it skin side down on a plate. Pound the peppercorns and coriander in a mortar and pestle and mix with the sugar and salt. Chop up half the dill and press this into the fleshy side of the fish, then rub in the spice mixture on top of it.

**2 •** Sandwich the fillets together so that the dill spice mixture is in the center. Rub any residual dill spice mixture into any exposed areas of flesh, then wrap the fish tightly in plastic wrap and place in a casserole dish or baking tray. Refrigerate for 48 hours.

**3 •** For the sauce, simply blend all of the ingredients and you're good to go.

**4 •** After a couple of days, remove the plastic wrap from the fish, wipe the herb mixture away and pat dry. Signe Johansen recommends then putting the remaining fresh dill onto the skinless side of each fillet, pressing it down without squashing the fish. Then slice each fillet into thin strips, on the diagonal. Serve on rye or sourdough bread with a little of the sauce drizzled over.

# • PICKLED CUCUMBER SALAD •

This recipe is ubiquitous across Scandinavia, although the ingredients vary from kitchen to kitchen. The three staple ones are cucumber (unsurprisingly) and a delicate balance of sugar and white wine vinegar. Some like to spice it up with caraway or celery seeds, but I keep my salad straightforward with a combination of black and white pepper. In terms of herbs, dill is a winner, although if you're eating this with the gravlax then you might face dill overkill, so perhaps use parsley instead.

### • SERVES 6 •

2 cucumbers
3 tbsp white wine vinegar
3 tbsp granulated sugar
big pinch sea salt
½ tsp ground white pepper
½ tsp ground black pepper
1½ tbsp dill or parsley, stalks discarded and leaves chopped
lemon juice (optional)

**1** • To prepare the cucumbers, slice off the ends and peel as much of the skin as you like. You can leave a few strips of dark green skin if you prefer, or remove the whole lot—it's purely an aesthetic judgment. Cut the cucumber flesh into very fine disks.
**2** • Mix the remaining ingredients together—including the lemon juice if a little extra acidity is to your taste—reserving some of the herbs for serving.
**3** • Arrange the cucumbers in a bowl, pour the dressing over the top and refrigerate for half an hour or so to give the flavors a chance to mingle and seep into the cucumber without making it too soggy.
**4** • To serve, sprinkle the last of the herbs on top and enjoy with fish dishes such as gravlax or poached salmon.

# • DANISH DREAM CAKE •

My mum's recipe for dream cake—pilfered from a Danish friend in the 1990s—is scribbled in an ancient notepad of handwritten cake recipes. I've been eating it since I was a kid but until recently hadn't had it for quite some time. True to its name, my memories of this delightfully basic white sponge cake, encrusted with a coconut and brown sugar topping, had acquired a dreamlike quality. A dream to make and eat, indeed.

## • SERVES 12 •

6 tbsp (¾ stick) unsalted butter, softened, plus more for
    greasing the springform pan
1¾ cups whole milk
5 large eggs
1¾ cups superfine sugar
3¾ cups all-purpose flour, sifted
3 tsp baking powder
2 tsp vanilla extract

FOR THE TOPPING
9 tbsp unsalted butter
1½ cups shredded coconut
1 cup dark brown sugar
3 tbsp whole milk

**1** • Preheat the oven to 350°F. Grease a deep 9½-inch springform pan and line the bottom and sides with parchment paper.
**2** • Put the milk and butter in a small saucepan and melt over medium heat, stirring frequently. Set aside to cool.
**3** • Meanwhile, in a large bowl whisk the eggs with the superfine sugar for 8–10 minutes, until light and fluffy, then add the flour, baking powder and vanilla and whisk to combine until the mixture is completely smooth.
**4** • Fold in the buttery milk and transfer to the prepared springform pan. Bake in the oven on a baking tray (a little of the liquid will leak from the pan) for 35–40 minutes until golden brown.

**5** • Put all of the ingredients for the topping in a small saucepan and stir over medium heat until combined. Once the sponge cake is cooked, remove from the oven and spread the topping evenly over it immediately.

**6** • Raise the oven temperature to 400°F and put the cake in, complete with topping, for another 5 minutes. Remove from the oven and cool in the pan before turning out and eating once the topping is fully set.

# UNITED KINGDOM

Tongue sandwiches with lettuce, hard-boiled eggs to eat with bread-and-butter,
great chunks of new-made cream cheese, potted meat, ripe tomatoes
grown in Mrs. Lucy's brother's greenhouse, gingerbread cake fresh
from the oven, shortbread, a great fruit cake with almonds crowding
the top, biscuits of all kinds and six jam sandwiches!
• ENID BLYTON, *Upper Fourth at Malory Towers* •

THE TWENTIETH CENTURY was one of bad press for British food. Denigrating comments (often from American personalities) abound about the kingdom's food, giving it a regular proverbial thump. Comedian Jackie Mason once said in a stand-up performance that "Britain is the only country in the world where the food is more dangerous than the sex," while U.S. wine expert Bill Marsano (who should definitely know better) is rumored to have once commented, "The British Empire was created as a by-product of generations of desperate Englishmen roaming the world in search of a decent meal." Even Laurie Colwin, a self-proclaimed devotee of English food (see page 1), writes in *Home Cooking* that one has to "work up the courage to confess that you like English food" and that people are "apt to sneer."

Comments like these may perhaps be better described as playground taunts than well-researched attacks, but the fact remains that the bad British food to which Mason and Marsano refer lasted well into my own school days, perpetuating a decline of British cuisine that started with two world wars. School lunch ladies dolloped canned potatoes, claggy ravioli and disintegrating greens[*] onto our plates, making us young Brits question our nation's culinary greatness.[†] Having a family who took an interest in food, and

• • • •

[*]If, for some reason, you were intrigued to sample British school food on visiting London, the Stockpot restaurants (in Soho and Chelsea) serve the nostalgic misery of many a British youth at a suitably low cost. An epicurean experience it isn't, but I have been known to pop in for a fond fix of syrup sponge and custard.

[†]The quality, and nutritional value, of British school lunches is an issue that television chef Jamie Oliver has tackled head-on with shows such as *Jamie's School Dinners*.

a mother and grandmother who cooked from scratch, I was one of the lucky ones and privy to all that British food had to offer for the good.

Great Britain has a grand tradition of making magnificent food, from pasture to plate. From porky cold cuts like thickly sliced brined hams, pork pies and scotch eggs[*] to hardy northern lamb, roasted with garlic and rosemary on a Sunday, in Lancashire hot pot or Shepherd's pie, and from some of the world's great hard cheeses (cheddar! Wensleydale! Stilton!) to a rich coastline of sea treats and quietly voluptuous root vegetables, we produce raw materials of competitive quality and have a rich heritage of sustaining dishes—all the products of life in a cold climate. This is the kind of food which the famous Mrs. Beeton[†] gave Victorian housewives recipes and instructions for in her *Book of Household Management*—haunch of mutton, turnips in white sauce, fried vegetable marrow, and so on.

More than any other country's cuisine, Britain's is recognized for its complete meals—the Full English Breakfast, the Sunday Roast, the Afternoon Tea, the Picnic. These are our culinary institutions and, perhaps with the exception of afternoon tea (which is less conducive to modern life), they are institutions that we still visit with remarkable regularity. It is around my parents' table on a Sunday that the family still congregates most often (and if not there, then in a pub), and the British hangover would be a bleaker experience without a meal of eggs, bacon, sausage, beans, mushrooms, and friends. What's more, the Enid Blyton[‡] quote above reminds me of the British tradition of picnics, assembling an array of simple, native and largely cold foods that combine in a picnic basket. These meals, shared and picked at from a blanket (perhaps the origin of the English expression "spread" in reference to a meal laid out?) are uniquely reminiscent of a British upbringing. When my grandmother died, the most memorable letter of condolence to my father came from a friend who, as a child, remembered eating her tomato "and sand" sandwiches on a windy Blakeney Point on the Nor-

• • • •

[*] Beloved by many, scotch eggs consist of hard-boiled egg encased in sausage meat, rolled in bread crumbs and baked or deep-fried. Trendier, gentrified renditions of this classic picnic food use soft-boiled eggs—to which, I must admit, I am very partial.

[†] Isabella Beeton was a nineteenth-century housewife often regarded as the UK's first food writer, releasing her *Book of Household Management*, a compendium of tips on keeping house for middle-class housewives of her time. Known commonly as Mrs. Beeton, she is buried in West Norwood cemetery, right where I grew up in southeast London.

[‡] Famous for children's books featuring recurring characters like Noddy, the Famous Five, and the Secret Seven, Enid Blyton wrote in the middle of the twentieth century. My parents grew up reading her books, as did my generation, and they remain a staple read for British kids, harking back to the thirties, forties and fifties—bygone years when pleasures were simple. They provide an interesting point of reference in terms of food—predating the introduction of Mediterranean foods and ingredients, the foods to which Blyton refers are quintessentially British, the kinds of dishes that Tom Kerridge is now reviving in his books, TV shows and restaurants.

folk coast. Braving bad weather and determined to have a jolly good time, she made almost practical food for the most impractical of circumstances.

Sandwiches, incidentally, are a British creation, named for the eponymous fourth Earl of Sandwich, John Montagu, of the eighteenth century. A notorious gambler, Montagu sought a solution to greasy playing cards after eating cooked meats with his hands. The answer? To lay said meat between pieces of bread, sandwiching it in slices (yes, he even has an English verb named after him!). Indeed, British bakers have a history of pioneering bread-making techniques. We have our traditional loaves like multigrain, whole-wheat and crusty white that champion native crops like wheat (including rye and spelt) and barley, as well as region-specific varieties like Irish wheaten or soda bread. Though it is an ancient method of bread-making, sourdough, the result of fermenting yeast dough with natural yeasts for longer than other bread varieties, has also seen a revival in the UK in recent years. This resurgence of artisan bread in Britain becomes all the more significant when you know that we Brits are (brilliantly? shamefully?) responsible for the sliced loaf—or what Nigella Lawson has referred to as "plastic bread." In 1961, the Chorleywood bread process, also known as the "no time method" of bread-making, was developed to make bread in a fraction of the time using lower-quality wheat, churning out bread cheaply and in bulk. Chorleywood bread is yet another example of the downturn British food took in the middle of the twentieth century, now representing some 8 percent of the nation's bread production.

So what happened to British cuisine? Why the playground bullying from other nations? Sadly, no matter how good its native cuisine, war for an island country equals bad news for food. At the outbreak of World War II in 1939, Britain was already importing the majority of its food, including half its meat supply and even more of its cheese and fruit. Rationing was imposed incrementally over the course of the six-year conflict and, by the end, people were allowed as little as one egg per week and just ½ cup of butter. Ingredients that people had taken for granted before the war became scarce if not impossible to find, and with the continuation of rationing until well into the mid-1950s, many Brits either grew up with, or became accustomed to, a limited pantry—and a compromised palate as a result.

Tom Kerridge is chef patron of the Michelin-starred pub the Hand and Flowers in the English county of Buckinghamshire. His work, including a highly successful television series and book, *Proper Pub Food*, is dedicated to celebrating everything that British food does well: unpretentious and hearty food that can be dressed up or down. From Kerridge's perspective, the UK has taken its eye off the prize and fallen subject to a fifty-year distraction in the aftermath of wartime austerity. First there was rationing, then the introduction of tasteless canned products and then, in the 1960s and '70s, the rise of packaged holidays in the Mediterranean, exposing sojourning Brits to the cuisines of warmer climates. Imitation became a problem. Isolated on our little island and fed up with the restrictions imposed by geography, we wanted to feel part of the olive oil brigade in mainland Europe. Kerridge points to Spaghetti House (which opened in 1955), the inauthentic pasta restaurant chain, as indicative of this. Indeed, in her book *A Book of Mediterranean Food*, the great British food writer Elizabeth David championed this national appetite for Mediterranean food,* explaining where to find the base ingredients with which to reproduce it in London. But Kerridge cites another challenge: the British work ethic, "We work very hard in this country, which pays off in that we're in a more stable economic position than Mediterranean countries. But good food takes time and our cuisine has suffered for this."

Britain has only awakened to its culinary potential in the last ten years or so. Some of our most celebrated restaurants—Simon Rogan's L'Enclume in Cumbria, Restaurant Nathan Outlaw in Cornwall, not to mention Tom Kerridge's the Hand and Flowers—prize British ingredients, the produce of our cold climate. Now is something of a honeymoon period between Brits and their native ingredients and their traditional dishes, rediscovering the food with which our grandparents and antecedents before that were raised. In more recent years, chefs have been moved by what Kerridge calls the Redzepi effect: "We're suddenly realizing we are a Northern European country and have a cold climate. That Noma, one of the best restaurants in the world, is serving cold climate cuisine is inspiring to us. We have a food heritage we can be proud of, too. Yes, cabbages can be glorious!"

So what are our strengths, then, according to Kerridge? Root vegetables, he says, turnips, carrots, potatoes, and meats cured, smoked, braised or crafted into a host of family dishes with which my brother and I, and our friends, and our antecedents, grew up. Every cut of the animal was used, reflected in dishes still popular today, like steak and kidney pie, and the Brits know how to use leftovers like no other nation. Who *doesn't* love bubble and squeak (see page 150 for my recipe), a fried hash of leftover mashed potato and cabbage, or even a turkey curry.

If one of the problems with British food has been a tendency toward imita-

• • • •

* David's preface to the second (1955) edition of her book *A Book of Mediterranean Food* points to the decline of rationing in 1950s Britain and she gives instructions of where to find ingredients that, in many instances, have acquired staple status in the pantries of my generation: "So startlingly different is the food situation now as compared with only two years ago that I think there is scarcely a single ingredient, however exotic, mentioned in this book which cannot be obtained somewhere in this country, even if it is only in one or two shops."

tion in the second half of the twentieth century, the other has been with self-perception. Colwin wrote that "even the English" are down on their own cuisine because of that "dread substance" School Food, while Jane Grigson[*] wrote in *English Food* (1974), "The English are a very adaptive people. English cooking—both historically and in the mouth—is a great deal more varied and delectable than our masochistic temper in this matter allows." We are a self-deprecating lot, with a rhetoric that can be as entertaining as it is infuriating. Giving British food the makeover that it deserved was as much about convincing British people of its value as proving it to the rest of the world. It is about embracing our treacle tarts and our bread and butter puddings (see page 151) as "hearty," not "stodgy," and realizing that good food isn't by definition dwarfed by a giant white plate or best eaten with grated Parmesan. The Enid Blyton quote above captures the characteristic simple pleasure that is British food, unbastardized.

For such a small island, we have surprising regional diversity. The variation in accents for a start—a Liverpudlian lilt couldn't sound much more different from a Thames Estuary or Cornish twang, and that's before you've even branched into Scotland, Wales or Northern Ireland.[†] It follows, then, that our food varies accordingly. The fish dishes of the southwest, championed by chefs like Mitch Tonks and Nathan Outlaw,[‡] are standout, with oysters to rival northern France and chunky white fish served in golden batter alongside chunky chips, the much-loved British institution of fish and chips.[§] There's also the smoked salmon and soused herring of Scotland—dishes that reflect the country's latitudinal positioning and which echo Scandinavian staples made with the same

• • • •

[*] Jane Grigson was a British food writer known for her interest in English food (she wrote a book on the subject) as well as (most notably) fruit, vegetables and herbs of the English garden—not to mention her caustic wit and tone of voice.

[†] The United Kingdom consists of Great Britain (England, Scotland and Wales) and Northern Ireland. In this chapter, I use the word "British" to encompass the UK rather than its literal meaning, pertaining to Great Britain but not Northern Ireland.

[‡] Both British restaurateurs and chefs who specialize in seafood of the south coast. Tonks runs the Seahorse in Dartmouth. Outlaw is chef patron at Restaurant Nathan Outlaw in Rock, Cornwall.

[§] This traditionally working-class meal consisting of battered haddock or cod served alongside chips that are doused in salt and vinegar (and sometimes mushy peas on the side too), before being wrapped in old newspaper, has like so many British food traditions become gentrified in recent decades. There are several mentions of both components in the work of Charles Dickens (a "fried fish workhouse" in *Oliver Twist* and "husky chips" or fried potatoes in *A Tale of Two Cities*) but it is not known when the two became united in newspaper. When I was little, we used to walk down to our local chippie (the colloquial name given to fish and chip shops where jars of pickled eggs and onions lined the Formica countertop) each Friday. Indeed, "Fish Fridays" are a familiar ritual in the Christian calendar (no meat on Fridays, the day of Christ's sacrifice), although in my family I imagine it was more of a reflection of my tired parents at the end of a working week.

ingredients—as well as haggis, the minced sheep's offal dish encased in the animal's stomach, served with neeps and tatties (turnips and potatoes, respectively). You'll find superior lamb in the north of the country, where sheep roam sometimes perilous gradients, bracing themselves against harder weather conditions than farther south. The meat is athletic and lean. There's Yorkshire pudding (a baked batter of eggs and flour, served with roast beef, potatoes and vegetables as part of a Sunday roast), Cornish pasties (pastry parcels of minced beef, rutabaga, potato, onion and seasoning), Welsh cakes (small spiced dried fruit rounds) and, native to my family's stomping ground in Norfolk, famous Cromer crab.

Then there are the cuisines that we've adopted as our own, most notably Indian. Curry, a narrow slice of Indian cuisine as a whole but its most popular incarnation in the UK, has become known as one of Britain's national dishes alongside roast beef and fish and chips. Today our appetite for curry is insatiable. We can boast twelve thousand restaurants that welcome 2.5 million customers each week and which serve 43 million portions of chicken tikka each year. Every autumn we host National Curry Week and, since the press announced a "crisis" in curry (a shortage of chefs to feed the aforementioned masses), there has been talk of launching our own British curry academy. Anglicized versions of northern Indian (mainly Punjabi) food have emerged over time—chicken tikka, sometimes with a masala sauce; korma and dopiaza, the creamy Persian-influenced dishes developed by the Mughals who settled in the central north, around Delhi and Lucknow; *jalfrezi*, a favorite from the British Raj in Bengal that involves stir-frying leftover meat and vegetables; and, most famously, the *balti*. *Balti* (meaning "bucket") is a uniquely British invention, a marinated meat or vegetable dish in light sauce that arrives in a wok-style serving dish. Originating in the city of Birmingham, whose landmarks include the Balti Triangle of curry restaurants, the dish has firmly become part of the culinary landscape. Chef April Bloomfield of the Spotted Pig in New York, but originally from Birmingham, has a recipe for "My Curry" in her book *A Girl and Her Pig*: "My life in England was filled with curry . . . [it] tastes especially fantastic with a beer in the wee hours after a night of clubbing." There's the implication of ownership here; that "curry," not "Indian food," belongs both to her hometown, alongside all its other cultural mainstays like beer and northern nightclubs.

Last, there are the traditional British desserts and cakes—heavy on fruit and syrup and pastry—that Laurie Colwin said "cannot be surpassed." And they can't. Blackberry and apple or rhubarb crumbles are easily whipped up and define the simple pleasures yielded by the British seasons. Fruits are stewed with sugar, topped with a flour, sugar and butter mixture, baked and then eaten with thick yellow custard. Victoria sponge, scones, bread and butter pudding, treacle tart, sticky toffee pudding, spotted dick, Christmas pudding . . . the list goes on. One interesting, and perhaps alarming, ingredient to our steamed puddings, like spotted dick and Christmas pudding, was traditionally suet, the raw meat fat found around the kidneys of mutton or cow. Suet has a high melting point, which means that, over the course of a long, slow steaming period, it imparts moistness without making the pudding too dense. Though it may not sound particularly appealing, suet has a particularly English character to it and harks back to the puddings enjoyed in Dickensian times to stave off the chill of British winters and make use of our native ingredients. I like to imagine characters in my favourite period novels—*Pride and Prejudice*, *A Christmas Carol*—eating from this traditional British larder, suet included, before the introduction of postwar temptations from the Med.

That's right, British food, it's my love in a cold climate.

**PANTRY LIST** • root vegetables (potatoes, rutabaga, turnips, carrots, leeks, onions) • meat and offal • fish (cod, haddock, whitebait, kippers) • seafood (mussels, oysters, shrimps, scallops, prawn, crab) • hard and blue cheeses (most famously, cheddar, Double Gloucester, Wensleydale, Stilton and Shropshire Blue) • shortcrust pastry, bakery goods from bread to cakes, cookies and scones • condiments (mustard, Worcestershire sauce, brown sauce, ketchup, chutneys)

• • •

# • COTTAGE PIE •

Traditionally a dish made with whatever remains from a joint of roast meat, Cottage Pie is the homely, delicious result of leftovers. Nowadays, we're more likely to buy mince for mince's sake, but it's nevertheless one of the cheaper, less glamorous forms of meat, and (I feel) it needs to be amplified by wine, plenty of spice and bold seasoning. Wash a helping of this down with a glass of red wine on a winter's night and feel your seasonal sorrows slip away. Make this recipe with lamb mince and it becomes Shepherd's pie.

• **SERVES 4–6** •

FOR THE FILLING
2 tbsp olive oil
1 ⅓ lb lean beef (or lamb) mince
2 white onions, finely chopped
1 large carrot, peeled and finely diced
2 celery sticks, finely chopped
4 garlic cloves, finely chopped
4 tsp tomato puree
3 ½ oz dry white wine
1 cup beef stock
1 heaping tsp granulated sugar
1 tsp ground cinnamon
½ tsp ground nutmeg
1 sprig fresh sage
pinch salt
freshly ground black pepper

FOR THE TOPPING
2 ¼ lb large potatoes, peeled and
        chopped into chunks
2 tbsp butter
⅓ cup whole milk
½ tsp ground nutmeg
big pinch salt
freshly ground black pepper
2 ½ oz grated cheddar cheese

**1** • Preheat the oven to 375°F.

**2** • In a deep, wide pan, heat 1 tablespoon olive oil, brown the mince (in batches if necessary), remove from the pan and set aside.

**3** • Add the remaining tablespoon of oil to the pan and sweat the onions, carrot and celery for 3–5 minutes, moving regularly, then add the garlic for another minute. Add the browned mince and stir in the tomato puree, wine, stock, sugar, spices and seasoning and cook over low heat for 15 minutes, stirring regularly. Remove from the heat and into a large pie dish and set aside to cool.

**4** • Meanwhile, place the potatoes in a large pan of cold salted water. Bring the water to a boil and cook the potatoes until they are soft but not breaking apart—about

15 minutes or so. Drain, return the potatoes to the pan, add the butter, milk, nutmeg, salt and pepper, and mash until creamy. Don't worry if there are a few lumps.
**5** • Once the meat has cooled, spoon the mashed potatoes over the top and sprinkle with the grated cheddar. Place in the oven for 15 minutes, then reduce the heat to 300°F for another 20 minutes, or until the cheese is golden and the sauce is bubbling around the edges of the filling. Serve hot with some greens and plenty of condiments like English mustard and chutney.

# • BUBBLE AND SQUEAK •

Another British classic that glories in leftovers, particularly those from a Sunday roast, and which became popular during wartime rationing when the pressure to use up every morsel of food was at its height. The slightly eccentric name is onomatopoeic, alluding to the noises its ingredients make as they cook in a frying pan. Americans might call this a hash, the Irish a colcannon—ultimately, regardless of name, they all just put the remaining potatoes and vegetables from previous meals to use, meaning no two ever bubble or squeak in quite the same way. An optional addition (suited to brunch time) would be to make little wells in the mixture before turning it and to break eggs into them. An English answer, if you like, to the Israeli shakshuka recipe (see page 182).

## • SERVES AS MANY AS YOU LIKE •

Potatoes, coarsely mashed (essential)
Cabbage, carrots, peas, sprouts (or whatever you have),
    coarsely shredded and at room temperature
2 tbsp salted butter
salt and freshly ground black pepper
mustard, ketchup or brown sauce to serve

**1** • Combine the potatoes and shredded vegetables in a bowl and set aside.
**2** • Melt the butter in a nonstick frying pan over medium heat and, once hot, transfer the vegetable/potato mix to the pan and sauté for 10–15 minutes, flattening with a spatula as it cooks.
**3** • Once the sides and base are golden and crisp, tip it onto a plate and then back into the pan, the other way up. Cook for another 10 minutes, or until a nice even crust has formed. Serve with lots of condiments.

# • BREAD AND BUTTER PUDDING •

All hail my favorite pudding—and not one for the carb conscious! This here is a very classic recipe, though the beauty of b&b pudding is its adaptability. I've often made it with panettone instead of white sliced bread, sometimes adding rose water and swapping lemon zest for orange to echo the Middle Eastern pantry. You might want to try adding chocolate chips, nuts or even snazzier flavors like grated tonka beans, which are my latest discovery from Kiwi chef Anna Hansen of the Modern Pantry restaurant in London.

## • SERVES 6 •

7 tbsp salted butter, softened, plus more for greasing the pan
1 ½ tsp ground cinnamon, plus more for sprinkling
1 ½ tsp freshly grated nutmeg, plus more for sprinkling
zest of 1 lemon
8–9 slices white bread, crusts on
½ cup mixed raisins, sultanas and currants
3 cups whole milk
1 cup light cream
½ cup superfine sugar, plus more for sprinkling
3 eggs
1 tsp vanilla extract

**1** • Preheat the oven to 350°F and grease a medium-sized oven-proof dish.

**2** • In a bowl, blend the butter with ½ teaspoon of the ground cinnamon, ½ teaspoon of the nutmeg and half the lemon zest, then spread this mixture over each of the slices of bread. Place the buttered slices in the bottom of your dish so that the pieces fit together snugly. Sprinkle the raisins, sultanas and currants over the top and set aside.

**3** • In a bowl, whisk together the milk, cream, sugar, eggs and vanilla with the remaining lemon zest, cinnamon and nutmeg, then pour into the dish over the bread.

**4** • Sprinkle a small amount of superfine sugar, nutmeg and cinnamon over the top and bake in the oven for 30–40 minutes, or until the top is golden and the bread crusts are browning.

# THE MIDDL

# E EAST

# SUGAR AND SPICE
# AND ALL THINGS NICE

...

Our lives would scarcely be the same without sugar, spice and some of the aromatic ingredients featured on this map —not least for regular sweet fixes. All the ingredients here have become indispensable to cooks across the globe; the use of spice in particular defines many cuisines, distinguishing one from another according to the variants, quantities and different blends used. Along with a brief history of sugar and the Spice Route on the facing page, this map shows the origins of some of my favorite aromatic and sweet ingredients, which have since been grown and used in domestic kitchens all over the world—often far from their original homelands.

**UNITED STATES &**
**CANADA**
Maple syrup

**MEXICO**
Vanilla

**MAYAN**
**CENTRAL AMERICA**
Chocolate

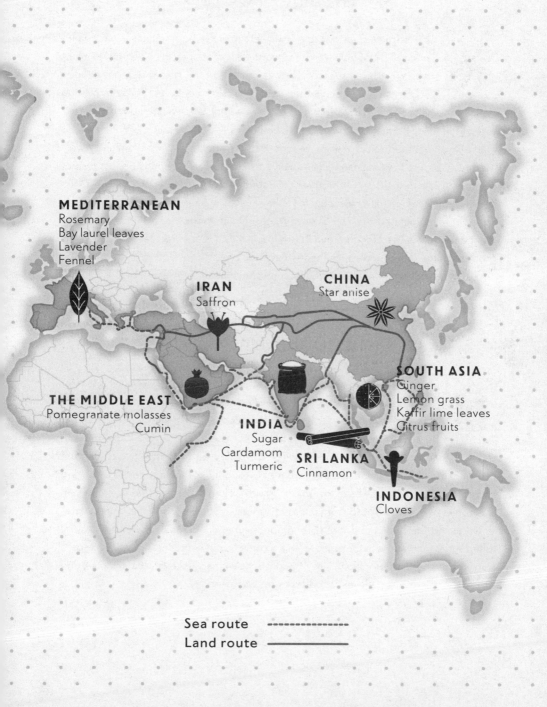

**MEDITERRANEAN**
Rosemary
Bay laurel leaves
Lavender
Fennel

**IRAN**
Saffron

**CHINA**
Star anise

**SOUTH ASIA**
Ginger
Lemon grass
Kaffir lime leaves
Citrus fruits

**THE MIDDLE EAST**
Pomegranate molasses
Cumin

**INDIA**
Sugar
Cardamom
Turmeric

**SRI LANKA**
Cinnamon

**INDONESIA**
Cloves

Sea route  ----------------
Land route  ——————————

## • THE SPICE ROUTE •

Historically, spices were a valuable currency—both financially and diplomatically. Not only were they worth a lot of money in trade between East and West but the Spice Route (pictured on the previous page) defined relations between countries and empires for centuries. For example, the Ottomans' rise to prominence on the world stage coincided with their seizure of the Spice Route from the Byzantine Empire in 1453 (see page 159). The map is marked with the theoretical "homes" of some of the world's most important and widely used spices, most of which can be narrowed down to points in the Indian subcontinent and the Middle East. When Christopher Columbus discovered the New World in 1492, he was in fact looking for a new route to Cathay, or Asia, because the Ottomans and the Portuguese dominated the two existing routes. He thought he had arrived in India (hence the terms "Red Indians" and "West Indies"), but had in fact fallen upon a land proffering very different wares indeed—from chilies (see pages 266–69) to corn, potatoes and tomatoes (see page 326) and chocolate to vanilla (see below).

## • THE SUGAR JOURNEY •

Sugar also originated in the East, purportedly in India where it was first refined. It was, however, the Chinese—the great imperial power of Asia at the time—who first kept sugar plantations in the seventh century. Sugar gradually migrated to the Middle East, where it became a staple ingredient of sweet foods and was often combined with spices such as cardamom and cinnamon. In the twelfth century, Crusaders brought back sugar from the Holy Land and it was subsequently taken to the Americas with Columbus in the fifteenth century. In the tropics of the New World, from the southern states of what is now the United States down to the Caribbean and Central and South America, European colonizers established sugar plantations in the eighteenth and nineteenth centuries. And so the expansion of sugar began; before long it had become the culinary necessity that we know and love—for better or for worse—today.

## • CHOCOLATE •

Chocolate comes from the area of Central America associated with the Mayans—communities that were at their height between AD 250 and AD 900 around present-day Mexico, Guatemala, Belize and Honduras. Our word comes from the Mayan term *chocolatl*, which translates as "hot water," suggesting that it was first enjoyed as a hot drink—albeit a bitter one (without sugar)—as far back as 1,100 BC. This cacao drink was embellished with ingredients such as vanilla and chili when the Aztecs took control of Mesoamerica in the fifteenth century, but it was the arrival of the Europeans that precipitated chocolate's international popularity. Very quickly, plantations started growing cacao in volume and sugar was blended with it to create what we today would recognize as solid chocolate.

## • VANILLA •

Unlike chocolate, the origins of vanilla can be traced to a very specific area of Mexico in the modern-day state of Veracruz. It was first used by the Totonac people who were native to this area in the fifteenth century, but quickly spread to Europe with the arrival of the conquistadores who named it vainilla or "little pod." It is now one of the most popular flavorings of chocolate, desserts and drinks worldwide. Its biggest producer is Madagascar, closely followed by its native Mexico.

# TURKEY

Colour is the touch of the eye, music to the deaf, a word out of the darkness.
• ORHAN PAMUK, *My Name Is Red* •

THE WORD "COLOR" encapsulates everything that left me entranced by Istanbul. Orhan Pamuk, Turkey's most celebrated contemporary writer, captures the spectrum of it in one neat sentence. Istanbul is a wonderful racket of visual splendor. From the breathtaking interior of the Blue Mosque, the Bosphorous shimmering at sunset and the colored glass lamps that create multihued silhouettes on the walls of the Grand Bazaar, to the mountains of dried fruits and nuts, and piles of brightly colored spice dusts, Istanbul is a feast for the eyes.

Happily, it's also a feast for the nose, mouth and palate, the arresting colors of everyday market stalls mere clues to all the flavors that Turkey has to offer: pyramids of cinnamon and rosebuds, golden sultanas and gnarled walnuts, dried figs and glistening plump olives of many colors, drizzling honeycomb and vats of fresh yogurt, fruit stalls boasting dark red apples, eggplants of deepest purple, pomegranates and the odd pineapple. Istanbul feels like a living museum dedicated to Turkish food, both ancient and modern.

My own experience of visiting Istanbul was the very definition of "food tourism." We spent our days eating, then walking to the next opportunity to eat and eating again. We waddled from fresh yogurt, honey and nuts at breakfast to *pide* at lunch, via snacks of *lokum* (Turkish Delight) and baklava and on to Efes beer and raki to wash down stews and kebabs at night. I was constantly full, but I'm not one to turn down the opportunity to try something new—and everything looked and tasted novel to my west-European palate.

Turkey is a land of seventy million people and fifty different ethnic communities, a country on the cusp of Christianity and Islam, Europe and the Middle East. Istanbul is at the heart of this divide, a city spread over three spits of land that jut out from the mainland—two of these sit in Europe and the other, to the east, is in Asia. The two continents are separated by a strait of water called the Bosphorous. While to Europeans, Istanbul might feel as unfamiliar as other cosmopolitan Muslim cities (such as Beirut or Marrakech), it is equally separated from its Arabic neighbors, with a secular government and quite different language. It doesn't sit comfortably in either Europe or Asia—no coincidence, then, that the Anatolian Peninsula was once referred to as "Asia Minor."

I have chosen to explore the food of Istanbul over any other part of Turkey not only because you find there a true cross section of Turkish food, as in many capital cities, but also because the city is home to the Topkapi Palace, where Ottoman cuisine was developed over the centuries. The Ottomans' legacy of international dominance outlined the shape of modern-day Turkish cuisine, and it is these lines I want to trace in this chapter, shading them in with a little of the color evoked by Orhan Pamuk.

For centuries—623 years to be exact—the interventions of the mighty Ottoman Empire punctuated European politics. When the Ottomans conquered the Byzantine Empire[*] in 1453, they took hold of the Spice Route (see page 156), a move that spread Ottoman influence far and wide but also brought inspiration from abroad back to Anatolian soil.[†] Flickers of dishes you might recognize from elsewhere—meze appetizers with hummus and yogurt-based dips, stuffed vegetables, pastries, sweet and sour—originate in Turkey and were spread by the Ottomans. Meanwhile, the varied spices collected on the Spice Route, from India to Morocco, came back to the Empire's capital; sugar, sweet foods (like *gaz*—see page 35—which may well have shaped the *lokum*, or Turkish delight, of today),[‡] and rice were lifted from Persia; wine came in from Greece and the kebabs and grilled meats for which Turkey is perhaps best known abroad reflect the nomadic life led by many an Ottoman crusader.

Today, Turkish grills and kebab shops stud the pavements of many European streets—beyti, schwarma and shish are a few varieties that might sound familiar. In Turkey there are many more regional variations, for example *Adana* and *Urfa*, most of which can be found somewhere in Istanbul. Taking their

• • • •

[*] Led by the Greek speakers and centered around modern-day Istanbul (then known as Constantinople), the Byzantine Empire was a continuation of the Roman Empire in the eastern Mediterranean.

[†] "Anatolia" refers the Asian side of Turkey. Though Istanbul straddles both European and Asian Turkey, the latter nevertheless comprises 97 percent of the whole country.

[‡] *Lokum*, or Turkish delight, joins baklava as a specialist phenomenon out of which Istanbul's shops make an art—they are almost galleries to edible beauty. This is Turkish delight as you have never seen it before, forget the bright pink, cloying stuff you grew up on and imagine soft, delicate rose-infused rolls hugging walnuts, dates, lemon peel or mint, finished with a dusting of confectioners' sugar.

names from their cities of origin (in south and southeastern Turkey respectively), both *Adana* and *Urfa* are made with a blend of lamb mince, tail fat* and bulgur wheat molded into long strips, then grilled and eaten with salad and yogurt. *Adana* kebabs are strongly seasoned with *pul biber*,† the flaming hot chili pepper that adorns numerous Turkish dishes in flake form. My Istanbul authority, Rebecca Seal—who published a cookbook about the city's culinary delights, titled simply *Istanbul*—also told me that offal is devoured ubiquitously and in various ways: fried, deep-fried, grilled, with onions or in wraps—this is food that reflects the nomadic lifestyle of both shepherds and Ottoman crusaders. Examples include *kokorec*, spiced sheep intestines wound around a spit and grilled, and *mumbar*, intestines stuffed with ground meat, bulgur wheat and onion. Both are typically eaten with bread and a chopped salad.

The heritage of Ottoman cuisine is still relevant to contemporary Turkish cooking, and so too should it be in your kitchen. Luckily, the ingredients required to make Turkish food at home are readily available in specialty shops, especially those run by native Turks in larger cities. As a starting point, stock up on fresh herbs, aromatic spices, *pul biber* flakes, plain yogurt and well-sourced lamb or chicken. It will help in your quest if you have a good grill and your stove has an open flame for the authentic chargrilled meats and vegetables that define the Ottoman feast.

The cuisine of Anatolia, today's Turkey, was developed on the home front as well as on battlefields and trade routes. As in Morocco (see page 283), modern Turkish cuisine has a lot to thank its royal heritage for—many of its cornerstones, such as filo pastry, pilafs, soft breads and yogurt-based dishes were developed and mastered by palace cooks in the royal kitchens of Topkapi Palace. Sources suggest that there were up to fourteen hundred live-in cooks at the court who, due to laws regulating the freshness of food, became experts with fresh ingredients. To this day, ripe vegetables and fruit, freshly sourced meat and seafood and just-made dairy, dough and pastry are permanent fixtures on Turkish menus—preserved fare remains rare. What's more, yogurt is a Turkish invention. When I first became enamored with Middle Eastern and Indian food, perhaps the biggest revelation was the use of yogurt. Like many Brits, I'd grown up eating it as part of dessert, but I now view it as a much stronger ingredient in savory dishes, complementing meat and grains with a light creamy texture and delicious sour notes.

• • • •

*Tail fat is an ultra flavorsome fat base popular in the Middle East and is derived from Awassi sheep, bred for the purpose. Apparently, rams can store up to 26½ pounds of fat in their tails.

†Sometimes known as Aleppo peppers (employing a Syrian name, somewhat confusingly).

Arguably the Turks have mastered pastry better than any other nation, rolling filo pastry, known locally as *yufca*, into membrane-thin leaves and making of it an art form. When layered up it acquires an unparalleled crispness that serves as a canvas for savory and sweet dishes alike: *borek*, a fried pastry filled variously with minced meat, cheese, potatoes and spinach are a staple meze, or baklava, known and loved the world over: sweetened pastry layering nuts (pistachios, almonds, walnuts) and honey syrup. Specialist shops sell baklava in squares, rectangles, circles and triangles, decorated with different colored nuts—it really is a thing of beauty. Pastry is another Ottoman delicacy that has traveled. Today it is enjoyed all over the globe, not least in the Muslim world with the likes of *bastilla* in Morocco and *knafeh*, a Palestinian delicacy made in the Levantine countries and Israel (see page 177).

Dolma (stuffed vegetables—"dolma" is the generic term for anything stuffed) and pilaf (a rice-or grain-based dish with other ingredients mixed in)* are ubiquitous not only in Turkey but across the Muslim world. This book is full of examples of stuffed vegetables—from Lebanon to Sicily and southern Spain—and blended rice dishes—pilau in India, *polow* in Iran—that descend from common culinary practices native to the Middle East. Once again, these are recipes that were perfected in Topkapi: the textbook fluffy pilafs and the stuffed dishes just dry enough to remain intact but juicy enough to write home about. These might include eggplants (the hero vegetable of Turkish cuisine), artichokes, squid and even melons. All are stuffed with a mixture of rice or bulgur wheat, mince and spices. *Midye dolma* are particularly typical of Istanbul—mussels in their shells, packed with an aromatic rice pilaf containing raisins, garlic, pine nuts and herbs.

Another ubiquitous Turkish food is *simit*, braided or twisted bread that is dipped in pomegranate molasses and sprinkled with sesame seeds. *Simit* vendors can be found on almost every street corner and, though it's a typical breakfast bread to be devoured with yogurt or jam, *simit* is eaten throughout the day, perennially. It most closely resembles pretzels, while *pide* and *lahmacun* are incarnations of a flatbread reminiscent of pizza, topped with minced meat and pickles, roasted vegetables and herbs.

As you'd expect from a city surrounded by coastline, Istanbul has fantastic seafood. Freshly caught fish sourced from the Bosphorous and the Sea of Marmara glow on market stands in the Kumkapi district by night,

• • • •

*Pilaf can be made with rice, bulgur or another grain, seasoned and blended with pulses like chickpeas. Another typical grain-based dish is *kisir*, which is usually enjoyed as an accompaniment: bulgur wheat blended with tomato paste, parsley, onion and the sweet-and-sour kick of pomegranate molasses.

illuminated by stark lightbulbs that show off blue, pink, gray scales and dripping fins. Tuna and bonito, horse mackerel and sardines, swordfish and—most important of all—anchovies (*hamsi*—which can grow to up to 6 inches) are a major feature of the cuisine. Anchovies fried in a corn batter, known as *hamsi tava*, are a specialty and are presented laid out in a star or fan shape (see my recipe at the end of the chapter). *Balik dolma* (stuffed fish) is common, as is *pilaki*, for which fish are cooked in a sweet vegetable sauce based on onion, tomato, olive oil, carrot and sugar. Fish is prepared in myriad ways—fried, grilled or poached—and served most simply with lemon and parsley, or in soups or casseroles.

Ottoman cuisine is one that people, including the Turkish, tend to imagine in black and white—the food of a bygone time. As Musa Dagdeviren, one of Turkey's most celebrated chefs, says,[*] it would be impossible to re-create Ottoman cuisine authentically, and restaurants claiming to do so have their sights set on luring tourists hungry for a taste of Turkey's colorful history. Ottoman guilds were famously secretive about their working methods, but we can still speculate and connect the dots linking the territories along the Spice Route that the Ottomans controlled. In this way we create an outline, a line drawing, which we can color in with the vibrant spectrum of what Turkish cuisine offers us today, and which Istanbul so beautifully showcases for the hungry traveler. To once again borrow the words of Orhan Pamuk, color really is, in this sense, "a word out of the darkness."

**PANTRY LIST** • pomegranate molasses • red pepper paste • yogurt • cumin • sumac • red pepper flakes • paprika • parsley • mint • dill • nuts (pistachios, hazelnuts, walnuts, almonds) • filo pastry • citrus fruits • minced meat (lamb and chicken) • orange blossom water • rose water

• • •

• • • •

[*] Musa has committed himself to unraveling the complex web of his country's cuisine, not only pinpointing regional differences but unearthing dishes that seem to have disappeared with history. Food at his restaurant Ciya Sofrasi, on the Asian side of Istanbul, has been known to make old ladies cry, with its Proustian reminders of bygone times.

# • DEEP-FRIED ANCHOVIES •

This dish of anchovies fresh from the Bosphorous and then deep-fried is an Istanbul delicacy. They are often arranged on a plate in a star pattern with wedges of lemon to douse their crispy battered skins. They are like the whitebait of Turkey, but bigger and of fuller flavor. Rebecca Seal recommends using the even bigger alternative of sprats if you can't find fresh anchovies.

## • SERVES 6 •

2 cups sunflower or vegetable oil for deep-frying
¾ cup all-purpose flour
big pinch sea salt and freshly ground black pepper
20–30 fresh anchovies (or 20 sprats)
lemon wedges to serve
flat-leaf parsley, to serve

**1** • Heat the olive oil (a good 1½–2 inches), in a wok or a deep saucepan and gauge its readiness with a bread crust—drop one in and see if it sizzles and browns. If it does, you're good to go.
**2** • As the oil is heating, mix the flour and ample seasoning in a bowl, then thoroughly smother the fish in the mixture.
**3** • When you're ready to fry, dust off the excess flour and drop the fish into the oil in batches. They shouldn't take longer than 2–3 minutes to go golden brown, at which point lift them from the pan with a slotted spoon and place on paper towels to absorb any excess fat.
**4** • Arrange on a plate in the shape of a star, the fish fanning out from a central point. Scatter lemon wedges, parsley and black pepper all over.

# • BEEF KOFTE •

These beef meatballs showcase the use of yogurt with meats in Turkey and the surrounding countries. They also make a refreshing change from the prevalent use of lamb in the Middle East. Rebecca Seal, who contributed this fantastic recipe from her book *Istanbul*, says in her introduction that there are many variations on *kofte* in Turkey and encourages you to exercise some creative license in making your own—in other words, play around with ingredients and quantities. The one thing I will add is that although the sumac is optional here, I recommend it for a lemony spice kick that marries the beef and yogurt brilliantly.

## • SERVES 2–4 •

FOR THE MEATBALLS
3–4 tbsp bread crumbs
10½ oz minced beef
1 garlic clove, very finely chopped
¼ onion, very finely chopped
1½ tbsp flat-leaf parsley, very finely chopped
1 tsp sumac plus extra to garnish (optional)
1 tsp ground cumin
1 tsp hot Turkish red pepper paste or ½ tsp hot
    paprika
1 tsp Turkish tomato paste or 2 tsp concentrated
    tomato purée
¼ tsp freshly ground black pepper
½ tsp salt
1 medium egg
vegetable oil for deep frying

FOR THE GARLICKY YOGURT
¾ cup plain Greek-style or Turkish yogurt
½ garlic clove, very finely chopped
    (or more, to taste)
1½ tbsp flat-leaf parsley, finely chopped

**1** • If the bread crumbs are fresh, toast them gently in a dry frying pan. In a bowl, mix the beef with the garlic, onion, parsley, sumac, cumin, red pepper paste, tomato paste or purée, black pepper, salt, and 3 tablespoons of the bread crumbs.

**2 •** Add the egg and mix quickly but thoroughly. If the mixture is very wet, add the remaining bread crumbs and mix again. Divide the mixture into 12 portions and shape into balls.

**3 •** To make the garlicky yogurt sauce, mix the yogurt with the garlic and parsley. Taste and adjust the seasoning. Keep in the fridge until it's time to serve.

**4 •** Heat the vegetable oil for deep frying until a cube of day-old bread sizzles and browns in 30 seconds, then reduce the heat to low. If you don't have a deep fryer (and as you know, it's a luxury in my view), then I recommend using a wok (inauthentic, sorry), which quickly heats up the oil. A deep saucepan will also work fine. Deep-fry the meatballs in batches for 4 minutes each, or until the meat in the center is cooked through and the outside is a deep golden brown. Lift out with a slotted spoon and drain on paper towels. (Alternatively, flatten into patties and sauté for about 3 minutes on each side until golden and cooked through.)

**5 •** Serve immediately, with the yogurt sauce and sprinkled with a little extra sumac.

# THE LEVANT

By nature, a storyteller is a plagiarist. Everything one comes across—each
incident, book, novel, life episode, story, person, news clip—is a coffee bean
that will be crushed, ground up, mixed with a touch of cardamom, sometimes a
tiny pinch of salt, boiled thrice with sugar, and served as a piping-hot tale.
• RABIH ALAMEDDINE, *The Hakawati* •

IN ARABIC, A *hakawati* is a teller of tales, and in the
novel of the same name, it is the narrator's grandfather who is the storyteller. Rabih Alameddine com-
pares the process of telling stories—of absorbing
information from several sources and embellishing
it—with that of making a strong, spiced Arabic coffee.
It is an elegant analogy, and one that reminds me of all
the culinary mixing that goes on in this small, densely
populated space, divided into compact yet varied countries.

"The Levant" refers to the area of the Middle East encompassing Lebanon,
Syria, Jordan, Israel and the Palestinian territories. It is the Holy Land, home
to the Mount of Olives, the land flowing with milk and honey, where the sun
shines in Jacob's ladders over craggy hills softened to mauve and ocher by
their converging beams of light, striking through the shadows. Despite this
natural splendor, sadly the Levant is not a region that gets good press, with
turf wars and religious frictions regularly flooding our headlines. But for a
place so torn up by conflict, its food has an amazing ability to unite people,
a quality embodied by the meze culture of sharing plates, but also the sheer
number of dishes in common across different countries or religious communities. It's almost impossible to dislike the bright, hard-hitting flavors of
dishes like tabbouleh and baba ghanoush, which are eaten in all five of the
countries comprising the Levant. Good food is universal. When communities are divided in head and heart, sometimes the stomach still binds them—
we are all made of flesh and blood.

There is, however, one major unsettled Middle Eastern conflict of an
epicurean nature. This battle—between Lebanon and Israel—is over hum-

mus. Both countries claim to have invented the creamy chickpea dip, but given the relative youth of the Jewish nation-state, it seems sensible to say that hummus comes from the communities inhabiting the landmass known as the Levant. Incidentally, although I don't want to perpetuate the divide, it seems sensible to do so from a culinary standpoint, so I'm keeping Israel separate from the Arab cuisines of the Levant. With so many influences at play, Israel's food culture has burgeoned into a rich and complex fusion cuisine that warrants its own culinary tour.

The obvious Arab cuisine to explore is that of Lebanon, the fresh flavors of which have been successfully exported all over the world. But while there are many similarities between the cuisines of Lebanon and Syria—not least because they were part of the same country, Greater Syria, until the mid-twentieth century[*]—Syrian food is arguably more nuanced. Given its superior size to its neighbors, Syria offers some interesting regional variations, including the cuisine of Aleppo—which my friend Anissa Helou, a Middle Eastern cook and author, refers to as "the gastronomic capital of the Middle East." As well as looking at Lebanon and Syria, I've included some Palestinian recipes, one of which has become native to Jordan, where over two and a half million Palestinians now live.

Anissa, whose recent book *Levant* is a veritable Bible (or your own preferred religious text) of Levantine recipes, grew up in Lebanon but spent her summers in Syria with paternal relatives. She highlights the common ground between the cuisines— raw foods, the use of herbs as ingredients (not just a garnish), tart flavors, sweet spicing, nuts, pulses and grains, flatbread, the important distinction between black and white pepper, and olive oil. But there are some crucial points of difference too. While Lebanese food is built on simplicity and freshness—lots of salads, lemon juice, olive oil, garlic—Syrian food adds complexity with more fat, and sweet-and-sour elements.

Cooking techniques and the way that food is eaten are broadly very similar across the Levant. Meze culture, whereby people share finger foods such as dips, salads, pickles or deep-fried falafel, is omnipresent. Flatbreads (known as *khobez*) are the edible utensil used to scoop foods, particularly the creamier dishes for dunking such as hummus (whereas in Ethiopia they use *injera*; in West Africa, *fufu*; in Asia, rice). Wrapping and stuffing are common

• • • •

[*] "Greater Syria" was the combined name of today's Syria and Lebanon under the Ottoman Empire. This was subsequently broken up by the League of Nations following World War I.

ways of preparing food, either using flatbread (think meat, halloumi or *lab-neh* wraps) for what we would liken to a sandwich, or vegetables such as peppers filled with rice, lamb, tomatoes and mint.

The freshness of Levantine food is the result of using outstanding produce, grown locally. The blistering Middle Eastern sun ripens fruit and vegetables into their very best selves; with ingredients this good, the work is really done for you, and cooking becomes about curating rather than concocting. Which is not to be sniffed at. The simple combination of fresh salad with other local flavors—olive oil, some lemon juice, fresh green herbs, white pepper—is inspired. *Fattoush*, the classic Arab salad, for example, combines lamb's lettuce with cucumber, tomato, radish, toasted flatbread, parsley and mint with a simple dressing.

A key quality of Levantine food is the use of herbs, which refuse to sing backing vocals as they do in most Western cuisines, and instead frontline in many dishes (this is also the case in nearby Iran where a bowl of fresh herbs, *sabzi khordan*, is set in the middle of the table as an accompaniment to almost every meal; see page 184). Tabbouleh, another typical and well-known salad, is a veritable jamming session for finely chopped mint and parsley in which bulgur wheat, scallions, and tomatoes add some rhythm. For me, one of the best things about discovering the cuisines of the Levant was discovering a new approach to ingredients that were for the most part familiar to me: salad materials, bulgur, garden herbs, for example. Without much hassle (save for locating the likes of pomegranate molasses and tahini, which you may need to buy online if you live outside a big city), I was able to bring many seemingly mundane ingredients to life in a dish that tasted new and intriguing to those I was cooking for.

Nuts and seeds are also prevalent across the Levant, perhaps none more so than the humble sesame seed, whose presence in many Middle Eastern dishes is fundamental yet understated. Sesame seeds are frequently used to flavor breads, falafel, salads, and sweet biscuits and are one component of *za'atar*, the classic Levantine spice mixture.[*] They also form the basis for ta-

• • • •

*Za'atar* is a spice blend of dried wild mountain herbs oregano and marjoram, lemony sumac, sesame seeds and salt (see page 198). *Baharat,* which simply translates to "spice," is the standard Levantine spice mix used in numerous recipes such as kibbeh, and combines cinnamon, nutmeg, allspice berries and black peppercorns. Sumac is an ingredient in *za'atar* and is also used on its own for a tangy, lemony flavor—sprinkled over hummus or in *fattoush.* It is found across the Middle East and is the ground fruit of a subtropical plant whose name in Arabic means "red" owing to its earthy deep red color.

hini, a thick, dark oil extracted from broiled sesame seeds that has a honey-like texture and is added to hummus and baba ghanoush, among other dishes. (To add cheap and easy Arabesque character to white fish such as cod or vegetables such as eggplant or butternut squash, you can't go wrong if you douse with shop-bought tahini mixed with lemon juice, water and sea salt and finish with some fresh parsley and a sprinkling of za'atar.)

Pine nuts and pistachios are also popular in foods both savory and sweet. One of my favorite examples is knafeh, a Palestinian dessert combining pastry with soft white cheese soaked in rosewater or orange blossom–tinged syrup, and coated in nuts. I have rarely been so hypnotized by the visual majesty of food as I was in Habibah in Amman, Jordan, a Palestinian bakery that specializes in knafeh. It was full of vast rounds of variously decorated knafeh varieties—dusted with vibrant green pistachios, for example, or patterned with geometric designs in sesames and walnuts, the nablusi cheese and sugar syrup in which it was drenched creating strings of spiders' web-thin sweetness whenever it was cut into.

On to chickpeas, which are responsible for the Levant's most recognizable dish—wonderful hummus. Chickpeas fed me almost single-handedly as a penniless vegetarian student and as such are very close to my heart. And no, I didn't tire of them. Chickpeas are very versatile, particularly when combined with other elements of the Levantine pantry—most obviously, to make hummus and falafel but also in salads such as balilah (mixing the chickpeas with scallions, lemon, garlic and parsley), enjoyed with fat Levantine couscous, or in fatteh (toasted pita bread covered with hot chickpeas and yogurt sauce). In some dishes, chickpeas can be exchanged for broad beans or butter beans. Broad beans (fava beans) form the basis for the famous garlicky Egyptian dip fuul—which has become popular across the Middle East—while butter beans embellish many a soup or salad, alongside the typical olive oil, lemon, garlic and herbs combo dressing.

In the Middle East, dairy is not the rich, heavy entity of Western cuisine. Cheeses such as feta or halloumi are made from ewe's or goat's milk. Fermented curd cheese—known as kashk or kishk—is also popular, made by separating yogurt curds from whey, rolling the thickened curds in herb mixtures and leaving them for a few days to mature. A similar principle is applied when making labneh, thick yogurt strained through cheesecloth and eaten with olive oil and flatbread as a meze, sometimes flavored with herbs and spices. Anissa makes hers with goat's yogurt, coriander and garlic to accompany stuffed zucchini, lamb and meat dumplings. Perhaps my favorite use of yogurt, however, is in the Jordanian dish *mansaf*—lamb cooked in dried yogurt sauce and served with bulgur or rice, pine nuts and almonds. Have a go—Yotam Ottolenghi has contributed his spectacular *mansaf* recipe on page 175.

Grains are another important feature of Levantine cuisine, the most important being bulgur wheat. This is made from wheat that has been boiled, dried and ground and plays a starring role in classic Lebanese dishes such as kibbeh (meatballs, either eaten deep-fried, baked or as *kibbeh nayyah* with raw lamb, for which I have included Anissa's recipe) and tabbouleh. Available in brown or white, and in three different textures (coarse, fine and very fine), bulgur is enormously versatile and its use is widespread across the Middle East. Green wheat, known as *freekeh*, however, is more Syrian and has a nutty, almost smoky, flavor.[*]

Syrian cuisine builds complexity onto the common flavors, ingredients and techniques of the Levant region. It is a truly multi-climatic country—with desert, mountains, plains and coast, offering diverse ingredients with which to play—and surrounded by other countries with rich and ancient cuisines. To the north it borders Turkey, and its easternmost point reaches out almost to Iran—flickers of Ottoman and Persian cuisine will often flash before you at the Syrian table. Examples of this include the cooking of meat and fruit together, for example in cherry kebabs (typical of Aleppo), the prevalence of pistachios from the north, and the use of ghee (clarified butter)—which most people think of as the fat base for Indian food. While the fresh fruits and vegetables of Lebanon abound, Syrians can match them and also boast a vibrant array of preserved goods. There are candied fruits such as apricots, figs, prickly pears, walnuts, even eggplants; and dried vegetables to rehydrate, such as zucchini, okra and, again, eggplants—the darling of Levantine vegetables (see my baba ghanoush recipe on page 173).

The ingredient I most associate with Syrian cuisine is pomegranate molasses, and if Levantine and Persian cuisines get your mouth watering, then it's worth investing in a bottle. It can usually be found in the speciality section in supermarkets. It is so strong that you only need tiny amounts and its dark tartness adds sweet-and-sour oomph to many dishes, particularly those from Aleppo. The ancient city in the north of the country had a prime location on the Silk Road, making it a hub for colorful ingredients and spices from afar, and a pit stop between North Africa, Europe and the Orient.

• • • •

[*] The wheat undergoes a similar process to bulgur but is picked at an earlier stage, which accounts for its greenness.

Syria is also set apart from Lebanon by its broader use of herbs and spices—such as tarragon (sometimes added to *labneh*) and Aleppo pepper, a fruity dried capsicum of medium heat, which gives distinctive flair to Aleppian dishes including *muhammara*. This is a meze dip made with blended roasted red bell peppers, walnuts, pomegranate molasses, garlic, olive oil and lemon juice.

Some Levantine ingredients are niche and may need to be bought online, although as the popularity of the cuisine rises, so too does the profile of ingredients like *za'atar*. However, for the most part it's easy to reproduce these dishes at home. Like so many of the cuisines in this book, their authentic reproduction is reliant on the quality of ingredients you buy. Once you're over the incongruity of combining molasses with peppers and nuts, or eating lamb spiced and raw, your eyes will be open to a gamut of punchy, young, healthy flavors that both challenge and soothe your palate. Plagiarize from this cuisine and, trust me, you'll have a story or two to tell—like the most seasoned *hakawati*.

**PANTRY LIST** • lemons • pickles • sesame • fermented yogurt and sour fruit • olives • tahini • meats (lamb, goat, chicken) • chickpeas • broad beans • bulgur wheat • herbs (parsley, mint, tarragon) • spices (allspice, nutmeg, cinnamon, *za'atar*, sumac) • yogurt (fresh and dried) • *labneh* • white cheese such as feta

• • •

# • FATTOUSH •

This is my favorite salad, combining crunchy toasted flatbread with gorgeous ripe vegetables, herbs and a bright, uncomplicated dressing of good-quality extra virgin olive oil, lemon juice and sumac. If you are less concerned about protein, this serves as a meal in its own right, but of course it accompanies grilled meats, falafel and dips beautifully, too.

## • SERVES 4 •

2 tablespoons extra virgin olive oil, plus more for coating the
pita bread
pinch sea salt plus more for the pita bread

3 pita bread
2 little gem lettuces, coarsely chopped
handful lamb's lettuce, coarsely chopped
4 large ripe tomatoes, sliced into half moons
1 cucumber, sliced into half moons
8 radishes, coarsely chopped
1 green bell pepper, finely chopped
6 scallions, finely sliced
1½ tbsp mint, finely chopped
1½ tbsp flat-leaf parsley, finely chopped
juice of 1 lemon
1 tsp sumac

**1 •** Preheat the oven to 350°F. Slice the pita thinly and coat in a little olive oil and sea salt. Bake for about 20 minutes, turning regularly, until crisp and golden.

**2 •** Combine all the chopped vegetables and add most of the mint and parsley. Dress with the darkest, richest extra virgin olive oil you can find, the lemon juice, sumac and salt before adding the toasted pita, breaking it into smaller pieces as you do so. Sprinkle over the remaining mint and parsley to serve.

# • TABBOULEH •

When making tabbouleh, the most important thing is to get the ratio of herbs to bulgur wheat right. That means putting parsley and mint in the spotlight, and being sparing with the bulgur (avoid the temptation to treat it like couscous). The Arabic word *tabil* (from which the word "tabbouleh" is formed) means "seasoning," which is integral to this intensely flavored salad. Your tabbouleh should be a sea of green, punctuated by glimmers of tomato and specks of wheat.

## • SERVES 4 •

¼ cup bulgur wheat
juice of 3 lemons
4 large tomatoes, coarsely chopped and drained
2 tbsp flat-leaf parsley, finely chopped
2 tbsp mint, finely chopped
6 scallions, finely sliced
4 tbsp extra virgin olive oil

pinch ground cinnamon
pinch sea salt and black pepper
little gem lettuce, to serve

**1** • Rinse the bulgur in water several times and then let it soak in the juice of one of the lemons for 10 minutes. Fluff with a fork and drain.

**2** • Combine the tomatoes, herbs and scallions. Sprinkle the bulgur wheat over the top, then dress with the remaining lemon juice, extra virgin olive oil, cinnamon, salt and pepper.

**3** • Serve with some little gem lettuce leaves dipped into the salad around the bowl's edge. These can be used to scoop it up.

# • BABA GHANOUSH •

The name of this smoky dip means "the darling of her father"—or "daddy's girl dip," as I like to call it. The secrets to perfect baba ghanoush are balance and smoke: don't let the quantities of the ingredients fall out of kilter and do char the eggplants over an open flame—don't grill them. Smokiness is fundamental to getting this right. If you have an electric cooktop, I'm afraid you'll have to light the barbecue and hold the eggplants over it on a prong. It's worth it.

## • SERVES 4 •

3 large eggplants
1 tbsp tahini
1 tbsp plain yogurt
juice of 1 lemon
2 garlic cloves, very finely chopped
pinch sea salt and black pepper
1 tbsp extra virgin olive oil
pinch *za'atar* (see page 198)
flatbread, to serve

**1** • With a fork or prong, pierce the top of each eggplant and hold it above as big an open flame as possible to let it blacken all over. This will take 15–20 minutes, and the eggplants will be left looking charred, flaky and soft.

**2** • Peel the skins from the flesh and discard. You will be left with a little bit of blackened skin, but try to keep it to a minimum. With a knife and fork or—even better—a potato masher, break the flesh apart. Don't be tempted to put it in the blender—you want to maintain some of the texture. Transfer to a sieve and set over the sink for 5–10 minutes, to drain off excess liquid.

**3** • Combine the drained flesh with the tahini, yogurt, lemon juice and garlic. Some recipes don't use yogurt, but I prefer to balance out the sesame strength of tahini with some light creaminess. Add salt and pepper to taste.

**4** • Lastly, drizzle your best extra virgin olive oil on top so that it makes little wells between lumps of eggplant. Sprinkle with *za'atar* and enjoy with good-quality fresh flatbread.

# • MUHAMMARA •

This dip is local to Aleppo in Syria, and is typical of its wonderful sweet-and-sour flavors—charred red bell peppers, pomegranate molasses, lemon, garlic, walnuts. *Muhammara* is usually eaten with pita bread as a meze dish, but it goes very well with grilled meats as a relish (you should end up with a pesto-like consistency) if authenticity is less of a priority. *Muhammara* benefits from being left to sit and mature in the fridge for a few hours before serving—this will soften the garlic and allow the flavors to combine.

## • SERVES 4 •

3 large red bell peppers
extra virgin olive oil, sea salt, plus freshly ground black pepper
1 cup walnuts, plus a handful to serve
½ white onion, finely chopped
1 clove garlic, finely chopped
1 tbsp pomegranate molasses
1 cup fresh bread crumbs
pinch dried chili flakes
juice of ½ lemon
flatbread to serve, lightly toasted

**1** • Preheat the oven to 400°F.

**2** • Bake the bell peppers on a rimmed baking sheet with a large tablespoon of olive oil and some salt and pepper until they are blackened and slightly wilted—this can take up to half an hour.

**3** • Put the walnuts on a baking tray and toast in the oven for 6–7 minutes, moving regularly. You should be able to smell their oily, nutty aroma without letting them burn.

**4** • Remove the bell peppers from the oven and when they are cool enough to touch, pull out the stems and seeds and discard. Place the flesh in a blender along with the nuts, onion, garlic, pomegranate molasses, bread crumbs, three tablespoons of olive oil, chili flakes and lemon juice. Blend until combined. Taste and gauge the balance of flavors—sweet should be equal to sour.

**5** • When ready to serve, put into a bowl with a dash of extra virgin olive oil and sprinkle over the remaining walnuts. Enjoy with good-quality flatbread.

# • MANSAF •

I discovered *mansaf* in Jordan, where it originated with the Bedouin community. It is the Hashemite kingdom's national dish, eaten communally off big, flatbread-lined plates over which the lamb, yogurt, rice and nut concoction is spread. There are even fast-food outlets dedicated to it. *Mansaf* is a brilliant example of how yogurt is combined with meat and other savory ingredients to startlingly delicious effect in the Middle East, adding a depth of umami flavor largely unfamiliar to European palates. The yogurt in this instance is *kashk*, a dried fermented yogurt native to Persian cuisine (known as *kishk* in the Levant), described by Yotam Ottolenghi—who kindly contributed this sumptuous recipe—as similar to whey, available either as a liquid or in dried form ready to reconstitute with water. If you can't get hold of it, Yotam recommends replacing the *kashk* and the Greek yogurt with either 2 cups goat's yogurt, or 1 cup sour cream mixed with 1 cup crème fraiche, three tablespoons of finely grated Parmesan and five finely chopped anchovy fillets. Serve with a fresh green leaf and pomegranate salad.

## • SERVES 4 •

2 tbsp olive oil
4–8 lamb chops (2¼ lb total)
3 bay leaves
1 tsp whole allspice berries
¼ tsp black peppercorns
1 onion, quartered
sea salt
1 cup liquid *kashk*
1 cup Greek yogurt
1 egg
pinch saffron
1¼ cups basmati rice

3 tbsp unsalted butter
1 x 14-oz can chickpeas, drained
½ cup sliced almonds
1 tsp dried Aleppo chili flakes
    (or another mild heat type)
1 tsp sumac
3 large flatbread, slightly warmed (Indian
    chapatti works well, as does lavash)
half a lemon
2½ tbsp flat-leaf parsley, chopped

**1** • Heat a tablespoon of the olive oil in a large saucepan over medium-high heat. Add the chops and sear for 4 minutes on each side, to get some color. Pour in 2½ cups water and add the bay leaves, allspice, peppercorns, onion and ½ teaspoon of salt. Bring to a very gentle simmer and cook, covered, for about 70 minutes, until the meat is completely tender. Once done, skim the fat off the surface.

**2** • Whisk together the *kashk*, yogurt and egg, along with 2 tablespoons of the hot cooking broth. Slowly add this to the lamb, stirring as you pour, and then add the saffron. Bring to a very low simmer—if the temperature is too high the mixture may split—and cook for about 20 minutes, stirring gently from time to time, until the sauce thickens a bit.

**3** • Meanwhile, pour some boiling water over the rice and soak for 20 minutes. Drain, rinse and drain well again. Melt 2 tbsp of the butter and the remaining tablespoon of olive oil in a medium saucepan and add the rice, along with ¾ teaspoon of salt. Add 1¼ cups water, bring to the boil, stir once, reduce the heat to low, cover and cook for 20 minutes. Remove from the heat, stir in the chickpeas, season again to taste and cover the pan.

**4** • While the rice is cooking, place the almonds in a small frying pan with the remaining tablespoon of butter, chili flakes and a small pinch of salt. Cook for about 5 minutes over medium-low heat, stirring often, until the almonds are nicely toasted. Remove from the heat; stir in the sumac.

**5** • Arrange the flatbread on a large, round metal tray or ceramic platter, making sure it covers it completely. Spread out the rice and chickpeas on top, leaving a clear rim of bread, and squeeze the lemon over the rice. Top the rice with the lamb and spoon over as much of the sauce as you want, leaving the aromatics behind in the pan. Sprinkle with almonds and parsley and serve.

# ISRAEL

Where life was chaotic, because that is what life is. Where the past was murky and tragic and the future had to be grasped by the throat. Where Europe ended and the East began and people tried to live inside that particular, crazy contradiction.
• LINDA GRANT, *When I Lived in Modern Times* •

ALL CUISINES ARE in flux, but perhaps none to quite the same extent as Israel's, which, like the country itself, is an evolving kaleidoscope of the ancient and modern, the Jewish and Arab, the Halal and Kosher traditions . . . a "particular, crazy contradiction," indeed.

Israel's western side looks onto the Mediterranean, while its other borders are with Egypt, Jordan, Lebanon, the West Bank, Gaza and Syria. It shares much of its native produce with these countries and territories, drawing heavily on Arab cuisine. From 1948 onward, the Ashkenazi and Sephardic Jews who have come to plant roots in Israel over the last fifty-odd years—en masse after World War II and then in the 1970s and '80s respectively—brought with them their own culinary traditions, creating a hybrid cuisine, something entirely new.

Israeli cooks have defined a national cuisine by applying new twists to ancient components. Yotam Ottolenghi calls his home city of Jerusalem a "soup," his take on "the melting pot." This is also a good analogy for Israeli cuisine as a whole. If the three base ingredients are a *sofrito* of the Arab, Ashkenazi and Sephardic Jewish traditions, then the soup is continually seasoned by new arrivals. Ottolenghi himself is a testament to this: of Italian-German parentage, Jerusalem-born and raised and now based in London. With his acclaimed cookbooks and restaurants he is playing an important part in raising the profile of Middle Eastern recipes and ingredients abroad, drawing on the flavors of his upbringing to create a unique culinary style of his own.

Ottolenghi tells the history of Israeli cuisine as a story of immigrant peoples mixing together and embracing the land—with a beginning, a middle and a not-quite-end. I say "not-quite-end" because he is quick to underline the open-endedness of present-day Israeli food, a cuisine that is still forming and finding its feet.

The story starts in the late nineteenth century, when Zionist ideas were budding in eastern Europe. In the wake of state-sponsored pogroms in Russia in the 1880s, large numbers of Russian Jews made their way to Palestine (though even more headed for the United States). From 1909 a second wave of Jewish immigrants arrived in the Promised Land, founding the city of Tel Aviv on land purchased from local Arabs. From 1948 onward they arrived en masse, bringing with them the sort of Jewish food we associate with New York delis—schnitzels, knishes, matzo ball soup and quark cheese.

Jewish immigrants started to pick up on local Arab cooking traditions and ingredients. This was probably inspired partly by necessity—feeding dozens or even hundreds of kibbutz* laborers quickly and cheaply required the use of readily available food sources. The classic Israeli chopped salad, made with a base of finely chopped tomatoes, cucumbers, olive oil and lemon juice (and the optional additions of radishes, red bell pepper, onion, scallion, parsley and coriander) is one such adopted dish. In contemporary Israeli cuisine, concoctions of bright, sweet fresh vegetables are served with every meal, from breakfast with eggs and flatbread to wraps and sit-down spreads. My friend Zac Frankel is native to Melbourne, Australia, of Egyptian-Jewish descent, a Claudia Roden devotee and an expert at hummus-making—his recipe is included at the end of the section. He lived on a vegetarian kibbutz for six months. Breakfast consisted of raw vegetables, boiled eggs, white cheese similar to feta and home-baked sourdough. At lunch they would eat a hot stew like *matbutcha* (tomato and eggplant) or *majadra* (lentils with rice). Dinner consisted of simple salads like tabbouleh except on Friday nights when they would mark the coming of Shabbat,† by eating "*challah* bread with tahini, fish cooked in a Yemeni tomato and black olive sauce, grilled and marinated eggplant, and white rice."

From the 1970s onward, greater numbers of Sephardic Jews began arriving from North Africa, elsewhere in the Middle East (in particular Iraq and Iran) and the eastern Mediterranean. The Sephardic use of spice and pulses has had a defining effect on today's Israeli food. For example, the ingredients of Morocco and Tunisia such as couscous, date syrup and harissa are used in dishes such as *chraime* stew (a Sephardic fish dish popular during Rosh

• • • •

* A kibbutz is an Israeli community with, for the most part, a self-sufficient economic model based on agriculture. Kibbutz culture started at the beginning of the twentieth century as a means of cultivating the harsh, dry environment of the Galilee Valley, but became over the decades a utopian approach to Jewish life in the Holy Land.

† Saturday is the Jewish Sabbath (Shabbat). Its arrival is marked by a dinner each Friday night, with which challah—sweet "Jewish brioche"—is always eaten.

Hashanah,[*] which features chili and caraway), as well as in tagines and the breakfast dish *shakshuka* (originally from Tunisia), a sweet and spicy tomato and red bell pepper stew in which eggs are poached. Egypt, just next door, has also inspired several omnipresent Israeli dishes such as *fuul* (mashed broad beans with an oily garlic kick), and *koshari*, combining lentils with rice, pasta and garlicky onions and tomatoes.

And so, Israeli cuisine started to become a coherent culinary movement. As Yotam Ottolenghi puts it, "The introduction of Sephardic dishes was intrinsic to the recognition of an 'Israeli food.' It was more joyous, more colourful, more flavoursome and a lot more suited to the climate and *terroirs* than Ashkenazi fare."

Perhaps the biggest influence of all on Israeli food has been that of the Palestinian Arabs with whom the Jewish population shares home soil. Some dishes are virtually inextricable from those we discovered in the Levant: hummus, for example, which Israeli cooks have deftly mastered; kibbeh (meatballs of ground meat, finely chopped onions and bulgur wheat); all manner of stuffed vegetables and pastries filled with cheese. Yotam says that in the 1990s, the schnitzels and other Ashkenazi foods suddenly seemed like "the food of your grandparents," and that local Palestinian food acquired new appeal. Ingredients were lifted from it and applied by Israel's newest natives.

Has Israel colonized Arab food, then? Perhaps. But as Ottolenghi notes in *Jerusalem*, Israel is a place where "food cultures are mashed and fused together in a way that is impossible to unravel." No one can definitively lay claim to a dish—be it hummus or anything else—any more easily than you can extract the individual ingredients out of a soup.

As a Jewish nation, Israel has a very particular relationship with meat and seafood. Kosher dietary law[†] dictates that only animals with cloven hooves that also "chew the cud" are acceptable for human consumption. Pigs are the most conspicuous unclean animals (they have a cloven hoof but do not eat grass). Fish without fins and scales are also unclean. This rules out creatures such as eels, crustaceans such as lobster and prawns and mollusks such as mussels and squid. While lots of young Israelis have a more liberal attitude to keeping kosher, it still prevails in restaurant culture and dictates what is

• • • •

*The Jewish New Year that is celebrated every September and is believed to mark the anniversary of Adam and Eve's creation.

†It's complex, but the fundamentals state that animals must be slaughtered according to kosher rituals (one clean slit across the throat) and meat, milk and wine must be produced in supervised conditions and stored and prepared separately from one another.

available in shops. Lamb, goat and chicken, all of which thrive on the dry craggy hillsides of the Holy Land, are eaten abundantly, grilled, stewed or minced into concoctions rich in local flavors. As a rule, however, Middle Eastern cuisines are particularly well versed in vegetarian dishes. Anyone with an interest in eating less meat would do well to take inspiration from the cuisines of Israel, Lebanon and Syria. While meat is important to these cuisines, meals are frequently enjoyed without it.

The Israeli pantry is virtually identical to the Levantine one. To emulate it, make sure you have good extra virgin olive oil, plenty of lemons and a spectrum of fresh herbs and dry spices like parsley, mint, *za'atar* and sumac for brightly flavored salads and meze with chutzpah.

**PANTRY LIST** • lemon • parsley • mint • white pepper • pickles • sesame • fermented yogurt and sour fruit • olives • tahini • meats (lamb, goat, chicken) • chickpeas • broad beans • bulgur wheat • herbs (parsley, mint, tarragon) • spices (allspice, nutmeg, cinnamon, *za'atar*, sumac) • yogurt (fresh and dried) • *labneh* • white cheese

• • •

## • HUMMUS •

The best homemade hummus I've ever eaten—that is to say, hummus prepared by the hands and in the home of someone I know—is that of my dear friend Zac Frankel, who lived on a kibbutz in Israel for six months. For that sentimental rather than any rigorous culinary reason, this recipe is in the Israel section of the book. Zac says that while soaking dried chickpeas, and subsequently shelling them, might seem pedantic, this method is absolutely worth it. While the use of canned chickpeas with their shells on may take a fraction of the time, the fundamental simplicity of hummus demands perfectionism when it comes to texture. This more long-winded method produces a dip as smooth as it is authentic. In Israel, hummus is often served with additional ingredients in the middle of the bowl—*ful medames* (stewed broad beans), for example, a boiled egg, sautéed mushrooms—as well as pickled vegetables and salad alongside. So, try any or all of the above for extra authenticity.

• **SERVES 4** •

1 ½ cups dried chickpeas
1 tsp baking soda
4 garlic cloves, coarsely chopped
8 oz tahini paste
juice of 2 lemons
1 ½ tsp salt, plus more to taste
extra virgin olive oil, to serve
paprika, to serve

**1** • Soak the chickpeas overnight. You can shell them after you cook them, but I find that it's slower and a lot messier. My trick is, once I've soaked and drained them, to pour boiling water over them and let them sit for a few minutes. This should make the shells separate from the chickpeas, so they look paler in color. If it doesn't, drain again and repeat the process. I then take each chickpea between my thumb and forefinger and squeeze until it pops out, leaving the shell in my hand. Yes, it's laborious, but once this process is complete, you've done half the work of the recipe.

**2** • Place the chickpeas in a saucepan, cover with water, add the baking soda and bring to the boil and simmer until cooked, scooping the foam off the top as you go. The baking soda is very important here: it softens the chickpeas and helps to create a lovely texture. When the chickpeas are done, they should be tender and almost melt in your mouth.

**3** • Strain the chickpeas, setting aside the liquid in a bowl. Place the chickpeas in a food processor along with the garlic and blend until smooth. Now add the tahini paste, ¼ cup of the strained liquid, the salt and most of the lemon juice. Blend and taste to see if it needs more lemon juice or salt. Then add more of the liquid (or water if there's not enough) until you've reached the desired consistency. Lemon juice thickens tahini and will affect the consistency of the hummus as a whole, so if you add more lemon juice you may need to add more water afterward. Remember that the hummus will thicken up and the flavors will become stronger once you've put it in the fridge.

**4** • To serve, dollop into a flat bowl, use a spoon to flatten out and then make a shallow well in the middle with as many little crevices around it as possible. Drizzle the hummus with some extra virgin olive oil and lightly sprinkle sweet and/or hot paprika over it.

# • SHAKSHUKA •

Lovely word, isn't it? I first ate *shakshuka* in Israel, though it is native to Tunisia and North Africa. It's commonly eaten at breakfast or brunch, although I find it a complete meal at any time of the day. It's essentially a simple, sweetened, spiced pepperonata with eggs poached into it. Nothing not to love . . . including its name.

## • SERVES 4 •

pinch saffron
1 tsp cumin seeds
2 tbsp extra virgin olive oil
2 yellow or white onions, finely sliced
4 bell peppers (any color but green),
    sliced lengthways
2 garlic cloves, finely sliced
1 tsp freshly ground black pepper
½ tsp dark brown sugar
1½ tsp thyme leaves
1½ tbsp coriander, chopped
1 tsp sweet paprika (or, instead of cayenne
    and paprika, a heaping tsp of harissa)
pinch cayenne pepper
1 x 14-oz can chopped tomatoes
big pinch sea salt
4 large organic eggs

TO SERVE
sea salt
sprinkling of *za'atar* (see page 198)
1 tbsp flat-leaf parsley, leaves chopped
good soft, crusty bread

**1** • In a bowl, soak the saffron strands in a tablespoon of warm water and set aside.
**2** • Toast the cumin seeds in a large frying pan over medium heat for 1–2 minutes or until they start to give off a rich scent, then add the olive oil, onions and bell peppers and sauté for 3–5 minutes or until starting to soften. Next, add the garlic, black pepper, sugar, thyme, coriander, saffron water, paprika and cayenne (or harissa) and cook for 2 minutes before adding the chopped tomatoes. Simmer for 10–15 minutes,

making sure there's always a saucy consistency. If the liquid provided by the tomatoes threatens to dry up, add a splash of water.

**3 •** Season with salt, create little wells in the mixture and crack the eggs into them. Spoon some of the pepper mixture over the top. Some people choose to bake their *shashuka* in the oven at this stage at 375°F/340°F fan/gas 7 for 5–10 minutes (your pan will obviously need to be ovenproof to do this), but I prefer to do mine on the cooktop. You need to make sure the heat surrounds the eggs to cook them through, however, so either way, they must be covered. Give them 10–15 minutes. You'll know when the eggs are done when the whites are no longer clear. Don't leave them in a second longer, as you want the yolk to remain runny.

**4 •** Serve sprinkled with sea salt, *za'atar* and parsley and enjoy dunking and scooping with lovely bread.

# IRAN

Sedi Mohammadi embodied the latest incarnation of the hospitable Iranian wife
... the choice and variety of dishes on her table, the steaming khoreshts, mountains of saffron-stained rice, the "belly-full" of stuffed fishes, yoghurts sprinkled
with crushed dried rose petals and mint and a myriad of pickles and salads.
• KAMIN MOHAMMADI, *The Cypress Tree* •

THERE IS A convention around how things originating in Iran are defined. Contemporary culture is "Iranian"—cinema, rap music, people—whereas anything
predating the twentieth century is "Persian"—art, literature, rugs and food. Kamin Mohammadi's mother
is a "hospitable Iranian wife" but the colorful dishes
on her table are most definitely Persian.

Persian cuisine is ancient, steeped in tradition and
has been deceptively influential, spreading its roots
into present-day Arab, Indian and Iberian food cul-
tures. And yet for such a historically important, not to mention delicious cuisine, Persian food's profile is surprisingly modest and too often eclipsed by
the better-traveled cuisines of Turkey, Morocco and Lebanon.

The nation named Iran is less than eighty years old, yet it is home to one
of the world's oldest cultures. In 1935, the Middle Eastern territory known to
foreigners for thousands of years as Persia changed its name to Iran, meaning
"Land of the Aryans" in Farsi.* It is a vast country of over 579,000 square miles,
a country of temperature extremes, rugged mountains, interior basins and ancient culinary traditions. Persian cuisine has stayed virtually unchanged for
centuries, unlike that of nearby Israel, where food is forever evolving. In recent
times, Iran's history of political and cultural isolation from the West has en-
sured that its food culture is preserved; the big fast-food chains have no presence and (thankfully) the same masterfully executed dishes—stews (*khoresht*),
soups (*aash*) and rice (*polow*)—continue to adorn Iranian tables.

• • • •

*Though now inevitably associated with the hateful eugenics of the Nazis, the English term
"Aryan" was coined in the nineteenth century as a neutral label for those of Indo-European descent.
Persian people themselves had referred to their country by the name "Iran" for thousands of years.
"Persia" was in fact an invention of the ancient Greeks.

It strikes me that the West is perhaps less acquainted with Persian food than with other cuisines of the Western world, such as those Lebanon, Morocco and Turkey, with which it has a great deal in common. Herbs, yogurt, and grilled or stewed meats, particularly lamb, are familiar to them all, as are styles of eating and food preparation such as meze and one-pot dishes. The tagines of Morocco (see page 283) and Palestinian *maqluba* (an upside-down rice dish into which meat, nuts and vegetables are stirred) both have equivalents in Persian cuisine, for example. (Some say that the cuisines of the Middle East can be separated according to their choice of water essence: rose water in Iran and Turkey, orange blossom in the Levant and Morocco. Really, of course, this is no more than a handy generalization.)

Given the spices used (fenugreek, cumin, coriander) and the strong reliance on rice, however, Persian food is in some ways more aligned with northern Indian and Pakistani cuisines than those of the Middle East and North Africa. The Persian Mughals planted deep roots in northern India, which are expressed in the Awadhi cuisine of Lucknow to this day (see page 201).

One possible explanation for the fact that Persian food has traveled less prolifically than that of Turkey or Lebanon is the rather narrow restaurant culture in Iran, limited to kebob and *chelo* (rice). "Why pay for something that I can make better at home?" many Iranians will ask. Why, indeed? Aside from kebob, which requires expensive specialist equipment, the best and most authentic food in Iran is to be found in home kitchens. I learned this for myself when I met Pury Sharifi, to whom I was introduced by Yotam Ottolenghi. Having met her at one of his cookery masterclasses, Yotam realized that *she* could teach *him* a thing or two about Persian cooking. Her north-London kitchen table welcomed me with a spread of bright purple eggplants, oranges, sultanas, creamy white yogurt, *kashk* dishes (fermented yogurt) and bunches of fresh herbs in intricately painted bowls.

Pury's cooking showed me that, despite the similarities among Persian and other Middle Eastern cuisines, there is an art to Persian flavor pairing that produces dishes unlike anything you've ever tasted. Imagine eggplant with walnuts, crowned with thick whey; morello cherries with lamb; chicken with oranges and saffron; spinach, yogurt and raisins; ingredients such as pomegranate molasses, dried buttermilk and dried limes for natural sweet and sour. While meat slow-cooked with fruit sounds like it could just as easily be Syrian or Moroccan, for instance, the Iranians use such a vast number of ingredients—each of which plays a small but crucial role in the alchemy of a given dish—as to render their cuisine inimitably complex.

Persian food requires an enormous volume of fresh herbs (known as *sabzi*, meaning "green"), which represent growth and health. *Sabzi polo*, or rice with herbs, is eaten on Nawrooz (the Persian New Year, on March 21) and requires a huge quantity but delicate balance of coriander, chives, dill, parsley and fenugreek. At every Iranian table you will find *sabzi khordan*, a plate of fresh, raw herbs including tarragon, basil, mint, and chives (also radishes and scallions), at which diners will nibble between mouthfuls or dishes to cleanse their palates. Tarragon is particularly effective, with a light aniseed burn to ready your mouth for the next dish. Lesser-known Persian herbs found on the *sabzi khordan* plate include *marzeh* (savory in English, an aromatic mountain herb that tastes a bit like a blend of marjoram, thyme and sage) and costmary (or "balsam herb," a large-leafed plant from the juniper family).

A spectrum of spices is also central to Persian cuisine but, noticeably, there is no chili. Fenugreek, mustard, cumin and coriander seeds are all used, as well as turmeric and sweeter, warming aromatic spices such as cinnamon and cardamom. *Advieh* (see page 197) is the classic Persian spice blend, which, although it varies regionally, always contains cinnamon, cardamom, coriander, cumin and rose petals in equal parts. This can be sprinkled on rice just before serving or added to *khoreshts* (stews), for which there might be any number of spices on top of the essential five—dried limes, cloves, black pepper, turmeric. All spices are delicately balanced and combine harmoniously. As Pury says, "The subtlety of Persian cuisine is in part because we use so many ingredients. But we never overuse any of them . . . except for saffron. But that's subtle anyway, and used at the last minute."

Luminous orange and with an incomparable hay-like scent, saffron is a hallmark of Persian food and is used generously. A pinch of saffron hairs infused in a little warm water makes dishes light up before serving. Pury's dip *borani esfanaj*, spinach with yogurt, shallots and raisins, is one example. Little pools of the saffron liquid filling grooves in the dip's surface gave it a final boost of color and fragrant zing as it arrived on the table.

Barberries (*zereshk*) are sour, ruby-colored berries, a typically Persian ingredient that adds a gorgeous injection of tartness to many dishes. They are used as another agent of sweet and sour, combining well with chicken or appearing as little glistening gems atop rice and stews such as *khoresht-e-mast*. Light yet hearty, and piercing yet comforting, this is a stew of chicken, yogurt and orange peel, showcasing the two Persian traditions of sweet and sour and meat and fruit, all crowned with saffron water and barberries.

There are countless other *khoreshts* displaying similar traits, however. *Khoresht nanah jafari gojeh* (lamb with mint, parsley and greengage) is par- .

ticularly tantalizing. Stews are most commonly lamb-based, but chicken, beef and sometimes fish are used, too. Another classic *khoresht* is *fesenjan*, a dark, grainy stew eaten in autumn and winter that blends chicken, pomegranate molasses, caramelized onion and walnuts. But perhaps the most famous is *ghormeh sabzi*,* the almighty Persian stew of slow-cooked lamb and herbs. Barberries, almonds, walnuts, prunes, cucumbers, zucchini and turnip are just some of the ingredients accompanying meat in myriad Persian stews. But the most important ingredients in *khoresht* are often the least conspicuous: the yogurt or buttermilk, the dried lime, or the spice mix. Despite not speaking Farsi, I've never had any problem remembering the name of *ghormeh sabzi* because, aptly, "ghormeh" sounds just like "gourmet."

Soups are an important part of Persian cuisine, thicker and heartier than you would find in Europe and a cheap form of sustenance for the nation, particularly during winter months in the north. *Eshkeneh*, for instance, is an onion soup thickened with flour and eggs and seasoned with turmeric and fenugreek. Pulses such as kidney beans, mung beans and orange or green lentils are a major feature of some soups—particularly those known as *ash*. Pury's favorite is *ash-e-jo*, a barley soup made with chickpeas, lentils, kidney beans, spinach and parsley. With healthy (and affordable) components like this, it's easy to understand why soups have a reputation for being medicinal in Iran—a bit like the "Jewish penicillin" chicken soup found in Ashkenazi Jewish communities across the globe.

Rice comes in various outfits in Iran: plain (*chelow*), fluffed and mixed with other ingredients (*polow*), and *tahdig*, meaning "bottom of the pan," where the rice is molded into the shape of a cake, with an upper crust created with eggs, yogurt and saffron. The diner chisels into it. The word *polow* (any rice dish with something mixed in) signposts Iran's link to India, from which the better-known Indian word "pilau" came,† and indeed to the "pilaf" in Turkey—they all share the tradition of lightly spicing rice, letting it stick to the base of a pan and go golden with the help of butter and saffron. The simplest *polow* uses just saffron and butter, but the cook may throw in herbs, pulses or sour cherries (to create a dish known as "Blushing Rice"). "Jeweled Rice" (*morasa polow*) combines barberries, pistachios, almonds, orange peel, raisins, *advieh* and, naturally, saffron water. Soaking saffron in warm water

• • • •

*On a personal note: you may have gathered that I have something of an aversion to lamb, but Pury's *ghormeh sabzi* was so seductive in its painted bowl that I tried a mouthful. And I liked it. Fifteen years of lamblessness and Persian *khoresht* turned me. Lamb and I are currently working on our relationship.

†Introduced into India by the Persian Mughals in the sixteenth century.

allows you to get the most out of it (it's a notoriously expensive spice). I soak between five and ten strands (depending on the intensity of flavor desired) in a small splash of boiling water and let it stew for five minutes or so. The water will turn amber—it's a beautiful process to watch as the red seeps out of the strands—and it can then be added to the dish you are making.

Everything comes to the table at once in Iran. The European way of serving food in courses gives way to a grand spread of stews, raw herbs, meze and bread. Dips are scooped up with nan (flatbread, another similarity to India, where it is naan), which comes in several guises. These range from thin and flaky (known as *nan-e-lavash*) to thick, almost downy *nan-e-taftoon*, which Pury serves alongside dips such as *borani-e-labu* (roasted beets with yogurt and fresh mint), *borani esfanaj* (spinach, yogurt, onion, raisins and saffron) and *kashk-e-bademjan* (eggplant, walnut, fermented whey and dried mint).

In the quote from Kamin Mohammadi's memoir, *The Cypress Tree*, at the beginning of the chapter, food—the vividly colored spread of rice and stews and yogurts—is inextricably linked to hospitality. I'd heard much about Iranian hospitality (but experienced little of it) before I met Pury Sharifi, whose food, though alien to me, was instantly comforting. She told me, "The concept of a guest is very significant in Iran. Especially if they're a stranger. A good Iranian welcome is a source of national pride." My first experience of Iranian hospitality certainly did Iran proud. I even came away with a couple of Pury's recipes, so even if I can't give an authentic Iranian welcome, I can at least make authentic Persian food.

**PANTRY LIST** • saffron • rose water • herbs (tarragon, mint, savory, basil, chives) • spices (fenugreek, cinnamon, coriander, cumin, cloves, black pepper, turmeric) • rose petals • yogurt (fresh and dried, *kashk*) • dried limes • orange • dried barberries • almonds • pistachios • kidney beans • lamb

• ◆ •

# • CHICKEN WITH BARBERRIES, YOGURT AND ORANGE PEEL •

Known in Farsi as *khoresht-e-mast*, this beautifully balanced dish sounds and looks exotic, but uses ingredients that are readily available in much of the United States. The dried barberries pose the biggest challenge and can be found in most Middle Eastern grocers or online. Before you use them, they'll need soaking in a bowl of warm water for ten minutes, then draining. They have a unique, authentically Persian tartness and are worth tracking down, but if you really struggle to find them, you could try using cranberries, currants or sour cherries. This is Pury Sharifi's family recipe.

## • SERVES 4 •

7 heaping tbsp Greek yogurt
5 tbsp olive oil
2 medium onions, finely sliced
sea salt
4 chicken legs (drum sticks and thighs separated
    and skin removed)
freshly ground pepper to taste
2 large oranges
big pinch saffron
1½ tbsp dried barberries, rehydrated (see above)
2 tbsp sliced almonds to garnish (optional), toasted

**1** • Strain the yogurt through a muslin bag for several hours, preferably overnight—you can do this by hanging it from the tap over your kitchen sink.
**2** • Heat the olive oil in a heavy pan and fry the onions, sprinkled with a pinch of salt, over medium heat, until golden—10–15 minutes. Add the chicken to the onions and fry for 2–3 minutes, in a single layer or in batches, to seal the meat. Half cover the meat with water and add salt and pepper to taste. Cover the pan and simmer for 30–40 minutes.
**3** • Meanwhile, peel the oranges with a potato peeler, taking care not to include any pith with the peel. Cut the peel into matchstick-sized strips. In a small pan of boiling water, simmer the strips for 3 minutes. Drain and rinse with cold water.
**4** • Grind the saffron in a mortar and pestle and soak it in 4 tablespoons of warm water for 10 minutes. Add the saffron water, orange peel and barberries to the

chicken, turning the meat from time to time. Test for seasoning and simmer for 10 minutes. Remove the chicken pieces and keep them warm. Keep the sauce on a gentle simmer, add the strained yogurt and stir until it is dissolved. Then return the chicken pieces to the pan and turn them over in the sauce for 2 minutes to heat through. Place the chicken in a serving dish, pour the sauce over the chicken and garnish with the sliced almonds. Serve with *chelow* rice (see page 192).

## • LAMB WITH SPLIT PEAS, DRIED LIME AND EGGPLANTS •

This traditional *khoresht* ("stew") is one of Pury's family favorites and is known as *khoresht-e-gheimeh bademjan*. Dried limes (*limou omani*) are widely used in Persian cooking, lending a distinctive aroma and tangy taste to *khoreshts* and other dishes—not unlike preserved lemons in Moroccan cuisine. They should always be pierced with a fork or a sharp knife before cooking to release their full flavor. Some people enjoy eating the cooked limes with the *khoresht*, while others find them too sour.

### • SERVES 6–8 •

sea salt
4 large eggplants, peeled and halved lengthways
pinch saffron
6 tbsp olive oil for frying the onions
2 medium onions, thinly sliced
2½ oz yellow split peas, rinsed and drained
1½ lb shoulder or leg of lamb, cut into ¾-inch cubes
1 tsp turmeric
5–6 whole dried limes, pierced
freshly ground black pepper
vegetable oil for frying the eggplants
2 heaping tbsp tomato purée
1 tsp *advieh* mixed spice (see page 197)
2 tomatoes, quartered

**1** • Salt the eggplants on both sides and stand in a colander for at least an hour.

**2** • Grind the saffron in a mortar and pestle and soak it in 4 tablespoons of warm water for 10 minutes.

**3** • Heat the olive oil in a heavy pan and sauté the onions, sprinkled with a pinch of salt, over medium heat, until golden—10–15 minutes. Add the split peas and stir for 2 minutes so that they are coated with oil. Then add the cubed meat and stir until sealed on all sides, 5–6 minutes. Once the meat is lightly browned, add the turmeric and sauté for another 2 minutes. To prevent the mixture from sticking to the pan, you may need to add a little more oil.

**4** • Pour enough cold water to just cover the meat and add the dried limes together with salt and pepper to taste. Cover the pan, slowly bring to a boil then simmer for 30–40 minutes.

**5** • While the *khoresht* is cooking, scrape any excess water from the eggplants with the back of a knife, add the vegetable oil to a large frying pan and fry the eggplant in batches over medium-high heat until brown on all sides—approximately 10 minutes per batch—and set aside.

**6** • After the 30–40 minutes, stir the tomato purée, saffron water and the *advieh* spice mix into the *khoresht*. Gently press the limes with the back of a wooden spoon to release their full flavor, cover and simmer for another 15 minutes.

**7** • Add the eggplants and tomatoes to the *khoresht* so that they are partly covered by the sauce. Simmer for another 25–30 minutes, checking the eggplants regularly to make sure they don't overcook. Serve with *chelow* rice.

# • CHELOW RICE •

This method of soaking, parboiling and steaming the rice, known as *chelow*, results in fluffy grains and a delicious crust (*tahdig*) at the bottom of the pan. Pury assures you there's no need to be put off by what might appear to be a complex method—once you've made *chelow* a couple of times, you'll find it as easy as (or, rather, easier than) pie . . .

### • SERVES 8 •

3½ cups basmati rice
salt
pinch saffron
5 tbsp olive oil

**1** • Place the rice in a large bowl, cover with water and gently swirl it around with your fingers, then drain. Repeat several times to get rid of the excess starch. Cover the rice with fresh cold water, add 2 tablespoons of salt and soak for at least 3 hours and up to 24 hours. The salt prevents the rice from breaking up.
**2** • Grind the saffron in a mortar and pestle and soak it in ¼ cup of warm water for 10 minutes.
**3** • Fill three quarters of a large, nonstick heavy pan with water, add 2 tablespoons of salt and bring to a boil over high heat. Pour the washed, rinsed and drained rice into the pan, return to a boil and cook over high heat for 6–10 minutes, gently stirring a couple of times. This is the crucial point, as you need to taste the rice periodically to make sure it's neither under- nor overdone. It should have just a little bite to it. Pury's mother's advice is to take the rice off the heat a couple of minutes after the water is boiling from the center out and the rice has risen to the top. Transfer the rice to a large colander, rinse with tepid water and drain.
**4** • Put 6 tablespoons water in the pan over medium heat and, as soon as it starts to boil, add the saffron water and swivel the pan to spread the saffron evenly, then add the olive oil. When the oil mixture starts to boil, add the drained rice a little at a time and form it into a pyramid. Make several 2-inch-deep holes in the rice with the end of a wooden spoon and, as soon as the steam begins to rise from the holes, reduce to medium-low heat. Cover the underside of the lid with a clean dish towel and place it firmly on the pan so that no steam escapes. Cook the rice for 50 minutes or until the grains are soft and fluffy.
**5** • Remove from the heat and place the pan on a damp dish cloth for a few minutes—this will allow the crust to come off easily. Place a large serving dish over the

pan and, holding both firmly together, turn the pan upside down. This way the rice arrives at the table shaped like a cake with a golden crust. Alternatively, you can reserve some of the saffron water and mix this with 3 tablespoons of the cooked rice. Spoon out the rest of the rice and spread on a serving dish; garnish with the saffron grains. You can then break up the crust and place it on a separate serving dish.

# AS

# IA

# SHAKING UP THE SPICE ROUTE

...

All along the ancient Spice Route, countries and regions use local spice blends that encapsulate their key flavor characteristics. These can either be integrated into dishes or sprinkled over to finish, a peppering of fragrant garnish.

Note that spice blends vary from country to country and town to town, and even from home to home. Every one is different—these suggestions are really just a rough guide. Generally, I've worked with teaspoons rather than larger quantities. You'll need a mortar and pestle to make many of your own spice blends—kitchen equipment at its most basic and satisfying! A large granite set is heavy and solid enough to grind your seeds or pods into a powder, either coarse or fine. Note though that *dukkah*, *ras el hanout*, *panch phoron*, and *za'atar* are all whole spices mixes that should not be ground. With thanks to Pury Sharifi for her *advieh* spice blend.

## CHINESE FIVE SPICE (CHINA)

1 tsp ground Sichuan pepper
1 tsp ground star anise
1 tsp ground fennel seed
½ tsp ground cloves
½ tsp ground cinnamon

## PANCH PHORON (WEST BENGAL)

1 tsp cumin seed
1 tsp fennel seed
1 tsp fenugreek seed
1 tsp mustard seed
1 tsp nigella seed

## BERBERE (ETHIOPIA)

2 tsp salt
3 whole cloves
2 tsp coriander seeds
1 tsp fenugreek seeds
5 white cardamom pods
5 tbsp dried onion flakes
5 dried chilies de árbol,
stemmed, seeded and
broken into small pieces
1 tsp ground nutmeg
½ tsp ground ginger
½ tsp ground cinnamon
½ tsp black peppercorns
¼ tsp whole allspice
3 tbsp paprika

## ADVIEH (IRAN)

2 tbsp ground cinnamon
1 tsp ground cardamom
1 tsp ground black pepper
1 tsp ground nutmeg
1 tsp ground coriander seed
½ tsp powdered cloves

## RAS EL HANOUT
### (MOROCCO)

## GARAM MASALA
### (NORTH INDIA)

1 tsp ground black pepper
1 cinnamon stick, ground
1 tsp ground cloves
1 tsp ground cardamom
1 tsp ground cumin
¼ nutmeg, ground

1 tsp nutmeg
1 tsp cumin
1 tsp coriander
1 tsp ground ginger
1 tsp ground cinnamon
1 tsp turmeric
1 tsp rose petals
½ tsp black pepper
½ tsp paprika
½ tsp sugar
½ tsp cardamom powder
½ tsp ground cloves
½ tsp allspice

## ZA'ATAR
### (THE LEVANT
### AND ISRAEL)

4 tsp sumac
2 tsp sesame seeds
2 tsp thyme
1 tsp sea salt
1 tsp cumin
1 tsp oregano
1 tsp marjoram

## LA KAMA
## (NORTH AFRICA)

2 tsp ground cinnamon
1 tsp ground turmeric
1 tsp ground black pepper
1 tsp ground ginger
1 tsp grated nutmeg

## DUKKAH
## (EGYPT)

10 hazelnuts
1 tbsp sesame seeds
1 tsp coriander seeds
1 tsp cumin seeds
1 tsp fennel seeds
1 tsp nigella seeds
1 tsp peppercorns
big pinch sea salt

## BAHARAT
## (TURKEY)

2 tsp dried mint
2 tsp dried oregano
1 tsp ground cinnamon
1 tsp ground mustard seed
1 tsp ground coriander seed
1 tsp ground cumin
1 tsp ground black pepper
1 tsp ground cloves
1 tsp ground fennel seed
1 tsp ground nutmeg

# INDIA

Indians are the Italians of Asia and vice versa. Every man in both countries
is a singer when he is happy, and every woman is a dancer when she walks to
the shop at the corner. For them, food is the music inside the body and
music is the food inside the heart.
• GREGORY DAVID ROBERTS, *Shantaram* •

PARALLELS BETWEEN FOOD and music are not
new—it was in Shakespeare's *Twelfth Night* that music was termed "the food of love," for example—but
Gregory David Roberts's comparison is particularly
apt for India. Just as music exists as an infinite number of genres, styles, combinations of notes, keys,
rhythms and so on, Indian food is so much more than
a single cuisine. From the plains of the Ganges to the
peaks of the Himalayas and the coconut-flecked
beaches of Kerala and Goa, India is a land of stagger-
ing geographical and culinary diversity. It is the spice capital of the world,
with hundreds of regional and historic cuisines and innumerable recipes
adapted and interpreted by every home cook.

It is somewhat depressing, then, that despite the significant British-
Indian, -Bengali and -Pakistani population and the long history of British imperial administration in India, our understanding of south Asian food in the
West, particularly in my native Britain, is staggeringly narrow. Indian restaurants line busy streets all over the UK and, unlike more marginal minority cuisines, this is not just a metropolitan phenomenon—few small towns
are without their own tandoori joint. "Going for a curry" is a singularly British institution: eating mildly spiced, sauce-based dishes lifted from Punjabi
cuisine is part of everyday life for millions. The British have so commandeered these diluted renditions of Punjabi food that, along with roast beef
with all the trimmings and fish and chips, the likes of chicken tikka, korma
and biryani have become national dishes. To my mind, though, the Brits' exposure to Indian food and the regularity with which it's eaten has had the
two-pronged effect of creating a huge appetite for this delicious cuisine but
also stunting awareness of Indian (and Bengali and Pakistani) food.

I remember my granny, who was born in Nainital, northern India, in 1919, making her superlative kedgeree for supper for my brother and me, when we were children. We devoured the butter-clad grains of basmati rice interspersed with fried onions, hard-boiled egg and smoked haddock (admittedly we drenched it all in ketchup). I didn't believe her when she told me that this dish, which we associated so strongly with her Norfolk kitchen, actually hailed from India and was traditionally eaten at breakfast. It's also only relatively recently that I, fairly well versed in Indian cuisine (given my career choice and the large Indian community that surrounded me when I was growing up in the almost-suburbs of south London), really discovered some of the vegetarian delights offered by south Indian cuisine: *pani puri*, *masala dosa*, curries of coconut milk and red chili.

So how did this situation come about? After World War II many Bangladeshi and Pakistani immigrants opened restaurants across the UK—perhaps most famously on London's Brick Lane, or the Balti Triangle and Curry Mile in Birmingham and Manchester respectively—and traded on their "Indian" provenance. For many Britons this conjured up our rich colonial heritage: there was familiarity and maybe even some glory to the food's otherness. Relatively quickly, anglicized versions of Indian food emerged, of which the balti is the best example:* a uniquely British invention from Birmingham. The word means "bucket" in Punjabi and baltis are served in a wok-style dish, concoctions of lightly marinated meat and vegetables. Dishes like the balti no doubt have an important place on the British culinary landscape—indeed, they signpost some fascinating anthropology—and can be great. But they represent a scant slice of a deep and nuanced pie, clouding our understanding of what Indian food, in all its glory, can be.

To understand true Indian food, you need to grasp the sheer scope of variety and potential in this cuisine. The number of spices required for, say, a simple chicken curry—a different version of which you will find in virtually every Indian municipality, village and even home—means that one is never the same as another. An obvious point maybe, but it strikes me that Indian food is perhaps more open to variation than any other cuisine in the world. The different spices and spice blends† are infinite, which means that "classic" or

• • • •

*But there are so many others. Chicken tikka, sometimes with a masala sauce; korma and *dopiaza*, the creamy Persian-influenced dishes developed by the Mughals who settled around Delhi and Lucknow; *jalfrezi*, a favorite Bengali dish of stir-fried leftover meat and vegetables.

†For example, cumin; garam masala; ginger, which could be fresh or ground; mustard, the seeds, the oil or the leaves; turmeric, fenugreek, cinnamon, coriander, cardamom, saffron, cloves, Kaffir lime leaves, Kashmiri chilies and black pepper.

"definitive" versions of dishes don't really exist. That's worth bearing in mind when cooking Indian food from recipes, even those excellent examples kindly contributed by cookbook writer Meera Sodha, author of the book *Made in India* and chef Anirudh Arora of London's Moti Mahal restaurant.

You also have to understand the importance of personal touch in this cuisine. India remains a country of home cooks. Every mother or household cook will vary their use of ingredients, even if only slightly. There can be surgical precision to Indian cookery but it also involves an enormous amount of creative license, which I urge you to take when making these recipes. Try things out—add a little bit more garam masala or turmeric to your dal and see if you like it. The great thing is that it's also very easy to redress the balance in curry-style dishes like dal simply by, in this case, adding more lentils or water.

The population of India is over 80 percent Hindu, the ancient religion espousing karma, multiple gods and holy cows, which are not so much worshipped as respected for their ability to produce dairy. In northwest India particularly, dairy forms a vital part of the daily diet in the form of ghee (clarified butter), paneer (curd cheese), creams, milks and yogurt. The country's minority religions include Islam (most prevalent around the borders of Pakistan and Bangladesh, in Kashmir and Bengal respectively); Christianity, predominantly around the coasts of Goa, Kerala and East Bengal; Jainism,* in the central and western regions such as Rajasthan and Gujarat; Buddhism near the Nepali border and Sikhism, which is particularly concentrated around Punjab.

It would take a whole book (or two or three) to cover India's multitude of regional cuisines, so I have taken the liberty of splitting the country in two—north and south—a crude regional divide dictated by broadly different climates and geographies (as well as religious and some postcolonial differences). Broadly speaking, the coast, coconut and hot chili define the food of southern India, while in the north there is a prevalence of dairy, mustard and tandoori meat. In the north, we will take a journey up the ancient trading route of the Grand Trunk Road, which will allow us to map shifts in the food culture.

In this chapter, I hope to give you a taste for Indian food as it exists outside your local Indian buffet and show you how, in India, food is "the music inside the body."

••••

*Jainism is an ancient religion, and a minority one in India, that emphasizes the equality of all beings.

# NORTH INDIA

Dinners were fairly generous affairs . . . venison kebabs laden with
cardamom, tiny quail with hints of cinnamon, chickpea shoots stir-fried
with green chillies and ginger, and small new potatoes browned with flecks
of cumin and mango powder.
• MADHUR JAFFREY, *Climbing the Mango Trees* •

NORTHERN INDIA OFFICIALLY spans eleven Indian states,[*] but I'm using the term loosely to encompass the eastern region of West Bengal, too. It is a land of hot summers, cold winters and monsoon rains, of the dramatically purple-lit Himalayas leading down into the verdant green North Indian River Plain—a zone of fertile, well-drained land spreading out from the Ganges and Indus Rivers. Traces of man's activity pepper the landscape: skinny roads weaving tightly around mountain terrain, dustings of settlements, the odd temple, the tinkling bells fastened around goats' necks. But nature looms large here.

The Grand Trunk Road[†] is an old trading route that stretches across fifteen hundred miles of what used to be the British Raj: Bangladesh, India and Pakistan (and farther up into Afghanistan). Named by the British colonizers for the amount of cargo that was carried up and down its length, the Grand Trunk Road spans an enormous stretch of northern India and, as you might expect, cultures and cuisines shift as you journey along it; dishes echo the geographical, historical and religious nuances of the changing landscape. Here we will explore a handful of culinary "hot spots" as an introduction to the scale and fascinating diversity of northern Indian cuisines.

The trail stretches from Kashmir through to Punjab, Delhi, Lucknow and West Bengal, and ranges from the freshwater-fish curries of West Bengal to

••••

[*] Bihar, Chhattisgarh, Haryana, Himachal Pradesh, Jammu and Kashmir, Jharkhand, Madhya Pradesh, Punjab, Rajasthan, Uttarakhand and Uttar Pradesh.

[†] In *Kim*, Rudyard Kipling referred to it as "such a river of life as nowhere else exists in the world," which creates a charming parallel between this, the man-made "river of life" and the actual, natural river that at various points runs alongside the GTR, the river Ganges.

the Mughal-infused Awadhi cuisine of Lucknow, and from the tandoori of Delhi and Punjab to the delectable grilled meats of Kashmir. As well as differences there are similarities, the common flavors touched on by Madhur Jaffrey in the introduction to her autobiography, *Climbing the Mango Trees*. A profusion of greenes, ginger and cumin awaits you.

Kashmir crowns northern India, bordering Pakistan to the north and facing south down the snow-carpeted Himalayas onto lush green valleys, lakes and subtropical pine forests. Food needs to be versatile here, able to grow in wildly diverging temperatures and maintain those who eat in a climate of extremes.

Ingredients are fewer than in other Indian cuisines—there is a smaller array of spices and more meat, particularly lamb. Freezing winters are a time for feasting on the summer's dried produce and simple, tasty curries like *rogan josh*, a hot lamb curry for which I've included a recipe (see page 210). Meaning "hot oil" in Farsi, this is the classic, most exported Kashmiri dish and, as the language of its name suggests, has Persian roots. Lamb is cooked in oil, fennel seeds, ginger, paprika and Kashmiri chilies for a smoky, hearty defense from the cold.

Kashmiri chilies (see Hot Stuff, page 268) are internationally famous for their deep red color and mild heat. They add a lot of flavor but not too much spice, which, along with the large amounts of dried ginger used in Kashmir, makes for feel-good dishes to be eaten with lots of rice. Spicy red gravies and sauces with a curd-like texture define Kashmiri curries, but meats such as leg of lamb are also roasted on spits over an open fire.

*Tava* grilling, when food is seared on a convex, plate-shaped cast-iron griddle, is the typical approach to cooking both meat and bread in Kashmir. The use of meat intensifies in northern India, and still more in Pakistan, where offal and offcuts join red meat and chicken on the *tavas*. Think lamb's brain, kidneys, liver, shanks and trotters.

The use of the *tava* extends down into Punjab, although here the famous tandoor oven takes precedence. Cooking from this pocket of northwestern India (known collectively as Punjabi food but actually encompassing dishes from Delhi, Haryana and Himachal Pradesh) is the most widely known of all Indian cuisines and has traveled all over the world. It's Punjabi cooking that has inducted many a Brit and American to the wonders of Indian food, and some of the flavors and ingredients we most associate with India—cumin, tomatoes, onions, lemons and coriander—accompany meat, curd cheese and vegetables in numerous familiar tandoori dishes.

Criss-crossed by five rivers, Punjab was once plagued by flooding but, since the construction of canals by British colonial powers in the nineteenth century, has been drained more effectively and now boasts an abundance of crops such as wheat, rice and sugarcane, earning it the nickname of India's "bread basket." Unsurprisingly, the region boasts wonderful bread, which is fired in the tandoor oven, a piece of equipment so fundamental to the cuisine of northwestern India that it almost defines it. Traditionally, a charcoal or wood fire would have been lit inside a cylindrical clay pot, generating and circulating heat around the vessel, lending earthy, charred flavors to its contents. Nowadays, stainless steel tandoors mimic the work of the conventional clay pot, allowing the temperature to be maintained for longer.

As a boy in Delhi, Anirudh Arora,[*] now head chef at Moti Mahal in London, would take his family's dough to the *tandooria*, a man with a tandoor oven at the end of the street, who blasted it into succulent rounds of naan. The equivalent in rural Punjab is the *sanja chula*, or "evening stove," a tandoor set in the ground to which the ladies of the village would take their dough to be cooked each evening. Naan is only one of many varieties of bread: there's also *kachori*, a deep-fried bread stuffed with vegetarian fillings (not unlike a samosa), *paratha*, a flatbread cooked on a *tava* and ideally suited to scooping up curries and stews and numerous others.

The base tandoori ingredients in Delhi are different from those in Punjab. In Delhi, ingredients are doused in cumin, green chili and onions, which are sometimes pickled, while in Punjab, chili, garlic, mustard oil, lemon juice and—crucially—yogurt are used. Punjab is a verdant green land of dairy farming, abundant vegetables, tandoori meats and breads. Dishes are cooked in ghee, cream and butter, and curd cheese, or paneer, is also widely used. Paneer is native to Punjab and combines brilliantly with green vegetables— you may be familiar with curries such as *saag paneer* (spinach and paneer) or *muttar paneer* (peas and paneer).

Punjab is also notable for its mustard cultivation. The mustard leaves are used, as well as the seeds and oil, an important point of difference from the mustard use in West Bengal. Dishes include *sarson ka saag*, in which mustard leaves are cooked with spinach, garlic, ginger, chili and spices, which is particularly delicious devoured with roti flatbread.

Winding down through Uttarakhand (the region containing the town of Nainital, where my paternal grandmother was born in 1919) and into the state of Uttar Pradesh, the northeasternmost state of India, we come to the

• • • •

[*] The son of a colonel in the Indian army, Ani spent much of his childhood traveling around northern India and developed a passion for regional Indian cuisine. He now specializes in the food of the Grand Trunk Road, his menu transporting restaurant guests through the plains of the Ganges and into the rugged hills of Pakistan.

city of Lucknow. The Ganges continues to provide natural irrigation to the land and agriculture once again dominates industry. Oils give way to ghee, and tomatoes to yogurt, with creamier-style curries such as korma coming into the fray. Dairy becomes integral—a sign not only of changing terrain and agriculture but the region's rich cultural history.

Before it was known as Lucknow, the city was named Awadh. The term "Awadhi," however, still stands in reference to the local cuisine, which is the product of three factors plaited together: first, the adoption of northern-Indian tandoori and grilling that we saw in Punjab and Kashmir; secondly, the lasting effects of India's sixteenth- and seventeenth-century Mughal colonizers, the Persian emperors who made Lucknow their capital; and lastly the influence of the holy city of Benares (or Varanasi) some two hundred miles away, home to around fifty thousand vegetarian Brahmin Hindus and where, historically, butchers were illegal.[*] The result is a mixture of vibrant dishes, both carnivorous and vegetarian.

The Awadhi griddle of choice was and is the *tava*, used to cook kebabs. This technique of grilling was borrowed from regions farther north, Kashmir (and even Pakistan), where the *tava* reigns supreme. Lucknow is famous for its minced lamb kebabs, which are cooked on an open griddle with various masalas (spice mixes). These locally pounded and grilled meats are famous for their softness, for the prevalence of fat that melts in the mouth, of which chef Ani says, "It was said that people from Lucknow were so lazy that they didn't want to chew their food."

The characteristic style of cooking in Awadhi cuisine, though, is *dum* (short for *dum phukt*, which literally means that the food "takes in air as it cooks," very slowly). *Dum* remains integral to Awadhi cuisine today and is the process by which biryanis are made, allowing the ingredients to absorb one another's flavors gradually, in a sealed container over a low heat, surrounded by charcoal.

There are loud echoes of ancient Persian cuisine in Lucknow. Ingredients such as saffron, nuts, gold and silver leaf, cardamom and yogurt are key to Awadhi cuisine and reminiscent of contemporary Iranian food, but have bred with the region's other influences to create the very particular Awadhi

••••

[*] Hinduism was traditionally a vegetarian religion. The sacred Hindu text, the Atharva Veda, states: "Those who eat flesh uncooked, and those who eat the bleeding flesh of men, Feeders on babes unborn, long-haired, far from this place we banish these." Over time, however, the conventions have been modified and it's now estimated that less than a third of all Hindus maintain a strict vegetarian diet. But Brahmins, being the highest priestly caste in Hindu society, still refrain from eating any animal flesh.

cuisine. Semantically, the link to Persia is also clear—pilau rice is descended from *polow* and biryani comes from *birian*, which means "fried before cooking."*

Also clearly descended from the Mughals is the korma curry. It is rich in butter, yogurt, cream and nut pastes and lightly spiced with the likes of cumin and coriander. An indulgent curry, korma takes its name not from the creamy texture with which we instantly associate it but from the technique of braising the meat. A vegetarian version, the *navratan korma*, is named for the nine vegetables it contains. Vegetarian equivalents of most meat dishes (even kebabs, which might be based on yams or beans) are available for those stricter Hindus who maintain total vegetarianism.

Moving to the southeast, we reach West Bengal. Bengal is split into two parts, with its eastern side in Bangladesh and its western side in India.† Culturally and geographically rich, West Bengal has a lively state capital in cosmopolitan Calcutta and a topography that ranges from the Himalayas in the north (site of jungles and home of the eponymous Bengal tiger) to the Ganges delta in the south (think mangroves and crocodiles), making it both a tourist magnet and important agricultural producer for the whole country. This is home to some of India's most fertile terrain, the plains of the Ganges being rich in alluvial soils on which rice, potatoes and grains flourish, while the river itself is a source of highly prized freshwater fish.

Around fifty miles inland, in Calcutta, river fish are a particular delicacy. Varieties such as *rohn* (similar to carp) and *hilsa* (very bony, very oily and very popular) command lobster prices and are usually used in curries, where they can be cut up into smaller morsels so as to stretch farther. Mustard and mango or ginger and tomatoes are characteristic flavor combinations in the fish curries of West Bengal. These river fish have a more intensely "fishy" flavor than the Arabian sea fish used in south Indian curries and the Bengalis prefer to spice their curries with a lighter touch, emphasizing the flavor of the fish. Chef Ani explains that "the fish can be tasted before the spices in Bengali curries whereas in Goa you are overwhelmed by chili, spice and coconut first." The Bengalis even have their own way of cutting fish—not filleted but resembling neat steaks with a bone hole just off-center.

• • • •

*The mutton used in an Awadhi biryani is indeed fried before the dish is cooked as a whole, and contains more distinctly Persian ingredients: rose water, mint leaves and cinnamon.

†Bengal was split in half in 1947 for religious reasons. The West was a Hindu territory belonging to India, the East was a Muslim state that became part of Pakistan. In 1971, this eastern side became the independent nation-state of Bangladesh.

The Bengali-American author Jhumpa Lahiri, known for her sensitive portraits of Bengali immigrants and their first-generation children in America, infuses her narratives with food. Vibrant, lightly spiced fish curries and vegetable dishes prepared with mustard oil become for her characters a reassuring link to India and a way to instill belonging in their American-born offspring. In the short story "When Mr. Pirzada Came to Dine" she writes of a "succession of dishes: lentils with fried onions, green beans with coconut, fish cooked with raisins in a yoghurt sauce . . . ," a string of ingredients and dishes typical of the region. What's more, the "succession" of dishes served like courses—not all brought out at once as you might find elsewhere in India—suggests European influences, namely those of the British Raj and the French. (Chandannagar, a small area of Bengal, was administered by the French East India Company from the seventeenth century onward. It was only ceded to India some three years after the nation's 1947 independence, then incorporated into West Bengal with its formation in 1955.)

Tomatoes, lemon, lime, some coconut milk and a little chili form the typical Bengali curry base, while the preferred fats in which to fry ingredients are mustard oil, peanut oil and, increasingly, sunflower oil. Ghee and butter are considered expensive luxuries in Bengal and dairy is much less prevalent than it is farther north in Punjab. The inconsistent delta terrain can't support the cows required for the large-scale production of yogurt butter and ghee, and cattle are instead kept to plow the fields for grain crops.

Rice, vegetables and lentils are all important components of the Bengali diet. Okra, eggplant, cauliflower, pumpkin, beans, potatoes and green bananas might be curried, shallow fried, steamed in a banana leaf (a popular local technique) or included in a biryani rice dish.[*] The Bengalis are known for their creativity with vegetable offcuts, the peel and the rind, ingeniously finding roles for them in curries and stews—a "nose to tail" approach to vegetables, if you like. (Peel to pith, perhaps?) Lentils, particularly black ones (known as *kaali dal*), are often eaten as a side dish and provide a wonderful "wet" accompaniment to drier dishes like fried eggplant or steamed fish. (You haven't tried dal until you have tasted it made with black lentils, which acquire a creamy texture and smoky flavor on cooking. I'd be happy with this as my main course, let alone as a side dish for fish or vegetable dishes).

Bengali food is mellow and subtly spiced. The spice blend local to Bengal (and East India more generally) is *panch phoron* (or "five spices"—see page

• • • •

[*] Biryani is a one-pot rice dish lifted from Mughal cuisine. Rice is spiced and fried; meanwhile a separate curry is made. The two are then layered upon each other.

197), and combines fenugreek, nigella, cumin, fennel and black mustard seeds. It is thrown into curries or on top of dal—its gently fragrant components are kept whole, delicately speckling curries with their assorted shapes and colors. Whole mustard seeds are used frequently, as is *kasundi*, the Bengali mustard paste with oil, garlic and spices, which is used as a condiment or to flavor river fish.

West Bengal's tea rituals date back to the British Raj. Black tea was first cultivated in the mid-nineteenth century, in the northern area of Darjeeling. By the turn of the century tea gardens had become big business. Darjeeling black tea now has protected product status, much like the AOC produce in France and other parts of Europe, and is known as the "Champagne of teas" for its fine grapy flavors, which enhance the taste of more or less any given food.

In Calcutta, bakeries such as Nahoum's draw attention to a dwindling Jewish subculture. Calcutta's Jewish community, thought to be Baghdadi in origin and present in the city since the end of the eighteenth century, has been steadily moving to Israel since that nation's formation. But Nahoum's, a baker and confectioner in the New Market quarter of the city, still serves delicacies such as cashew macaroons and pineapple pastries, which compliment a cup of Darjeeling tea to perfection.

If your cupboards are anything like mine, cooking the food of northern India takes a little more forward planning than that of the south, because of its emphasis on animal protein. Buy some ghee (it is ubiquitous in grocery stores in areas where there is an Asian population, and can also be found in all good supermarkets) and good-quality meat in advance of trying some of the recipes here—perhaps Meera's chicken tikka or Ani's *rogan josh*—and give making your own spice blend a whirl, with the inspiration of the chart on pages 197–99. Individual spice blends mark one cook's creations apart from another's, and it's here that you can really exercise your creativity in the kitchen.

**PANTRY LIST** • an infinite variety of spices and spice blends (see pages 197–99) • fennel seeds • mustard seeds • mustard leaves • Darjeeling tea • ghee • cream • yogurt • paneer • lentils (black and orange) • lemon • lime • tomatoes • chilies • naan bread • river fish • lamb

# • CUCUMBER AND MINT RAITA •

The Indian cousin of the Greek dip *tzatziki*, *raita* is a condiment that soothes the palate as you eat hot and spicy main dishes. The crunch of the cucumber and freshness of the mint enhance the zingy comfort of yogurt on a burning mouth. Eating a hot curry like *rogan josh* is, for me, unthinkable without *raita*.

## • SERVES 4 •

1 large cucumber, peeled and halved
16 oz Greek or plain yogurt
20 mint leaves, chopped, plus extra for serving
½ tsp cumin powder
sea salt and freshly ground black pepper
dusting of paprika (optional)

**1** • Grate one half of the cucumber and leave it in a sieve over the sink to drain off excess water. Coarsely chop the other half, avoiding the central line of seeds as much as possible (discard the seeds when done—they will add too much moisture).
**2** • Now simply stir the yogurt, mint and cumin together in a bowl, add the cucumber and season to taste.
**3** • Refrigerate until ready to serve, at which point dust with some paprika and sprinkle with a little extra fresh mint.

# • ROGAN JOSH •

The heat and bright red color of *rogan josh* (literally "hot oil," a classic Kashmiri lamb dish descended from the Mughals) is sometimes associated with passion. If your passion for chili and hot flavors is unrequited by this wonderful recipe of Anirudh Arora's, try adding some finely chopped red chilies before serving. (Madhur Jaffrey's version also calls for paprika and cayenne pepper for a different kind of complexity, or sweet heat.) And, if you're anything like me, you'll want either plenty of *raita* or more yogurt on serving, to offset the heat of the curry.

2¼ lb lamb, diced

¼ cup vegetable oil

6 cardamom pods (preferably a mixture of
    green and black ones)

6 whole cloves

1 cinnamon stick

1 bay leaf

2 onions, coarsely chopped

1 tbsp ginger paste

1 tbsp garlic paste

2 tsp red chili powder

½ tsp turmeric

1 tsp ground coriander

4 medium tomatoes, skinned and puréed

3½ oz plain yogurt

salt to taste

TO SERVE

1 red chili, deseeded and finely chopped (optional)

1 tsp garam masala (see page 198)

few sprigs coriander, chopped

more plain yogurt (or *raita*—see page 210)

**1** • Rinse the lamb under cold running water, then drain and pat dry with paper towels.

**2** • Heat the vegetable oil in a large, heavy frying pan. Add the whole spices (cardamom, cloves, cinnamon, bay leaf) and cook over a gentle heat for a few minutes to allow their flavors to infuse.

**3** • Add the onions to the pan and cook for 5–7 minutes, until golden brown, then add the lamb and cook for another 4–5 minutes over high heat, until well seared all over. Add the ginger and garlic pastes and cook, stirring frequently, for 2 minutes.

**4** • Stir in 1¾ cups water and simmer gently for about 30 minutes, adding more water if necessary. Stir in the remaining spices and cook for another 15 minutes.

**5** • Add the puréed tomatoes and yogurt and cook for another 15 minutes, or until the lamb is cooked through and tender.

**6** • Remove the whole spices and bay leaf, season to taste and then sprinkle with the red chili if using, garam masala and chopped coriander before serving.

# SOUTH INDIA

May in Ayemenem is a hot, brooding month. The days are long and humid.
The river shrinks and black crows gorge on bright mangoes in still,
dustgreen trees. Red bananas ripen. Jackfruits burst. Dissolute bluebottles
hum vacuously in the fruity air.
• ARUNDHATI ROY, *The God of Small Things* •

THE HEAVY, OPPRESSIVE heat of the south Indian state of Kerala steams off the pages of *The God of Small Things*. Arundhati Roy's seminal novel is set among a Syrian Christian community (an ancient group known as the Saint Thomas Christians of Kerala), in the fictional village of Ayemenem. Roy explores life in postcolonial Kerala, with its mix of religions, entrenched caste system, long coastline, hot climate and the backwaters—the lagoons alongside the Arabian Sea. You can veritably hear the bluebottles buzzing around overripe fruit and half expect one to fly out from the book as you read.

South India covers the four major states that slot into the country's triangular tip—Kerala, Tamil Nadu, Karnataka and Andhra Pradesh—as well as tiny Goa, which stands apart from the others owing to 451 years of Portuguese colonization, the legacy of which is a unique fusion of cultures and cuisines. There are lots of similarities among the cuisines of the south—the emphasis on coconut and chili, for instance, or the consumption of *dosas* (filled pancakes made from rice flour) at breakfast—and though each state's cooking boasts its own character, reflecting its unique ethnic mix and geography, the differences between the regional cuisines of southern India appear less defined than those of the north (which, it has to be said, covers a much larger area).

If you struggle with the heavy, oily curries of northern India—or, indeed, those of your local curry house—then south Indian food provides a lighter and fresher alternative to a heavy korma. Cream and yogurt are, for example, replaced by coconut milk, and spitting tandoori meats give way to tender chunks of fish punctuated with chili. The requisite ingredients for making south Indian dishes are a good range of spices including curry leaves and fenugreek, a can of coconut milk, hot chili, fresh herbs and beautiful, meaty sea fish. (Have your fishmonger on speed dial. Good fish is about the only investment this cuisine demands—everything else is an affordable item to keep in your pantry, and in my experience the quality of the fish can make or break a dish.)

Souther Indian cuisine is the product of a climate that yields vibrant tropical fruit, brilliant vegetables, and which demands the sensible preservation of fresh food with spice and salt. Coconuts and hot Byadagi chilies[*] are rife and both play a central role. Coconut, Kerala's largest export,[†] is used for its flesh, oil and milk, the latter marking apart the famous fish curries of the south from those of Bengal. Coconut oil is usually the fat base of choice, following which, some dishes are embellished with ghee to "finish." Coconut flesh is usually used as a dessert, sweetened with *jaggery* (unrefined cane sugar) or dried into shavings, which are often stuffed into vegetables or added to curries with a coconut milk base.

Fruit plays a larger part in savory food than you find in the north—as an ingredient in curries and as a medium with which to cook and to serve. For example, banana and plantain leaves frequently serve as plates or vessels in which to envelop fish before cooking. There's also *kokum*, a distinctive regional fruit not unlike a tomato to look at, which is south India's characteristic sour spice. Its function is not dissimilar from that of tamarind, adding tartness to curries and lentil dals (incidentally, tamarind is also widespread—see page 222). And then there is bitter gourd, or bitter melon, which originates here and can be found in curries on its own, alongside other vegetables or stuffed with coconut shavings.

The intense heat of red and green chilies characterizes much south Indian food, a feature that grew from the need to preserve produce in the face of hot weather. Historical necessity shaped the modern-day palate, it would seem, for spicy food remains central to Kerala and the other southern states to this day. Chili is used in tandem with fenugreek (which has a nutty flavor with celery notes), aromatic curry leaves (otherwise known as sweet *neem*), mustard, ginger, garlic and black pepper. Cumin is less important in south Indian cuisine than in the north, but still used fairly widely. As Vivek Singh, executive chef of London's famous Cinnamon Club restaurant, explains in his book *Cinnamon*

• • • •

[*]Byadagi is a town in Karnataka that produces the deep red chilies that season food from much of southern India.

[†]Over 90 percent of Indian coconuts are grown in the southern states and Kerala alone accounts for over half of this.

*Kitchen*, spices are "tempered" all over India—meaning that seeds are briefly added to hot oil in order to release and fully express their flavors—to create a seed and oil blend called a *tadka* (or sometimes *chaunk*), which is then added to curries at the end of cooking, before serving. The more nuanced southern *tadka* will include fenugreek, mustard seeds, lentils and curry leaves, while a northern equivalent might be limited to cumin and garlic.

In this hotbed of food preservation, chutneys and pickles are very popular and are commonly served with poppadums beside curries. Unique to south India, a *pachadi* is another condiment: pounded boiled vegetables with varying amounts of chili, spices, yogurt and peanut oil, served with rice or breads like *dosa* and *uttapam*. Native to south India, and it is thought specifically to Karnataka, the *dosa* is a crisp pancake made from fermented rice flour and lentils, wheat flour or semolina. It can either be a light finger food stuffed with curried potatoes and onions (known as a *masala* filling) or served plain alongside chutneys and *pachadis*. Not unlike the *dosa* but thicker, *uttapam* are like southern Indian pizzas—airy round flatbreads with toppings such as chili, onion and tomato that are cooked into the batter.

The south Indian meal revolves around rice, which is often a constituent in dishes (not just a side). The mulligatawny soup, for example, originally a Tamil[*] dish but later adapted by the British Raj, combines meats such as chicken or lamb with rice and a curry-flavored broth.

With a large Hindu majority, southern India is still largely vegetarian, despite changes in cultural practices that mean many Hindus are less observant of food laws than previously. Vegetarian dishes such as *rasam* (lentil and tamarind soup), *sambar* (lentil and pigeon pea[†] stew), and dal eaten with *dosa* or *uttapam* are staples consumed all over, with subtle variations in spicing that mark the differences between each state's rendition. Kerala, though, has the largest Christian population in India and there is also a substantial Muslim community, making the use of fish and meat more common than elsewhere. Fish and seafood define the cuisines of Kerala and Goa, and fish types include shark, tuna, pomfret, sardine and mackerel. The Goan fish or prawn curry (*humann*) is a mainstay on Indian restaurant menus all over the world while the *moily* curry of Kerala is also well-loved: an unusually simple base

• • • •

[*]The Tamil are a race native to south India and the southern area of the Indian subcontinent including Sri Lanka and Malaysia. They speak their own (Tamil) language and a large majority are Hindu.

[†]Pigeon peas are a semitropical and tropical green legume important in the vegetarian diet of southern India and are used particularly in Tamil cuisine.

of coconut, turmeric, ginger, onion, green chilies, curry leaves and whatever fish or seafood you might choose to use. This makes it perfect for adapting in your own kitchen, which I encourage you to do with the recipe below.

A word on Goan cuisine: for such a tiny state (well under fifteen hundred square miles), Goa's food culture is almost incomparably diverse. Though it has many of the same foundations as the food of Kerala and other southern Indian fare, the introduction of tomatoes and potatoes by the province's Portuguese colonizers, as well as tropical fruits such as pineapple and nuts such as cashews from Brazil, gave Goan cuisine extra flair—flourishes from the New World via the Old World. Goa even has its own spicy sausage, or *chouriço*: pork (often, pig intestine), red chili, palm vinegar, turmeric and garlic create a rich array of flavors unlike those of any sausage you've tried before. Goan *chouriço* is always cooked and usually enjoyed with local bread.

South Indian food has a wonderful spectrum of hot, sunny flavors and a trip to this land of ripening red bananas and bursting jackfruit can easily be taken from home.

**PANTRY LIST** • curry leaves • coconut • chilies (red and green) • mustard • fenugreek • tamarind • black pepper • kokum • coconut oil • chutneys and pickles • good fresh fish and seafood

• • •

# • COCONUT FISH CURRY •

Meera Sodha, who contributed this recipe, calls this delicious fish curry "Kerala on a plate" since it brings together coconuts and fish (both of which run amok there) in one dish. Any firm white fish such as cod, pollock or monkfish will do for this recipe, but Meera's favorite is haddock.

### • SERVES 4 •

2-inch piece ginger, coarsely chopped
4 garlic cloves, coarsely chopped
1 green chili, deseeded and coarsely chopped
pinch coarse salt

3 tbsp coconut or rapeseed oil

2 medium white onions, thinly sliced

2 big ripe tomatoes, quartered

1 ½ tsp salt

¾ tsp turmeric

½ tsp red chili powder

20 fresh (or dry will do) curry leaves (optional)

1 ¼ cups coconut milk

4 fillets of haddock or another firm white fish
(approx. 5–6 oz each), skinned

1 lime to serve, quartered (optional)

1 • In a mortar and pestle, pound the ginger, garlic and green chili along with the coarse salt until the mixture turns into a pulp.

2 • In a frying pan large enough to accommodate all the ingredients (and for which you have a lid) heat the oil over medium heat, add the onions and stir every now and then until they are pale gold. This will take 10–15 minutes. Add the ginger, garlic and chili and cook for another 2–3 minutes. Then add the tomatoes, salt, turmeric, chili powder and curry leaves if you're using them. Put the lid on and cook for a couple of minutes.

3 • Meanwhile, combine the coconut milk with 6 tbsp water. Pour into the pan and when the milk starts to bubble, add the fish fillets; cover and cook for about 5 minutes or until the fish is cooked through. Serve with rice and a squeeze of lime.

## • OVEN ROASTED CHICKEN TIKKA WITH MINT CHUTNEY •

Chicken tikka is one of the most popular Indian dishes in restaurants—a classic of the northern Indian tandoori that's usually served as a starter. The chicken tikka we are familiar with is bright, almost neon, red-pink in color but this, Meera Sodha's family recipe, is an altogether different beast. Less luminous and with beautiful intensity of flavor (particularly when served with the mint chutney below), Meera's chicken tikka shows that, though it may turn fewer heads on sight, the proof is most certainly in the pudding (or starter).

### • SERVES 4–6 AS A STARTER OR AS PART OF A SPREAD •

1 ⅓ lb chicken thighs, bones and skin removed

1 ½-inch piece ginger, coarsely chopped

4 garlic cloves, coarsely chopped
1 green chili, deseeded and coarsely chopped
pinch coarse sea salt
½ cup plain yogurt
1¼ tsp salt, or to taste
½ tsp chili powder (mild or hot according to
    preference)
½ tsp turmeric
¾ tsp cumin seeds, crushed
1 tsp sweet paprika
½ tsp garam masala (see page 198)
¾ tsp superfine sugar
salad leaves, to serve

FOR THE MINT CHUTNEY
½ green chili, deseeded and finely chopped
juice of ½ lemon
1 tbsp mint leaves, finely chopped
2 tbsp Greek yogurt
2 tsp superfine sugar

**1 •** Pick the chicken thighs over to remove any excess fat, then chop into pieces around 1 inch x ¾ inch and set to one side in a large bowl.

**2 •** In a mortar and pestle smash the ginger, garlic, green chili and sea salt until it turns into a paste. Add the paste to the chicken pieces, followed by the yogurt, salt, spices and sugar, mix thoroughly and cover. Marinate for at least 5 minutes and up to a few hours (the longer the better).

**3 •** Preheat the oven to 400°F.

**4 •** Line two roasting pans with foil and coat with a thin layer of oil. Distribute the chicken between the two pans so that you don't crowd the pieces, leaving any excess marinade behind. Bake for around 20 minutes, turning over halfway through to cook evenly.

**5 •** Meanwhile, blend all the ingredients for the mint chutney in a blender until smooth.

**6 •** Serve the chicken tikka on a bed of salad leaves with a drizzle of mint chutney.

# • BANANA PANCAKES WITH COCONUT AND JAGGERY •

Coconuts and bananas abound on fertile Keralan soil. Meera's recipe for this mouthwatering local dessert of honeyed bananas and toasted coconut was inspired by her Keralan friend Kumari's dish. In her book, *Made in India*, Meera paints a picture of being served banana pancakes by Kumari at her home, next to the cow and under the mango tree. Channel that image as you tuck into these—you're in for some tropical travels. Jaggery is a type of Indian sugar made from the sap of palm trees with a flavor not unlike fudge. If you can't find any, you can substitute brown sugar—a light brown sugar works well.

### • SERVES 4 (MAKES 8 PANCAKES) •

FOR THE PANCAKE BATTER
1 ¼ cups all-purpose flour
½ tsp ground cinnamon
pinch salt
2 medium eggs
1 cup 2% milk
unsalted butter for cooking the pancakes
crème fraiche, for serving

FOR THE FILLING
½ cup jaggery (or 6 tbsp light brown
     brown sugar)
3 bananas, sliced into ¾-inch rounds
½ tsp ground cardamom (or well-ground
     seeds of two cardamom pods)
1 ¼ cups shredded coconut

**1** • Sift the flour, cinnamon and salt into a bowl; make a well in the middle and add the eggs. Start to mix together using a fork or small whisk and slowly trickle the milk into the flour, mixing as you go, until you've used up all the milk and have a smooth batter without lumps. Set aside.
**2** • To make the filling, take the jaggery and break up any lumps, either in a mortar and pestle or with a rolling pin. Put it in a saucepan, ensure it's all in one layer and warm for about 15 minutes over low heat. Don't stir, but keep a watchful eye over it until it melts, caramelizing into a lovely golden brown color—make sure it doesn't

stick. Stir in the banana slices and cardamom—it will spit and bubble and the bananas will release some liquid so cook through, stirring occasionally, for another 2–3 minutes. Remove from the heat and fold in the coconut.

**3 •** To make the pancakes, rub the inside of a nonstick frying pan with butter using a piece of paper towel and then get the pan nice and hot. Pour in a small ladle of the batter (3 or 4 tablespoons should be enough), and quickly swirl from side to side until the batter has coated the bottom. Heat through for around 30 seconds, until the batter has set in the middle and loosened around the edges. Add an eighth of the banana mixture and carefully spread it across one half of the inside of the pancake. Fold the other half over to close it and press the edges shut using your spatula. Heat for 15 seconds on each side until nice and golden.

**4 •** Shuffle the filled pancake out onto a plate, serve with a dollop of crème fraiche. And repeat!

# THAILAND

Thai cooking is the opposite of Western cuisine, where two or three flavours are
blended in an elegant way to arrive at a distillation of the requisite flavours.
Thai food creates a locus of flavours within each dish, through its components,
producing a complexity that can be dazzling.
• DAVID THOMPSON, *Thai Food* •

THE FIRST TIME we visited him in Pattaya—the Thai
beach resort to which he retired—my grandfather
thumped his fists on the restaurant table and shouted
out words in Thai that, to our English ears, sounded like
"you cow, you cow!" Deferential waitresses laughed a
little nervously but seemed essentially unfazed by the
brash Englishman. Grandpa then went on to explain
wryly that "you cow" (*hiu kao*) meant "I'm hungry," the
exact translation of which is "I want rice." He took great
joy in shocking his guests, allowing us all momentarily
to mistake his appetite for rudeness. (To be fair, he made a habit of throwing his
substantial weight around, so calling a waitress a cow unprovoked wouldn't
have been wholly out of character. Back home in the UK, when we ate out in Italian restaurants, every waiter was called "Pasquale," to our shame.) This incident
with my grandfather was my first lesson in how central rice is to the Thai diet.[*]

A plate or basket of cooked white rice is the focus of the Thai meal. Despite
the enormous regional variations in Thai cuisine, there is an unwavering
devotion to rice all over the country. Served sticky[†] in the north, abundant in
the central plains ("the country's rice bowl" of paddy fields)[‡] and plain and

••••

[*] David Thompson notes, in *Thai Food*, that a colloquial greeting in Thailand is "gin kao ruu yang?"
which is used to mean "how are you doing?" but literally translates as "have you eaten rice yet?"

[†] Sticky (or glutinous) rice is widely grown in Asia, with opaque grains that stick to one another
when cooked. It is always soaked for several hours before cooking, then steamed on bamboo for
just under half an hour. Sticky rice is the staple rice of the Thais in central, northern and northeastern Thailand, as well as being the dominant ingredient in the cuisine of Laos, where it is eaten
with every meal.

[‡] Thailand's rice paddies lie in the central alluvial plains, where five rivers meet in the Chao Phraya
basin. The potential for agriculture means this region is both heavily populated and the country's
economic center, with a rich and varied cuisine. Peanuts, maize and taro are also grown here.

fragrant in the south,* rice is the undisputed ruler on Thai tables. Rosemary Brissenden, author of *South East Asian Food*, a book revered by Elizabeth David when it was published in 1969 as one "every serious cook should possess" and still in print today, notes that all other dishes—whether meat, fish or curry—are called "side dishes," a perspective that "asserts the primacy of rice." When the white rice, piled high, arrives at the table, you take a spoonful and garnish it with whatever else is served. And as in many other global cuisines, the northern European culture of going to a restaurant and ordering a dish just for yourself is counterintuitive to Thai eating habits. Rice and its side dishes are shared among one and all.

Thailand was a big part of my life when I was growing up. Long before he retired there my grandfather went regularly on holiday, and the scent of lemongrass and coconut wafted more or less permanently through his Norfolk farmhouse, arresting the senses. For as long as I can remember, the Far East was an important annex to his otherwise very British sensibility; "Oxford, Norfolk, Pattaya" was his very own "New York, Paris, London." In the late 1990s, he upped and moved to the Gulf of Thailand, to his beloved Pattaya, and spent the majority of his last years reading English newspapers in the sun and, crucially, delighting in the food of coastal Thailand. Pattaya is where American GIs used to take holidays between stints on the front line in Vietnam, indulging in all for which Thailand has become famous—good, bad and ugly. It is perhaps the best known of Thailand's "high-rise beachfront strips, which swarm with free-living tourists" (Brissenden), but like many tourist-driven metropolises on the sea (Cancun, Mexico, springs to mind), its popularity can be explained by profound natural beauty and an alluring culture of which food is no small part. Our times in Thailand were punctuated by bright flavors that remain illuminated in my memory: breakfasts of egg-fried rice; mango and sticky rice on the beach; neon sunsets and heady nights seasoned with hot chili, tamarind and coconut. And, of course, more rice.

There are many and varied cuisines to be found in Thailand, but the food of the Gulf is the food for which Thailand has become best known abroad—we're far more acquainted, for example, with the coconut curries balancing sour tamarind, lime and gorgeously sweet palm sugar than the gamy cuisine of the north. This is in part a reflection of the dishes and ingredients that have traveled but also of where the majority of tourists choose

• • • •

* Although steaming is a popular and common method for cooking rice, the traditional Thai technique is to cook it slowly in a clay pot over a very low heat, little more than the embers of a fire.

to visit. This is the Thailand of full-moon parties, of scuba diving, strong cocktails in buckets, fish dishes and hot chili.

Ingredients such as coconut milk, chilies and turmeric are rife in food from the Thai Gulf, in common with other South and Southeast Asian coastal cuisines like that of Malaysia, Indonesia and Goa and Kerala in India. They are often paired with fish and seafood, which eclipses meat as the prominent animal protein. Fish is particularly important in Buddhist Thailand, where killing large, four-legged mammals was traditionally taboo and remains less than desirable. While, for example, pork has risen to greater prominence in Thailand, Thais often still rely on Chinese butchers for slaughter.

As in much of Southeast Asia, China has been a key influence on Thai cuisine. This is most visible in Bangkok (owing to large-scale immigration at the beginning of the last century), where stir-frying and deep-frying are integral, but has trickled down to the coast, too. Egg-fried rice and saucy sweet-and-sour fish (which I remember most strongly, thick in red sauce and dotted with pineapple), the use of noodles (rice noodles can be bought fresh at Chinese markets), and *kaeng jut* (a thin mouth-cleansing soup) are all products of Chinese presence. In *Thai Food*, David Thompson posits that "the true genius of Thai cuisine is its ability to incorporate the unfamiliar," citing the Thais' absorption of the chili into their native cuisine "within a century" (and comparing this to Europe's relative resistance to the tomato, which took a good two hundred years to be accepted into the culinary canons of, say, Spain and Italy).

I've already alluded to tamarind several times and it is one of the Thais' most important ingredients. A matte brown paste, it is derived from the tamarind fruit. Tart in flavor, there's nevertheless fruitiness to its texture, sort of how I imagine dates would be if pummeled to a liquid paste. No coincidence, then, that its name means "date of India" in Arabic—an ironic moniker given that it is indigenous to the African tropics. Nevertheless, these days tamarind is most commonly found in Mexican cooking (in which it is used for drinks, eaten raw as fruit or candied for sweets) and Southeast Asian cuisines like those of Thailand and Vietnam. Lime is the other crucial sour flavor in Thai cuisine and, given the prevalence of fish, is particularly suited to the local palette of ingredients. I still find there's something very exotic about limes, despite the fact that they are now widely available in Western countries. Their citrus notes are more nuanced than the kick provided by lemons, a little sweeter and altogether more intriguing.

Both lime and tamarind are beautifully balanced by palm sugar, which marries the sweet to their sour. Little tan crystals offer a very distinctive sugary kick and illustrate how subtle differences in ingredients can create vastly different results from one cuisine to another. Derived from palm trees, the sap of which is boiled several times, the rich flavor of palm sugar reminds me of hazelnuts and coffee. Juxtaposed with the wince-inducing combination of lime and tamarind, it's no surprise that together they inject energy to the tired and hungry.

Chili, garlic, lemongrass and coriander are all important, vivid ingredients in Thai cuisine—adding flavors and sensations on a sliding scale that ranges from delicate to powerful in dishes like red or green curries. Interestingly, though we usually associate red chili with a more intense heat than green ones, this is a common misconception. Thai green curry has on several occasions taken me down with its intense heat—if in doubt, go for the milder red option. Coriander is a common garnish in countless dishes, while Thai basil—its leaves are sweeter than those of its European counterpart, with an extra tang of licorice—is often thrown into curries and soups.

The ginger family plays a critical role in south Thailand's "temple food" qualities. (This is an expression I have been borrowing from Nigella Lawson[*] for many years. She used it to describe foods we cook as healthy comforts. I'd argue that much Thai cuisine falls into this category, the country's wealth of magnificent Buddhist temples giving the term an added cuteness.) Ginger root, galangal (a stronger, Southeast Asian version of the more familiar ginger) and turmeric all boost the fragrance and color of dishes. Turmeric is a particularly interesting addition because it is so much more common in Indian cuisine, where it gives dishes like dal an extra shot of orange hue—more South than Southeast Asian.

Umami is delivered to Thai cuisine in the form of fish sauce (*nam pla*) and shrimp paste (*kapi*). Both are critical ingredients in a wide range of dishes and are also used as condiments in their own right. It's especially useful to have a bottle of *nam pla* in your cupboard—it's an agent of concentrated umami that crops up across so many of the Asian cuisines. Add a small amount to a pad Thai or noodle soup and it will take your creation to the next level, transporting you from the realm of your kitchen to the heady heat of Siam.

Fish sauce is Thailand's answer to Roman *garum* or Japanese dashi: fermented anchovies blended with sugar and salt. As a seasoning it is even more important than soy sauce, which is imported from China and has a less complex flavor. This is an ingredient that needs to be used with care—too

• • • •

[*] As much as I love Nigella's notion of "temple food," I also fully buy into Anthony Bourdain's theory in *Kitchen Confidential* that "your body is not a temple, it's an amusement park. Enjoy the ride." In conclusion, treat your body with respect but balance that with adventures in gastronomy. A combination to make you feel truly alive. . . .

little or too much can underwhelm the palate and murder it respectively. The Thais add it to curries, soups and all manner of sauces, but also use it as a dipping condiment with garlic and chili.

While fish sauce is added directly to curries, shrimp paste is an important component in the curry paste. Shrimps are salted, dried in the sun and then ground to form pastes that vary in saltiness and color (ranging from light brown to chocolate) and, with garlic, shallot and galangal, provide the wetter, more adhesive elements of curry pastes—the rest being dried chilies and spices such as cumin and peppercorns.

To minimize oiliness in curries, the Thais add curry paste to the pan only once the fish, spices and coconut milk have been added (rather than frying their paste in oil, as the Indonesians and Malaysians might). This means that the paste cooks in the fat from the other ingredients, keeping oil to a minimum without compromising the release of all the different flavors.

Coconut milk is used in curry dishes across South and Southeast Asia, but in my mind it will always be a particularly Thai ingredient. To my palate, it is an ideal canvas for the complex array of flavors of Thai cuisine. (Give me a Thai fish curry with lemongrass, tamarind, lime and fish sauce over a Goan equivalent, any day.)

I've given you a selection of essential Thai recipes here. That said, I decided to leave out some of my favorites, on the grounds that I was offering something relatively similar elsewhere. I've omitted the quintessentially Thai *tom yam* soup, for example, because you'll find equally delicious Asian soup-style dishes elsewhere in this book (*udon* broth from Japan—see page 256—and a *pho* from Vietnam—see page 228). I've also excluded pad Thai, simply because it is so incredibly popular in the West and so many cookbooks offer great recipes. Instead I've given you some helpful basics including an easy homemade curry paste followed by a curry, which will forever remind me of Pattaya beach holidays with my grandfather, and lastly my mum's Thai pork mince, a staple chez Holland.

When the Thais make a toast they say *chok dee* (meaning "good luck"). Ever the attention seeker, my grandfather typically inserted an expletive to this for emphasis. As a final tribute, I'm afraid I am tempted to do the same.

*Chok* effing *dee* to you all.

RICE

**PANTRY LIST** • tamarind • lime • fish sauce • shrimp paste • coconut milk • ginger • galangal • turmeric • chili • palm sugar • coriander • lemongrass • Thai basil • mint • kaffir lime leaves • fresh fish and seafood

• • •

# • THAI VEGETABLE CURRY •

Recipes instructing me to make my own curry paste used to make me run a mile. As a student, I relied on (actually pretty decent) jarred curry pastes to make Thai curries and *tom yum* soups. But the homemade, real deal is just so much better. If you have a decent mortar and pestle it's very quick to whip up your own paste, and I firmly believe that you can't call a dish your own if you've used a ready-made product . . . sorry. This is my recipe for a vegetable curry, offered on the basis that if you want to elaborate with chicken, prawns, tofu etc., you can. I like the vegetable version as it is, but feel free to treat it as the mere foundation to something carnivorous or more elaborate, if you wish. If you struggle to find tamarind paste, just add the zest and juice of an extra lime. While their flavors aren't particularly comparable, the lime will nevertheless supply that extra kick of acid sourness.

## • SERVES 4 •

FOR THE PASTE
½ tsp cumin seeds
½ tsp coriander seeds
½ tsp black peppercorns
2 dried chilies, rehydrated in hot water
    for 10 minutes
½ tsp dried chili flakes
1 stalk lemongrass, outer layers discarded,
    coarsely chopped (or 1–2 tsp from a jar)
3 large garlic cloves, coarsely chopped
¾- to 1-inch piece ginger, coarsely chopped
½ tsp shrimp paste

FOR THE CURRY
1 x 2-oz package creamed coconut
1 x 14-oz can coconut milk
7 oz water
2 tbsp fish sauce
2 tsp palm sugar
3 tbsp tamarind paste
1 large zucchini, sliced lengthways into batons
2 bell peppers (I use one orange, one red), finely sliced lengthways
10 baby corn
3½ oz sugar snap peas
8 button mushrooms, sliced
zest and juice of 1 lime (juice to taste)
soy sauce, to taste
few sprigs coriander, chopped, to serve

**1** • Toast the cumin and coriander seeds in a pan until brown and fragrant, then grind in a mortar and pestle with the rest of the paste ingredients and set aside.

**2** • Put the creamed coconut into a large pan and gently melt over low heat. Add the paste, stir and let the mixture cook for a minute. Raise the heat and add the coconut milk, water, fish sauce, palm sugar and tamarind paste. Bring to a boil, stir and simmer for 10 minutes.

**3** • Add the vegetables, reduce the heat and cover. Test the vegetables intermittently to see if they are cooked—it should take 10–15 minutes, depending on how crunchy you like your vegetables. Stir in the lime zest and taste to gauge the balance of salt and acidity before adding soy sauce and lime juice accordingly. Serve with steamed rice (fragrant rice is good) and a generous sprinkling of chopped coriander.

# • MUM'S THAI PORK MINCE •

My mum has been making this for as long as I can remember. It has such complexity of flavor that I was convinced she was the only person who could cook it . . . I was wrong (sorry, Ma). This is super easy. Just stock up on a few Southeast Asian staples (all big supermarkets will have the likes of rice wine vinegar, fish sauce and lemongrass) and you're good to go. You could even replace the fresh garlic, chili, ginger and lemongrass with bottled pastes if you're caught without fresh ingredients on hand. Serve with boiled rice for an uncomplicated but nuanced midweek supper that will transport you straight to Siam.

3 tbsp vegetable or sunflower oil
1-inch piece ginger, finely chopped
2–3 garlic cloves, very finely chopped
1 green chili, deseeded and chopped
1 stalk lemongrass, outer layers discarded,
    finely chopped (or 1–2 tsp from a jar)
2 tsp palm sugar
1⅛ lb good-quality pork mince
juice of 2 limes
1 tbsp fish sauce
1 tbsp rice wine vinegar
3 tbsp soy sauce
3–6 tbsp water

TO SERVE
1 scallion, chopped
few sprigs coriander, chopped
big pinch dried chili flakes

**1** • Heat the oil in a large pan and sauté the ginger, garlic, green chili and lemongrass for 2–3 minutes without allowing them to burn. Then add the palm sugar and pork mince. Sauté for another 3–5 minutes, stirring to break the mince up so that it browns all over.

**2** • Add all the liquids (lime juice, fish sauce, rice wine vinegar, soy sauce and water) and simmer for 5–6 minutes, until the meat is cooked through. NB: I like to use 6 tbsp water because it leaves a lot of juice, which is lovely with rice or simply scooped in spoonfuls from the pan after you've transferred the meat and some sauce to a serving bowl. It's utterly delicious, although rather too liquid if you serve the whole dish with it all. So do what feels right!

**3** • Scatter with the scallions, coriander and chili flakes and serve with boiled rice.

RICE

# VIETNAM

They say whatever you're looking for, you will find here. They say you come to Vietnam and you understand a lot in a few minutes, but the rest has got to be lived. The smell: that's the first thing that hits you, promising everything in exchange for your soul. And the heat. Your shirt is straightaway a rag. You can hardly remember your name, or what you came to escape from.

• GRAHAM GREENE, *The Quiet American* •

GRAHAM GREENE'S VIVID description of Vietnam, of what makes it invigoratingly different from British soil, is palpable and multisensory. How it feels, smells, looks—"the colours, the taste, even the rain"—his explanation of loving this little country, which curves voluptuously around the Chinese peninsula, bowls the reader over in a sensual flurry. Perhaps it is no coincidence that Greene's senses appear so inextricable from one another. Vietnamese culture, and more importantly Vietnamese cuisine, is after all founded on groups of five entities that need to be kept in balance: five elements, five colors, five nutrients, five organs and—yes—five senses.[*]

This of course echoes some of the traits we will see when we get to China and Japan. Again, no coincidence. Rosemary Brissenden notes that Vietnamese cuisine is "most closely akin to that of China, overlaid with the occasional French influence—except that it uses less oil, more sugar and more fresh uncooked herbs and vegetables than Chinese cuisine." Vietnam may be geographically closer to its neighbors of Thailand, Cambodia and Laos, but the cultural impact of several colonizations has been enormous. In a (cashew) nutshell, the Chinese ruled Vietnam for about a thousand years, during which time they spread their roots into the Vietnamese cultural

••••

[*]These sets of five often correspond with one another, for example tastes with elements: spicy (metal), sour (wood), bitter (fire), salty (water) and sweet (earth). The colors are the same that we will see in Japanese cuisine: red, green, yellow, white and black.

consciousness.* Then came the French. Then, in the middle of the twentieth century, during the Cold War, the country became the battlefield of competing political ideologies.

Vietnam has long been a hub of violence and changing allegiances that have, over time, helped to create a culture that's both lively and resourceful. While colonization of one territory by another demands adherence, it also breeds departure. Vietnam may have wanted to cook with all the sophistication of the Chinese—with their myriad rice varieties, complex sauces and marinades—but China's confiscation of the best Vietnamese ingredients prevented this. For hundreds of years, the most prized ingredients went straight to the imperial capital of Beijing, leaving the Vietnamese to make do with whatever was left over. The proverbial short straw maybe, but over the centuries (and partly through necessity) Vietnamese cuisine has developed into a healthy and nuanced one, currently enjoying popularity all over the world.

In general terms, Vietnamese food is fresh, quickly executed and inexpensive. It honors the true flavors of ingredients rather than masking them with sauces. Foods are often served raw or are cooked only minimally in dishes like *pho* (a light brothy and highly restorative noodle soup). *Pho* couldn't be more different from the cheap, saucy Chinese food found in UK takeouts, though London's Vietnamese community, who remain concentrated along the Kingsland Road in Shoreditch, historically made and sold Chinese dishes in their restaurants in answer to the voracious British demand for starchy, MSG-rich dishes such as chop suey. It is only relatively recently that the record has been set straight and perceptions started to change about the nature of "Vietnamese food."

For the most part, the Vietnamese will cook ingredients with water and broths rather than oil and fat, allowing the flavors of each ingredient to shine through with nutritious *and* delicious results. This is nowhere truer than in *pho*, the clear, sweet broths that are flavored with spices such as cinnamon, star anise and ginger that are first roasted then infused into the liquid with a tea strainer. This mixture is subsequently boiled for twenty-four hours. Quickly executed this part isn't, but as long as your stock is prepared the day before and the meat is added a few hours before serving, the final

• • • •

*Vietnam continues to be designated as part of the Sinosphere, the group of territories influenced by China, and is generally considered to have a Confucian moral code. In the words of Rosemary Brissenden, "Chinese rule placed an indelible Confucian stamp on the culture and institutions of Vietnam—at least at the upper levels—and it remained unique among South East Asian cultures in not having been 'Indianised' in its arts, culture and religion.".

flourishes can happen quickly. You can poach rice noodles (known as *banh pho*) in just thirty seconds and simply throw bean sprouts and herbs like coriander, sweet basil or lime over the soup moments before serving. Importantly, no fat is added and any droplets of oil you might see on the resulting broth's surface probably derive from the meat.

*Pho* originated up north in Hanoi—the capital city, usually also considered Vietnam's street food capital—but quickly gained popularity in the south after the country's partition in 1954, when around a million people fled the communist north. There's an etymological tussle between China and France regarding the history of the word. Whether it came from *luc pho*, Cantonese for "beef with noodles," or was inspired by the French *pot au feu*, *pho* can only trace its history back about a hundred years, soaring to prominence at home and abroad during a period of great change in Vietnam.

*Bún riêu* and *bánh cuon*, two other signature dishes, also hail from the country's north. *Bún riêu* is another noodle soup, of spiced minced crab and vermicelli rice noodles swimming in a tomato broth enriched with fermented shrimp paste, tamarind and scallions. Made with a fermented rice batter, *bánh cuon* look like the love children of dim sum and spring rolls: long rolled dumplings containing ground pork, mushrooms and shallot and enjoyed with a fish-based dipping sauce at any time of day. Northern Vietnamese cuisine is generally better suited to home cooking—restaurants are rarer in Hanoi than in Ho Chi Minh City, where Chinese influences are felt more keenly. The eventually global spread of these delicious northern street food dishes really began with the migration from north to south in the middle of the twentieth century.

Beef wasn't eaten in Vietnam in any real volume until the French arrived in the middle of the nineteenth century. This European intervention in Vietnam's history enriched the cuisine beyond compare; the ingredients and recipes introduced by France (culinary capital of the world, no less) have proved integral to many signature Vietnamese dishes today. As we have seen, beef *pho* is one, as is *bo luc lac* or "shaking beef," named for the quick shaking action in which beef sirloin is tossed to fry in the pan. Typically simple and easily assembled, *bo luc lac* is served as a hot salad with lettuce, watercress and onion, the beef marinated in the most characteristic Vietnamese flavors: fish sauce, soy sauce, lime, chili, Thai basil and garlic. Though herbs such as mint, Thai basil and coriander have long been present in Vietnam, eating them (and other green leaves) raw is a relatively recent phenomenon, mirroring European influence. When France colonized Vietnam in 1858, introducing the likes of dill and watercress to the existing herb canon, Vietnamese people were emulating the Chinese tradition of cooking herbs into dishes.

Perhaps France's greatest contribution to Vietnamese cuisine after beef, however, was the baguette. The Vietnamese put their own national spin on the classic French bread, making it lighter and airier than the European original. With a robust crust and extra space inside, it makes an excellent vessel for sandwich fillings, which is exactly how the Vietnamese use it. *Banh mi* (simply "bread" in Vietnamese) are something of an edible reminder of Vietnam's imperial past, fusing the bread of colonizer and fillings of the colonized. Salad, pickled cucumber, daikon radish, coriander, chili sauce and Kewpie mayonnaise* join pulled pork, chicken, egg or tofu in one of the great success stories of fusion cuisine.

A *banh mi* sandwich is a fantastic route into Vietnamese food. It is both an introduction to the crisp acid flavors and a morsel of edible history. Try buying some light baguette, fresh herbs, Kewpie mayonnaise and marinating some meat or fish, or, if you're feeling more adventurous (and time rich!) make a *pho* with the help of the recipe below, contributed by Hieu Trung Bui, London-based Vietnamese restaurateur and proprietor of the Cây Tre restaurants and Kingsland Road's Viet Grill. The flavor, feel and smell of these dishes will seduce you—but don't worry. I shouldn't think you will have to "exchange . . . your soul," as Graham Greene had it. You're in your own kitchen, after all.

**PANTRY LIST** • coriander • mint • Thai basil • star anise • red chili • dill • limes • fish sauce • ginger • soy sauce • watercress • scallions • bean sprouts • lettuce • daikon radish • Kewpie mayonnaise • vermicelli rice noodles • beef brisket

• • •

• • • •

*Kewpie mayonnaise is a Japanese take on mayo made with rice vinegar, which has spread across Southeast Asia.

# • GREEN PAPAYA SALAD •

This is a little bit like a Vietnamese slaw, composed of shredded carrot and under-ripe papaya blended with chili and umami dressing. It is admittedly far more delicate in its balance of flavors than a Western coleslaw, but I sometimes use it in the same way: on a warm summer's evening it accompanies barbecued meats brilliantly. You will have no trouble getting green papaya in Asian shops.

## • SERVES 4–6 •

1 large green papaya, peeled and deseeded
1 large carrot, peeled
2 garlic cloves, very finely chopped
2 scallions, very finely sliced
5 tbsp fish sauce
3 tbsp granulated sugar
juice of 2–3 limes, plus zest of ½ lime
2 Thai bird chilies, finely sliced

TO SERVE
handful roasted cashews or peanuts, coarsely chopped
few sprigs coriander, chopped
1 scallion, chopped

**1** • Slice the papaya and carrot into batons the shape and size of large matchsticks.
**2** • Now simply combine the remaining ingredients, making sure the sugar is dissolved before pouring it all onto your slaw and tossing well.
**3** • Refrigerate for an hour before serving so the flavors can really mingle. Then top with the nuts, coriander and scallion.

# • BEEF PHO •

Making *pho* is a long-winded process, to be tackled when you have a spare after-noon. It's worth making a large batch and freezing half for a rainy day—it makes a warming broth ideal for coughs, colds and winter blues. Hieu Trung Bui's beef *pho* usually includes beef tenderloin as well as the marrow bone, oxtail and brisket in the recipe below, but I've taken the liberty of excluding it here because I like the economy of using beef offcuts. *Pho* is in essence an unsophisticated street food, albeit one with myriad sophisticated flavors.

## • SERVES 6 •

3 1/3 lb beef marrow bone
1 1/2 lb oxtail
2 1/4 lb brisket
1 1/2 tbsp salt, plus a pinch for the meat
4–5 large shallots, halved
2-inch piece ginger, finely sliced
1 tbsp coriander seeds
5 cardamom pods
3 star anise
12 scallions, chopped
2 1/2 tbsp coriander, chopped , and more to garnish
7 oz dry pho noodles (flat rice noodles)
3 oz fish sauce
1/4 cup sugar
freshly ground black pepper

TO SERVE
handful beans prouts
lime wedges
hoisin sauce

**1** • In a big bowl, soak the bone and meats. Add a big pinch of salt, cover with water, soak for 2 hours, then wash and pat dry.
**2** • Preheat the oven to 400°F.
**3** • Place the shallot, ginger, coriander seeds, cardamom and star anise on a rimmed

baking sheet and roast in the oven for 15 minutes, shaking the tray every now and then to prevent burning.

**4** • Place the marrow bone in a large pot, cover with water and bring to a boil. Then reduce the heat to low and simmer for 30 minutes before skimming the foam from the top, until the liquid is clear. Simmer this mixture for an hour, then add the oxtail.

**5** • In a big mortar and pestle, grind the roasted star anise, coriander seeds, cardamom, ginger and shallot. Put this mixture into a cheesecloth or muslin, fasten it tightly and then add to the pot. Simmer for another 30 minutes before adding the brisket. Bring to a boil again, reduce the heat and skim again. Cook for 2½ hours.

**6** • In the meantime, cook the pho noodles as instructed on the package and set aside.

**7** • Remove all the meat and discard the bone. Soak the brisket and oxtail in cold water until cool, then place in a colander set over a bowl to drain the juices and dry out the meat. Thinly slice the brisket. Pick the meat from the oxtail and discard the fat. Season the broth with the fish sauce, sugar and 1½ tbsp salt.

**8** • Put the cooked noodles in a bowl with some of the brisket and oxtail and top with scallions and coriander. Cover with ladlefuls of boiling broth, add some black pepper and serve with more chopped coriander leaves, bean sprouts, lime wedges and hoisin sauce.

# CHINA

He that takes medicine and neglects diet wastes the skills of the physician.
• CHINESE PROVERB •

IN CHINA, NOTIONS of harmony—balancing your five elements of wood, fire, air, earth and water—are an accepted doctrine by which to live. In the West, these ideas are still deemed alternative, or even "New Age" (despite predating most of the big monotheistic religions), but to the Chinese, living a balanced life is just common sense.

What I like about Chinese medicine—and about Eastern health principles generally—is their proactive, preventative approach to keeping well. Each element goes hand in hand with a feeling, a color and a taste, as well as a dominant yin and yang body part, aiding not only diagnosis (for instance, a preference for sweet foods could imply a problem with your spleen) but suggesting a diet by which you can keep these elements balanced in a sustainable way. As such, food has an actively health-giving role in Chinese medicine.

Foods themselves are either yin or yang. Carbohydrates, vegetables and anything that cools the body down are yin while yang products are stronger—proteins, spices, coffee. The Chinese eat a balanced combination of yin and yang foods to keep their bodies stable, although as Western eating habits creep in—principally eating more meat and sugar—there is the impending threat of the yin and yang falling out of kilter.

Ideas about harmony translate to the Chinese kitchen and plate. It is this, combined with the brilliance of Chinese cuisine at every socioeconomic level that makes it one of the world greats.* The typical Western perception

• • • •

*I have heard mumblings of the "Three Great Cuisines of the World" being, unofficially, French, Chinese and Turkish. In *The Last Chinese Chef*, Nicole Mones justifies China's position as one of "the greats," thus: "Three qualities of China made it a place where there grew a great cuisine. First, its land has everything under heaven: mountains, deserts, plains, and fertile crescents; great oceans, mighty rivers. Second, the mass of Chinese are numerous but poor. They have always had to extract every possible bit of goodness and nutrition from every scrap of land and fuel, economising everywhere except with human labour and ingenuity, of which there is a surfeit. Third, there is China's elite. From this world of discriminating taste the gourmet was born. Food became not only a complex tool for ritual and the attainment of prestige, but an art form, pursued by men of passion."

of Chinese food, however, is that it is "unhealthy" or "junk food." I grew up associating the addictive food additive monosodium glutamate (MSG)* directly with Chinese cuisine. MSG is responsible for the intense and addictive savoriness of Chinese food but also, allegedly, the symptoms of what is now known in the West as "Chinese Restaurant syndrome"—tingling, palpitations and drowsiness following a meal of Westernized Chinese food. Here lies a fundamental paradox—a sorry outcome for Chinese cuisine—and an opportunity for education. Maybe, just maybe, if people in the West can learn a bit more about the realities of Chinese cuisine outside of their local take-outs, they might simultaneously pick up some basics of Chinese medicine—a lifestyle choice that doesn't preclude conventional medicine but works with it (and keeps visits to the doctor to a minimum).

Another ancient Chinese teaching outlines the seven necessities with which to begin a day, all of which pertain to food: firewood, salt, sauce, rice, oil, vinegar and tea. The seven necessities set up a framework for all that is integral to Chinese cuisine in terms of flavors, textures, techniques and the rituals around dining.

The firewood, or fuel, with which to apply heat is crucial to the various methods of cooking employed in China, from steaming to stir-frying and slow-cooking. The flavor imparted by firewood also lends smokiness to foods such as tofu, duck smoked with black tea, or indeed teas with smoky flavors such as lapsang souchong.

The intensely savory food of China relies heavily on salt, which is derived both from soy sauce and in its purest form. Soy sauce is the product of fermented soybeans and is a powerful agent of umami, giving it an added layer of complexity over simple sea salt.

Sauces are, as a rule, fundamental across the regional cuisines of China and capitalize on fermented or sweet-and-sour flavors in viscous liquid form. Plum sauce, often enjoyed with Peking Duck,† straddles the sweet and tart flavors of fruit, reducing these down with sugar, vinegar and ginger to create a condiment for meat, noodle and vegetable dishes alike. Generic sweet-and-sour sauce is a simpler version of this—just soy sauce, sugar, rice vinegar and cornstarch heated to give a more complex seasoning to dishes than salt, soy sauce or vinegar alone could offer.

• • • •

*MSG is used to give the intense umami flavoring associated most with Asian foods. It is made by fermenting wheat or molasses proteins with bacteria that are often genetically engineered, following which sodium is added.

†An imperial dish of roasted duck, served with pancakes, scallion and plum or hoisin sauce.

Rice is a staple in the Chinese kitchen, simply steamed to absorb the diverse flavors that emanate from colorful protein and vegetable dishes. Though not one of the original seven necessities, noodles, and more generally wheat, have been so embraced by the Chinese as to render them equally important in the Chinese kitchen. Wheat noodles, which originate in China and date back to as early as the Han Dynasty (around 206–220 BC), are a staple across Asia, and can also be made from buckwheat or rice (sometimes called glass noodles or vermicelli).

Oil is also an essential ingredient, as with any cuisine that involves a lot of shallow and deep-frying. For stir-fries, oils are selected on the basis of their smoke point—the temperature at which they begin to give off smoke. The higher, the better, because smoking oil turns the wok contents bitter. Peanut, rapeseed, sunflower and corn oils are the usual choice for frying in Chinese cuisine. Stir-frying in a wok needs to be a brief process during which heat is imparted to the ingredients quickly, the oil lightly sautéing and flavoring vegetables, noodles and meat, ideally without reaching its smoke point. Sesame oil, with its strong nutty flavor, is used after cooking to dress stir-fries, dumplings and spring rolls.

Given the importance of sweet and sour in Chinese cuisine, vinegar is another key ingredient outlined in the seven necessities. Both bitter and sour, it is believed to have powerful energetic qualities that are much celebrated in Chinese medicine, as well as the ability to relieve pain and toxicity. Rice vinegar can be used for curing and pickling herbs and vegetables such as radishes, bamboo shoots and garlic. Red rice vinegar has a sweet-and-sour edge and is often used as a dipping sauce in Cantonese cuisine.

Tea drinking is the seventh necessity, an ancient custom that is ingrained into Chinese daily life. The practice is thought to have originated with the Shang Dynasty (as early as 1600 BC) and now forms a communal daily ceremony called yum cha ("drink tea") in regions such as Guangdong. Tea is a powerful source of antioxidants, with both anti-inflammatory and calming properties.

Interestingly, meat and fish are not included in the seven necessities. Chinese cuisine is not founded on the regular consumption of animal protein, although an increasing proportion of people eat meat with every meal. Small amounts of meat traditionally went a long way for China's poor, not unlike Lazio's quinto quarto or the use of pork offcuts in southern and central Spanish cocidos. Soybeans, preserved or pickled vegetables, rice and noodles, and all the seven necessities outlined above were and remain the essentials of Chinese cuisine, but are nowadays embellished more and more with meat or fish.

I've chosen to cover two cuisines from the south of China because, on the whole, they possess a wider spectrum of flavors, ingredients and dishes than elsewhere. Historically, the imperial cuisine belonged to Beijing—where the Emperor resided—while Shanghai, home to wealthy traders, was the capital of commercial food. Rather than look at either of these, I have chosen to explore Guangdong and Sichuan, two "poor man's" cuisines steadily growing in popularity all over the world. The cuisine of Guangdong, or Cantonese food, has spearheaded the rise of Chinese cuisine overseas while the food of Sichuan was developed by the region's resourceful working class, and has subsequently become the most flavorsome fare in all of China, in spite of its humble roots. It's also interesting to see how various local ingredients from these regions—such as oyster and hoisin sauces from Canton, and Sichuan peppers—have become accepted into the Chinese national culinary canon.

The Chinese philosopher Confucius[*] said that "the way you cut your meat reflects the way you live," a culinary conceit that sheds light on your state of mind, but also demonstrates the symbolic role of food in China—both in society and as a factor in a balanced life. Food is intimately linked to physical and mental well-being, as well as to class, wealth and breeding. What and how you eat are not just an indication of your circumstances, but a way of changing them.

• • • •

[*] Confucius, who is believed to have lived between 551 and 479 BC, placed great emphasis on the study of old texts to help shed light on the moral issues of the present. Though he referred to questions of spirituality, his teachings were less a religion than a philosophy of morality and justice. They were hugely important to successive generations of Chinese government, and Confucian ideals in turn influenced governance in the Chinese colonies, like Vietnam. Apparently, more people worldwide have read the teachings of Confucius than have read the Bible.

# RICE

• • •

Rice is thought to have originated in China many thousands of years ago and is now in the running for the title of world's most important foodstuff, feeding millions across the globe. The only crop grown more prolifically is corn (see page 310), but while rice is grown mainly for human consumption, corn is often intended for other purposes, like fuel.

Rice is a staple in cuisines across the world, from the sticky versions enjoyed perennially in East Asia to the jollof rice of West Africa (page 277), rice and peas of the Caribbean (page 319), risottos of Italy, *chelo* of Iran and pilafs and pilau of Turkey and India respectively.

As a crop it is remarkably versatile and can grow in myriad conditions, although the plant needs a lot of water and thrives in the paddy environment famous in East and Southeast Asia. Fields of young rice plants are flooded, allowing them to flourish in the abundance of water while keeping pests to a minimum. On harvesting, husks are removed from the grains—this makes for brown rice, which can be further milled to create white rice. Though its nutritional value is inferior, white rice can be stored for a long time and is a simpler, quicker ingredient to cook with—and thus a sustainable and easy food solution for people across the world who have only rudimentary cooking equipment.

In its native China, rice is one of the Twelve Symbols of Sovereignty—a symbolic interpretation of the universe that bolstered the emperor's self-image as second only to God. Rice represented his ability to feed his people, a symbol of fertility and prosperity.

• • •

# GUANGDONG (CANTON)

Anything that walks, swims, crawls, or flies with its back to heaven is edible.
• CANTONESE PROVERB •

GUANGDONG, FORMERLY KNOWN as Canton,* is the southwestern province of China that occupies a long stretch of coastline on the South China Sea. The Dong Jang, Bei Jang and Xi Jang (east, north and west, respectively) rivers flow into the province and out into the sea, forming the Pearl River delta. The delta has long been both a window to the rest of the world and a historic inlet to China; it was the first stop on the Maritime Silk Road. There is an enormous concentration of people living in Guangdong, particularly around capital Guangzhou, often lured here from other parts of China (like nearby Hong Kong) by the economic opportunities presented by low taxation and a high demand for labor in the province's manufacturing industries.

Thanks to its geographical accessibility, the food of Guangdong is the best-traveled of all the Chinese cuisines—China's equivalent to Punjabi food, if you like, exported and reproduced, if not necessarily authentically, all over the world. (If as a student you stumbled home during the early hours and ordered "Chinese food"—soggy with sauce, oozing with MSG—then your takeout of choice probably claimed Cantonese origins.)

In essence, Cantonese cooking is deceptively simple. In contrast to the Sichuan style, which prizes more complex flavor combinations, a lot of Cantonese food is lightly infused or decorated with ingredients such as garlic, scallion, or one of several sauces, to release natural, fresh flavors.

Cantonese eating centers around the ritual of yum cha—literally "drink tea"—during which bite-sized foods are enjoyed with tea (ranging from black, green and white to red, oolong and pu-erh) in local teahouses. The English concept of tea as a beverage to complement cakes or scones could hardly be more different. Teas with spicy overtones, such as oolong and pu-

••••

*Though "Guangdong" is now the name by which it is known, the cuisine and people of the province are still referred to as "Cantonese."

*erh*, are considered thirst quenchers and suited to any meal, although certain foods (like dim sum) were designed with the purpose of accompanying tea drinking. Literally "touch the heart" in Cantonese, dim sum are little buns or dumplings filled with meat, shellfish or vegetables. They are either steamed or fried and served in stacking bamboo boxes to keep them warm and moist. The popular *cha siu bao*, or *baozi*, are a delicious example—steamed buns stuffed with barbecue pork, which have been marinated in sesame oil, Shaoxing wine,* oyster, hoisin and soy sauces.

As you might expect for a coastal region, fresh seafood has traditionally dominated Cantonese cuisine. Fish is usually steamed whole and served with garlic, ginger, scallions, and soy sauce—simple flavor flourishes to enhance the taste of the fish. Squid, lobster, shrimp and clams are variously prepared but almost always adorned with green rings of scallion, and bright "O's" of red chili. Guangdong is a center for the production of dried shrimp and oyster sauce flavorings, which feature heavily in the cuisine. Dried shrimps may be added to stir-fries and dim sum, soups and noodles for umami kick, while oyster sauce (a reduction of cooked oysters, sugar and salt) is a common condiment across Cantonese cuisine, added to anything from pork and simply prepared vegetables to chow mein.

Pork, chicken and, to a slightly lesser extent, beef are the common meats in Cantonese cuisine. The carnivorously inclined Cantonese enjoy *siu mei*, the practice of cooking meat (pork, chicken, duck, goose) unadorned, on a rotisserie spit, and embellished only on serving with rice and a sauce. Another style of meat preparation, known as *lou mei*, involves the slow-cooking of offal and entrails (gizzards, brisket, tongue) in a stock before serving with yet more hoisin or oyster sauce.

Garlic, scallion, and chives—all members of the onion family—are vital ingredients throughout China, but the simplicity of Cantonese cuisine amplifies their presence. Fuchsia Dunlop, food writer and specialist in the cuisine of Sichuan, devotes a whole chapter of her book *Every Grain of Rice* to these ingredients, showcasing both their value in Chinese cookery and the way in which meat, eggs and tofu often take a backseat to vegetable ingredients. Dishes such as stir-fried chives with pork or venison slivers, and garlic stems with bacon, are just two examples of a healthy, sustainable and authentic way of using meat: almost like a seasoning for vegetables (and

• • • •

* An essential Chinese ingredient, Shaoxing wine tastes a bit like dry sherry and is made from fermented rice. If you struggle to find it, try substituting with a dry sherry such as an Oloroso rather than a Japanese rice wine, which has an altogether different flavor.

counterintuitive to our prevailing "meat and potatoes" mentality).[*] Nevertheless, the Cantonese are very open to eating living things, as evidenced by the proverb quoted above. Their sparing attitude to meat simply serves the Chinese ethos of balanced "yin and yang" eating.

**PANTRY LIST** • scallion • sugar • salt • soy sauce • rice wine • cornstarch • vinegar • scallion oil • sesame oil • garlic • chives • ginger • Shaoxing wine • oyster sauce • hoisin sauce • chili • offal meats • fish and seafood

• • •

# • CANTONESE STEAMED FISH •

Proof that Chinese, and more specifically Cantonese, cuisine isn't as unhealthy as is commonly believed. What's more nourishing than briefly steamed fish with ginger? My choice would be bream, but any meaty white fish will do nicely—a nod to the seafood riches of the South China Sea.

### • SERVES 1–2 AS A MAIN OR 2–3 AS PART OF A SPREAD •

1 tsp rock salt
1 whole white fish such as sea bass, sea bream
    or pomfret (around 10½ oz), gutted and cleaned
2 tbsp Shaoxing wine
2 tbsp fresh ginger, finely chopped
2 tsp sesame oil
1 tbsp peanut oil
1 garlic clove, finely chopped (optional)
3 scallions, sliced lengthways
1–2 tbsp soy sauce
1½ tbsp chives and coriander to serve, chopped

• • • •

[*] It is, however, what Hugh Fearnley-Whittingstall and, more recently, Bruno Loubet have been talking about for a while: "vegevorism," to use its cringe-worthy moniker—putting vegetables at the center of a plate and garnishing with animal protein. Another example of how we can learn from Chinese dietary principles.

**1** • Salt the fish thoroughly, inside the cavity and out. Put it on a plate, pour a tablespoon of the Shaoxing wine into the cavity, and the other over the top of the fish. Place half the ginger inside the fish and the rest sprinkled over the top. Then either in a steamer or on a rack above a large pan of boiling water, steam the fish for 12 minutes. When it's done, it will be an opaque white in color.

**2** • In the last minute of steaming, heat the sesame and peanut oils together in a wok (or a frying pan) for about a minute, adding the garlic, if using, for the last 30 seconds.

**3** • Transfer the fish to a serving dish, throw the scallions over the top and drizzle with the garlicky oils and the soy sauce. Finish by sprinkling the chives and coriander over the top.

# • STIR-FRIED BOK CHOY •

This makes a great accompaniment to the steamed fish and can be whipped up in a matter of minutes. *Bok choy* means "white vegetable" in Cantonese—a little odd, perhaps, as despite its white crunchy stems, its leaves are dazzlingly bright green. The shape and thin sides of woks make them ideally suited to stir-frying a substantial volume of ingredients—if you have one then so much the better, but it is not essential. Just heat the oil for a little longer if you're using a standard frying pan and perhaps fry ingredients in smaller batches.

## • SERVES 4 •

2 tbsp peanut or vegetable oil
2 garlic cloves, finely chopped
4 heads bok choy
2 scallions, coarsely chopped
2 tbsp soy sauce
2 tbsp oyster sauce
1 red chili, deseeded and cut lengthways
    into long strips

**1** • Heat the oil in a wok until it starts to steam and add the garlic, moving it constantly to prevent burning, for 2 minutes.

**2** • Add the bok choy and scallions and, once the bok choy starts to wilt—around 2 minutes—add the sauces and two tablespoons water. Serve immediately with the strips of chili scattered over the top.

# SICHUAN

From Sichuan came the food of the common people, for, as we all know,
some of the best-known Sichuan dishes originated in street stalls.
• NICOLE MONES, *The Last Chinese Chef* •

THE SICHUAN PROVINCE (sometimes written "Szechuan") is also in the south of China, but farther inland from Guangdong. It has long been known as "the land of plenty" in recognition of its verdant scenery—high mountain plateaus of around two and a half miles in the west and a basin and plains surrounding the mighty Yangtze River—and its abundant natural resources, which support highly profitable agriculture. Rice, pork and fruit are produced here, and even vines are grown successfully around the city of Yibin, in response to an escalating demand for Chinese wine overseas.[*]

This is the home of China's best and hottest peasant food, lent its heat by a combination of chili and the Sichuan pepper. Sichuan cuisine has become popular in cosmopolitan centers in the West: simple dishes belie complex flavors and hot spice. This is food that arrests the senses, often surprisingly so for those previously unacquainted with it.

Meat was, as in Guangdong, traditionally used sparingly here and Sichuan cooks excel at producing vegetable and tofu dishes of extraordinary vibrancy, relying on intense flavors such as lots of garlic, peanuts and the eponymous Sichuan pepper. Sichuan cuisine is defined by its simplicity, its affordability and its savoriness.

That said, an absolute classic of Sichuan cuisine is twice-cooked pork (for which I have included a recipe), a belly cut of meat that is first boiled and then stir-fried with leeks or wild garlic, before being doused variously in Sichuan's chili condiments (see below) and fermented bean paste. Beef is more prevalent

• • • •

[*]In 2013, London wine merchants Berry Bros. and Rudd announced that they would be stocking four wines from China's largest and oldest winery, Changyu. Changyu is in fact in the Shandong province, not Sichuan, but this nevertheless demonstrates a mounting appetite for Chinese wine outside of Asia.

in Sichuan than in Guangdong and can be found boiled and swimming in spicy red broth or dry-fried with chili bean paste and ginger. True to form, however, nothing of the animal is wasted and the cuisine utilizes offal in many guises; for example *fuqi feipian* combines cold tripe, tongue, heart and stomach with Sichuan peppercorns, peanuts and a spice mix including star anise and ginger.

Sichuan peppers add aromatic pungency to dishes and create a numbing sensation in the mouth. Despite their name, they are not chili peppers at all but come from a prickly ash tree called Zanthoxylum. They are little red berries or seed pods and are subjected to a drying process before being added to dishes to give a powerful but cleansing experience to the eater. This feeling is known as *ma* in Chinese and is complimented by *la*, the spicy heat lent to food by capsicum chili peppers. The two are often a duo in local dishes such as the "numbing spicy" *mala* sauce of Sichuan pepper, chili, spices and oil that is eaten with barbecued meats. Sichuan pepper is also one of the five spices in the Chinese five-spice mix (see page 197).

Chili defines the food of Sichuan and the province's chili peppers can be used in a number of ways: dried and whole (known as "facing heaven" because their stalk "hats" look to the sky), in the form of a fermented chili paste, or infused into oil. The dried peppers are often chopped into ½-inch-squared chunks and thrown in just like that. I remember mindlessly popping one into my mouth along with some black beans at Soho's Bar Shu—not quite realizing what it was—and regretting it for the rest of the meal. A certain amount of caution is useful when eating Sichuan food for the first time.

Chili is eaten abundantly and with everything—asparagus and mushrooms; string beans; spiced or smoked tofu; Malabar spinach and cucumber; broad beans and soybeans, not to mention noodles and rice—all just a few examples of the vegetarian ingredients that Sichuan cooks adorn with their cocktail of "big" ingredients—chili, garlic, peanuts. Chairman Mao even purportedly had chili cooked into his bread, famously asserting to a Russian diplomat that "you can't be a revolutionary if you don't eat chillies."

Sichuanese "red oil" wontons put a regional spin on the wonton, a filled, deep-fried dough ball found all over China.* They also have a local name, "folded arms," because of the distinctive shape in which the dough is folded

• • • •

*Wontons are made with a flour- and egg-based dough, spread into a square-shaped wrapper that sits in the palm of the cook's hand. The center is then filled with (most commonly) pork, though the addition of leek is popular in the north, as is a combination of shrimp and pork in Guangdong. Wonton soup is a popular way of serving them, but they can alternatively be deep-fried and dipped into a sauce. "Red oil" wontons are unique to Sichuan.

into dumplings, perhaps reflecting the posture of Sichuanese people bracing themselves against the region's cold winters. They are typically stuffed with seasoned pork, their Sichuan character given via a red dressing of chili oil, garlic, scallions, and soy sauce or tamari.[*]

Glutinous rice balls, or *tang yuan*, are ultra local to Chengdu, the capital of Sichuan. Long-grain rice is soaked for several days before being ground down into a dough or damp flour, which is rolled into balls. These are then stuffed with sesame seeds, sugar and a fat base (lard or coconut oil) and boiled for a short time before being served with a dip of more sweetened sesame. They are sometimes added to a sweet rice soup that, according to Fuchsia Dunlop, has traditionally been given to Sichuan's women after childbirth—doubtless a quick and effective source of energy-giving glucose.

Shaoxing wine, a fermented rice wine, is not actually native either to Sichuan or Guangdong but has found a home in the cuisine of both. It is a key ingredient in the marinade for "drunk" meat dishes, but you also find it fairly ubiquitously in recipes demanding smaller amounts. Though the fermentation adds a more complex note, the effects of adding Shaoxing wine are not unlike those you get with sherry—it provides a sweet, rich alcohol kick.

As poor man's food goes, I don't feel too sorry for the Sichuanese. Their spectrum of bold flavors and punchy dishes testifies to the fact that a little can go a long way if you have the right resources. This is the kind of food that reminds you you're alive: mouth-stinging shots of heat and strong flavors that really make your palate work. Invest in some classic Chinese condiments—oyster sauce, tamari, Shaoxing wine—and, of course, some Sichuan peppers and transform even the least prepossessing of vegetables into a delicacy fit for a king, albeit one inspired by the "common people."

**PANTRY LIST** • sichuan pepper (whole and ground) • chili • tamari • scallions • bean sprouts • Shaoxing wine • sesame seeds • peanuts • tofu • oyster sauce

• • • •

[*]Tamari is a concentrated soy sauce, made with less wheat than regular soy sauce. This creates intensity of flavor and makes it a good dipping sauce.

# • TWICE-COOKED PORK •

A Sichuan classic, using the holy trinity of regional fermented pastes—chili bean, sweet bean and fermented black bean, all of which can be found easily online or in Chinese shops. As its name suggests, the belly pork is cooked twice for this recipe—first boiled in salted water until tender, left to cool and firm up, then sliced and stir-fried with the bean pastes until a little crispy at the edges. Serve with rice and my stir-fried green beans.

## • SERVES 2–4 •

14 oz belly pork (boneless and with rind removed)
2 tbsp vegetable or peanut oil
2 tbsp chili bean paste
2 tsp sweet bean paste
2 tsp fermented black bean paste (or miso paste will do)
2 tbsp soy sauce
2 tsp sugar
6 baby leeks or 12 scallions, sliced

**1** • Bring a pan of water to the boil, reduce to a simmer and add the pork. It needs to be cooked through, which will take 20–25 minutes. Remove the meat and let it cool, in the fridge, for an hour or two.
**2** • Cut the pork into pieces—½- to 1-inch slices are ideal. Heat the oil in a wok or large frying pan and stir-fry the pork slices over medium to high heat for 4 minutes until they are brown and crisp on both sides.
**3** • Remove pork from the pan, add the chili bean paste so that the oil turns red, then add the sweet bean and fermented black bean pastes. Return the meat to the pan and mix in the soy sauce and sugar. Add the leeks or scallions and stir-fry for another minute before serving.

# • STIR-FRIED GREEN BEANS •

You could serve these as an accompaniment to almost any of the pork and fish dishes I've included in the book, but I like them best with plain rice, the spicy Sichuan sauce smothered over each grain. Enjoy them with tea to offset the intense heat—my favorite is jasmine.

## • SERVES 4 •

1 lb green beans
2 tbsp peanuts, coarsely chopped
2 tbsp vegetable oil
6 dried red chilies, cut into ¾-inch pieces
¼ tsp Sichuan pepper
4 garlic cloves, very finely chopped
½-inch piece ginger, very finely chopped
3 scallions, sliced

FOR THE SAUCE
2 tsp Shaoxing wine
2 tsp chili bean sauce
1 tsp sesame oil
1 tsp sugar
pinch salt

**1** • You need to start with dry beans, so carefully pat them dry after rinsing. Cut each bean into two or three (depending on length).
**2** • Stir together all the ingredients for the sauce until the sugar has dissolved; set aside.
**3** • Toast the peanuts in a dry pan over medium heat until fragrant and turning brown; set aside.
**4** • Heat a wok on a high flame for a couple of minutes, then add the vegetable oil. Stir-fry the beans for about 5 minutes, until they start to darken and blister. Then set aside on paper towels, to drain off the excess oil.
**5** • Discard all the oil except for a tablespoon's worth, then stir-fry the chilies, Sichuan pepper, garlic, ginger and scallions for 30 seconds. Add the sauce, the beans and the peanuts. Stir-fry for another minute or so before serving immediately.

# SOYBEANS

...

Soybeans originated in East Asia and to this day they play a starring role in the cuisines of China, Japan, Korea and Southeast Asian countries, where they feature in whole form (edamame, for example) and in almost endless variations and by-products. Tofu and soybean paste, miso and *natto* in Japan (see page 256), *doenjang* and *ganjang* (see page 250) in Korea, not to mention the omnipresent soy sauce, are all quintessentially Asian ingredients and condiments derived from the humble soybean.

Nowadays, the Americas (particularly Argentina, Brazil and the United States) are the largest producers of soybeans. As well as being exported to Asia, they are used locally in the production of milk, oil and soybean meal. Soybeans are one of the world's most concentrated sources of protein—in theory a supremely healthy and less environmentally damaging alternative to meat. However, the scale on which they are now grown has created significant controversy. Genetic modification of American soy crops has compromised the reputation of soybean-derived products in recent years. In South America their cultivation is linked to deforestation, soil erosion, the loss of biodiversity and the destruction of traditional ways of life. Perhaps not such a good alternative after all.

...

# KOREA

Gosh but there's a lot of admin with Korean food. Everything has to be dredged
or dipped and rolled and dipped again. Fiddle here. Turn there. Flip this.
• JAY RAYNER, *Observer Magazine* •

THERE'S NO DOUBT about it, Korean food makes you
work hard. Whenever I go to a Korean restaurant, I am
struck by just the same thing Jay Rayner was: there's a
huge amount of preamble to eating from the Korean
table. One of the pillars of Korean cuisine is *ssam*,* the
custom of wrapping rice, *banchan* (side dishes) and
condiments in a leaf (either lettuce, seaweed, cabbage
or pumpkin). Filling, rolling and readying your lettuce
leaf for consumption can feel arduous, especially
when you're hungry, but luckily the final result boasts
an explosion of exotic flavors that make all the effort worthwhile.

Though clearly drawing on a similar culinary heritage as other parts of
East Asia—the flavors of soy sauce, sesame oil, chili and fermented ingredients spring to mind—there is a singularity to Korean food that belies its
fraught history of subjugation, first at the hands of Chinese and Japanese
colonizers and subsequently in the Cold War spat between the United States
and Russia, which has resulted in the division of the Korean peninsula into
two mutually hostile states. Korean food is almost a metaphor for the way
the country has absorbed influences while resisting domination. I like to
imagine Korea as the leaf for wrapping, the location and canvas for powerful
flavors and full textures—China might be the rice, Japan the kimchi, Russia
some pickled garlic and America some grilled meat.

During the occupation by Japan, Koreans were kept in a state of poverty.
Meals consisted of little more than plain rice and other, even cheaper, grains;
enough to keep people fed and functional but fundamentally unsatisfied. In
1945, Japanese rule gave way to the Korean and Cold Wars consecutively. Nutrition in what became North Korea continued to be totally inadequate. Ameri-

••••

*A word that fans of the Korean-American chef David Chang might recognize from one of his New
York restaurants, the Momofuku Ssäm Bar.

can journalist Barbara Demick's *Nothing to Envy* is an examination of everyday life in the country in the 1990s. "At mealtimes, the women would huddle together over a low wooden table near the kitchen, eating cornmeal, which was cheaper and less nutritious than rice, the preferred staple." Demick draws attention to the discrepancy between the landscapes not just of North Korea and the surrounding countries of Southeast Asia, but also its South Korean counterpart. "The lush green patchwork of the rice paddies so characteristic of the Asian countryside can be seen only during a few months of the summer rainy season." We read of people who resort to eating tree bark. Insufficient, and as bleak as the fading landscape, the food eaten in North Korea for much of the twentieth century was so poor that malnutrition was endemic.

South Korea, on the other hand, experienced a boom in exciting new flavors and food technology. All sorts of varied ingredients became readily available, not least an abundance of meat, which started to be farmed on a grand scale. Meat consumption rose, rice consumption fell, Chinese noodles and American bread began to be imported. A spectrum of edible delicacies became accessible but, true to form, rather than simply following the American food model in the 1960s and '70s—to which Britain fell prey, abandoning its own national cuisine in favor of convenience—South Korea built on the dynastic royal court cuisine that predated Japanese occupation. *Bulgogi* restaurants, eateries serving marinated and grilled meat, once again rose to prominence, frequented by a new South Korean middle class. The *ssam*-style eating culture now popular both at home and all over the world is based on the *bulgogi*—a fiercely hot metal grill in the center of the table on which marinated beef, chicken, pork and fish is blasted before being wrapped, alongside rice and fermented condiments, in a humble lettuce leaf.

Before grilling, *bulgogi* meats are marinated in sesame oil, sugar, soy sauce and garlic. Standard cuts of meat include grilled short ribs, known as *galbi*, which are soaked in a similar marinade with the addition of chili and *ganjang* (fermented soy beans) and pork belly, or *samgyeopsal*, which looks like thick cuts of bacon. Two meat dishes very particular to Korea are *soondae*, boiled blood sausage (a membrane of pig intestine stuffed with pork blood and cellophane noodles—eat it at your peril—I'll pass, thanks) and, to my mind more appetizingly, *hobak ori* or "pumpkin duck," quite literally gamy smoked duck served inside a sweet squash.

Given the long Pacific coastline, fish such as mackerel and pike are key Korean ingredients, usually eaten salted and grilled whole on a smoking barbecue. Historically fish was an important source of protein, particularly in

South Korea, while, as we've seen elsewhere, rich red meats were reserved for the wealthy. (This explains why the new accessibility of meat in the 1970s was such a novelty, and why its regular consumption became a status symbol for a burgeoning middle class.) As is the case elsewhere in Asia, a lot of fish is dried and then fermented—particularly anchovies and shrimps, which together with the intestines of larger fish, make a seasoning known as *jeotgal*, used to flavor kimchi, soups, stews and *soondae* blood sausages.

The technique of fermentation is rife across Asia. All the principle agents of umami—soy, shrimp paste, and so on—are created by this natural process of turning sugar into acid to create an intriguing sour flavor. Fermented food products have achieved a status near to super food in recent years. The lactobacilli (or "healthy bacteria") produced during the process help to keep the gut in good working order, thereby battling obesity and digestive complaints. (And fermented food also tastes great, obviously.)

The Koreans have taken fermentation to a whole new level with their national dish, kimchi. There are up to two hundred varieties, depending on the region and the time of year, but they usually have a base of white (*napa*) cabbage or daikon radish and varying degrees of brine, chili, scallion, herbs, salted fish such as anchovy or shrimp and sometimes even pear juice. Kimchi is a true Korean staple, eaten with almost every meal and the most important *banchan* (side dish) on the Korean table, kick-starting the palate and balancing the flavors of grilled meat and crunchy raw vegetables. (TV cook Gizzi Erskine loves kimchi so much that she named her kitten after it . . .)

Several other pillars of Korean cuisine also rely on fermentation, including *doenjang* (fermented bean paste) and *gochujang* (fermented red chili paste), which are used both as relishes and central ingredients in their own right. *Doenjang* soup (*doenjang jjigae*) is a popular accompaniment to most meals (like miso in Japan), a cheap and simple broth of *doenjang* paste watered down and embellished with vegetables and tofu. The pop star Psy, who soared to fame in 2012 with his single "Gangnam Style" about life in the Seoul ghetto of Gangnam, poked fun at "*doenjang* girls"—a Korean stereotype of the woman of limited means who eats the soup at home so she can afford to appear flashy in public—in his music video. *Gochujang*, another fermented condiment of sticky rice, chili and soy beans, makes for a well-loved combination with *tteok*, or Korean rice cakes, starchy oblongs very different from the rice cake disks we know in the West. Combining these two fermented sauces of *gochujang* and *doenjang*, *ssamjang* is the classic sauce with which to top *ssam* leaves before loading with meat, fish, rice and vegetables.

*Gochujang* might also be used to garnish noodles, which often come in the form of *naengmyeon*, a popular street food sold by *pojangmachas* (street hawkers) and, increasingly, specialized fast-food outlets. *Naengmyeon* are cold buckwheat noodles served in a cold meat broth, topped with boiled egg, scallion, sliced pear and cucumber and slices of beef. Alternatively, *japchae* are sweet-potato noodles stir-fried with vegetables such as mushrooms and carrots, beef, soy and chili. They are often served with rice.

*Bibimbap* is probably the best-known incarnation of rice in Korea, meaning simply "mixed rice." This is, in essence, Korea's answer to *polow, Se* or paella, variations of which can be found all over the world, blending rice with meat, vegetables and the very Korean addition of fermented red chili paste. Unlike its foreign equivalents, however, *bibimbap* arrives in front of the diner unblended—a bowl of rice topped with a colorful mosaic of different toppings to mix and match according to taste. Porridges and rice cakes are also popular. This isn't porridge as we know it, but a kind of rice-based gruel with chicken, garlic and scallions, typically served without spice, called *dakjuk*.

To those unacquainted with Korean cuisine, novelty awaits. Both in the "fiddle" of preparing your first few *ssam* wraps and the flavors each stuffed leaf delivers. When you first try it, a lone piece of kimchi pickled cabbage might make you wince, but, like other Asian cuisines (namely those of China and Japan), Korean food emphasizes balance: a leaf, a hunk of grilled beef, a sprinkle of white rice, a slice of raw daikon, some kimchi and a lick of *ssamjang* in equilibrium can make this a deeply satisfying, delicious and healthy way to eat. Despite the "admin" of eating Korean to which Jay Rayner referred, this is the hardest you'll have to work for Korean food . . . the eating of it, I've discovered, is remarkably easy.

**PANTRY LIST** • *doenjang* (fermented bean paste) • ginger • chili flakes and *gochujang* (fermented red chili paste) • cabbage • daikon • *tteok* (Korean rice cakes) • *japchae* (sweet potato noodles) • egg • pear • *jeotgal* (fermented fish seasoning)

◆ ◆ ◆

# • KIMCHI •

Kimchi splits opinion, but I love its fizzy, fermented flavor. Enjoy on its own or as an integral part of a Korean spread. Chinese cabbage is tight-leaved and, in shape and texture, looks like a cross between a Savoy cabbage and a cos lettuce, but whiter. It can be found in most supermarkets. Daikon, sometimes known as *mooli*, look like white carrots and have a texture not unlike that of radishes. Again, you should be able to find them in larger supermarkets or an Asian supermarket.

## • SERVES 4–6 •

1 head Chinese cabbage
4 tbsp table salt
6 garlic cloves, very finely chopped
¾-inch piece ginger, very finely chopped
1 tsp sugar
2 tbsp fish sauce
2–4 tbsp chili flakes (preferably Korean *gochugaru*),
    or to taste
2 daikon, peeled and cut into matchsticks
4 scallions, cut into 1-inch pieces

1 • Cut the cabbage into quarters, each quarter into 1-inch pieces, and then, in a bowl, rub the salt into each piece to soften the leaves. Cover with water, then place a large plate over the top and put something heavy on the plate, to compress the cabbage. Leave for 2–3 hours.

2 • Next, you'll need to rinse the cabbage of all the salt. Thoroughly. Do so two or three times and let the water drain off for a good 10 minutes.

3 • Pound the garlic, ginger, sugar, fish sauce and chili flakes in a mortar and pestle. Combine this with the cabbage, daikon and scallions, then stuff into a sterilized jar. Push down firmly until the vegetables are covered by the cabbage's residual brine.

4 • Let the kimchi ferment at room temperature for 4 or 5 days. Keep checking it, pushing the cabbage mixture down to keep it submerged. After 4 of 5 days it should be ready to eat—at which point keep it in the fridge until you are ready to indulge in a Korean feast.

# • BEEF BULGOGI •

This Korean "fire meat" (the literal translation) consists of thin strips of rib-eye steak, typically marinated and barbecued, though it is also found fried. Provided you prepare it in advance and invest in good-quality steak, it's relatively undemanding. You could serve it with plain boiled rice, kimchi and an array of Korean sauces such as *gochujang*, or you could ditch the rice and shove it all into a baguette for a makeshift Korean answer to the Vietnamese *banh mi*.

## • SERVES 4 •

3 tbsp soy sauce
1 tbsp sesame oil
2 garlic cloves, very finely chopped
1 tbsp superfine sugar
2 tbsp sesame seeds, toasted
½ tsp salt
1 tsp freshly ground black pepper
1 lb rib-eye steak, fat removed and cut into thin strips
2 scallions, sliced into ¾-inch pieces
1 carrot, sliced into thin batons
1 white onion, finely sliced into half-moons

**1 •** Take a sturdy, sealable freezer bag and place it inside a bowl or jug. Pour the soy, sesame oil, garlic, sugar, toasted sesame seeds, salt and pepper into the bag and seal. Shake vigorously to make sure the sugar is dissolved.

**2 •** Drop the beef, scallions, carrot and onion into the bag, seal it and rub the marinade all over the meat from the outside. Place in the fridge for at least 4 hours, but preferably overnight.

**3 •** To barbecue, drain and discard the marinade and seal the strips of beef and carrot and the onions inside a packet of aluminum foil. Cook for 15–20 minutes. Alternatively, sauté in a little vegetable or peanut oil over medium heat for 3–5 minutes, until the beef starts to go crispy.

# JAPAN

I'd rather have dumplings than flowers.
• JAPANESE PROVERB •

ETHEREAL IMAGES OF Kyoto's cherry trees in blossom, with their twisted, pink-clouded hanging branches, are quintessentially Japanese. They feature in art and film alike, from *shin hanga* woodcut prints to the film adaptation of Haruki Murakami's novel *Norwegian Wood*. On a metaphorical level, our perception of Japan is just as ornate; it feels like a nation of intricacies—of delicacy in volume—from the social customs of its people to innovations in electronics, animation and, in food, sushi.

Traditional foodstuffs don't come much more intricate than sushi. Restaurants where uniform *maki* rolls line up like monochrome armies and slabs of *nigiri*—raw salmon lounging across bricks of sticky white rice—seduce us not only because sushi is so delicious, but because it is so completely and beautifully other. The surgical precision with which it is made—elaborate structures from which soft-shell crab poke deep-fried claws; the little jewels of luminous *tobiko* (flying fish roe); and all the gear with which to eat it—from chopsticks to piles of pickled ginger and wasabi paste to pierce your palate—is mesmerizing.

So many of the cuisines we consider very different from our own still use the basic techniques and ingredients with which we are familiar—stews containing meat, pulses and vegetables are sometimes only distinguished by the local ingredients and seasonings applied, from Spain all the way to India. But sushi is an absolute departure from Western cooking, a novelty. It might contain familiar ingredients—rice, fish, vegetables—but its assembly shakes up our understanding of how to treat these items. Raw fish? Rice wrapped in dried sheets of seaweed?

Although sushi has now been exported all over the world, it remains semi-shrouded in mystery—because how many of us know how to make it? Training to be an *itamae*, or sushi chef, can take decades, and chefs aiming to make it in the sushi business literally dedicate their lives to the art of it.

This is touched on in 2011's *Jiro Dreams of Sushi*, a documentary about the legendary Tokyo sushi restaurant Sukiyabashi Jiro and its octogenarian chef patron. The restaurant's shrimp dealer is quoted, saying, "When you work at a place like Jiro's, you are committing to a trade for life."

In any cuisine, it is as much the arrangement of ingredients as the ingredients themselves that form dietary conventions. Perhaps because Japanese food in the West typically commands a hefty price tag, Japan's international reputation for edible intricacies has been amplified above the food of its normal working people. True to the proverb with which I started, though, much of Japan's cuisine is, as we will see, more practical than its more aesthetic attributes would suggest. Dumplings rather than flowers.

Novel and infinitely marketable, sushi is usually our first culinary association with Japan. The thing is, the Japanese don't eat it very often, and if you've been lucky enough to visit, you'll know that it's noodles and rice that make up the staple diet of most Japanese people. The most traditional arrangement of a Japanese meal is "one soup, three sides," comprising a bowl of soup (usually miso, complete with tofu dice and seaweed lurking at the bottom, to be eaten once the eater has finished slurping), and three side dishes, one of which is always a bowl of white rice (*gohan*), pickles (*tsukemono*) and an *okazu*, a dish that might be fish-based (such as sashimi), meat or vegetarian.

Buddhism prohibited the consumption of meat from four-legged animals until as recently as 150 years ago, so the Japanese became resourceful with their seasonal vegetables and the plentiful seafood surrounding their island nation. The Japanese attitude to meat resembles what scientists increasingly endorse in the West—eat less meat of better quality. It is eaten, but not every day. The lesser importance of meat in comparison to its place on Western tables is reflected in Japanese table settings. Eaters sit with their chopsticks immediately before them and with a bowl of soup and another of rice closest to hand. Any meat dish will be positioned to their far right, next to the pickles on the left. (There is a delightful geometry to the Japanese table setting, which you can see on a more miniature scale in bento boxes. "Bento," meaning "convenient," condenses the layout of the Japanese table into a cute packed box of rice, pickles, meat or fish and, if freshly served, some soup.)

The taboos that existed around meat help to explain why Japanese cuisine is arguably less varied than that of its Asian cousins such as China, Thailand and India. Less meat called for smaller quantities of spices, and fewer varieties of them. Flavorings are relatively minimal in Japan, limited to garlic, ginger (in myriad forms: root, salt-pickled, vinegar-pickled and shoots), some chili and cloves, *yuzu* (a round yellow citrus fruit used for

sushi marinades and salad dressings), mirin (a sweet rice wine used to flavor fish and teriyaki sauces) and wasabi (a hot green paste not unlike horseradish). Even curry, now an institution in Japan (in the form of dishes like
chicken *katsu* curry), only arrived in the late nineteenth century, introduced
by the British. But in contrast to the meticulous blends of spices involved in
making an Indian curry, Japanese curry*—eaten with rice, *udon* or wrapped
in a sealed piece of dough—simply combines garlic and curry powder.

Traditionally, cows were kept for plowing, so even dairy is not widely
found in Japan. The Japanese diet was almost entirely free of meat, butter
or cheese until the nineteenth century, and consequently the Japanese are
not acclimatized to the rich, heavy foods we know well. Vegetable, sunflower
and sesame oils are the fat bases of choice for frying—the first two for deep-
fried dishes like tempura and the latter for shallow frying the likes of egg
pancakes, known as *okonomiyaki*.†

Japanese cuisine prizes a balance of colors and flavors. There are five of
each—red, yellow, green, black and white, and sweet, sour, bitter, salty and
umami respectively (some would add hot or spicy to the latter list). The color
of a food might reflect how it has been cooked—black might mean dried seaweed or charred eggplant, for example, or red could just as easily be a *katsu*
curry as some beads of *tobiko*. Balancing these on a table spread or in a bento
box appeals to the Japanese appetite for aesthetic intricacy as much as dietary equilibrium.

When it comes to flavor, the Japanese pride themselves on the discovery
of umami.‡ This is perhaps the single most important element of Japanese
cuisine, a glutamate known as the fifth of the five basic tastes, which, although now well established, remains notoriously more difficult to define
than sweet, sour, salty and bitter. Umami is a savory flavor that stimulates
receptors at the back of the mouth and though it is by no means exclusive
to Japan, is perhaps harnessed more self-consciously in Japanese cuisine
than others. There is a sense of ownership about the flavor. Fermented soy-

• • • •

*Katsu curry has become very popular in the West, particularly when made with chicken. The
meat is breaded, fried and served with rice and Japanese curry sauce.

†*Okonomiyaki* are delicious Japanese pancakes cooked on hot plates, from the Kansai and Hiroshima
regions of the country. Their batter is made from eggs, dashi, shredded cabbage and flour, after which
meat, seafood or tofu is added during the cooking process. *Okonomiyaki* are topped with fish flakes,
seaweed, pickled ginger or mayonnaise to serve.

‡Umami was discovered in 1908 by Professor Kikune Ikeda at Tokyo Imperial University, so Japan
is regarded as its birthplace. Ingredients rich in umami include green tea, vegetables, aged cheeses
like Parmesan, seafood and fish—particularly anchovies.

beans are powerful agents of umami, for example, and are used to make soy sauce, miso (a paste of fermented soy beans) and *natto* (whole fermented soy beans), all of which feature heavily as condiments and ingredients in Japanese dishes. Tofu is also made from the processed curd of soybeans and is a crucial source of protein in the Japanese diet.

Japanese broths are very rich in umami, the basis for which is dashi, a kind of concentrated umami water not unlike *garum* (the anchovy-based seasoning used in Ancient Rome. Essentially a stock made from *iriko* (anchovy) and fermented bonito flakes (skipjack tuna—though sometimes mackerel, sardines or kelp seaweed are also added), dashi simultaneously adds flavor to dishes and releases it from other ingredients such as meat, fish, eggs and noodles. Junya Yamasaki is head chef at Koya, London's first restaurant devoted to *udon* noodle broths—a dish eaten every day, several times a day, in much of rural Japan. He says that dashi is now used by chefs all over the world but remains absolutely "at the heart of food in Japan. For example, you differentiate noodle restaurants less by their noodles—which don't vary very much—but by their *dashi*." Junya's own dashi at Koya is as pure as it comes, with no added seaweed, shiitake or vegetables; it is a simple but intense fish broth. It's no wonder that he describes good dashi as "an art."

Noodles are the food of workingmen and make for soups that are absolutely integral to the Japanese diet. These can be hot—hot broth with hot noodles—or cold, or a refreshing combination of cold noodles dipped in hot broth. These soups, into which ingredients such as duck, prawn, seaweed or mushroom might be mixed, are Japanese fast food—quickly slurped standing up or on the go. (Doesn't this put American fast food to shame?) In Junya's words, "this is not food you linger over, it is labourer's food. It is made by the truckload and it is inexpensive both to produce and to buy." He explains the broad differences between broths eaten across Japan. While broths in the West are lighter, clear and eaten with *udon* noodles (the fat, white, wormlike variety made with wheat flour), the whiter broths of the East, often made with pigs' feet, are more likely to use soba (thinner noodles made from buckwheat).

Koya specializes in *udon* over soba or any other variety of noodle partly because Junya is from western Japan but, more important, because *udon* have become something of a cult food trend in the last ten years.[*] The most famous variety, known as Sanuki *udon* from the Kagawa prefecture (on Japan's fourth-

• • • •

[*] *Udon* fever reached such a crescendo that, in 2006, a movie was made titled just that—*Udon*. Other movies with noodle-based narratives include 2008's *The Ramen Girl*, in which Brittany Murphy trains to become a ramen chef, and *Tampopo* (1985), set in a family-run noodle shop and dubbed the first "ramen western." Spaghetti Westerns head east . . .

largest island, Shikoku) has risen in profile since the arrival of Hanamaru—the first chain restaurant to take *udon* broths nationwide in Japan. While on the one hand Hanamaru has commercialized this poor man's meal, they've also created an almost religious national appetite for *udon* in all its forms. At the end of every April, hordes of *udon* anoraks descend on Kagawa for a Sanuki *udon* pilgrimage, looking for the best, nichest, weirdest noodle broths. "It's quite extraordinary," says Junya. "There are over seven hundred restaurants in Kagawa and three hundred in the capital of Tamakatsu alone. People will queue for miles down the road for some of them, and each specializes in something different." Some are experts in hot dashi broths with hot noodles, others with cold noodles, some without a dashi at all.

Ramen, another kind of noodle soup using Chinese wheat noodles that originated with the Chinese community living in Japan in the early twentieth century, is more elaborate than its simple *udon* counterpart. Noodles swim in a rich stock and are decorated with a mosaic of toppings that can be blended or eaten separately by the eater. The *tonkotsu* ramen, for example, has a thick and milky broth made by hours of boiling pork bones. It is then topped with cuts of meat such as pork belly, some pickled ginger and possibly marinated boiled eggs* before serving. Miso ramen bases its broth stock on miso, unsurprisingly, but this is often combined with meat stocks as well. Vegetables, cuts of meat and sesame seeds might be used to garnish it. Of course, there are infinite variations on how to serve and garnish a ramen broth—despite its simplicity, it's always a varied and novel eating experience.

The Japanese word for "cuisine" is *ryori*, the sum of which is "*ryo*"—meaning a measured thing—and "*ri*," which means "reason." Implicit in the word *ryori* is the idea of sensibly curating custom-made meals for the recipients of your cooking. It sounds simple—but then, that's what healthy eating is. Low in fat, low in meat and rich in produce sustainably farmed and found locally†—more dumplings than flowers—we in the West would do well to follow a diet modeled on Japanese cuisine. In food as much as any other facet of Japan's culture, the words of Canadian novelist William Gibson ring true: "Japan is the global imagination's default setting for the future."‡

• • • •

*Onsen tamago* are another form in which the Japanese enjoy eggs. Named for the *onsen* hot water springs in which they were originally cooked, *onsen tamago* are poached in their shells, which leaves the yolks runny and the egg white milky yet firm. They are enjoyed with chopped scallions and dashi or soy sauce.

†The irony here is that, according to Koya's Junya, "the food we eat in Japan is not from Japan, even the rice. Ninety-nine percent of the flour we use for *udon* comes from Australia."

‡From an interview in the *Observer*.

**PANTRY LIST** • miso • pickled vegetables (*tsukemono*) • ginger (pickled and fresh) • mirin • wasabi • dashi • *natto* • *udon* noodles • soba noodles • tofu

• • •

## • BEGINNER'S UDON •

This simple noodle soup is a haiku to Vietnam's epic poem, the *pho*. It can be thrown together in half an hour, a delicious hit of umami. There's no fat whatsoever here save for a tablespoon of vegetable oil in which to fry the (optional) tofu. *Ichiban dashi* is a simple dashi recipe to induct you into *udon* soup making. Freezing dashi is a point of contention—some argue it compromises the flavor but I personally like to have it on hand. Slurp the soup from the bowl (a great excuse to eat noisily) then shovel the noodles into your mouth with chopsticks.

### • SERVES 4 •

FOR THE DASHI (MAKES 3½–4 CUPS)
¾ oz kombu (dried kelp) or wakame seaweed
½ oz *katsuo bushi* (dried bonito flakes)

FOR THE UDON
2 x 7-oz packages *udon* noodles
1 tbsp vegetable oil
7 oz tofu, cut into ½- to ¾-inch square pieces
3½ cups dashi (see above)
2 tbsp soy sauce
1 tbsp mirin
2 tsp sugar
6–7 scallions, finely sliced

**1** • To make the dashi, soak the kombu in a pan with 4 cups of water, for 20 minutes. Place over medium heat and, just as the water is starting to boil, remove from the heat and scatter in the *katsuo bushi*.
**2** • Return to the heat and boil for 3–4 minutes, by which time the *katsuo bushi* will have sunk to the bottom of the pan, then strain through a cheesecloth, muslin or a

coffee filter. The resulting liquid can be used immediately or will keep in the fridge for a few days.

**3** • Cook the *udon* as instructed on the package, taking care not to overcook. Drain, rinse in cold water and set aside.

**4** • Heat the vegetable oil over medium heat and sauté the tofu for 5–6 minutes, until it acquires a golden brown color on all sides. Set aside.

**5** • Reheat the dashi in a pan and add the soy sauce, mirin and sugar. Bring to the boil, then reduce the heat. Add the *udon* and simmer for 2 minutes. Serve topped with the scallions and tofu.

# • PAN-FRIED SALMON WITH MISO-MAYONNAISE DIPPING SAUCE •

Japanese mayonnaise is generally apple or rice vinegar based, the most famous being Kewpie, a brand that specializes in thick, creamy Japanese mayo made from egg yolks and a blend of malt and apple cider vinegar. Combining this mayonnaise with white miso paste (both available online) produces a dipping sauce or condiment not unlike "Dijonnaise" (European mayonnaise and Dijon mustard), a creamy indulgence with a peppery, umami buzz. It makes a fantastic sauce for salmon steaks fried simply in some oil, soy and lemon—a dish I like to accompany with the soused spinach recipe (see page 263). If you can't find Kewpie mayo, try making your own version by adding two tablespoons of rice vinegar and one tablespoon of superfine sugar to your regular mayonnaise and mixing well.

## • SERVES 4 •

4 salmon steaks or fillets (5 oz each)
2½–3½ tsp table salt
3 tbsp Kewpie (or other Japanese
    mayonnaise, or your own version—see above)
2 tbsp white (or brown) miso paste
4 tbsp vegetable oil
1 tbsp soy sauce
juice of ½ lemon
½ lemon, cut into 4 wedges

**1** • Lay the salmon on a chopping board lightly scattered with salt. Sprinkle a layer of salt on the side facing upward. Let sit for up to an hour.

**2** • Combine the mayonnaise and the miso paste thoroughly; set aside.

**3** • Heat the oil in a large frying pan over high heat and fry the salmon steaks for 3–4 minutes on each side. Add the soy sauce and lemon juice so it bubbles and becomes fragrant. After 5–6 minutes of frying the salmon, remove from the pan and plate up.

**4** • Serve with a dollop of the miso mayonnaise on the side, a wedge of lemon and some soused spinach (recipe follows).

## • SOUSED SPINACH SALAD •

Cold, wilted spinach drenched in the Japanese flavors of mirin, soy and dashi makes a delicious accompaniment to meat, fish and even plain boiled rice. Prepare this in advance to have it at the ready. One thing: my dashi alternative here is a massive cheat and, I hasten to add, will not achieve the kind of complexity you get with authentic dashi. It's a basic vegetable stock enhanced with a kick of umami from the fish sauce. If I'm in a hurry, it suffices. Apologies to dashi purists.

### • SERVES 4 •

7 oz fresh spinach, washed and trimmed
1 cup dashi (see page 261) or 1 cup vegetable
    stock with 1 tsp fish sauce
1 tsp mirin
1 tbsp soy sauce
pinch salt

**1** • Wilt the spinach in a splash of water over medium heat for 2–3 minutes. You want it to be completely wilted but not to have lost its vibrant color. Keep moving the leaves from the bottom of the pan to the top, making way for fresh leaves to be subjected to the heat. Remove from the heat, chop into chunky 2-inch lengths, place in a colander over a bowl to drain and set aside.

**2** • Bring the dashi (or stock and fish sauce mixture) to a boil, then reduce the heat to a simmer. Now add the mirin, soy sauce and salt and simmer for another 2 minutes. Remove from the heat and place in a bowl inside a bowl of ice cubes to force cool it.

**3** • Add the spinach to this mixture and refrigerate for 5–6 hours. Serve alongside the pan-fried salmon, miso mayonnaise and boiled rice.

# AFR

# ICA

# HOT STUFF

## THE INTERNATIONAL
## CHILI PEPPER

...

Chilies have traveled all over the world and play an integral role in countless modern cuisines from Ethiopia to West Africa (and the West African disapora that traveled to the New World) and from India to Europe. They were most likely spread by the Portuguese (who colonized pockets of the East, like Macao and Goa), the first nation to access Asia by looping around Africa by sea.

This inclusion of the chili in so many international cuisines is relatively recent—within the last five hundred years. Originating in South and Central America, they were discovered by Christopher Columbus on his arrival in the New World in the late fifteenth century and quickly spread to Europe. Their exact New World provenance is contested; opinion appears to be split between Mexico and Peru, and they play an important role in both of these cuisines—albeit in the form of different varietals. A few of these are detailed here, each expressing the *terroirs* and taste buds of the cuisine to which they have become linked—like the Kashmiri Chili of Kashmir, and the *pul biber* of Turkey.

**CARIBBEAN**
Scotch Bonnet

**MEXICO**
Habanero
Jalapeño
Chipotle

**PERU**
Aji Amarillo
Aji Panca

**FRENCH GUIANA**
Cayenne Pepper

**ITALY**
Capsichina

**AFRICA**
Piri Piri Chili

**THE MIDDLE EAST**
Pul Biber

**NORTH INDIA**
Kashmiri Chili

**SOUTH AMERICA**
Rocoto Chili

**SOUTH INDIA**
Byadagi Chili

## • KASHMIRI CHILI (KASHMIR, NORTH INDIA) •

Beautiful deep red color, mild heat. Kashmiri chilies add a lot of flavor but not too much spice, making for feel-good dishes. Try using semi-dried Kashmiri chilies, which you re-hydrate in water, for butter chicken, *jalfrezi* curries or any tandoori dish.

## • BYADAGI CHILI (KARNATAKA, SOUTH INDIA) •

Bright red, with medium heat. *Byadagi* chilies are native to a town of the same name in Karnataka and are responsible for the hot chili flavor in South Indian curries, chutneys, sambar and more.

## • PUL BIBER (THE MIDDLE EAST) •

Burgundy color, mild heat, rounded flavor. The provenance of *pul biber* chilies is hazy because they are known variously as Turkish chilies and Aleppo peppers, which suggests they are Syrian. They are often eaten in flake form and peppered over meze dishes to serve, not unlike the way the Spanish might apply *pimentón*. Personally, I love a few flakes sprinkled over avocado on toast.

## • SCOTCH BONNET (CARIBBEAN) •

Orange or red, blisteringly hot and with a voluptuous shape, the Scotch Bonnet is the predominant chili in the cuisines of the Afro-Caribbean and West Africa. AKA habañero chili, its Mexican alter ego—not quite the same but similar.

## • JALAPEÑO (MEXICO) •

Green, punchy Mexican chilies renowned for their vigor! Jalapeños are most familiar in their sliced, pickled form as an addition to Mexican dishes and fast foods like burritos or fajitas (see page 311). Jalapeños also play a key role in the fusion cuisine of California (see page 297).

## • CHIPOTLE (MEXICO) •

Fiery and fruity. The Mexican smoked chili, chipotles are jalapeños that have been smoke-dried and are used in *adobo* sauces (see page 313), salsas or with bean dishes.

## • AJI AMARILLO (PERU) •

As fiery as its yellow color and name suggests. Celebrated Peruvian chef Gastón Acurio calls this the most important ingredient in his national cuisine, used in ceviches and in the popular sauce, *salsa criolla* (see page 332).

## • AJI PANCA (PERU) •

Dark, smoky and milder than its yellow brother, *aji panca* is used in its dried (and subsequently rehydrated) form or in a paste, particularly as a rub for meats, lending fruity heat without overwhelming spice. The everyday Peruvian chili.

## • ROCOTO (SOUTH AMERICA) •

Fierce, intense, rounded, with black seeds and hairy leaves, the *rocoto* chili is set apart from the other chilies here. It looks like a fruit and has a flavor that matures from pleasantly sweet to scorching in the mouth. Definitely one for those who can take the heat.

## • CAYENNE PEPPER (FRENCH GUIANA) •

Tropical bright red chili, intense heat. Native to French Guiana but widely used throughout the world, perhaps most famously in its dried, powdered form in the cuisines of the United States' Deep South.

## • PIRI PIRI CHILI (AFRICA) •

Small, compact and fiercely hot. Piri piri chilies grow in Africa, including West African countries like Nigeria and Ghana (see page 277) and Ethiopia (see page 270). After their discovery in the Americas, the Portuguese took these little chilies to Africa; "pili pili" means "pepper pepper" in Swahili, becoming "piri piri" and then, in the popular Portuguese marinade, "peri peri"—in which it is combined with garlic, citrus and herbs.

## • CAPSICHINA CHILI (CALABRIA, ITALY) •

Known locally as *piparedduzzu*, these curvy, bloodred chilies give Calabrese cuisine its signature heat and mark it apart from food elsewhere in Italy.

# ETHIOPIA

Those who eat from the same plate will not betray each other.
• ETHIOPIAN PROVERB •

THE PRACTICE OF *gursha*—the Ethiopian word for preparing handfuls of food and feeding them to one's companions—is testament to this proverb. *Gursha* symbolizes both trust and affection—almost like giving a hug via the medium of food, but charged with the responsibility of feeding another person well. In most cultures, food can be a vehicle for bringing people together and demonstrating love and hospitality. But Ethiopian *gursha* takes this a step farther. Food unites people over the table and feeding one another becomes a demonstrative act of care and kinship.

Before launching into an exploration of Ethiopian cuisine, I think it's worth noting the obscurity with which African food—and the continent as a whole—has been veiled. Geographer George Kimble's observation[*] that "the darkest thing about Africa has always been our ignorance of it," strikes me as true of all aspects of the African continent, from language and geography to culture and cuisine. It's somewhat shaming that, in my native Britain, our knowledge of Africa, and our strongest links to it, are often limited to the territories we colonized—a best-forgotten "master/servant" dynamic that ended over fifty years ago.[†] For the most part, the food of Africa is shrouded in mystery in much of the West (excluding, perhaps, that of North Africa—Morocco, Algeria, Tunisia—which is often considered an extension of the Mediterranean). African food is rarely seen as newly glamorous or "emerging," like that dished up in the Vietnamese or Peruvian eateries that grace cosmopolitan streets to the excitement of food enthusiasts. Ethiopian cuisine, however, has been around under the radar for some time—one hears mutterings about the multitasking "big pancakes" (*injera*, which we will discover below), which are eaten, eaten off and eaten with. But what else, if anything, do we know about Ethiopian food?

• • • •

[*] In *Africa Today: Lifting the Darkness*.

[†] Ghana gained its independence from Britain in 1957, Nigeria in 1960.

Sitting in the Horn of Africa (the peninsula that juts into the Arabian Sea), the Ethiopian landscape is one of massive skies, flat desert plains and lone baobab or acacia trees feeding on the crusty soil. It has a precarious kind of visual majesty, suspended between dramatic beauty and the challenges of erratic weather patterns and war.[*] Doris Lessing captured this fragile balance, writing of the Ethiopian horizon, "I knew how far below in the swelling heat the birds were an orchestra in the trees about the villages of mud huts; how the long grass was straightening while dangling locks of dewdrops dwindled and dried; how the people were moving out into the fields about the business of herding and hoeing." Daily life falls prey too easily to natural disasters and political upheaval. Despite plenty of sunshine and several good water sources (twelve of which lead into the river Nile), the climate flits unpredictably between tropical monsoons and drought, making agriculture (which accounts for just over 40 percent of Ethiopia's domestic production) difficult and the GDP low.

Life is still largely pastoral in Ethiopia (although, as in many African countries, rapid urbanization is a reality—the population of the capital, Addis Ababa, is growing at just under 4 percent a year). Small farms predominate in Ethiopian agriculture. Coffee, pulses, cereal and maize are the main crops while citrus, bananas, grapes, pomegranates, figs and custard apples (the fruit from a semi-evergreen tree cultivated in tropical climates) are the less commercial, more colorful products of Ethiopian soils (concentrated in the southwestern Oromiya region). Ethiopian coffee is prized by chi-chi coffee purveyors—its quality competing with the likes of Colombian and Brazilian coffees—and is a key international export.

Given the importance of agriculture, and of man's rather shaky relationship with nature, the congregation of people around the Ethiopian table is racked with significance. Mealtimes are an opportunity to unite after a long day's work in the field and to celebrate food on the table. Dishes are simple but flavorsome, with brightly spiced pulses and sharing platters. Ethiopian cuisine is a lesson in the delicious potential of vegetarian food—pulses such as chickpeas, peanuts and lentils, not to mention vegetable dishes, are the centerpieces of a meal during times of fast. The centrality of religion[†] and

• • • •

[*] A seventeen-year-long civil war blighted Ethiopia between 1974 and 1991, followed by the Eritrean-Ethiopian War between 1998 and 2000.

[†] Over 60 percent of the Ethiopian population is Christian, and about 30 percent Muslim.

particularly the preeminent Coptic Church,[*] means that fasting plays a major role in Ethiopia's culinary life and customs. While lamb and goat, beef and chicken are all eaten in stew form, vegan food is prevalent during the seven fasting periods, which include Lent and every Wednesday and Friday. This has led to widespread creativity with vegetarian ingredients, down to the use of fat bases such as oil from the safflower—an ancient crop that looks like a dandelion. Safflower is used for its oil, seeds and flowers, which, when dried, make for a cheap alternative to saffron.

Ethiopian food is perhaps the hottest in Africa and uses a lot of red chili. This is dried and blended with up to fifteen other spices to make *berbere*, Ethiopia's signature spice blend, containing garlic, fenugreek, ginger, coriander and allspice. *Berbere* is thrown into most Ethiopian stews, which are known as *wat*. *Niteh kibbeh* is another crucial base ingredient for Ethiopian meals, a ghee-like clarified butter seasoned with spices and often kept cool in banana leaves. Together, *niteh kibbeh* and *berbere* are made into an emulsified paste called *awaze*, with the addition of finely chopped onions, water and, sometimes, *tej*—Ethiopian honey wine. *Awaze* can be a marinade or a condiment and sits in the middle of an Ethiopian spread. It is used in much the same way as harissa in North Africa, soy sauce in Asia or—dare I say it—ketchup in England. Visit an Ethiopian restaurant such as Addis, near where I work on Caledonian Road in London, and your table will quickly resemble a mosaic of reds, browns and yellows, either in little bowls or loaded in separate mounds onto an *injera*, on which the Ethiopian meal is founded.

*Injera* are hardly the most ubiquitous product on the North American market, but if you can't find it in a specialty store, you could try making your own (see Further Reading, page 349). An *injera* is a large unleavened soft pancake made from teff[†] grass grains. Finely ground teff flour is mixed with water and fermented for several days before being fashioned into *injera*, which measure around 12 inches across. These are laid out on platters to create an edible tablecloth, onto which stews (*wat*) are ladled. The most famous of these is *doro wat* (chicken and hard-boiled eggs), although they can be made from any meat sautéed with onions and *niteh kibeh* (minced beef and spices

● ● ● ●

[*] Ethiopia became Christian in the fourth century and today's Ethiopian Orthodox Church is an off-shoot of the Coptic Church, which is the largest Christian grouping in the Middle East and Africa.

[†] Teff is a highly nutritious grain (not unlike quinoa or millet in nutritional value) that is native to Ethiopia. It accounts for approximately a quarter of all grain production in Ethiopia.

is called *kifto*, for example) or as vegetarian dishes for fast days. Vegetarian stews include *miser wat* (with red lentils), *kik pea alechi* (a chickpea vegetable stew) or *gomen wat*. This last stew uses *gomen*, Ethiopian collard greens sautéed in garlic (you can substitute kale), *niteh kibeh* and *berbere*. *Gomen* might also be combined with *iab*, a kind of Ethiopian curd cheese mixed with yogurt and seasoned with lemon and salt.

Aside from general lack of awareness of African food, one of the barriers to making Ethiopian food at home is the unfamiliarity of the ingredients. Really, however, once you've bought your *injera*, substituted *niteh kibeh* for ghee and prepared your *berbere* spice mix (see page 197) and *awaze*, the protein staples are actually very similar to those of European food cultures: meat, chickpeas, eggs. As with West African cuisine, cooking from the Ethiopian kitchen is a lesson in extracting full flavor from a few local ingredients, amplifying them into simple delicacies to feed a large brood.

Once the *injera* is laid out with a rainbow of different *wat* mounds, eaters sit around tearing from the pancakes and scooping up meat, chickpeas, vegetables and *awaze*. The *injera* fills three roles: a vessel for serving, a utensil for eating and the food itself. When Ethiopians practice *gursha* they tear at the *injera*—deconstructing the vessel as they build a social bond. The *injera* is the "same plate" to which the proverb at the beginning of the chapter refers, the basis for an Ethiopian meal and an ancient symbol of trust.

**PANTRY LIST** • chickpeas • peanuts • red lentils • *berbere* spice mix • clarified butter (*niteh kibbeh*) • *awaze* sauce • teff grass grains (to make *injera*) • white curd cheese (*iab*)

• • •

# • CHICKPEA STEW •

This is a cheap, easy and nutritious *wat* that is delicious as is or can be embellished with meat if you prefer. You can eat it with rice, although I'd recommend seeking out some *injera* and investing in some *awaze* dipping sauce to re-create the full Ethiopian spread.

## • SERVES 6–8 •

3 x 14-oz cans chickpeas, drained
3½ tbsp unsalted butter
1 large onion, finely chopped
4 garlic cloves, very finely chopped
1-inch piece ginger, very finely chopped
2–3 tbsp *berbere* spice mix (see page 197)
1 x 14-oz can chopped tomatoes
2–3 cups stock (chicken or vegetable)
5 oz frozen peas
7 oz fresh or frozen spinach (optional)
sea salt and freshly ground black pepper

**1 •** Preheat the oven to 400°F.

**2 •** Pour the chickpeas into a large baking dish in a single layer and roast in the oven for 15 minutes, stirring every so often. This will add depth of flavor.

**3 •** In a saucepan or deep frying pan, heat the butter and sauté the onions for 2–3 minutes, until they are soft and translucent, then add the garlic, ginger and spice mix and sauté for another 2–3 minutes.

**4 •** Add the chickpeas, chopped tomatoes and stock, bring to a boil and simmer for 20 minutes to reduce it a little, then add the peas, and spinach if using, and cook for another 10 minutes.

**5 •** If your *wat* is still too liquid to imagine scooping it up with an *injera*, take a couple of ladles of the chickpea mixture and blend, then return it to the stew. Serve in a mound on a bed of rice or an *injera*.

# • GOMEN STEW •

Another delicious *wat* that combines beautifully with chickpea *wat*, *injera* and *awaze*—all the usual suspects on the Ethiopian table. I also enjoy it on its own. It injects a dose of excitement into eating your greens!

## • SERVES 4–6 •

1½–2 lb spring greens or kale, shredded
1 tbsp olive oil
1 onion, coarsely chopped
6 garlic cloves, very finely chopped
1 green bell pepper, deseeded and coarsely chopped
juice of 1 lemon
big pinch salt
½ tsp paprika
½ tsp turmeric
½ tsp ground allspice
¾-inch piece ginger, very finely chopped

**1 •** Bring 2 cups water to boil in a large pan and boil the greens, covered, until tender. This will take about 15 minutes. Drain, but reserve the water to use later.
**2 •** In a large frying pan, heat the olive oil and sauté the onions until translucent. Then add the garlic and sauté for another 2 minutes without letting the garlic brown. Add the greens and the cooking water and cook until the water evaporates.
**3 •** Now simply add the rest of the ingredients, cover and cook for another 5–10 minutes, until the pepper is slightly softened and the room smells fragrant.

# CASSAVA

• • •

Cassava is the brown, slightly whiskered root vegetable with hard white flesh that you often see on market vegetable stalls or in ethnic shops. It's fair to say that most Europeans don't know what to do with it, or even what it is called, but cassava makes up the staple diet of millions in the developing world.

Both potatoes and cassava entered Europe from South America but cassava, otherwise known as manioc, is able to flourish in dry and tropical soils—unlike the potato with which we are so much more familiar. Cassava is particularly important to the cuisine of West Africa where it is pounded with yams to make *fufu* (see page 278). Tapioca, or manioc flour, is the ground starch or flour of cassava used to thicken stews and to make farofa in Brazil, the crunchy, buttery condiment often eaten as a side dish (see page 335).

• • •

# WEST AFRICA

A man who calls his kinsmen to a feast does not do so to save them from starving. They all have food in their own homes. When we gather together in the moonlit village ground it is not because of the moon. Every man can see it in his own compound. We come together because it is good for kinsmen to do so.
• CHINUA ACHEBE, *Things Fall Apart* •

I HAVE NEVER visited West Africa but it has always been alive in my imagination. My dad was born and brought up in Nigeria, the son of a colonial district officer in the eastern city of Enugu. His early years have always sounded carefree and exotic to my English ears: throwing overripe mangoes down onto imperial wives (in their finest clothes) from his parents' roof; snapping sugarcane straight from the crops to suck raw—equatorial Africa's answer to the penny sweets of my own childhood. My granny had a framed picture of four-year-old Dad, chunky and blond-haired, standing in a line with his Nigerian friends from their village, his little white hand waving keenly at the camera—quite literally sticking out like a sore thumb. I've always had the impression that his was a happy infancy, blissfully innocent to all the moral question marks and inequalities introduced by colonialism.

When I asked my dad about the kinds of food he grew up with in Nigeria, his response came as a list of wonderful words: "*fufu, sasa*, groundnut stew, stink fish." They somehow encapsulated the beautiful, very rich simplicity of West African cuisine.

The region consists of sixteen countries,[*] many of them tucked around the Gulf of Guinea and facing out toward the Atlantic Americas. Though each country has its own variations on common dishes (not to mention each cook having his or her own method), and of course dishes that are unique

• • • •

[*]Benin, Burkina Faso, Cape Verde, Ivory Coast, Gambia, Ghana, Guinea, Guinea-Bissau, Liberia, Mali, Mauritiana, Niger, Nigeria, Senegal, Sierra Leone and Togo.

to them—Ghana has *kenkey*,[*] for example—West African food as a whole specializes in dressing up local produce to provide affordable meals in large volumes. Executed well, I can think of few cuisines that are able to nourish and delight the crowds to quite such great effect.

Information is passed on via the oral tradition in West Africa, and spreads organically across the region's diverse landscapes, ranging from Saharan desert to tropical rain forest. This means that tribal traditions frequently transcend national borders, with folktales, stories and proverbs shared between generations without necessarily being written down. The inheritance of recipes and culinary traditions is no exception. Dishes have spread with communities but gently mutated from one generation to another. Though popular *jollof* rice originated in Sierra Leone, it is native to the Igbo tribe of southern Nigeria, suggesting that the Igbo community have settled and spread their culinary traditions well beyond the borders of Nigeria. This sharing of recipes at community level has created numerous ubiquitous dishes such as groundnut stew and *fufu* that draw on the ingredients readily available across the region.

The food we will be cooking on this leg of the journey is straightforward so long as you have access to good ethnic stalls or supermarkets. This isn't a problem in most big cities, where the likes of cassava and plantain can be found in many corner shops or markets. (If you live out of range of the bigger cities you might have to search a little harder, though online shops are a fantastic option.) Between them, cassava and plantain are essentially the potatoes of West Africa and are heavily relied upon across the region for regular, staple sustenance. They happily tolerate hot, dry conditions and poor soil quality and are relatively low-maintenance—hardy native carbohydrates suited to the terrain (see box on page 276). Cassava is most often boiled with plantain (green banana), yams (sweet potatoes, which, along with maize, grow all over the region) or cocoyam (another tropical tuber with edible leaves—see opposite page), and then pounded to make *fufu* (see page 281), a starchy dough which the eater presses between their fingertips. This can then either be dipped into one of many soups or a small crevice is made in the dough and filled with the thick soup.[†]

Two of Europe's staple carbohydrates—potatoes and rice—were intro-

• • • •

[*]Fermented, ground maize forms the basis of *kenkey*, boiled corn dumplings that are wrapped in maize husks and enjoyed with stews or fried fish. It can also be made with plantain skins.

[†]Brazilian tapioca and Jamaican dumplings/patties (see page 322) are two New World *fufu* equivalents.

duced to West Africa by imperial Europeans, brought in from their other colonies (South America and Asia respectively) by imperial Europeans. Potatoes prefer cooler growing conditions to those of West Africa and as such remain scarce (and expensive) here, but rice is the basis for one of the region's principle dishes, *jollof* rice—an accompaniment to meat and fried fish, often finished with fried plantain. This is almost like West African paella, made with a "*sofrito*" base of onions, tomato and tomato paste, which Ghanaian home cook Veronica Binfor told me is used to start almost every West African dish (see *sofrito* chart, page 74). A spice mix is then added. A typical mix would include garlic, ginger, nutmeg, Scotch bonnet pepper and, often, curry powder (which was brought in by imperial Britain from the Indian colony). In more recent years, Veronica tells me, *adobo* has gained popularity. This Iberian seasoning that blends paprika, garlic and salt for meat rubs and stew flavoring traveled with the Spanish and Portuguese all over the New World, from Latin America to the Philippines. It is now a popular agent of sweet spice in West African cooking.

Distinctions among sauces, soups and stews are unclear in West Africa. They all have similar consistencies and are enjoyed in largely the same way—with *fufu*, yams or rice. Peanut and palm nut soups are made with meat such as lamb shoulder or smoked fish while chicken soup and the West African classic groundnut stew (*maafe*) are made with peanut butter, offcuts of meat and varying quantities of peppers, corn and okra. The *palaver* sauce of tomatoes, onions, *igushi* (like pumpkin seeds), meat or fish, cocoyam leaves and cassava is essentially another stew. Its name is thought to come from the Portuguese word for a long-winded discussion and according to Bea Sandler, author of *The African Cookbook*, was probably inspired by cooks arguing in the kitchen, slapping each other with the wilted cocoyam leaves[*] (sometimes called "elephant's ears") that they would later add to the dish. What a palaver!

Dried, smoked or preserved fish such as saltfish, herring or mackerel is often used to flavor soups, but the fresh fish and seafood of the West African coastline is also of fantastic quality. In the southern Ashanti and coastal regions, snapper, tilapia, octopus and shrimp are fried simply with salt until very dry and served with yams or, in Ghana, *kenkey*. Fresh and quickly assembled, this is absolutely typical street food. In some settings it might be

• • • •

[*] The crop is very particular to the region so I recommend substituting with spinach or even canned callaloo (available in some supermarkets, especially those in areas with a big Caribbean community). Cocoyam is also widely prepared with saltfish (or, as my dad used to call it, "stink fish"). This approach to combining wilted greens with preserved fish, or with okra, was clearly carried over to the Caribbean, where similar dishes are breakfast staples (see page 319).

accompanied by *waakye*, smoky black-eyed beans cooked with rice to accompany meat and fish. *Waakye* informed the well-loved Caribbean dish rice and peas (see page 324), demonstrating once again the West African inheritance in the Americas.

Though West African restaurants pepper those areas of cities in which its population has settled, this is food that's best enjoyed in a home, made by a family cook, with a big group of people. As the quote from Chinua Achebe at the beginning of the chapter suggests, these are dishes around which people flock, as much for a sense of community as for sustenance. So, I'd recommend trying a couple of the recipes below at home when you have a few people to cater for. They're easy, tasty and, coming as they do from a culture founded on the oral tradition, are open to infinite interpretation—the best kind of recipes from which to cook.

PANTRY LIST • curry powder • nutmeg • ginger • *adobo* • saltfish • palm oil • coconut oil • peanut oil • palm kernel oils • shea butter • groundnut oil • cassava • yam • plantain • peanuts

• • •

# • IJE'S HOTPOT •

My friend Ije Nwokerie, who comes from Enugu, Nigeria, kindly provided his hotpot recipe. It's easy, he says, to visit his homeland from his London kitchen, but he created this specific recipe in order to eat plantains in a more healthy way than the standard option of deep-frying them. This recipe combines chicken and plantains, which Ije says were both treats when he was a child in Nigeria. It takes a mere fifteen minutes to prepare and if you're worried about finding plantains—don't. They are never far away if you've a good market on hand.

### • SERVES 4 •

5 tbsp vegetable or peanut oil
2 yellow or white onions, halved
1 Scotch bonnet pepper, deseeded and halved

1 ½ tsp ginger paste (or 1 ½ tsp fresh
    ginger, very finely chopped)
1 ½ tsp garlic paste (or 3 garlic cloves,
    very finely chopped)
1 lb skinless chicken pieces—4 thighs
    would work well
2 x 14-oz cans plum tomatoes
1 tsp paprika, or to taste
salt to taste
4 ripe yellow plantains, peeled and
    chopped into 1-inch-long pieces
1–2 tbsp honey
7 oz fresh spinach

**1** • Preheat the oven to 400°F.

**2** • In a large ovenproof pot, heat the oil and sauté the onions until translucent. Add the Scotch bonnet and ginger and garlic and fry for another couple of minutes. Reduce the heat and chuck the chicken in. Keep stirring for 5–7 minutes until it starts to smell good and the meat has browned on all sides.

**3** • Add the tomatoes, paprika and salt and cover with a lid. Let it cook for another 4 minutes or so. Add the plantains, honey and spinach. Stir, cover and bring back to the boil. Transfer to the oven for 45–60 minutes.

**4** • Serve straight from the pot with *fufu* or boiled rice.

# • FUFU •

*Fufu*, the West African carbohydrate base of pounded starches or roots to accompany soups and stews, can come in several guises. I've chosen the most basic West African rendition here—seasoned buttered yams. (When I was growing up, I would pass piles of rather indecent-looking barky root vegetables in the likes of Brixton market or Peckham Rye, with no idea how to cook them.) But *fufu* can also be made with cassava, or a combination of yam, cassava, sweet potato and plantain. It can be rolled and formed into an edible spoon with which to scoop soups and stews. It's also pretty yummy in its own right, a West African mashed potato, if you like.

## • SERVES 4–6 •

2¼ lb white yams
7 tbsp unsalted butter
sea salt and freshly ground black pepper

**1** • Place the whole unpeeled yams in a big pan of cold water and bring to a boil over high heat. Once boiling, reduce the heat to medium and simmer for 20–30 minutes, until they are tender.

**2** • Drain the yams and allow them to cool before peeling and chopping into chunks. Return to the pan, add the butter and seasoning, then simply mash this mixture together. In order to get the kind of smooth consistency you are after, I would favor a potato ricer, but a potato masher will do just fine.

**3** • *Fufu* is served in a big ball from which people take a little, forming it into mouthful-sized morsels with which to scoop their stew. Transfer your mixture into a serving bowl and form it into a large, smooth ball. (Wet your hands first, so it doesn't stick to them.)

# MOROCCO

*To visit Morocco is still like turning the pages of some illuminated Persian manuscript all embroidered with bright shapes and subtle lines.*
• EDITH WHARTON, *In Morocco* •

MOROCCO IS QUITE the adventure for food tourists, a visual and prandial feast that arrests the senses with luxurious aromas and market bustle. The smell of sweet spice wafting from kitchen doorways; the swirls of vapor that rise from piles of fluffy couscous; deep-fried sardines spitting from a hawker's stall; a tagine lid lifted to reveal rich stew beneath a cloud of steam. Such is the magic of Moroccan cuisine that, amidst these eddies, you half expect a genie to emerge...

The opulence of Moroccan food is unmatched by any other African cuisine. Here at the top of the continent, just twenty miles from the Spanish coast and, historically, the final stop on the Spice Route before goods entered Europe, there has always been a huge wealth of influences and ingredients on which to draw. Perhaps the most important influence, and the factor that differentiates Morocco from her neighbors Algeria and Tunisia, is a monarchy. Palace kitchens played a significant role in developing the cuisine; here native ingredients—like saffron from Taliouine in the south, honey from the High Atlas Mountains[*] and dates from the Sahara desert—met imported ones, and indigenous Berber cooking techniques were fused with those of Europe and the Middle East.[†] Palace cooks quite literally built up a cuisine that was fit for royalty.

The influence of the Berbers, the nomadic tribes based to the west of the

• • • •

[*] The Atlas mountains stretch across northwestern Africa from Morocco through Algeria and into Tunisia. In Morocco, they separate the Sahara desert from the coastline, dividing its Mediterranean north (which, in many ways, not least in food, bears more resemblance to southern Europe than to Africa) and its dry, more typically African south.

[†] What these palace cooks did reminds me of a quote from Jane Grigson's *English Food*: "No cookery belongs exclusively to its country, or its region. Cooks borrow—and have always borrowed—and adapt through the centuries ... What each individual country does do is give all the elements, borrowed or otherwise, something of a national character."

river Nile in North Africa, also differentiates Moroccan cuisine. In modern times the Berbers have been concentrated in Morocco and Algeria and their presence is the key to why Moroccan cuisine is so different from that of Tunisia and Egypt. Rustic methods of food preparation such as the tagine and making couscous by hand derive from the Berbers, as do the powerful combinations of sweet and savory ingredients. Examples of this remain strong in Marrakech. Jemaa el-Fnaa square is home to street food traders heavily influenced by Berber cuisine: chicken with nigella seeds, or one-pot dishes cooked in a tangia pot.* The latter might contain meats or vegetables blended with orange water, or dried fruit such as apricots and prunes, nuts such as almonds and pistachios, or sesame seeds. They are cooked over the course of the day, always with a preserved lemon.

The cuisine is as much the product of the seasons as the people who have settled there. The climate can be blazing hot in summertime in Marrakech and freezing in the High Atlas during winter, and what ends up on your plate (or in your tagine pot) depends on what the land yields at any given time. Seasonal eating is not just a necessity in Morocco but a sensibility bestowed upon Moroccan cooks. At the Moorish Lounge, my local Moroccan café in Streatham, south London, chef Ahmed has the choice of countless supermarkets, grocery stores and market stalls from which to buy produce that is available year-round. Yet he still prefers his tagines to echo the seasons. I always order the tagine *du Rif*, a vegetarian tagine of mixed seasonal vegetables crowned with goat cheese, but I've *never* had the same one twice. It's both romantic and enthralling—you never know exactly what you're going to get.

The components of a Moroccan dish are easily obtained and affordable—seasonal meat, fruit, nuts and spice. While there is nothing intrinsically complicated about the ingredients, however, the bigger challenge when embarking on cooking Moroccan is that doing so requires a certain level of knowledge and skill. It is about practice making perfect, and respecting time-honored techniques honed in palace kitchens some four hundred years ago. In my experience, Moroccan food doesn't turn out brilliantly if you attempt to take shortcuts. Be prepared for lots of pans to wash at the end of the process, but don't let that put you off. After two hours of chopping and grinding, I was exhausted when I made my first squash and chickpea *kedra*† but the time and elbow grease were

• • • •

* An earthenware pot for cooking, similar to the better-known tagine. A tangia is shaped like a vase with handles on either side.

† Like a tagine, the *kedra* is a dish named after the vessel in which it is cooked. A *kedra* pot is taller, thinner and deeper than a tagine and the resulting sauce has a more brothy consistency.

well worth it. I couldn't believe that *I* had made something that tasted like *that*! Moroccan food is among the most rewarding I have ever cooked.

All that said, in my experience, it is possible to cook tagines and *kedras* without the authentic pot apparatus—these recipes work well on the stovetop. Do remember though that without the tagine or *kedra* pot you are missing out on the intensity of cooking and steaming the contents at the same time, so you will want a good flame on your stove to compensate.

Because Moroccan food can be technical and time-consuming, many of us resort to eating it outside of the home. I'm fortunate to have grown up with a little corner of Marrakech just down the road from my parents' house in Streatham, but Morocco sees millions of tourists each year—all hungry for a piece of the pie, or in this case, a piece of the *bastilla*.[*] It is perhaps in part due to the huge international appetite for Moroccan food—which could be seen as a touristic fantasy set in the Morocco of four hundred years ago—that young Moroccans are eating at home less, eschewing their native cuisine in favor of Western alternatives. Moroccan food expert Paula Wolfert, who first visited as a beatnik in 1959, says, "Everything feels fragile around Moroccan food now. Young people eat out more because they're bored of traditional dishes. But to me they look less happy."[†]

Though traditional Moroccan food is still eaten widely, particularly on weekends and during festivals, home-cooking these dishes using historic techniques is a dying art. Modernity brings with it the apparatus to cut corners. These days, tagines are often made in pressure cookers, and the tradition of making couscous by hand at home—a long and messy job at the best of times—is dissolving slowly but surely.

Couscous is made by rolling semolina and salted water between the palms before adding semolina flour and more water to turn the dough into the "beads" we recognize as couscous. This is then finely sieved and steamed while raking through the couscous with a fork, left to rest, and then steamed again. The volume of couscous swells with every round of steaming, making Moroccan hospitality—defined as the ability to fit more people around the

• • • •

[*] *Bastilla* is a pie of spiced pastry, traditionally made with pigeon (and now, more often, chicken), which is thought to have originated in Fez, Morocco's second-largest city. The pastry of choice is ultra-thin *warqa*, structured into crisp layers and stuffed with the meat, cinnamon and toasted almonds and dusted with confectioners' sugar. Like much Moroccan food, it treads a fine line between sweet and savory.

[†] Speaking to Wolfert, I got a strong sense that, for her, Moroccan cuisine is almost synonymous with happiness and upholding close relationships. Indeed, relationships were integral to Wolfert in establishing her Moroccan cooking skills, which, she says, she acquired with "kisses, cuddles and measuring spoons."

table at the last minute—an easy feat. Couscous is enjoyed with a broth and marinated grilled meat or seafood. These three components of a couscous meal are plated separately but often use the same flavors intrinsic to tagines and *kedras*.

Eating a tagine is an act of sharing, symbolic of the generous Moroccan national spirit. People sit around the dish and scoop up the thick sauce with bread. As with couscous meals, tagines always allow room for more people, simply by serving more bread. Wolfert says, "There's always room for one more. It always struck me that, really, good food is a sign of friendliness in Morocco." Ingredients might include chicken with prunes and almonds, or caramelized quinces and walnuts, or dried apricots and pine nuts, or lamb with Medjool dates* and green apples, or artichokes and lemon.

As the last stop on the Spice Route before goods entered Europe, Morocco received a wealth of spices from Asia. Cinnamon, ginger and turmeric, three spice pillars of Moroccan cuisine, arrived from India, which, incidentally, is the only other country where the use of spice rivals the volume and diversity of Morocco's. *Ras el hanout*, for instance, a complex blend of more than nine spices† used to sprinkle on dishes or as a rub for meats, originates in Morocco‡ and means "top of the shop"—a blend of the best spices that shop had to offer. Each spice merchant will have his signature blend of *ras el hanout*, which is usually only semi-ground and, with ingredients like rose petals and ash berries, adds both warmth and a pretty flourish just before serving. Food confetti, if you like. Traditionally, spice blends have also varied from one region to another, thanks to the diverse Moroccan landscape. (This is changing, though, as people leave the countryside to pursue lives in cities like Marrakech, the country's throbbing capital, and coastal towns like Casablanca and Fez, where tourism flourishes.)

Preserved lemons (lemons aged in jars of salt and spices) are used all across North Africa in everything from salads to couscous and tagines, giving dishes a deeper, richer citrus edge. Most other cuisines simply preserve their lemons in brine, but Moroccans go further by aging them in their own juice. Wolfert maintains that preserved lemons are the most important con-

• • • •

*The king of dates—big, fleshy and with an almost caramel flavor. Wonderful.

†*Ras el hanout* can contain the following in shifting proportions: allspice, cardamom, cinnamon, clove, coriander seeds, ginger, mace, nutmeg, turmeric, black pepper, white pepper, cayenne pepper, star anise—see page 198.

‡Elsewhere in North Africa people traditionally used a simpler five-spice mix a bit like *la kama* (a ground mix of cinnamon, black peppercorns, dried ginger, turmeric and nutmeg from the north of Morocco—see page 199), without the complexity of *ras el hanout*.

diment in the Moroccan pantry. They are certainly essential to offsetting some of the sweetness you find in Moroccan food, a function similar to that of dried limes in Persian cookery.

One particularly frugal Christmas, I bought some large jars and made friends and family preserved lemons—try doing it yourself with my recipe below. Don't limit yourself to using them solely for Moroccan food, either; I once put them into the cavity of a chicken to roast (instead of fresh lemons), which made for really incredible flavors.

Another ingredient associated with Morocco, albeit wrongly, is harissa paste. Made from crushed red chilies, garlic, salt and olive oil, it is actually an import from Tunisia,* where it is famously used in dishes like *shakshuka* (which subsequently traveled to Israel), and has gained popularity in Morocco as the appetite for hot food has increased. (Wolfert says that Moroccans eat harissa "like ketchup" nowadays.) Though rich in spices, Moroccan food was not traditionally "spicy." Rather than adding neat chili to dishes, it makes sense to take inspiration from the Tunisians and temper the heat of chilies with other strong flavors.

I love Edith Wharton's allusion to "bright shapes and subtle lines." It reminds me of the big flavors, ingredients and cultural and historic influences present in Moroccan cuisine, so intricately woven together into delicate dishes that use carefully mastered techniques. Illuminate this manuscript by giving one of these simple Moroccan dishes a go for yourself.

**PANTRY LIST** • preserved lemons • orange blossom water • dates • honey • almonds • saffron • *ras el hanout* spice mix (see page 198) • cinnamon • caramelized onions • golden raisins • harissa paste • couscous • filo pastry

• • •

• • • •

*This explains its inclusion in many *shakshuka* recipes. Having been taken to Israel by Tunisian Jews, *shakshuka* is now a mainstay on Israeli breakfast tables, a spicy stew of capsicum peppers and tomatoes with eggs poached into it.

# • CHICKEN COUSCOUS •

Forget the horrible ready-prepared couscous salads with token morsels of red bell pepper or zucchini that became popular with yummy mummies in the 1990s. Paula Wolfert's couscous dish is soft and fluffy, and crowned with a gloriously sweet sauce. Don't let the long list of ingredients put you off—all are easily accessible and many you'll already have at home. For a vegetarian version, try replacing the chicken with chickpeas. You'll need to cut down the amount of stock (and opt for vegetable rather than chicken) and reduce the cooking time.

## • SERVES 4 •

3 tbsp olive oil

1 tbsp unsalted butter

1 medium chicken, jointed into drumsticks, thighs, wings and breasts (or a mixture of thighs and drumsticks, 8 in total, will do if you don't want to joint a chicken)

1 large white onion, sliced

1 large red onion, sliced

½ tsp ground ginger

3 pinches saffron

sea salt and freshly ground black pepper

2 cups chicken stock

1½ tbsp flat-leaf parsley, chopped, plus a little extra to garnish

1 tsp ground cinnamon

2 tbsp superfine sugar

2 tbsp honey

1 lb dried couscous

1 oz almonds, toasted (optional)

**1** • Heat the olive oil and butter in a large frying pan and sauté the chicken pieces for 2–3 minutes on each side, to brown. Remove from the pan and set aside. Add the onions, ginger, saffron and salt and pepper and sauté for 4–5 minutes, until the onions are translucent. Return the chicken to the pan, add the chicken stock and simmer for 30 minutes.

**2** • Preheat the oven to 450°F.

**3** • Add the parsley, cinnamon and sugar and simmer for another 5 minutes.

**4** • Remove the chicken pieces to a roasting dish and drizzle with the honey. Bake in the oven for 10 minutes or until the chicken turns a dark brown.

**5** • Meanwhile, keep the sauce warm over low heat and prepare the couscous. Place it in a large bowl or serving dish and pour over enough boiling water to cover it. Add a pinch of salt, stir quickly, cover with a plate and let sit for 5 minutes. Then, fork through the couscous to make it light and fluffy and so the grains are fully separated from one another.

**6** • Serve the chicken on top of the couscous, spoon over the onion mixture and sprinkle with the almonds (if using) and a little extra chopped parsley.

# • PUMPKIN "TAGINE" •

Strictly speaking, this isn't a tagine at all. Nor is it a *kedra*. Both those Moroccan dishes are named after the vessels in which they are cooked, so my cheat's stovetop version here is by definition neither—and would perhaps more accurately be called a "saucepan"! Nevertheless, many Moroccan cooks also bypass the tagine pot and, I find, this stovetop setup still produces dizzying flavors, tender vegetables and sauce of a good consistency for scooping with flatbread.

## • SERVES 6 •

pinch saffron
3½ tbsp unsalted butter
4 onions: 1 onion, finely chopped, plus 3 onions, finely sliced
    into half-moons
1 tbsp ground cinnamon
2 tsp ground ginger
½ tsp freshly grated nutmeg
1 tsp sea salt
1 tsp freshly ground black pepper
2 cups dried chickpeas, soaked overnight
3 carrots, cut into ¾-inch chunks
⅓ cup raisins
3¼ lb pumpkin or squash, peeled, deseeded
    and cut into 1-inch segments
10½ oz fresh spinach
2 tbsp honey
1 tbsp extra virgin olive oil

TO SERVE
1 preserved lemon, pulp removed and
sliced very finely (see below)
2½ oz blanched almonds, toasted
1 tsp *ras el hanout* (optional—see page 198)

**1** • Grind the saffron in a mortar and pestle and soak it in 2 tablespoons of warm water for 10 minutes.

**2** • In a very large, deep-sided pan or flameproof dish, place half the butter, the saffron water, the chopped onion, cinnamon, ginger, nutmeg and seasonings and cook over low heat for 5–6 minutes. The mixture will quickly become fragrant and deep orange in color, and the onion will begin to soften.

**3** • Add the chickpeas and cover with water, place a lid on the pan and raise the heat a little. Simmer like this for 30 minutes, then add the sliced onions and simmer for another 20 minutes.

**4** • Preheat the oven to 250°F.

**5** • Check the broth's seasoning and adjust to taste. Then add the carrots, raisins and pumpkin and simmer, covered, for 20–25 minutes, until the pumpkin and carrots are tender but still holding their shape.

**6** • Remove the vegetables, chickpeas and raisins and place in an ovenproof dish. Cover with foil and place in the oven to keep warm.

**7** • Wilt the spinach in a pan with a little water for 2 minutes and set aside.

**8** • Add the honey, olive oil and the rest of the butter to the broth, bring to a boil and simmer for 5–6 minutes until it reduces and thickens.

**9** • When you are ready to serve, remove the vegetables and chickpeas from the oven and arrange on a serving dish. Place the spinach over the top, then spoon the broth all over, sprinkle with the preserved lemon pieces, almonds and a little *ras el hanout*, if using, for extra spice and prettiness.

# • PRESERVED LEMONS •

Paula Wolfert calls preserved lemons "the most important condiment in the Moroccan pantry," and I have to agree. Such is the intensity and richness of these fermented, spiced lemons that fresh ones will not suffice as a substitute in Moroccan cooking. (You could try, however, using preserved instead of fresh lemons in the cavity of your roast chicken one weekend . . . works a treat and the gravy is to die for.) The addition of the spices adds a little more complexity and, for any budding culinary aesthetes, they look pretty in the preserving jar.

6 unwaxed lemons, washed
6 tbsp fine table salt
enough lemon juice to cover the lemons
cinnamon stick
3 whole cloves
10 coriander seeds
10 black peppercorns

**1** • Roll the lemons backward and forward on a chopping board to soften them, then cut them into quarters from the tops, stopping ½ inch from the bottom to keep the fruit held together.

**2** • Rub the salt in and around all the exposed flesh, then pack the lemons tightly into a sterilized preserving jar, adding a layer of salt in between each layer of lemons. This could be a bit of a squeeze, but it is possible—just apply lots of pressure!

**3** • You'll need plenty more lemons than the six noted above, because now you need to cover those in the jar with lemon juice—enough to submerge all the fruit.

**4** • Stuff the cinnamon stick in and scatter the spices in and around the lemons. Fasten the lid tightly and refrigerate for a month. Turn the jar every so often in order to distribute the salt, lemon juice and spice mix evenly. Top up with lemon juice during the process if need be.

# THE AME

RICAS

# MELTING POTS

...

Europe's discovery of the Americas in 1492 posed a massive opportunity to wield influence on a vast land-mass in a very short space of time—and that's exactly what happened. This map shows how the key European powers between the fifteenth and eighteenth centuries divvied up the majority of land in the Americas. The shaded areas of the map show which European powers colonized which parts of the continent at the height of imperialism in the mid-eighteenth century.

The arrows then indicate large-scale immigrations by peoples who, though not colonizers, have proved equally influential to the culture of different New World countries—and who have thus put their stamp on the various cuisines of the continent. Factors here include slavery starting in the sixteenth century, when millions of West Africans were enslaved to work the New World plantations or to be household staff; indentured slaves brought over from China and India to work the plantations once slavery had been abolished; and World War II (Jewish communities fleeing the Holocaust; Italian communities escaping the Mussolini regime).

This map is a (simplified) explanation of how the mixing of people in the Americas has been expressed in their cuisines—what melting pot populations have, quite literally, done to melting pots on the cooktop.

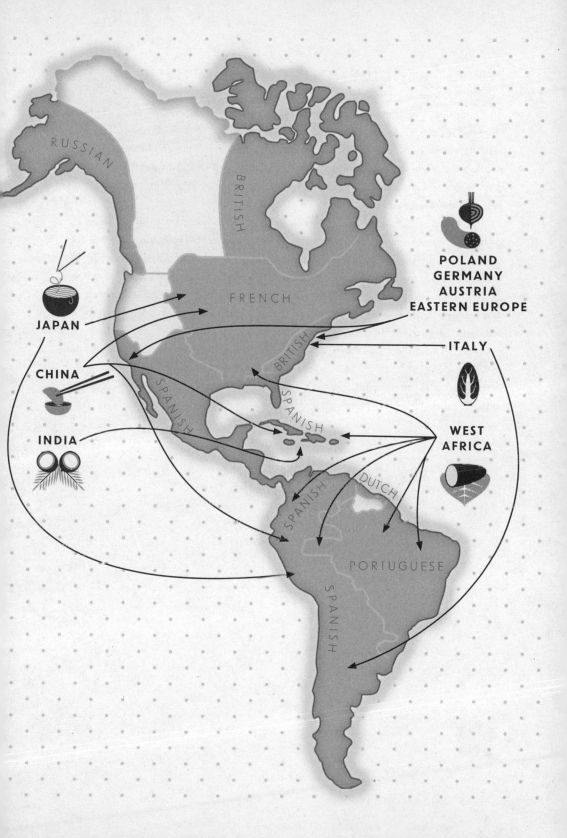

RUSSIAN

BRITISH

FRENCH

JAPAN

CHINA

INDIA

SPANISH

BRITISH

SPANISH

SPANISH

DUTCH

PORTUGUESE

SPANISH

POLAND
GERMANY
AUSTRIA
EASTERN EUROPE

ITALY

WEST
AFRICA

# • INDIGENOUS COMMUNITIES •

The indigenous communities of the Americas are known as pre-Columbian because they made up the New World's population before the arrival of Christopher Columbus and the conquistadores in 1492. The Maya, Aztecs, Inca, Apache and Inuits come from wildly different eras, geographies and cultures, yet have all been crudely labeled "Indians," in reference to Columbus's initial conviction that he had arrived in India, before the realization that he had in fact found an entirely New World.

The arrival of the Europeans imposed a huge and bloody compromise on the lives of these people, not only because they were quashed by imperial forces as violent as they were ambitious, but because the Europeans brought with them diseases to which the natives had no resistance. European diseases ranging from smallpox to influenza and the common cold were responsible for wiping out millions of indigenous Americans in the sixteenth and seventeenth centuries. (To put this into perspective, the death toll far exceeded even that of the Black Death in Europe.)

Nevertheless, their influences remain, as you can see in the food of countries like Mexico (see page 311), where indigenous customs are still celebrated in tandem with Spanish and African traditions in a hybrid culture (and cuisine) typical of the Caribbean, despite its uniquely Mexican chemistry.

# CALIFORNIA

A place belongs forever to whoever claims it hardest, remembers it most
obsessively, wrenches it from itself, shapes it, renders it, loves it so radically
that he remakes it in his own image.
• JOAN DIDION, *The White Album* •

WHEN I WAS twenty-one I moved to northern California with one suitcase and a volume of Joan Didion's collected writing. It was my year abroad at the University of California at Berkeley, where I would be continuing my degree in English. What I didn't realize was that I'd also be receiving an education in food.

At first, I didn't get it. Why did people make so much fuss about Californian cuisine when it drew so heavily on the cuisines of other cultures? Mexican, Chinese, Italian . . . I'd eaten plenty of food from those places. Was it fair to call food "Californian" when it flagrantly used the dishes and traditions of more established cuisines? Was this some kind of culinary plagiarism?

Quite quickly I realized that there was, of course, more to it than this. That California *did* have a cuisine in its own right, even if it was an offshoot of others. You see, Californian cuisine *is* derivative, and this is a trait in which its advocates take great pride. It parades the richness, diversity and possibility of the New World and gives the concept of the American "melting pot" edible expression, bringing together the disparate influences of its immigrant communities onto one plate.

California's Hispanic demographic is almost equal to its white one: nearly 40 percent of the state's population. Of these people, an overwhelming majority is Mexican, and they have integrated all the zesty staples of their homeland (see page 311) into the Californian canon (think chili, lime, pinto beans, avocado). A further 13 percent of the population is Pacific Asian, some of whom have planted deep roots—San Francisco's Chinatown is the biggest in the world and the city also boasts a Japanese population significant enough to have formed a Japantown. Add to this numerous smaller groups and cuisines such as the world's largest Iranian diaspora of 500,000 people around Los

Angeles; big Italian settlements like San Francisco's North Beach; over a million Jewish people, and plenty of good ol' home-on-the-range American fare, and suddenly you get a picture of food with huge diversity.

Dishes from these cultures have undergone a process of Californian adaptation, often with results that would be unrecognizable in their cuisine of origin. For example, the California sushi roll (which initiated America to sushi by hiding the seaweed within the roll, and, often, using imitation crab meat); Cioppino (an "Italian" fish stew that originated in San Francisco); and burritos that, ironically, surpassed any I ate in Mexico. Some of my favorite examples of Californian hybrid cuisine originate from Mission Street Food, a restaurant in the San Francisco Mission district. Octopus *a la plancha* with smoked yogurt, black olive, young turnip and pea sauce with *ras el hanout* (the Moroccan spice blend) or pork belly with marinated jicama (like a Mexican turnip) and pickled jalapeño, showcase the way cuisines can be crossfertilized and capture the essence of today's Californian food, blending East Asia with Mexico, North Africa and the Middle East.

Underpinning this patchwork of cultural influences is an ethos that prioritizes local and seasonal produce—cooking with whatever your surroundings produce in abundance at any given time of year. I remember one day eschewing a jaunt to San Francisco's Museum of Modern Art in favor of a trip to my local grocery store, the Berkeley Bowl. Brilliantly at odds with mainstream supermarkets, the BB is a gallery in its own right—an emporium, even—of local and seasonal fare fresh out of the ground and still muddy.

We're used to hearing buzz words like "local," "seasonal" and "organic" these days, but back in the 1960s—when much of the choice and exoticism introduced by foreign trade was still a novelty—California led the way in advocating a more sustainable approach to food. Figureheads like Alice Waters,[*] herself based in Berkeley—California's hothouse of alternative culture and the birthplace of the Free Speech Movement[†]—promoted ingredients sourced nearby and in season, going against the grain of consumer culture. "The timing and location encouraged my idealism and experimen-

• • • •

[*] Alice Waters gave Californian food a face and a voice. Latterly an activist for school lunch reform and a consultant on organic food, Waters opened the emblematic restaurant Chez Panisse in 1971, blending classic French cuisine with local Californian ingredients. Chez Panisse still resides in the same arts and crafts building on Berkeley's Shattuck Avenue.

[†] Between 1964 and '65 the Free Speech Movement became an organized student backlash against the university administration at UC Berkeley, which had banned student activism outside of its organized Republican and Democrat party clubs. The student activists successfully campaigned for the right to free speech and the movement became a landmark in the history of American civil liberties.

tation. This was during the late '60s, in Berkeley. We all believed in community and personal commitment and quality. Chez Panisse was born out of these ideals."[*]

Californian food might best be described more as an approach than a set of established dishes and flavors. It is less about "what" than "how." So while there are of course ingredients, dishes and influences that are typical of California, you don't necessarily need access to these in order to cook in a Californian style. Consider your current location. What fruits and vegetables are in season now? What foods are native to where you are? And which immigrant communities have moved there en masse? Blend the answers into your own concoction. Be creative according to what is in season and you will emulate Californian cuisine not just in flavor, but also in spirit.

In the words of Kim Severson from the *New York Times*, "[Californian cuisine] was the food of the gold rush and of immigrants, of orchards and sunshine." Of course, all cuisines are derivative in some way. What distinguishes California, aside from the staggering breadth of its constituent elements, is that, like Israel, its food culture is so new. Burgeoning over only the past two generations and still establishing itself, it isn't always seen as a cuisine in its own right. But I am convinced that Californian approaches to food have changed the way we eat irreversibly, epitomizing how we want to cook and eat now: fresh, healthy, with a touch of rebelliousness. It owns the right to make unexpected pairings with a steadfast belief in using ingredients available nearby and immediately.

I've often thought that the principles of Californian cuisine mirror those that winemakers have used for years, taking a self-conscious approach to their *terroirs* and respecting the power of home soil to reap its best results. But what I think I love most about Californian cooking—both in theory and in practice—is that it shows what food can be if we take an organic approach, choose our ingredients with integrity and pool our culinary traditions.

When *The White Album* was published in 1979, a journalist from the *New York Times* wrote that "California belongs to Joan Didion." Though the quote at the beginning of the chapter is open to interpretation (perhaps more a general reflection on the individual's relationship to a place than to any place in particular), it takes me back to California. It is the Golden State, molded by its inimitable collage of people, all looking to create something new. Californian cuisine is the product of that impulse, radically remade in the image of its people.

• • • •

[*]From *The Chez Panisse Menu Cookbook.*

When I was twenty-two I left California. But it never left me. Treat yourself to a trip to the land of immigrants and sunshine and feel your horizons expand.

PANTRY LIST • Think about combining what is in season where you are with whatever your readily available food resources are, based on the ethnic communities surrounding you, for example. For me in London, these might be Turkish or Indian ingredients, but in California they could include avocados and tortillas from Mexico, *ras el hanout* from Morocco (see page 198), polow from Iran, *labneh* from the Levant, noodles, ginger and *doenjang* from Asia. Seasonality and freshness of ingredients are key here.

• • •

# • CALIFORNIA SALAD •

This salad harks back to my salad days in California. It combines several influences and seasonal ingredients from the Golden State and can be made in a number of ways, depending on what you have in stock and what's in season at any given time. In my favorite incarnation, given here, it pairs quickly seared fresh prawns with the base ingredients of avocado, navel orange and an Asian-inspired dressing. You could add quinoa or bulgur wheat, with or without the prawns, for more of a complete meal. Both grains do a nice job of soaking up the dressing.

## • SERVES 4 •

1 shallot, finely chopped
½-inch piece ginger, coarsely chopped
1 clove garlic, coarsely chopped
1½ tbsp coriander leaves
1 tbsp extra virgin olive oil
2 tbsp rice wine vinegar
1 drizzle toasted sesame oil
2 tsp mirin or rice wine
1 tsp soy sauce
juice of ½ lime

½ cup quinoa or bulgur wheat, cooked in
        1¾ cups water and cooled (optional)
3 scallions, chopped into ¼-inch pieces
2 avocados, cut lengthways into slices
2 navel oranges, peeled and segmented with a sharp knife
20 raw prawns (optional)
pickled jalapeño peppers to serve (optional)
coriander to serve, chopped

**1** • For the dressing, pound the shallot, ginger, garlic and coriander leaves in a mortar and pestle until the coriander starts to stain the other ingredients green. Transfer the mixture to a small bowl and mix in the olive oil, rice wine vinegar, sesame oil, mirin, soy sauce and lime juice.

**2** • If you are using quinoa or bulgur, put it in a serving bowl, then arrange the scallions, avocados and oranges on top. If you are not using grains, then put the scallions, avocados and oranges straight in the bowl.

**3** • If you are using prawns, sear them in a frying pan for 2 minutes—they should have acquired color but still taste tender. Arrange these on top of the salad.

**4** • Then simply pour the dressing over the salad and, if you want to add some spice, scatter some pickled jalapeños and a handful of chopped coriander on top.

## • BBQ CORN ON THE COB WITH JALAPEÑO BUTTER •

Few things are better than chargrilled corn on the cob, when it's in season. This recipe guarantees tender kernels of sweet corn with lashings of Mexican-inspired butter, spiked with jalapeño and lime. The best way of grilling corn is 1) on a barbecue and 2) with the husks covering the yellow body of kernels. Sadly, summer is not perennial so I've given you instructions for indoor grilling; and since most supermarkets sell manicured corn without husks, I've assumed these are what you'll be using but have given you instructions just in case you do find the lovely whiskered corn in a blanket of husk.

### • SERVES 4 •

3 tbsp fresh or pickled jalapeños, chopped
        into small pieces
zest of 1 lime

pinch salt
1 tbsp coriander, very finely chopped
3½ tbsp unsalted butter at room temperature
4 corn on the cob, husks still on if possible
limes to serve, cut into wedges (optional)

**1 •** Light your barbecue or turn your grill on.

**2 •** In a bowl, mash the jalapeños, lime zest, salt and coriander into the softened butter very thoroughly. Use your hands to mold the seasoned butter into a cylinder (this will make it easier to slice when you come to serve) and refrigerate until ready to use. Ideally you will do this a couple of hours before cooking the corn so the flavors have the chance to infuse fully.

**3 •** Soak the corn in lightly salted water for 15–20 minutes. Drain.

**4 •** If you are grilling (or barbecuing) corn without husks, do so for 20–30 minutes, turning so that each side is exposed for a time. The kernels should be turning brown or black. If you are grilling with the husks on, they'll need a little longer—grill for 15 minutes until the husks appear blackened, then peel the husks back and discard them. Return the "naked" corn to the grill for another 10 minutes, turning all the time. The kernels should become charred.

**5 •** Arrange on a plate, slice the jalapeño butter, slather a piece over each cob and serve with wedges of lime, if using, for extra citrus spike.

# LOUISIANA

The minute you land in New Orleans, something wet and dark leaps on you and starts humping you like a swamp dog in heat, and the only way to get that aspect of New Orleans off you is to eat it off. That means beignets and crayfish bisque and jambalaya, it means shrimp remoulade, pecan pie, and red beans with rice, it means elegant pompano au papillote, funky filé z'herbes, and raw oysters by the dozen, it means grillades for breakfast, a po' boy with chowchow at bedtime, and tubs of gumbo in between.
• TOM ROBBINS, *Jitterbug Perfume* •

THERE'S A DISH called the Hoppin' John that is eaten in the Deep South, a Cajun risotto-like blend of black-eyed peas, rice, onion and bacon that makes me think of my dad. I've no idea whether he has ever eaten Hoppin' John but, given that his name is John and he loves the blues, it seems like the kind of thing he would love. I grew up in a semidetached south London house where John Lee Hooker and B. B. King boomed from the stereo, my father tapping his foot and playing air guitar along to songs like "The Thrill Is Gone" (his enthusiasm demonstrating that the thrill was definitely still there, in fact). He was the personification of a Hoppin' John.

Food and music often go hand in hand in the Deep South, working in harmony to express the soul of the black servant class that has come to define the area. Soul food, soul music. The names of some dishes sound so inspired that they could almost be song lyrics. This was certainly the case with country singer Hank Williams's 1952 song "Jambalaya on the Bayou." He sang of Creole and Cajun dishes such as jambalaya (essentially a Deep Southern paella, combining rice with stock and meats) and "filé gumbo" to the tune of his "pick guitar." Music and food both capture the unique character of life around the Louisiana swamps. When they join forces they powerfully evoke the subtropical moisture and braids of streams in which crayfish, catfish and even alligators dwell.

I've chosen to cover Louisiana over any other Southern state because it seems to me that there you will find the purest expression of the Deep South. When we cook and eat from the Louisiana kitchen, we bring to life the hum of New Orleans and the wetlands of the bayou,[*] not to mention the area's mixed social groups including the Creoles and the Cajuns. Louisianan food will give you the richest taste of the American South—but before you start cooking, line up a Southern sound track. The experience will be massively enhanced by having Muddy Waters or Slim Harpo to hurry you and your gumbo pot along.

As a whole, the American South takes up at least one third of the United States, stretching from Maryland down to Florida and west all the way to Texas. These eleven former slave states of the Confederacy, which claimed secession from the rest of President Lincoln's American Union between 1861 and 1865, formed a markedly different cultural space from the north and west of the country. Slavery was absolutely axiomatic to the economic model of the region in the nineteenth century—tobacco and cotton were farmed in scale on plantations—and there remains a cultural consciousness far removed from European notions of "America" as embodied by New York and California.

Louisiana, and the South as a whole, have a sizeable black population that has been instrumental in developing the cuisine that exists there today. Though a master-servant dynamic historically prevailed between the white and black populations, there is something heartening about the influence—control, even—that the black servant class had in Southern kitchens. This influence persists and, if you consider the size of the region, it is little wonder that Southern soul food (a term that came to describe African-American food of the South in the 1960s) is so popular.

Native American culture meets that of African slaves, America's European colonizers and Latin American neighbors in Louisiana.[†] The French tradition dominates[‡]—the roux sauce is key, for example—and is overlaid with African-American influences such as the use of okra and Scotch bonnet peppers in stews like gumbo and jambalaya, which can be cooked in either the Creole or Cajun style. These are the two leading culinary approaches in the South and, though both reconcile local ingredients with classical French

• • • •

[*]The bayou is the name given to the wetlands, or marshes, of the Southern states of America—most famously in Louisiana. Like so many words (and many names for food), it is a French term that has been adopted and creolized by English speakers in the Deep South. The Louisiana bayou is flat and low, home to a vast ecosystem of wildlife including fresh shellfish.

[†]The state was named after Louis XIV, who was king of France from 1643 to 1715.

[‡]The French colonized North America from present-day Louisiana through the Midwest and up to French-speaking Canada from the middle of the sixteenth century, reaching the height of their influence in the mid-eighteenth century.

cuisine and there are some dishes with the same names, they diverge stylistically on execution.

Creole cuisine, based around New Orleans in southeastern Louisiana, descended more immediately from that of the French colonizers. More "uptown" and less rustic than its Cajun cousin, Creole cuisine was probably developed by servants who blended colonial French influences (the use of butter and cream, garlic and fresh herbs, roux sauces, bisques and chowders) with diverse ingredients from some of the eclectic communities in the Southern melting pot. Potatoes can be traced back to the Irish; okra to African populations; peppers and sweet spice to the Spanish; allspice to the West Indians, and filé powder (the spicy powdered leaves of the sassafras tree (see page 305) to the Native Americans. French cuisine always lies at the base of a Creole dish, however, typified by what American food writer Colman Andrews describes as the "Holy Trinity of Creole ingredients": celery, onions and bell peppers. This trio echoes the French mirepoix used as a base in dishes like *moules marinières* or ratatouille, as well as countless dishes elsewhere in the Mediterranean.

The Cajuns, based in southwestern Louisiana, came to the American South from Acadia (now Nova Scotia) in French-speaking Canada in the middle of the eighteenth century, deported by the British who were expanding their territories in Canada. Their cuisine shares its French framework with Creole cooking but is altogether simpler, more rustic and spicier, applying more of the hot chili peppers inherited from the Spanish to the ingredients of the bayou and surrounding coast. Game meats play a big part, as they would have done in Canada, and include rabbit, skunk and even alligator. These are often smoked or marinated with Cajun seasoning, which, although it varies from one kitchen to another, always contains cayenne and black peppers, paprika and bell peppers. Charcuterie clearly descended from French equivalents such as andouille and boudin boiling sausage can also be found here.

Soups and stews using local fish and meats sit at the heart (and soul) of both cuisines and include pinto beans stewed with bacon, black-eyed peas in the Hoppin' John, conch chowder (using conch shell meat with tomatoes and bell peppers) and shrimp bisque, a light and creamy prawn soup with a dusting of cayenne. Perhaps the most famous Southern stew is the gumbo, which is shared by Cajun and Creole cuisines. Using a stock base, gumbo is a combination of local shellfish such as shrimp, and meats like chicken and sausage, all of which are blended and thickened with a roux (usually darker in Creole gumbos—a sign of a more complicated cooking process) and served over rice. An étouffée is a thicker, roux-based shellfish stew served over rice.

Its primary ingredient is usually crayfish* in a dark roux sauce made with *beurre noisette.*†

These stews are typically served with rice, grits or corn bread. Southern grits—the name is derived from Old English "grytt," which means "coarse flour"—are usually made with alkali-treated corn, known as hominy.‡ They have a porridge-like consistency and are eaten particularly at breakfast alongside *grillades* (slow-cooked vegetables with beef or pork) or eggs. Breakfast in Louisiana might also include biscuits—hard, savory scone-like dough mounds served with gravy, eggs or steak.

As in Mexico and farther south in Latin America, corn and cornmeal provide affordable and accessible carbohydrate in the South (see page 310). Louisianans can mold deceptively bland cornmeal into delicious, if cholesterol-rich, creations such as corn bread (my buttermilk corn bread is an annual contribution to Thanksgiving dinner and we will be cooking it later on—see page 308) and hushpuppies. These are deep-fried balls of cornmeal batter—a simpler, Southern take on Spanish *croquettas*, frequently served as a side dish with fish or seafood.

Cornmeal is also used as a dry batter or "breading" for meat, fish and vegetables such as catfish (soaked overnight to soften), okra and, most famously, chicken. Deep-fried chicken has become synonymous all over the world with the black population of the American South, and many chefs and cooks have tried to emulate it. In *Home Cooking*, Laurie Colwin refers to a fried chicken recipe that will make you want to "stand up and sing 'The Star-Spangled Banner'"—once again demonstrating that good food and the impulse to make music are almost inextricable in the South. Fried chicken is an artform perfected in the Deep South, an example of soul food that, true to its name, both comes from and nourishes the soul. Inject some soul into your kitchen with some of the recipes I've included below and keep the music playing.

• • • •

* Crayfish is known as "crawfish" in Louisiana and takes on a variety of colorful names across the American South including "crawdads" and "mudbugs."

† *Beurre noisette* translates as "hazelnut butter," butter that is left to darken and acquire a nutty flavor and hazelnut color on a low heat. It adds complexity to roux sauces.

‡ Hominy is called *masa* in Spanish. See page 312 for its various uses in Mexican cuisine.

**PANTRY LIST** • filé (ground sassafras) • dried shrimp • cayenne • bay leaf • oregano • okra • cornmeal • grits • crayfish • butter • bell peppers • pinto beans • paprika • celery • onion

• • •

# • CHICKEN GUMBO •

This Louisiana casserole can be made solely with chicken, as mine is here, or as a "surf and turf" dish with the addition of prawns. If you choose to use prawns, add them 1–2 minutes before you finish cooking so they are cooked through but still tender. Listen to Dr. John's "Gris-Gris Gumbo Ya Ya" while you eat it and be transported to the bayou!

## • SERVES 4 •

2 tbsp cayenne pepper
2 tbsp Cajun seasoning
1 tbsp freshly ground black pepper
2 big pinches salt
8 pieces organic chicken, thighs and
    drumsticks, skin on
5 tbsp vegetable oil
2 heaping tbsp all-purpose flour
2 onions, finely chopped
2 green bell peppers, deseeded and sliced
    lengthways
4 sticks celery, finely chopped
4 cups chicken stock
1 bay leaf
1 cup okra, chopped into ⅓-inch pieces
7 oz andouillette, chorizo or other smoked
    sausage, sliced
Cajun seasoning, to serve
boiled rice, to serve

**1** • In a bowl, combine the cayenne, Cajun seasoning, black pepper and salt. Rub this mixture into the chicken—including under the skin—and marinate for 20 minutes.

**2** • Heat 4 tablespoons of the vegetable oil in a wide, heavy bottomed pan or large casserole over medium-high heat and brown the chicken for 4–5 minutes. (Some recipes will tell you to remove the skin—I prefer not to because they impart lots of chicken-y flavor to the casserole.)

**3** • Remove the chicken from the heat and set aside, keeping the fat in the pan. Reduce the heat and add the remaining tablespoon of vegetable oil and the flour and stir into a paste. Let this cook for a couple of minutes, allowing it to brown into a nutty dark roux.

**4** • Add the onions, bell peppers and celery, cover and allow them to soften for 3–4 minutes. Next, add the chicken stock, a little at a time, until you have a thick, caramel-colored sauce. Add the bay leaf, then return the chicken pieces to the pan, cover, reduce the heat, and simmer for 45 minutes.

**5** • Add the okra and smoked sausage and once again cover for another 30–45 minutes. When you next check the mixture, the chicken meat should just be starting to come away from the bone. Leave the stew on the heat, remove the bay leaf and chicken and pull the meat off the bones. Discard the skin and bones and put the meat back in the pan for a final blast of heat. Serve with a sprinkling of Cajun seasoning, alongside boiled rice.

# • BUTTERMILK CORN BREAD •

Ever since we left America, my friends and I have celebrated Thanksgiving each November. It's an excuse to watch Whitney Houston's 1991 Super Bowl performance of "The Star-Spangled Banner" and to indulge in wicked food—candied yams, pumpkin pie and, my specialty, corn bread. I use this recipe, with its buttermilk for rich, sour moisture, as a base. Sometimes I throw some chili in the batter or some cheese on top if I'm feeling adventurous. Mostly, though, I like it as it is—a slightly sweet accompaniment to roasted turkey that makes a fantastic vehicle for mopping up juices, sauces and stray morsels that linger on otherwise clean plates.

## • SERVES 8 •

9 tbsp unsalted butter, plus more for greasing the pan or
  muffin tin
⅔ cup granulated sugar
2 medium eggs
½ tsp baking powder
1½ cups cornmeal/polenta or coarse semolina
1¼ cups all-purpose flour

big pinch salt
1 cup buttermilk

**1** • Preheat the oven to 350°F. Grease either a 4-cup loaf pan or (and this often goes down well) 15–20 cupcake molds.

**2** • Melt the butter in a saucepan over low heat and fold in the sugar. Remove from the heat, beat in the eggs immediately and blend thoroughly.

**3** • In a bowl, combine the remaining dry ingredients. Fold the buttermilk into the pan and then add the dry ingredients. Beat well until smooth and without lumps.

**4** • Transfer the batter to the loaf pan or molds and bake in the oven for 30 minutes (or 20–25 for molds) until a knife comes out clean when inserted to the center. Cool in the pan for 5–10 minutes before turning out.

# CORN

...

Unlike the bright yellow corn we are familiar with in Europe and the United States, the corn of the Americas—*choclo* in Spanish—is white, crunchy and has large kernels. This *maiz blanco* (white corn) is eaten whole on the cob, alongside beans, in salads, stews like *pozole* (a Mexican white corn stew) and, most important, is nixtamalized (dried with alkali) to make hominy (dried corn kernels), which are then ground into corn flour, or masa.

Though it is little known outside of the Spanish-speaking world, masa is perhaps the defining ingredient of the Latin cuisines, integral to the more recognizable corn-based pancakes, wraps and breads such as tortillas and tacos in Mexico and tamales and *humitas* (see page 344) in the Andes.

Sometimes known as Peruvian Corn, white corn is now grown across the Spanish Americas and, despite its origins, is most famous for its role in Mexican cuisine. Tortillas, soft corn pancakes griddled on a circular grill called a *comal* (see page 312), lay the foundations for the most-traveled Mexican dishes such as burritos, enchiladas, quesadillas and, of course, nachos. Deep-fried, triangular cut wedges of tortilla wraps (more authentically referred to as *totopos* in Mexico), nachos have risen to prominence in the English-speaking world—popularly loaded with salsa, sour cream and grated cheese—and are more a supremely unhealthy example of Tex-Mex "fusion" than a genuine Mexican snack. In Mexico, you're more likely to be served a bowl of home-fried tortilla chips with some equally homemade guacamole (see my recipe on page 315), zingy and bright green.

Tacos, essentially mini tortillas, can come with either hard or soft shells. The former are more popular in fast-food chains and supermarkets (they hit the big time when fast-food outlet Taco Bell opened in the United States in 1962) while the latter are fresher and more traditional. In Mexico they are a popular street food, served with grilled, fried or braised meats and garnished with typical adornments like jalapeños, coriander, lime, diced onions and an array of salsas.

# MEXICO

Tita knew through her own flesh how fire transforms the elements, how a lump
of corn flour is changed into a tortilla, how a soul that hasn't been warmed by the
fire of love is lifeless, like a useless ball of corn flour.
• LAURA ESQUIVEL, *Like Water for Chocolate* •

I SPENT SEVERAL months in Mexico the summer after I left California and at first it was a culture shock.
There was a palpable sense of things shifting as I
made my way from the United States into the tropics.
Oh sure, there were the obvious differences. Spanish
became the dominant tongue, complexions dark-
ened, the sun brightened and humidity set in. But
there was something more, something intangible.

In Mexico, the magic of the Latin Caribbean—of
which authors like Colombian Gabriel García Márquez
have written—joins with the spirit of capitalist America. It is a borderland,
connecting North and Central America, Old World influences with a New
World setting, the English with the Spanish. It is where McDonald's meets the
Maya, increasingly commercialized yet riddled with ancient relics. Nowhere
is this truer than in the Yucatán region. Billboards advertising Coca-Cola and
teeth-whitening solutions overlook the azure seas of Cancún, while just eighty
miles south in Tulum, tourists dance to trance music in the night breeze with
Mayan ruins as a backdrop. A world of crazy Caribbean juxtapositions.

Mexico displays many of the traits that food writer and chef Maricel Presilla sees as typically Central American, a "heritage of the Old World: foods
and cooking techniques, Catholicism, Roman law, Iberian rhythms" married
with indigenous and African slave cultures across a vibrant, clammy land-
mass spanning the Pacific to Caribbean coasts. It is truly Creole, or *criollo*—
literally meaning "of the land" (see page 322)—which Presilla explains to be
"our word to describe what is ours as Latin Americans."

Mexico is a vibrant place of geographical diversity, from rugged mountains to coastal plains, big stretches of desert and long coastlines looking onto
the Pacific to the west and the Caribbean to the east. For the traveler there
are bountiful opportunities for adventure—it is almost impossible to get

bored—and the food of Mexico reflects this. It veritably sings off the table—bright as a budding pink dahlia (the national flower), voluptuous as the beloved avocados, strong as a *lucha libre** wrestler and patriotic as a mariachi. The cuisine is a reflection of Mexico's diversity—geographical, cultural, and spiritual—and of the national instinct to channel love and nurture via food.

Stories, or the need to contextualize the edible, sit at the heart of the Mexican kitchen. How else might you explain some of the colorful names awarded to the food we might eat there? A little donkey, a wad of bank notes and some bloke called Ignacio translate respectively to burrito, taco and nacho—three Mexican dishes, or more accurately street foods, with which we are well-acquainted in the West. They are all based on masa, or corn flour dough, which is used to make products that are as staple to Mexican cuisine as bread is to European traditions.

The tortilla is the best-known masa† product. The corn flour is mixed with water, kneaded and cooked on a clay griddle (the more traditional option, known as a *comal*) or a tortilla press. Soft, white and dappled with toasted spots, tortillas come in many different guises and form the basis for burritos, fajitas, chimichangas, enchiladas and quesadillas (see the Corn box on page 310 for descriptions of each).

The explanation for the ubiquity of many of these snacks and dishes in the West is that the United States has somewhat commandeered Mexican food as its own and, until very recently, impressions of "Mexican" cuisine derived mostly from Tex-Mex—the Texan fusion of Mexican cookery with that of the American South. Fajitas and chili con carne are examples, perhaps the culinary equivalents of the *Looney Toons* character Speedy Gonzalez. That is starting to change as Mexican cuisine comes into its own.

Several varieties of avocado exist across the Americas; Maricel Presilla simplifies them into the three categories of Mexican, Guatemalan and West Indian. The Mexican variety are suited to cooler, highland terrains, have a green to black skin and buttery flavor and are used in salads, tostadas, soups and, most famously, in guacamole. This is an Aztec dish and, as we'll see, while "mole" refers to the sauce consistency, "guaca" is derived from the word *aguacate* (avocado). The real deal is a different beast from ready-made supermarket mush—chunks of soft, ripe avocado with finely sliced red onion, tomatoes, garlic, chili and lime juice.

• • • •

* *Lucha libre* is Mexican wrestling. The *luchadores*, or wrestlers, dress in brightly colored masks that evoke Aztec gods and animals.

† Masa is made from nixtamalized white corn, hominy in English, which is then ground down to form corn flour—the basis of tortillas and tacos.

Chilies are more than a popular ingredient in Mexican cuisine—they are intrinsic to it. Mexico boasts a chili family of different shapes, sizes and colors, with names that could just as easily—dare I say it—be members of a drug cartel: *guajillo, piquín, cascabel, pasilla*, ancho, *mulato*, habañero, jalapeño and chipotle. The type of chili used can define a dish, and range from citrusy and mild (*piquín*), and smoky and sweet (*guajillo*) to hot and spicy (habañero). In the West we are most familiar with jalapeños—usually green and pickled—and chipotles, which are smoke-dried jalapeños used to add smokiness to bean and legume dishes, moles (see below), and the *adobo* meat marinade (also used widely in the Philippines and West Africa and roughly comparable to North African harissa).

Mexican cuisine is heavily reliant on simple, flavorful sauces to embellish dishes, often balancing heat and acidity with careful combinations of chilies and vinegar or lime.[*] The Mexican-style tomato salsa to which we've grown accustomed is otherwise known as *salsa cruda* (meaning "an uncooked sauce," hinting at its plainness) or *pico de gallo* ("at which roosters peck," highlighting its bitty composition) and has the four basic ingredients of tomatoes, white onion, chilies and coriander. Oil and vinegar can be added thereafter. Mexican *salsa verde* is a wholly different creature from the tapenade-style sauce we know in Europe (with parsley, capers and anchovies). It is composed of green tomatillos,[†] coriander, lime, white onion and green chilies.

Moles are a typically Mexican sauce eaten alongside meat and rice and generally mark feasts or days of celebration such as Independence Day in September or the festivities around a young girl turning fifteen (her *quinceañera*). The word "mole" sometimes even doubles up to mean "wedding." Many regions have their own take on the mole—Oaxaca, for example, is known as the Land of the Seven Moles—but *Mole Poblano*, the variation that originates in the town of Pueblo, has become something of a national dish. Moles are made by roasting and frying a *sofrito* base, typically adding a lot of lard, chilies, peanuts, chocolate, plantain, bread crumbs, garlic, tomatillos and spices such as cinnamon and star anise. While moles are thought to have originated in South Central America, their varied ingredients suggest plural influences, from the Old World to Africa.

• • • •

[*] Even the bean dishes we will come to later are very liquid in consistency, functioning like sauces to complement the dryness of other ingredients such as tortillas, rice and spit-roasted meats.

[†] Despite their name, tomatillos have nothing to do with tomatoes. They resemble gooseberries, have a tart fruity flavor and originate in Mexico, where they are essential to green sauces like *salsa verde*.

Rice and beans are another manifestation of Mexico's multiple influences, their alternative name of *moros y cristianos* (Moors and Christians) once again drawing attention to the marriage of cultures. This sustaining dish, often with unexpected layers of flavor, combines the Old World *sofrito* base with Mexican bean varieties (pinto or black beans) and the African tradition of combining rice with legumes. Sometimes a little meat, chipotle or herbs are added to enhance the flavor. Refried beans are another popular rendering of beans in Mexico and are often added to burritos. They are boiled and mashed to a paste, then cooked a second time in fat, onion and garlic until sweet, mushy and oily.

Mexicans love meat, though it isn't considered essential to eating well. Pork and beef were largely introduced by European settlers and, due to their high cost, cooks and butchers will make sure that no part of the animal goes to waste. Offcuts like shreds of dark meat and bones add complexity to stews, soups, beans, tacos and street food alike. Chicken, however, is much more common. It is cheaply reared and makes a versatile addition to stews and soups. With two long strips of coastline, Pacific and Caribbean, fish and seafood are abundant coastal delicacies and include lobster, prawns, scallops, marlin, dorado (mahimahi), amberfish, tuna and snapper.[*]

A narrower canon of spices is used in Mexican cookery than many of the other cuisines you'll find in these pages. Allspice, cloves, cinnamon, cumin and star anise are the most important and pair well with other native ingredients such as chocolate (or cacao[†] in its raw form) and vanilla, which was first cultivated by the Aztecs in the Gulf of Mexico. The Mesoamericans offered tributes of raw cacao beans to the gods at religious ceremonies, or consumed them as a drink. The Spanish took cacao beans back to Europe where milk, sugar and vanilla (also taken from Mexico) were combined with it to suit the European palate. We're used to chocolate being a sweet treat or dessert ingredient, but its inclusion in dishes like the mole adds roundness of flavor and a smooth consistency to savory dishes as well.

Cooking from the Mexican kitchen can be a revelatory adventure in combinations of ingredients you might never have considered before. Chili chocolate may be gaining popularity in Europe, but pairing both of

• • • •

[*] I ate some wonderfully simple fish steaks with chili and rice in Tulum, the most beautiful beach I've ever visited, on Mexico's Yucatán peninsula. Fish in Mexican cuisine is a big subject in itself and, due to the mammoth undertaking that is Mexican national cuisine, I am not covering regional cuisines in this book. I refer you to other books that do on page 349.

[†] Cacao is the raw form of chocolate, the cocoa bean. Willie Harcourt-Cooze is a great authority on cacao, particularly that of Latin America.

these ingredients with meat, or putting avocado and corn chips together into soups, still seems incongruous. Embrace the incongruity and create bright, colorful hybrids for food that is truly unique, and absolutely Mexican.

**PANTRY LIST** • chilies (various, see page 303) • lime • allspice • cloves • cinnamon sticks • chocolate • vanilla • tomatoes • onion • avocado • white corn • cornstarch • rice • beans • sour cream • cheese • tomatillo • coriander • peanuts • plantain

• • •

# • GUACAMOLE •

Mexico in a bowl. Learn to make this and you'll never buy store-bought guacamole ever again. Serve immediately to avoid discoloration of the avocados.

## • SERVES 4 •

1 small red onion, finely chopped
2½–3½ tbsp coriander, chopped
3 green chilies, deseeded and finely chopped
sea salt
3–4 ripe hass avocados
juice of 1–2 limes, to taste
2 ripe tomatoes, deseeded and coarsely chopped
tortilla chips, to serve

**1 •** In a mortar and pestle, grind half the onion, most of the coriander, the chilies and sea salt into a lumpy pulp.

**2 •** In a bowl, mash the avocado flesh with a fork. Add the onion, coriander and chili mix along with lime juice to taste, and adjust the salt. Fold in the remaining onion and the tomatoes, taking care that the tomatoes don't lose their shape or become too mushy.

**3 •** Transfer it to a bowl and crumble a tortilla chip on top, sprinkle the remaining coriander over the guacamole and serve immediately with tortilla chips.

# • TOMATO SALSA •

Serve this potent salsa with tortilla chips, alongside guacamole or as a condiment, and watch mouths pucker with delight. You can, of course, amp up the heat with more jalapeños—for my tastes, the proportion of chili given here stays just the right side of the divide between enjoyable and masochistic—but adjust to your palate.

## • SERVES 2–4 •

4 ripe tomatoes, diced
½ red onion, finely chopped
2 oz jalapeños, chopped
2 tbsp coriander, chopped
small tbsp extra virgin olive oil
juice of 2 limes
sea salt and freshly ground black pepper

**1** • Combine all the ingredients in a bowl and season to taste.
**2** • Sprinkle with some chopped coriander and decorate with tortilla chips around the edge of the bowl.

# • FRUITY ONE-CHILI MOLE •

Moles are notoriously complex, using a panoply of chilies (usually at least three varieties) and spices. This one, kindly contributed by Maricel Presilla from her book *Gran Cocina Latina*, is her creation for those starting out in their mole-making careers. It's a distillation of everything she considers integral to a good mole: "a balanced taste that blends spiciness, tartness and fruitiness; just enough salt to bring out all the flavours; a background kick of heat to bring the creamy sauce to life; enough fat for unctuous smoothness; and evocative aromas." It only requires *mulatto* chilies, which are deeply flavored, sweet and can be bought, dried, online.

## • SERVES 8–16 •

6 *mulatto* chilies, deseeded
1 tsp allspice berries
½ tsp star anise seeds
1 tbsp sesame seeds

1 corn tortilla (store-bought brands like
    Old El Paso are fine)
3 medium plum tomatoes
1 medium white onion, halved but not peeled
3 garlic cloves, coarsely chopped
3–3½ oz pitted prunes
1 cup extra virgin olive oil
2 oz dark chocolate (at least 70 percent cocoa solids),
    finely chopped
1½ tsp salt
up to 7¾ lb poultry or pork
1 cup chicken stock

**1** • Heat a ridged pan if you have one, or a large frying pan, until a drop of water sizzles on contact. Add the chilies and cook, pressing with a spatula, until fragrant, for about 15 seconds on each side. Lift them out and into a bowl, pour 6 cups of hot water over the top and allow them to soften for 20–30 minutes. Reserve the soaking liquid to use later on.

**2** • Add the allspice berries and star anise seeds to the pan and toast lightly for 30 seconds. Remove and place in a bowl. Then toast the sesame seeds for a minute, stirring constantly, until they pop and turn golden. Scoop into the bowl with the allspice berries and star anise seeds. Transfer the mixture to a mortar and pestle, grind to a powder and set aside.

**3** • Toast the tortilla in the pan until charred; remove, crumble into pieces and set aside.

**4** • Add the tomatoes and onion to the pan and, turning occasionally with tongs, cook until lightly charred, about 8 minutes. Remove from the heat. When cool enough to handle, remove the onion peel and pick most of the skins off the tomatoes, leaving just a few bits. Cut the vegetables into two or three pieces. Set aside.

**5** • Place the chilies and 3–4 tablespoons of the reserved liquid in a blender. Process to a smooth purée. Pour into a bowl and set aside.

**6** • Place the spice and sesame seed powder, tortilla, tomatoes and onion in a blender with the garlic, prunes and another tablespoon of the reserved chili liquid; process to a smooth purée and set aside.

**7** • Heat the olive oil over medium heat in a large saucepan. Add the chili purée and simmer, stirring occasionally, for about 10 minutes, or until the fat begins to separate from the solids and starts to sizzle. Add the vegetable purée and cook, stirring, for 15–20 minutes, or until the fat again begins to separate from the solids and the sauce thickens to the point where you can see the bottom of the pot as you move the spoon. Add the chocolate and continue stirring until it is melted. Add the salt and taste for seasoning, adding a little more if necessary. Use a wooden spoon to force the paste through a sieve into a bowl.

**8** • You now have enough mole paste to season up to 7¾ lb of chicken, pork, duck or turkey. Add the chicken stock to thin the paste to the consistency of a tomato sauce. Then add the cooked or half-cooked poultry or meat to the sauce and let it simmer until it is heated through or completely cooked.

# CARIBBEAN (JAMAICA)

*Visual surprise is natural in the Caribbean; it comes with the landscape,
and faced with its beauty, the sigh of history dissolves.*
• DEREK WALCOTT, *"The Antilles: Fragments of Epic Memory"*
*(Nobel Lecture, given on winning the 1992 Prize for Literature)* •

AT ITS SIMPLEST, "the Caribbean" is the Caribbean Sea, azure blue and gently lapping onto the eastern shores of Central America and the clusters of island nations it encircles—some big, others small. It's also a cocktail of languages—a shot of French blended with another of English, all finished with a long glug of Spanish—proportioned like the perfect punchy piña colada. It's a place where colonizers and colonized are shaken up in great proximity, producing tensions and tragedy but also a collective outlook rooted in hope, no worries and a little bit of magic. Despite cultural, political and linguistic differences, Caribbeans are bound together by these qualities. For the purpose of this chapter, though, the Caribbean is the West Indies—the English-speaking islands of Jamaica, Trinidad and Tobago.

Writers agree on this common heritage rooted in an appreciation of the otherworldly. Magic realist Gabriel García Márquez has long acknowledged the blurry line between what is real and imagined in his work,[*] while Dominican-American author Junot Díaz wrote in *The Brief Wondrous Life of Oscar Wao*, "Dominicans are Caribbean and therefore have an extraordinary tolerance for extreme phenomena." This sense of the presence of the supernatural is common across the Caribbean islands and coastline, as far south as Colombia and Venezuela at the bottom and stretching up to the Yucatán coast of Mexico.

Positive rhythms, creative vision and a magical undercurrent define everyday experience in the Caribbean, a mind-set I've found contagious whenever I have traveled in that part of the world. Caribbeans celebrate life

• • • •

[*] "It always amuses me that the biggest praise for my work comes for the imagination, while the truth is that there's not a single line in all my work that does not have a basis in reality. The problem is that Caribbean reality resembles the wildest imagination." Gabriel García Márquez

itself, and food plays an important part in this. Colombian academic Oscar Guardiola-Rivera once told me, "We don't sit around a table as a distraction from the travails of daily life. We do everything else *in order to* sit around the table. What you share when you eat in the Caribbean isn't just food, it's stories. Words become a condiment to the food."

Caribbean cuisine in general, and West Indian in particular, bring together all its strands of ethnic and colonial influence, from European to African, Native American, Indian and even Chinese. Food is the lovechild of history here, and it has traveled with the West Indian diaspora far and wide. One of its new homes is my native London where, in the 1950s, arrivals from the Commonwealth colonies of Jamaica, Trinidad and Tobago came and put down roots. Theirs was not a seamless integration into British culture,[*] but despite—or perhaps because of—their struggle to assimilate, we have an annual celebration of London's Afro-Caribbean population, the Notting Hill Carnival, each August, when colorful floats and reggae music parade the grand streets while crowds of mixed faces feast on jerk chicken. Caribbean food from the former British colonies surrounded me as I was growing up and has real presence in the Big Smoke, hence my decision to cover West Indian food (over that of the Spanish- or French-speaking Caribbean) in this chapter.

The great irony is that, in London, it's easy to associate West Indian dishes with being a bit unhealthy—more fast food than temple food. West Indian food outlets are often singularly unglamorous, located in the traditionally ghettoized areas of London—Brixton, Tottenham, parts of Notting Hill—and rarely make claims about the nutritional virtues or health benefits of their food. But in reality, West Indian cuisine is largely healthy—low in saturated fat, high in protein, vegetables and full of cleansing flavors like ginger, chili and allspice.

The history of slavery in the West Indies explains much of its cuisine. People of African and mixed (African with European) descent form the majority demographic in Jamaica, and West African culinary traditions are reflected in the use of ingredients such as okra, plantain and ackee (the national fruit, not unlike lychee and often bought canned). Yet some of the dishes for which we know Jamaica best, like goat curry and roti wraps, are adaptations of Indian dishes, applying the tradition of currying to local meat or using favorite Jamaican flavors such as allspice berries, Scotch bonnet peppers, ginger and coconut milk.

• • • •

[*] Race riots punctuated their early decades in the British capital—the Notting Hill riots in the 1950s and '60s, Brixton riots in 1981. For those interested, read poet Linton Kwesi Johnson's brilliant poem "The Great Insurrection" about the "historical occasion" of the Brixton riots.

Following the emancipation within the British Empire of West African slaves after 1831, demand for cheap labor on British-run plantations remained. In the middle of the nineteenth century, plantation owners appealed to countries such as India and China, offering workers indentured servitude in return for their moving costs. Thousands of Chinese and Indians took up the offer and arrived on West Indian shores. This was common across the British Caribbean and created a substantial Indo-Caribbean population, of which writer V. S. Naipaul is an example, a descendant of indentured workers in Trinidad. Despite having famously written of his contempt for his homeland,[*] some poignant lines in a letter home to his father, written while he was studying at Oxford, are powerfully evocative of the Caribbean he left behind. "I long for the nights that fall blackly, suddenly, without warning. I long for a violent shower of rain at night. I long to hear the tinny tattoo of heavy raindrops on a roof, or the drops of rain on the broad leaves of that wonderful plant, the wild tannia."

The first West Indian dish that springs to most Londoners' minds is jerk chicken (or, to a lesser extent, jerk pork or goat)—a sweet, hot and smoky way of flavoring meat that defines the cuisine. Depending on the cook's approach, the meat is either rubbed in dry seasoning or marinated in sauce for a good few hours before grilling. The core flavors of jerk seasoning are allspice and chili. Allspice, otherwise known as pimento berry, is *the* Caribbean spice and gives jerk its unique smoky flavor. Though its dried fruit resembles black peppercorns, its taste is sweeter, like a blend of cinnamon, cloves and nutmeg. At their most authentic, jerk meats are even grilled over pimento wood, further infusing the flesh with smokiness while the skin becomes crisp. Of course, jerk also has a heat to it and the Jamaican chili of choice is the sweet but blindingly hot red Scotch bonnet.[†] Whether to use rub or to marinate is a point of conflict among jerk lovers. If you favor the "wet" approach to flavoring jerk meats, then some cooks use lime or soy sauce to give the chicken a lift of sharpness. (This rings of Asia, of course, and is a sign of the lasting Chinese influence on Jamaican cuisine.)

Jerk is usually eaten with rice and peas, a misleading name for white rice combined with kidney beans. This is easy to replicate on foreign soil (unlike some of Jamaica's other signature ingredients and dishes, which have a

• • • •

[*] In 1958, V. S. Naipaul wrote in the *Times Literary Supplement* that "superficially, because of the multitude of races, Trinidad may seem complex, but to anyone who knows it, it is a simple, colonial, philistine society."

[†] The Scotch bonnet is not unlike the supremely hot habañero of Mexico (see page 313). Most West Indian recipes requiring chili will specify Scotch bonnets.

singularly exotic ring to them) and I've eaten a lot of it over the course of my south London youth.

Other key ingredients include ackee fruit (red skin, creamy flesh, black seeds, with a flavor not unlike lychee), which was introduced by West African slave ships in the eighteenth century. This is often combined with saltfish (known elsewhere as *bacalao*), a widely eaten breakfast dish that was also inspired by West African cuisine (see page 277), and which has become Jamaica's national dish. Saltfish is combined with boiled or canned ackee fruit as well as onions, tomatoes, and trusty allspice and Scotch bonnet.

Other saltfish and vegetable side dishes include those made with okra and callaloo. The latter is the name given to both a green leaf vegetable (sometimes known as amaranth) and a dish enjoyed any time, anywhere in Jamaica. Not dissimilar from spinach, callaloo leaves are large, green and rich in iron and calcium. They are usually steamed but can also be cooked in coconut milk (more typical in Trinidad and Tobago), added to soups or enjoyed with saltfish from breakfast right through to the evening meal. Callaloo can also be prepared alongside okra, green plantains and breadfruit.

Green plantains are served chopped into chunks and fried. (I always find their savoriness alarming because, though they look like bananas, their under-ripeness means that plantains are treated more as vegetables than fruit in the Caribbean.) Another widely used fruit or vegetable (the line between the two often seems blurry in this part of the world) is breadfruit, which belongs to the mulberry family but has a starchy, carbohydrate-like texture and taste.

Creole languages exist all over the Americas—from the Deep South of the United States and across the Caribbean—but none of them are standardized, none the same as another. Jamaica is particularly famous for its unique brand of patois, the creolized language that developed as a result of the range of different peoples who have immigrated. Jamaican Creole language is almost embodied by Jamaican patties, which are shaped like Latin American empanadas but use local fillings such as goat or seafood, Scotch bonnet heat, and have the Indian and Chinese influences of turmeric and soy sauce respectively.

The land of patties and patois, the West Indies has a hybrid cuisine typical of the Americas. Its food, like the Creole language of Jamaica, is the living result of a fraught, often violent imperial history. But its dishes transcend the murky territory of postcolonial politics. To borrow the words of the great poet Derek Walcott, food—like the visual splendor of the Caribbean landscape he describes—makes "the sigh of history dissolve."

**PANTRY LIST** • allspice • Scotch bonnet chilies • salt cod • ginger • curry powder • coconut milk • ackee • goat • lime • soy sauce • kidney beans • okra • callaloo • plantain

• • •

# • JERK CHICKEN •

Caribbeans often cook jerk chicken until it is falling off the bone—almost dry. The word "jerk" or "jerky" is in fact thought to derive from the Spanish name for dried meat, *charqui* (a word from Quechua, a native South American language). So what strikes me as "overcooked" in jerk chicken is perhaps *au point* for Caribbean diners. In any case, I don't like dry meat, so forgive me for creating a jerk chicken recipe that keeps it tender. If you like, you can grill the chicken for five minutes each side, then bake it in the oven at 350°F for another fifteen to twenty minutes—but it's so much better on the barbecue. Reserve this recipe for hot days, when smoky coals combine with Scotch bonnet heat and charred chicken skins for an eating experience that really says "don't worry, be happy." A word of warning—be careful when you're handling the chilies (consider using plastic gloves): if you mistakenly touch your face afterward, you'll experience an almighty sting.

### • SERVES 6 •

1 tbsp black peppercorns
1 tbsp allspice powder
1 tsp ground cinnamon
1 tsp freshly grated nutmeg
2 shallots, coarsely chopped
4 scallions, coarsely chopped
few sprigs thyme
1 tbsp coriander, chopped
2–4 Scotch bonnet chilies (depending on how fiery
      you like it), deseeded and coarsely chopped
¼ cup dark brown sugar
1 tsp salt
2 tbsp soy sauce

juice of 2 limes
12 organic chicken pieces, thighs and drumsticks

**1** • Grind the peppercorns in a mortar and pestle, then mix in a blender with the allspice, cinnamon, nutmeg, shallots, scallions, thyme, coriander and chilies. Then add the brown sugar, salt, soy sauce and lime juice and blend into a paste. This is your marinade.

**2** • Place the chicken legs in a single layer in a large casserole dish and pour the marinade all over them, rubbing it into the meat and under the skin. Cover with plastic wrap and refrigerate for at least 3 hours, preferably more.

**3** • When the chicken has marinated for a good few hours, but before you start on your rice and peas (see below), light your barbecue. You will preferably have one on which you can control the height of the grill above the coals, which should be white before you start cooking and without any flames at all (very important—you want a bed of heat that exudes charcoally flavors but which doesn't burn your chicken to cinders!).

**4** • Sear the chicken on both sides so it acquires good depth of color, then raise the grill higher (where it will be cooler) and cook for 20–30 minutes. All barbecues differ, so look for meat that is starting to come away from the bone and juices that run clear. Serve with rice and peas.

# • RICE AND PEAS •

"Burn off your rice and *peeeeeas!*" was for several years the sound track to my spinning classes at Brixton Rec. dance hall pounding away as we worked. It isn't really a fattening dish, although the delicious flavors are delivered in part by coconut milk, and the "peas" are in fact kidney beans, so it's heavier than the name lets on. I particularly like this recipe because it's so intuitive—you don't need scales, just handfuls and aluminum cans! Be bold with your use of coriander to garnish; it enhances rice and peas as the perfect canvas for scorching jerk chicken (see above).

### • SERVES 4 •

1–2 tbsp vegetable oil
1 white or yellow onion, finely chopped
1½ cups long-grain or basmati rice (or if not
    using scales, take an empty 14-oz can
    and fill it three-quarters full with rice)

1¾ cups coconut milk (1 can)
1¾ cups water (1 can)
14 oz kidney beans (1 can)
big pinch salt and freshly ground black pepper
big pinch thyme leaves
iceberg lettuce to serve, shredded
handful coriander to serve, chopped

**1** • In a large, deep frying pan heat the oil over medium heat and sauté the onion for 8–10 minutes, until translucent. Add the rice, mix it thoroughly with the oil and onion, then add the coconut milk and water. Bring to a boil, then reduce the heat.
**2** • Add the kidney beans, salt, pepper and thyme, then simmer, stirring occasionally, for as long as it takes for the rice to cook and the liquid to be absorbed. It needs to dry out a little and become granular again—not sludgy. This should take 15–20 minutes.
**3** • Prepare a platter with the shredded iceberg and make a well in the center, then scoop the rice and peas into it. Crown it with the jerk chicken and sprinkle a generous handful of chopped coriander on top.

# PERU

Since it is impossible to know what's really happening, we Peruvians lie,
invent, dream and take refuge in illusion. Because of these strange circumstances,
Peruvian life, a life in which so few actually do read, has become literary.
• MARIO VARGAS LLOSA, *The Real Life of Alejandro Mayta* •

WHEN THE PERUVIAN writer Mario Vargas Llosa won the Nobel Prize for Literature in 2010, his inspiration was said to come from "the secret magic of Peru." This idea of Peru's "secret magic"—a kind of indefinable beauty—seems to be a common one, not least in terms of its food.

Peru's cuisine is incredibly rich, involving punchy flavors and bold techniques such as the marinating of raw fish for ceviche. But it's also very subtle. Peruvian restaurateur Martin Morales, from London's Ceviche restaurant, talks about "having *sazón*," a natural grasp of native flavors and balancing them to perfection. Having *sazón* is a bit like being born with rhythm, but that isn't to say you can't pick up the secrets of Peruvian cookery. Learning to cook like a Peruvian is a question of understanding balance and subtlety. Use of chili is a good example—it's a prevalent ingredient in Peruvian food but used in a more delicate way than in, for example, Asian cuisines—it seduces you with heat rather than dominating the palate.

The three main regions of Peru are coastal, Andean and Amazonian, but its cuisine doesn't necessarily follow the lay of the land. It is influenced as much by centuries of people's migration as by regional ingredients. Peru's first settlers are thought to have been Asian nomads, eaters of simple foods who cultivated corn, beans and chilies. Some of our now staple ingredients in the West—potatoes, tomatoes, peanuts, even popcorn—originated in or around Peru.[*] Native tribes, known collectively as the Incas, introduced them

••••

[*]This is a point of debate among food historians and anthropologists. Ingredients such as the tomato, potato, red bell pepper, chili, avocado and corn can be traced back variously to Mexico, Peru, Cuba and surrounding countries. It's safe to say, however, that these are all New World ingredients that originated in the Spanish Americas and were brought to Europe with the conquistadores in the sixteenth century.

to the Spanish conquistadores in the sixteenth century—who themselves introduced meats like chicken and beef to the New World. African slaves and Chinese and Japanese communities have since brought their own culinary traditions to the table, too, forming the Afro,[*] Chifa and Nikkei aspects of the cuisine.

Chifa is the cuisine of the Chinese immigrants who arrived in Peru from Guangdong (see page 240) in the nineteenth and twentieth centuries, and its most famous dish is chaufa rice—fried rice with chicken, pork, almonds, pineapple, ginger and scallions. Chifa recipes like this remain relatively loyal to the Cantonese kitchen but have been adapted to suit the ingredients most readily available in Peru. This influx of Cantonese cooks introduced Peru to Asian ingredients such as soy sauce and ginger, from which Peruvian cuisine has never looked back.

Nikkei, meanwhile, is the name given to the Japanese diaspora that has traveled and settled around the world. Peru has one of the world's largest Nikkei communities and its influence can be seen in the Peruvian national dish, ceviche, which echoes the Japanese approach to raw fish. This may all sound like fusion cuisine but, as with so much of the food of the Americas, Peru's unique cuisine is the result of diverse immigrant influences etching themselves onto the landscape and drawing on fundamental Andean building blocks such as corn, chilies, potatoes and Pacific seafood.

Peru's classic dishes are ideal for creative cooks because they are easy to adapt. This is partly because marinating is a key technique, so it's easy to play with quantities or to throw in something extra or different should you fancy it. One good example is ceviche, or marinated seafood. Though its key ingredients are fresh raw fish and a marinade of chili, lime, salt and onion, the balance of components can be tinkered with, different fish or seafood used, varying quantities of garlic, ginger, corn, avocado or tomato added, and so on.

The first time I ate ceviche, I was wary. Uncooked fish with chilies, citrus and raw onions? It sounded like the kind of food you most definitely wouldn't want to eat on a date (not that I was on one), and that you avoided when traveling (which I was, in fact, doing). I don't know what my expectations were, but I do know that the ceviche I eventually tried surpassed them.

• • • •

[*] The Afro-Peruvian population is concentrated around Peru's coast and in the capital city of Lima. Like its counterparts in Brazil, the Caribbean and the United States, this community has been instrumental in defining today's Peruvian cuisine, which is, by definition, a creolized one. Dishes like *cau cau*, a tripe stew of potatoes, chili, onion, garlic and turmeric, are reminiscent of the big one-pot stews you will find in West Africa, the Northern *paneladas* of Brazil (see page 333) or the gumbo of Louisiana—but with a particularly Peruvian, or Andean, character.

It contained white fish and lobster, avocado, corn, little pieces of tomato, plumes of red onion and, yes, lots and lots of chili and lime juice. It seemed to take everything that is brilliant about typically South American ingredients and apply them to seafood of the freshest caliber.

Another example of Peruvians' adaptability in the kitchen is *anticuchos*, an Afro-Peruvian specialty of barbecued meat brochettes. Originally made with beef heart (the Spanish kept the "good" meat for themselves and gave offal to their slaves), the meat is cut into cubes and marinated in vinegar, *aji panca* (fruity Andean chili), garlic and cumin, then grilled on skewers. Nowadays, octopus, chicken livers, salmon and tofu are also used for *anticuchos*, but the recipe's original use of beef hearts is testament to the ingenuity of Peru's slave communities. (This division of culinary echelons is of course a feature of many cuisines all over the world. See Lazio on page 86 and China on page 235 for examples.)

A contemporary (and onion-free) take on ceviche is the *tiradito*, more like a carpaccio or sashimi of finely sliced fish. This clearly evokes the Nikkei community but, garnished with Andean ingredients like white corn, takes on a Peruvian personality, too. Other seafood dishes include *chupe de camarones*, prawn chowder containing broad beans, rice, egg and oregano, and served with a slice of potato; or *jalea*, a mountain of lightly breaded seafood or fish resembling fritto misto. *Jalea* is delicious with the chunky onion relish known as *salsa criolla*, which is eaten in various guises all over South America (see Argentina, page 341). For this, red onions are finely sliced a la pluma ("like feathers") and then left to marinate with coriander, *aji amarillo* chilies, lemon, oil and seasoning. Literally translating to "Creole sauce," *salsa criolla* is enjoyed as a condiment with countless Peruvian dishes, from typically Andean delights such as *humitas* and tamales (see page 344) to dishes like *lomo saltado* (stir-fried tenderloin beef) and *arroz con pato* (literally, rice with duck), which also nod to Asia in their use of stir-frying and aromatic seasonings such as cumin, garlic and coriander.

Sweet root vegetables such as pumpkin, sweet potato and yucca (otherwise known as cassava or manioc—see Brazil, page 333) play a big part in Peruvian cuisine. Yucca can be fried or made into bread (*pan de yucca*), which uses yucca starch, cheese, egg and butter for a singularly soft and heavy South American bread roll. Root vegetables are also key to making *causas*, a typically Peruvian dish that hovers between a terrine and a potato cake. Finely mashed potato, yellow chili, lime, and salt are layered with the optional additions of crab, tuna, mayonnaise, tomato and avocado, all finished off with *salsa criolla*.

Quinoa is an Andean crop that thrives at high altitudes. It is thought to be native to Bolivia but is grown and used widely in the Peruvian, Argentine, Chilean, Ecuadorian and Colombian highlands, too. It makes a fantastic salad ingredient and accompaniment to fish dishes. Though it looks like a grain, it is botanically recognized to be a fruit and has a protein content of up to 18 percent, making it comparable to the protein value of meat. Andean farmers and their families have relied on it for centuries. (Quinoa has in recent decades rocketed in popularity in the developed world thanks to its superfood qualities, creating controversy around the nutritional repercussions this might have for Bolivians. So be sparing with your quinoa, readers!)

Finally, *picarones* are a popular dessert sold in the street: little pumpkin and sweet potato doughnuts eaten with a sauce of unrefined sugar known as *miel de chancaca* (a rich honeyed syrup flavored with orange zest). A *picaron* is a naughty, almost irresistible character—an apt name for this deep-fried treat and, given that *picar* means "to pick at" in Spanish, perhaps also an appropriate personification of Peru and its cuisine. Cheekily picking at the culinary heritage of its immigrant communities, maybe Peru itself is a crafty *picaron*? From a culinary perspective, could this ability to pinch and fuse other traditions with its own so seamlessly be the "secret" in Peru's "secret magic"?

**PANTRY LIST** • chili • lime • cumin • oregano • coriander and parsley • white fish (corvina, sea bass, sole) • prawns • scallops • squid • avocado • white corn • sweet potato • pumpkin • cassava • soy sauce • quinoa

◆ ◆ ◆

# • CEVICHE •

This really is Peru's signature dish, and with more than eight hundred varieties, there's clearly plenty of scope to tweak to your tastes. If you're looking for life-affirming food—this is it. The raw onion, kick of chili, acid prickle of lime juice and delicate raw fish combine to brighten the mood and cleanse the palate. I love that it's so easy to make and so simple to adapt. You can have fun with this one. I've made suggestions about where you can use some creative license. You could, for example, try using another citrus fruit in place of (or with) lime. Jason Atherton uses *yuzu* at Pollen Street Social, and I've heard grapefruit works well, too.

## • SERVES 4–6 •

1 lb skinless fillets of white fish (such as sea bass,
    sole or snapper)
sea salt flakes
handful raw shelled prawns, raw shelled lobster,
    raw roeless scallops (optional)
2 small red onions, finely sliced into half-moons
1 cup lime juice (about 15 limes' worth), strained
    to remove the bits of flesh
1 garlic clove, finely chopped
½-inch piece ginger, very finely chopped
2½ tbsp coriander, chopped
1 chili (yellow if possible, though green will do),
    deseeded and finely chopped

TO SERVE (OPTIONAL)
1 large hass avocado (ripe but not mushy), diced
2 tomatoes, halved, deseeded and diced
fresh sweet corn cut from 1 cob
1⅓ lb fresh podded broad beans, cooked in salted
    water for 5 minutes and slipped from skins

**1** • Put the fish fillets in the freezer for 20 minutes. This makes them easier to cut precisely. Remove and cut into 1-inch chunks. Roll in salt flakes along with any shellfish you are using and set aside.
**2** • You can also soak your sliced onion in cold water for a few minutes, which will mellow out the flavor a bit.

**3** • Mix the lime juice with the garlic, ginger and about half your coriander. Strain the mixture over the fish, making sure that it is evenly coated. Place in the fridge for an hour to "cook" the raw fish.

**4** • When you're ready to eat, create a bed of onions, remove the fish from its marinade and place it on the onions. Pour about half of the residual marinade in which you "cooked" the fish back over it, then throw over the chilies and remaining coriander before serving.

**5** • At this point add your extra ingredients. I'm a big fan of avocado and corn with my ceviche. The corn adds some lovely crunch while soft avocado really complements the fish.

# • RICE PERUVIAN-STYLE •

Known as *arroz a la Peruana* in Peru, this is a gently flavored rice dish with typically Peruvian white corn (otherwise known as *choclo*), some garlic, salt and pepper. It makes rice a bit more interesting without making it a main dish. It's really just a question of cooking the rice in a frying pan so that you can integrate the other ingredients more easily.

## • SERVES 6 •

1 tbsp olive oil
1 onion, finely chopped
2 garlic cloves, very finely chopped
2 cups long-grain rice
2 cups chicken stock
fresh sweet corn cut from 3 cobs
⅓ cup peas (optional)
2 tbsp unsalted butter
salt
1½ tbsp flat-leaf parsley, leaves coarsely chopped (optional)

**1** • In a large, deep frying pan heat the olive oil over medium heat and soften the onions for 5 minutes. Then add the garlic for a minute. Add the rice and stir constantly for 3 minutes or so in the oily onion and garlic mixture.

**2** • Add the stock, sweet corn, peas if you're using them, and butter all at once. Cover the pan and cook gently for 20–25 minutes, until the rice is tender.

**3** • Season to taste and serve, with parsley sprinkled over the top, if using.

# • SALSA CRIOLLA •

This simple salsa is a staple composed of Peru's holy trinity of flavors: red onion, lime and chili. It gives anything, best of all fish, a real lift. The conventional chili to use is *aji amarillo*—literally "yellow chili"—but seeing as this may be a challenge to find on home soil, any mild to medium (and preferably slightly sweet) chili, such as fresh jalapeño, will do.

## • SERVES 6–8 •

3 small red onions, finely sliced into half-moons
2 mild chilies (such as *aji amarillo* or jalapeños),
    deseeded and finely chopped
1½ tbsp coriander, leaves chopped
1½ tbsp flat-leaf parsley, leaves chopped
juice of 2 limes
1 tbsp red wine vinegar
3 tbsp olive oil
sea salt and freshly ground black pepper

**1** • Mix all the ingredients together in a bowl. Refrigerate for at least 30 minutes before serving, so the flavors mingle, then you're good to go.

# BRAZIL

Tupi or not Tupi: that is the question.
• OSWALD DE ANDRADE, *Manifesto Antropófago* •

IN THE *Cannibal Manifesto* (*Manifesto Antropófago*) of 1928, Brazilian poet and polemicist Oswald de Andrade proposed that Brazil should cannibalize other cultures to further its own. He used the cannibalistic Brazilian Tupi tribe as a metaphor to weigh up the pros and cons of such cultural cannibalism, ironically playing on Shakespearean verse to pose his central question. In recent decades Brazil has, to a certain extent, "consumed" first world culture, partly in order to bolster its perception in the West; for much of the last decade it has had the fastest-growing economy in Latin America.

Food is no exception to this program of assimilation. While the traditional hotpots (pan food, or *paneladas*) have continued to bubble away discreetly on cooktops for generations, Brazil's young cosmopolitans are keener on the perceived sophistication of Italian and Japanese food. Oh, misguided youth. The beauty of real, authentic Brazilian cuisine seems to be underrecognized nowhere more so than in Brazil itself. In most Brazilian cities you'll find pizza, pasta and sushi in abundance, particularly in the south, where cream-based spaghetti sauces are very popular (echoing the same appetite for cream- and cheese-based fare in Argentina—see *la fugazza* pizza on page 342). Culinary otherness has long been celebrated here and, because so few Brazilians have trumpeted their country's native edible riches, Brazil has failed to develop the international reputation for food that it deserves. This is only now starting to change with the rise of São Paolo as a serious food destination boasting world-class chefs like Alex Atala[*] of restaurant D.O.M.

Brazilian chef Samantha Aquim, known in Brazil for her chocolate brand

••••

[*] Alex Atala is the chef patron of Sao Paulo's D.O.M restaurant, voted sixth-best restaurant in the world in 2013's 50 Best Restaurants awards. Atala was number forty-four in *Time* magazine's 100 Most Influential People in the World. In the words of fellow chef René Redzepi of Noma, "He has surrendered to the enormous task of shaping a better food culture for Latin America. His philosophy of using native Brazilian ingredients in haute cuisine has mesmerised the continent."

Aquim, assured me that things are definitely changing and says a new, very genuine Brazilian artistic sensibility is emerging. Real pride is being taken in things that reflect authentic Brazilian lifestyle and culture. As she says, "Beans, samba and dancing mulattas are not our everyday Brazil." Happily, Brazilian food is seeing a revival and is increasingly being celebrated by those that matter—Brazilians themselves.

At well over three million square miles and nearly two hundred million people, however, Brazil is a complicated place to define. Massively concentrated around the coastline, its people are a mix of descendants of indigenous groups like the Tupi tribe, European colonizers (who began to arrive in the sixteenth century) and black slaves brought over from West Africa in the eighteenth century.* These three dominant social groups have mixed, perhaps more so than in other countries that could also be termed postcolonial melting pots, creating substantial mulatto (black and white) and *caboclo* (Indian and white) populations.

Geographically, Brazil spans a vast area of rain forest, grasslands, scrublands and mangroves, and, from a culinary perspective, can therefore only be divided—crudely—into four regions: Amazonian, northeast, southeast and south. While both Northeast and Southeast Brazil are on the Atlantic, seafood is more common in the north, upward from the state of Bahia, where stews like *moqueca de peixe* made with meaty white fish such as grouper, snapper and mahimahi (dorado) are popular.

Despite all the regional variation in Brazilian cuisine, however, there is one overarching feature, a real clue to Brazil's culture of conviviality—*paneladas*. That is to say, food cooked in just one pan large enough to feed a lot of people. Monotonous, did I hear you say? Oh no, *paneladas* are loaded with a spectrum of flavors to keep the palate interested well beyond the first few bites. "We don't cook for one, we cook for ten," Samantha Aquim says. "*Comida de panela* is family food, though no less interesting for it."

*Comida de panela* is a technique found all over Brazil, with flavors and ingredients that vary from region to region. Common flavors include coriander—thrown over many dishes—as well as *colorau* or *urucum* (essentially sweet paprika, like Spanish *pimentón*), dried beef (which can come two ways, *carne de sol*, sun-dried, and *carne seca*, salt-cured) and burnt garlic. While budding cooks all over the world are taught never to burn the garlic, in Brazil this is often a starting point. *Feijoada*, *the* classic Brazilian bean dish (a recipe for which my

• • • •

*Nearly 40 percent of all slaves brought to the Americas from Africa are reported to have been trafficked to Brazil.

friend Gizane Campos has contributed below), starts in this way and, like so many other *panelada* dishes, is thickened with manioc flour, the ground root of the tuberous manioc plant (also known as cassava or yucca), which offers a nutty flavor and mealy texture. Used in baking, frying and stews all over Latin America and the Caribbean, manioc flour is especially important to Brazilian cuisine because it is the key ingredient of *farofa*, the buttery toasted manioc flour "dust" served alongside *feijoada* and other stew-based main courses.

The legacy of the African diaspora (people whose ancestors arrived from countries such as the Congo, Nigeria, Angola) largely characterizes the cuisine of northern Brazil, with ingredients like palm oil (known locally as *dendê* oil) and coconut. From the sixteenth to the nineteenth centuries, about five million slaves were brought to Brazil to work the land, many of whom were sent up to the sugar plantations in the country's north—their huge influence is still very palpable today. Go to Salvador de Bahia, for example, and see the *baianas*, Afro-Brazilian women dressed in their colorful beaded attire, selling *acarajé*—black bean fritters fried in palm oil. Delicacies like *bobó de camarão* (prawn *panelada*, in a thickened sauce with manioc) or *casquinha de siri*, an appetizer of crab shells stuffed with the crabmeat, vegetables and Parmesan cheese, combine northern seafood ingredients with African culinary customs (and even a touch of Europe in the form of Emilia-Romagna's most famous cheese), to dizzying effect.

Seafood in the south is served more simply; indeed there is a general tendency toward blander food in the bigger southern cities of Rio de Janeiro and São Paulo (cue bad spaghetti!). Here meat starts to creep in more—the classic triptych of meat, beans and rice adorns many a plate. Brazilians love their meat and as a nation, they grow steadily more carnivorous as you travel south. Toward Argentina, steak, barbecues, sausages, pork and chicken hearts become the order of the day. I remember going to a Brazilian restaurant in east London with a group of friends from Belo Horizonte, a central southern city in Brazil, and being horrified when a pile of bulging, vein-striped hearts emerged from the kitchen. Apparently they are delicious—I'm afraid I'm an ex-vegetarian who's too squeamish to try.[*]

The seven states of Amazonia in the north and west of Brazil (home to the Tupi tribe to which Oswald de Andrade alluded) offer a unique spectrum of

• • • •

[*] Incidentally, I am not a food lover who subscribes to the belief that anyone interested in food needs to be so adventurous an eater as to completely depart from their comfort zone. Edible sojourns from your regular dietary choices are to be encouraged, but I object to an overt emphasis on edible novelties to the point where you are just plain freaked out.

age-old tribal dishes using ultra-local fare. *Colorau*, a spice similar to sweet paprika, made by grinding *annatto* tree berries, is particularly popular up here, seasoning a wealth of freshwater fish such as *surubim* (a river catfish that can be smoked like salmon) and meaty white *tambaqui*, the ribs of which are grilled or minced and added to *paneladas*. *Picadinho de tambaquí*, containing onions, garlic, hot chili, coconut milk and palm oil, is an example of one such *panelada*, served with rice, *farofa* and the ubiquitous local herb *jambú* (similar to sage), which has a disorientating anesthetic effect on the mouth. *Jambú* leaves (along with chicory and grated manioc) are also used in a sauce for marinated and roasted duck, known locally as *pato no tucupí*.

Brazil's culinary diversity is perhaps underexposed because so many of the ingredients are ultra local and don't travel well. Happily, all the recipes I've shared here are achievable in your own kitchen, not least Samantha Aquim's incredible (and simple) chocolate mousse recipe. Hundreds of species of cocoa grow in Brazil and much of the crop is exported to foreign chocolate companies (which dilute its rich natural taste with milk and vanilla), but some is retained to make native Brazilian treats like *brigadeiros*. These are truffles made with condensed milk, resulting in a brownie-esque texture. Divine.

Brazil's image—from Carnival to favelas and the "beans, samba and dancing mulattas" to which Samantha Aquim referred—is only one side of the story, a caricature. Returning to Oswald de Andrade, Brazil may have cannibalized other cultures as a strategic vehicle to furthering its own but, as I hope the recipes below will convince you, it's high time it fed upon its native delicacies. With such a rich heritage and landscape offering diverse culinary opportunities, Brazil is definitely one to watch.

**PANTRY LIST** • coriander • *colorau* (like sweet paprika) • coconut milk • cassava • manioc flour • dried beef (salt cured or sun dried) • *bacalhau* • freshwater fish in the north, saltwater fish on the coast (grouper, snapper, mahimahi) • black and brown beans • *dulce de leche*

• • •

# • BLACK BEAN STEW •

*Feijoada*, in Portuguese, is a Brazilian staple and a typical *panelada*, designed to feed a large group. In the words of my friend Gizane Campos, who contributed this recipe, "You never make *feijoada* for just two people—it is a very rich dish and should be enjoyed with a good group of friends over a lingering lunch—better on a Saturday or Sunday when you can take a siesta afterwards!" As with all stews, the leftovers make a great dinner or lunch next day, too. You can find all the authentic ingredients in Portuguese or Brazilian shops, and good alternatives for these in delis and supermarkets. Gizane suggests serving *feijoada* with some finely sliced spring greens, onion and garlic sautéed together for five minutes or so, as well as boiled rice and some slices of orange.

## • SERVES 8–10 •

2¼ lb dried black beans
14 oz sun-dried beef, cut into pieces, or 14 oz
    smoked pork ribs
14 oz smoked bacon, cut into chunks
8 tbsp olive oil
2 onions, finely chopped
6 garlic cloves, finely chopped
10 oz large smoked sausages, cut into big chunks
    (Portuguese sausage is best, but chorizo is
    a good alternative)
10 oz small Portuguese spicy sausage or *n'duja*
    (regular sausages will suffice here if neither
    spicy versions can be found)
14 oz salted pork ribs (or any other cut of pork
    on the bone from the butcher)
1 tbsp freshly ground black pepper
5 bay leaves
1 orange, peeled, whole
1 shot of cachaça (optional, but recommended)
1 orange to serve, peeled and segmented

**1** • In separate bowls, soak the beans, the sun-dried beef or smoked pork ribs (whichever you are using) and the smoked bacon in cold water, overnight. Change the water in the morning and continue soaking to get rid of excess fat and salt.

**2 •** Drain the beans and put them into a very large saucepan of cold water. Bring to a boil over medium heat, then simmer for 30 minutes until tender.

**3 •** Rinse the soaked sun-dried beef (or smoked pork ribs) and smoked bacon well, add to the beans and cook for another 30 minutes.

**4 •** Meanwhile, heat a very large, heavy saucepan over medium heat and pour in the olive oil, so it entirely covers the bottom of the pan. Add the onions and garlic and cook until softened. Add the sausages, salted pork ribs, pepper and bay leaves. Pour in the cooked beans and meat and top up with water to cover them. Place the peeled orange in the center of the pot. Let the stew simmer for 1½–2 hours or more, topping up with water as necessary, until the meat falls off the bone. Just before serving, fish out the bay leaves, add a shot of cachaça and serve with the orange segments.

# • SHRIMP STEW •

This recipe comes from chef Samantha Aquim—and, true to the ethos of the typical one-pot *panelada* feeding a large family, you'll see that this recipe deals in large quantities. Known in Portugese as *bobó de camarao*, and sometimes referred to as shrimp bobó in English, this is a dish of shrimp in a purée of manioc (cassava) meal, coconut milk and vegetables. Like many similar dishes, it is flavored with palm oil, called *dendê* in Brazilian Portuguese, and is traditionally served with white rice, but may also be treated as a stand-alone side dish. Shrimp bobó is one of the many iconic recipes from the Bahia region of Brazil, which is known for its Afro-Brazilian characteristics. You can find cassava in almost all ethnic markets (and some supermarkets) and palm oil is available online. If this is too tricky to get hold of, however, just use sunflower oil.

## • SERVES 8–10 •

2¼ lb cassava, peeled and cut into wedges
2 cups coconut milk
2¼ lb fresh prawns, descaled and cleaned
4 tbsp palm oil (or sunflower oil)
sea salt and freshly ground black pepper
3 tbsp extra virgin olive oil
1 white or yellow onion, thinly sliced
3 garlic cloves, finely chopped
½ small yellow bell pepper, deseeded and sliced lengthways

½ small red bell pepper, deseeded and sliced lengthways
2¼ lb tomatoes, peeled and diced
flat-leaf parsley and coriander to serve, chopped
scallions to serve, chopped

**1** • Boil the cassava in salted water for 20 minutes or so, until soft (as you would boil potatoes), then drain and transfer to a blender, blend it with the coconut milk and set aside.

**2** • Briefly fry the prawns (in batches if necessary) on high heat in 2 tablespoons of the palm oil or sunflower oil with some salt and pepper, then transfer to a bowl and put to one side.

**3** • Heat the olive oil in a frying pan and sauté the onion for about 30 seconds, then add the garlic and bell peppers and sauté for another 5 minutes or so. When all the ingredients have softened, add the tomatoes and sauté the mixture together until the liquid has been reduced.

**4** • Add the rest of the palm oil and stir for a few minutes to ensure it is well distributed. To this, add the cassava and coconut milk mixture and simmer for 2–3 minutes. The consistency should be creamy, but if it is too dense, then add some more coconut milk.

**5** • Add the prawns, season to taste and garnish with fresh herbs and scallions before serving.


# • INTENSE CHOCOLATE MOUSSE
# WITH CACAO NIBS •

This light but indulgent dessert comes from Brazilian chef and chocolate guru, Samantha Aquim. It has had my family in ecstasy on several occasions. It's also very easy to make, provided you have access to cacao nibs which, failing all else, are readily available online and in some supermarkets.

## • SERVES 4 •

2½ oz dark chocolate (at least 70 percent cocoa solids)
2 large egg whites
2½ tbsp superfine sugar
14 tbsp heavy cream
¾ oz cacao nibs, plus extra to garnish

**1** • In a bowl placed over a saucepan of simmering water, melt the chocolate. Let it cool down to room temperature for 15 minutes or so, without letting it harden again.

**2** • In a different bowl, whisk together the egg whites with the sugar for 5 minutes until tripled in volume and light and fluffy. Whisk in the melted chocolate and then the cream.

**3** • Stir in the cacao nibs, transfer to one large serving bowl or four individual bowls, sprinkle with a few nibs to garnish and put in the fridge to set for an hour before serving.

# ARGENTINA

The city kept reminding me of Russia, the cars of the secret police bristling with aerials; women with splayed haunches licking ice cream in dusty parks; the same bullying statues; the pie-crust architecture, the same avenues that were not quite straight, giving the illusion of endless space and leading out into nowhere . . .
• BRUCE CHATWIN, *In Patagonia* •

Bruce Chatwin's Buenos Aires is a mass of contradictions, serious yet silly to the point where the "splayed haunches," "bullying statues" and "pie-crust architecture" become cartoonlike. His experience of the city is in stark contrast to the Patagonian wilderness, perhaps a more familiar image of Argentina in its vastness and harshness: "We fixed on Patagonia as the safest place on earth. I pictured a low timber house with a shingled roof, caulked against storms, with blazing log fires inside and the walls lined with all the best books, somewhere to live when the rest of the world blew up."

Chatwin's telling of his Argentine journey, with all its contradictions, in fact exposes a truth about this country at the tip of South America, stretching up over two thousand miles from its Patagonian hinterland (described as "the uttermost part of earth" by Chatwin), through central grasslands of grazing cattle and up to its Andean borders with Bolivia, Peru, Chile, Brazil. Perhaps more than anywhere else in Latin America, visitors to Argentina are struck by the collision of old and new worlds, of Europeans and indigenous Americans, and the unique culture these—sometimes contradictory—influences have borne. Very little of Argentina is not enclosed by ocean or mountain range; it was the former that brought so many thousands of Europeans in the first half of the twentieth century and the latter—the Andes—which stopped them drifting farther west into the neighboring countries. Argentina is a haven of hybridity, remarkable for its diversity, from its population to its landscapes and with a cuisine that mirrors both.

Argentina's population looks and sounds very different from that of Chile next door. Most Argentines can trace some Italian, Spanish, French or

German ancestry within the last couple of generations. Around half of the Argentine population, for example, is estimated to be of Italian descent, indicated by the lilting accent with which Spanish is spoken, Italian surnames[*] and a widespread appetite for pizza and *helado* (ice cream). *La fugazza* is a favorite variety of pizza, topped with charred white onion, mozzarella and Parmesan, while the signature Argentine ice cream comes in *dulce de leche* flavor—a distinctly Argentine character (the super sweet and sticky caramel spread made from condensed milk is ubiquitous) applied to traditional European recipes.

But let's cut to the chase. It's not with pizza or ice cream which we instinctively associate Argentina, is it? No, it's steak, or the Sunday *asado* (barbecue) culture of dripping, bloody, voluptuous, fleshy cow crackling against a grill flame, left ever so slightly rare in the center and guzzled with Malbec wine. (Indeed, steak and Malbec make ideal bed partners and they are together Argentina's most exported edible items.) Yes, steak has been synonymous with Argentina since the middle of the twentieth century, conjuring romantic images of the equestrian Argentine—first gauchos, now polo players—which moneyed foreigners buy into. Edible aspiration. In *The Motorcycle Diaries*, Ernesto "Che" Guevara alludes to the Argentine diet as an altogether more "extravagant" affair when compared with the other Andean cuisines from which he and Alberto Granado will be eating on the rest of their trip.[†] Argentine food is the stuff of "kingly consumption."

Although steak is found all over Argentina, it is most closely associated with La Pampa, a vast three hundred thousand square miles of grassland in the country's center—just beside Buenos Aires. Plentiful space and rich grasses make this a fantastic roaming ground for some of the world's best beef cattle, which the Argentines shape into a range of steaks and offal by-products now enjoyed all over the world (nowhere more so than in Argentina itself, where vegetarians are a rarity and the average person consumes about 129 pounds of beef per year).[‡] Diego Jacquet, the Argentine chef patron of London's West

• • • •

[*] A nice example of this is the famous winery, Luigi Bosca. "Luigi" himself apparently never existed, but this archetypal Italian moniker was chosen to appeal to the hordes of Italians descending on Argentina at the start of the twentieth century.

[†] Starting in Buenos Aires, Guevara and Granado traveled through the Andes, the Atacama Desert, the Amazon basin and up to the Caribbean on a single motorbike, covering over five thousand miles of South American soil and witnessing how both the terrain and the lives of the people changed from one country, climate and culture to another.

[‡] According to the *New York Times*, the Argentines ate an average of 129 pounds of beef per person in 2012. That's more than double America's 57.5 pounds per person. Nevertheless, this is a sharp decline from Argentina's 222 pounds per person at its peak of consumption in 1956.

End restaurant Zoilo, says of Pampa beef, "It's definitely one of the best meats in the world. The texture is amazing because the cows have so much space to roam around in—their muscles can burn the fat in a unique way."

When Argentines go to a *parilla* (a traditional barbecue restaurant) or make an *asado* at home, they often eat meat and little else—baffling to a European, albeit a fallen vegetarian like myself—but there's no shortage of variety. Big *asados* are things of horrific beauty, mosaics of flesh, from hunks of tenderloin or slow-cooked rib-eye steak to twists of sausage (morcilla blood sausage or chorizo, often enjoyed alongside a wedge of melted cheese known as *provoleta*), *mollejas* (sweetbreads) and a whole host of offal. (Clearly "nose to tail eating" isn't the ethical choice or fashionable fad in Argentina that it is in the U.S. and the UK, but rather a cultural mainstay.) You can eat this stuff seriously bloody, brown or with infinite degrees of pink stripe running through it.

All this is usually served with two sauces, *chimichurri* and *salsa criolla*. The former is typically Argentine and contains olive oil, fresh oregano and parsley, garlic and chili. In Buenos Aires they include tomato sauce whereas in mountainous regions like Mendoza, they might add some *tomillo* (thyme) or *romero* (rosemary) while *salsa criolla* crops up in various guises all over South America—you'll find a sauce with the same name in Peru, for example. In Argentina it contains white onion, tomato, mild chili and oil. Diego Jacquet has contributed his recipe for *chimichurri* on page 346, guiding you to make and eat steak like a gaucho.

Though Argentine meat is of exemplary quality, it has somewhat eclipsed the country's other, more regionally based, cuisines on the world stage and Argentine cooking is more nuanced than *asado* culture would suggest. Patagonia in the south and Salta in the north both have their own particular cuisines, from distinct dishes to regional variations on national recipes. *Empanadas* are an example: essentially they are little envelopes of pastry holding *carne* (beef), cheese (a combination of a soft cheese and a stretchy white cheese that the Argentines call "mozzarella") or, in Patagonia, fish, seafood and mushrooms. The proportions of meat will vary from region to region. In Buenos Aires, for instance, you'll find roughly double the quantity of meat to onion than you would in Mendoza,[*] where the meat and onions will typically be spiced up with some cumin—and possibly some olives and eggs, too.

••••

[*] Mendoza is both a city and a region in western Argentina, which borders Chile. Its cuisine might lack definition but its wines do not. This is the Argentine wine country, internationally famed for its bold Malbecs oozing notes of blackberries, violets and vanilla. Irrigated and cultivated, the land here is just as suited to great vegetables (like bright juicy tomatoes) as it is to vines.

Like *empanadas*, you can find tamales all over South America, once again with differences from country to country. In Argentina they are an Andean specialty, concentrated around the northern regions of Salta and Jujuy, which borders Chile and Bolivia. These little parcels of corn dough (called *masa de maiz*—the same corn base that's used for tortillas elsewhere in the Americas) contain shredded meat—lamb, beef or pork—wrapped in a maize leaf and boiled or steamed. Meanwhile, *humitas* are similar to tamales, combining fresh corn, onions, green and red bell peppers, spices (and sometimes some cheese or chicken) all wrapped in a corn husk and baked in the oven. The texture of cooked *masa* is distinctively Andean—slightly starchy, coarser than polenta but fine enough to create a sticky dough.

Northern Argentina perhaps has the country's most distinctive cuisine, reflecting a harder lifestyle than people experience in the Pampa: extreme weather conditions, rugged mountains and poor irrigation. Stews and single-pot dishes offer practical, sustaining meals and include *carbonada* (beef, corn, potatoes and fruit such as peaches and pears, all served in a gutted pumpkin) and *locro*—the most famous of Argentine stews. Resembling a Spanish *cocido*, *locro* contains meat, bacon, sausage, pumpkin, corn and grains—a hearty, complete meal loaded with local ingredients in just one pan.

The only fish found all over Argentina is the relatively popular rainbow trout (*trucha*), which is usually farmed in artificial lakes. This can be baked, grilled, fried or cooked *en papillote* (wrapped up in local seasoning and some vegetables). Given that both countries have long coastlines, it is initially surprising that the Argentines eat relatively little fish compared with their Chilean neighbors.[*] Then again, Argentine culture has developed around the gaucho brand and a set of beef rituals—the Sunday *asados,* the *parrillas* and *choripan* stalls[†]—that are hardwired in most people's dietary choices.

Patagonian cuisine is the least quintessentially South American food in Argentina—that is to say, it is neither typically Andean nor steak-based—and has been molded to the limitations and bounties of a harsher climate. Lamb, wild boar and foraged foods such as mushrooms and berries are reminiscent of Scandinavian and German cuisines and point to the presence of different immigrant communities than you find elsewhere in the country.

• • • •

[*] Chile is bordered along one entire length by the Pacific, a rich source of fish and seafood such as razor clams, scallops and lobster—all of which are eaten in dishes from the west of the continent. Quite apart from the abundance of seafood, though, Chile simply doesn't have the landmass to cultivate cattle on an Argentine scale.

[†] Chorizo sausage in simple bread with *chimichurri* sold ubiquitously at Buenos Aires soccer matches and from street food stalls in parks.

In Patagonia the *terroirs* change and the cultural influences on gastronomy take a shift away from the Italian toward those of central and northern European. Aside from game and preserves, other dishes include Andean fondue, strudel and crêpes made with forest berries. The soil is ideally suited to the cultivation of Pinot Noir grapes and there are some stunning wines produced in the region.

Maté, the caffeinated hot drink beloved of Argentines (and Uruguayans, to an even more fanatical degree), is consumed all day and throughout the year. It is made from the leaves of yerba maté, an evergreen tree native to South America, which are dried, powdered and, when added to a vessel (also known as a maté), stewed in hot water. This brew is then sucked through a metal straw called a *bombilla* and, with subsequent top-ups of water, the contents gradually become more diluted. Personally, I prefer maté with a little sugar, though this would of course horrify die-hard maté fans. (I do understand. I'm a terrible snob about sugar in tea.) Maté or coffee might accompany a breakfast of bread with *dulce de leche* or an *alfajor*—an Argentine cookie not dissimilar from shortbread. These can have various flavorings but, most classically, two pieces of cookie sandwich a smooth filling of—you guessed it—*dulce de leche*.

Though there is more to Argentine cuisine than meets the eye—cooking with banana leaves and cornmeal takes some practice, not to mention access to those ingredients—I'd suggest keeping things easy on your maiden voyage to the Argentine kitchen, investing in a large quantity of really good skirt steak and fresh herbs to make an *asado* meal for your own simple "kingly consumption" alongside a glass of good Malbec. If you're feeling more adventurous, you could try making your own *dulce de leche* with Maricel Presilla's recipe (see page 347), perhaps even crafting it into ice cream for a glorious caramel kick (and lick whenever you need one). Just keep your haunches unsplayed!

**PANTRY LIST** • steak • trout • quinoa • white cheese (*provoleta*, mozzarella and Parmesan imitations) • blood sausage (morcilla) • sweetbreads • white corn • mild chili • *dulce de leche*

• • •

# • GRILLED SKIRT STEAK WITH CHIMICHURRI, GARLIC AND TOMATOES •

Here is Diego Jacquet's simple steak recipe with Argentina's signature sauce, the *chimichurri*. Like all uncomplicated dishes, its simplicity demands ingredients of superlatively high quality. There's no point in making it if you don't find a fantastic cut of beef skirt. Thereafter, monitor its (brief) phase over heat—coals, griddle or otherwise—to make sure the meat is *al punto* (just right) by your own standards. I like mine medium rare. If you can, make the *chimichurri* in advance as you will get a better flavor—the earlier the better.

## • SERVES 6 •

FOR THE CHIMICHURRI
6 garlic cloves, finely chopped
¼ cup flat-leaf parsley, finely chopped
1½ tbsp oregano, finely chopped
4 scallions, finely chopped
1½ tsp chili flakes
1 tsp paprika
juice of 2 lemons
3 tbsp balsamic vinegar
2 tbsp extra virgin olive oil
sea salt and freshly ground black pepper

FOR THE STEAKS
6 plum tomatoes, cut in half
3 garlic cloves, finely chopped
3 tbsp extra virgin olive oil
sea salt and freshly ground black pepper
3 skirt beef steaks, trimmed (about 14 oz each)

**1** • To make the chimichurri, combine the garlic, parsley, oregano, scallions, chili, paprika, lemon juice, and vinegar in a bowl, mix well and let sit at room temperature for an hour. Whisk in two tablespoons of olive oil and season with sea salt and black pepper; mix again and set aside at room temperature to allow the flavors to marry.
**2** • Put the tomatoes in a bowl with the garlic and enough olive oil to coat them thoroughly. Season with sea salt and pepper and let rest overnight in a cool space. I prefer not to refrigerate because I think it compromises the flavor of the tomatoes.

**3 •** Take the meat out of the fridge and allow it to come to room temperature for an hour or two. Don't season it before cooking; it's better to do it while it's cooking.
**4 •** If you are using a barbecue, preheat for 20 minutes or so before cooking. Alternatively, preheat a griddle pan over medium-high heat. Start by barbecuing or griddling your tomatoes on a low heat in a griddle pan, until they get lovely char marks—about 6–8 minutes. Then barbecue or griddle the steaks in the middle of the grill or pan for 4 minutes per side, seasoning as the meat is turned, until well charred. Once done, cover with foil and let it rest for 5 minutes—the meat will continue to cook and will finish to a medium cooked steak. If you prefer a rarer steak, opt for 2–3 minutes per side and for a well-done steak try 5 minutes per side.
**5 •** To finish, slice the steaks into diagonal strips cutting against the grain, transfer to a big platter with the grilled tomatoes and drizzle with large amounts of *chimichurri*.

# • DULCE DE LECHE •

The crude way of making *dulce de leche* is to boil a can of condensed milk in a pan of water, but the authentically Argentine way is almost as easy and reaps superior results that will delight adults and children alike at dessert time. This is Maricel Presilla's recipe from *Gran Cocina Latina*. Maricel learned to make it from an old woman in the northeast of Argentina, a region in which an old *criollo* cuisine lives on. Her tip was to caramelize some of the sugar before adding the milk, for a deep, rich dark color. Maricel is emphatic that this is not a recipe that you can abandon while it is cooking—you need to keep a close eye on it, especially toward the end—and recommends using a candy thermometer if you have one, cooking the sauce to no more than 225°F. For a variation on this recipe, try making a Mexican *cajeta* by using a combination of cow's milk and goat's milk and do not cook past a temperature of 222°F, for a more fluid texture.

## • MAKES 6 CUPS •

5⅓ cups superfine sugar
16¾ cups whole milk
1 vanilla pod, split lengthwise in half
1 tsp baking soda

**1 •** Heat a large, heavy saucepan over medium heat for a couple of minutes. Add ¼–½ cup sugar (½ cup will give a very beautiful dark golden brown color like *café con leche*). Cook, stirring, until the sugar caramelizes to a golden color.

**2** • Watching for spatters, quickly stir in the milk along with the remaining sugar, the vanilla pod, and the baking soda. The milk will turn a light beige color.

**3** • Continue cooking, stirring occasionally, for about 1½ hours. Then start checking the pan attentively while stirring more frequently. When the mixture starts to bubble steadily, check the state of doneness by spooning some drops onto a plate to see whether they flow or stay in place, or use a candy thermometer. Make sure you wait a couple of seconds for your sample to cool a bit. If it solidifies a little, or if it has reached 225°F on the thermometer, it is done.

**4** • Have ready a heatproof medium bowl placed over another bowl filled with cracked ice and a little water. When the *dulce de leche* has achieved the desired consistency, becoming a shiny, creamy custard that is still a bit liquid, pour it into the prepared bowl to let it cool and thicken. Store, tightly covered, in a plastic or glass container at room temperature or in the refrigerator. It will last for months.

# FURTHER READING

SHOULD YOU FIND yourself particularly inspired by any of the cuisines covered in these pages, here are a few books that will help you to dig a little deeper. There's a more extensive body of work about some cuisines than others, but perhaps those lacking an extensive bibliography will make for bigger adventures . . .

## • GENERAL / MUST HAVES •

The following four titles are not about any particular world cuisine, but they are all written by people who love to eat, to cook and to make their readers laugh. They inspired me and, though by no means an exhaustive list of food writing, I'd say they are a pretty good place to start if you like wit and food erotica in equal measure.

*Home Cooking: A Writer in the Kitchen* by Laurie Colwin
(Vintage Books, 2010)
*How to Eat: The Pleasures and Principles of Good Food* by Nigella Lawson
(John Wiley, 2002)
*Kitchen Confidential* by Anthony Bourdain (Ecco, 2012)
*The Man Who Ate Everything: And Other Gastronomic Feats, Disputes,*
*and Pleasurable Pursuits* by Jeffrey Steingarten (Vintage Books, 1998)
*The Table Comes First: Family, France, and the Meaning of Food* by Adam Gopnik
(Vintage Books, 2012)
*Tender at the Bone: Growing Up at the Table* by Ruth Reichl (Random House, 2010)

## • FRANCE •

*French Provincial Cooking* by Elizabeth David (Harper & Row, 1962)
*Mastering the Art of French Cooking* by Julia Child (Random House, 1961)
*The Alice B. Toklas Cookbook* by Alice B. Toklas (Perennial, 2010)
*The Little Paris Cookbook: 120 Simple but Classic French Recipes* by Rachel Khoo
(Chronicle Books, 2013)

## • SPAIN •

*Catalan Cuisine: Europe's Last Great Culinary Secret* by Colman Andrews
(Harvard Common Press, 2006)
*The Food of Spain* by Claudia Roden (Ecco, 2011)
*1080 Recipes* by Simone and Inés Ortega (Phaidon Press, 2007)

*Barrafina: A Spanish Cookbook* by Sam Hart, Eddie Hart, and Barragan
Mohacho (Fig Tree, 2011)
*Morito* by Sam and Sam Clark (Ebury Press, 2014)

# • PORTUGAL •

*Recipes from My Portuguese Kitchen* by Miguel de Castro e Silva
(Aquamarine, 2013)
*The New Portuguese Table* by David Leite (Random House, 2010)

# • ITALY •

*Polpo: A Venetian Cookbook (of Sorts)* by Russell Norman (Bloomsbury USA, 2012)
*The Geometry of Pasta* by Caz Hildebrand and Jacob Kenedy (Quirk Books, 2010)
*The Essentials of Classic Italian Cooking* by Marcella Hazan (Alfred A. Knopf, 1992)
*The Silver Spoon* (Phaidon, 2005)
*Bocca: Cookbook* by Jacob Kenedy (Bloomsbury USA, 2011)
*Made in Italy: Food & Stories* by Giorgio Locatelli (Ecco, 2007)
*Made in Sicily* by Giorgio Locatelli (Ecco, 2011)
*Heat: An Amateur's Adventures as Kitchen Slave, Line Cook, Pasta-maker
and Apprentice to a Butcher in Tuscany* by Bill Buford (Vintage Books, 2007)
*Claudia Roden's The Food of Italy* by Claudia Roden (Steerforth Press, 2003)

# • EASTERN EUROPE •

*Purple Citrus and Sweet Perfume: Cuisine of the Eastern Mediterranean*
by Silvena Rowe (Ecco, 2011)
*The 2nd Avenue Deli Cookbook* by Sharon Lebewohl and Rena Bulkin
(Random House, 1999)

# • GERMANY •

*The German Cookbook* by Mimi Sheraton (Random House, 1980)
*Grandma's German Cookbook* by Birgit Hamm and Linn Schmidt
(Dorling Kindersley, 2012)

# • SCANDINAVIA •

*The Nordic Bakery Cookbook* by Miisa Mink (Ryland Peters and Small, 2011)
*The Scandinavian Cookbook* by Trina Hahnemann (Andrews McMeel Pub., 2009)
*Scandilicious: Secrets of Scandinavian Cooking* by Signe Johansen
(Hodder and Stoughton, 2011)
*Scandilicious Baking* by Signe Johansen (Hodder and Stoughton, 2012)

# • UNITED KINGDOM •

*English Food* by Jane Grigson (Penguin Books, 1998)
*The Complete Nose to Tail: A Kind of British Cooking*
by Fergus Henderson (Ecco, 2012)
*Jamie's Great Britain* by Jamie Oliver (Hyperion, 2011)
*Historic Heston* by Heston Blumenthal (Bloomsbury USA, 2013)

# • TURKEY •

*Arabesque: A Taste of Morocco, Turkey and Lebanon* by Claudia Roden
(Alfred A. Knopf, 2006)
*Istanbul: Recipes from the Heart of Turkey* by Rebecca Seal
(Hardie Grant Books, 2014)

# • THE LEVANT •

*Lebanese Cuisine* by Anissa Helou (St. Martin's Press, 1995)
*The Art of Syrian Cookery* by Helen Corey (Doubleday, 1962)
*Levant: Recipes and Memories from the Middle East* by Anissa Helou
(HarperCollins, 2013)
*The Lebanese Kitchen* by Salma Hage (Phaidon Press, 2012)
*Casa Moro* by Sam Clark and Sam Clark (Ebury Press, 2011)

# • ISRAEL •

*Jerusalem* by Yotam Ottolenghi and Sami Tamimi (Ten Speed Press, 2012)
*The Book of New Israeli Food* by Janna Gur (Schocken Books, 2008)
*The Book of Jewish Food* by Claudia Roden (Alfred A. Knopf, 1996)
*Honey & Co.: Food from the Middle East* by Sarit Packer and Itamar Srulovich
(Saltyard Books, 2014)

# • IRAN •

*Food of Life: Ancient Persian and Modern Iranian Cooking and Ceremonies* by Najmieh
Batmanglij (Mage Publishers, 2011)
*The Legendary Cuisine of Persia* by Margaret Shaida
(Interlink, 2002)
*Persiana: Recipes from the Middle East and Beyond* by Sabrina Ghayour
(Interlink Books, 2014)
*Pomegranates and Roses: My Persian Family Recipes* by Ariana Bundy
(Simon and Schuster, 2012)

## • INDIA •

*Madhur Jaffrey's Indian Cookery* by Madhur Jaffrey (Barron's, 1995)
*India: The Cookbook* by Pushpesh Pant (Phaidon Press, 2010)

## • THAILAND •

*Thai Food* by David Thompson (Ten Speed Press, 2002)
*Thai Street Food* by David Thompson (Ten Speed Press, 2009)
*South East Asian Food* by Rosemary Brissenden
(Penguin Books, 1972)

## • VIETNAM •

*Vietnamese Home Cooking* by Charles Phan
(Ten Speed Press, 2012)
*Into the Vietnamese Kitchen: Treasured Foodways, Modern Flavors*
by Andrea Nguyen (Ten Speed Press, 2006)
*South East Asian Food* by Rosemary Brissenden
(Penguin Books, 1972)

## • CHINA •

*Sichuan Cookery* by Fuchsia Dunlop (Penguin Books, 2003)
*Every Grain of Rice: Simple Chinese Home Cooking* by Fuchsia Dunlop
(W. W. Norton & Co., 2013)
*The Revolutionary Chinese Cookbook* by Fuchsia Dunlop (W. W. Norton, 2007)
*The Hakka Cookbook: Chinese Soulfood from Around the World* by Linda Lau
Anusasananan (University of California Press, 2012)
*The Last Chinese Chef* by Nicole Mones (Mariner, 2008)

## • KOREA •

*Seoultown Kitchen* by Debbie Lee (Kyle Books, 2011)
*Eating Korean: From Barbecue to Kimchi, Recipes from My Home*
by Cecilia Hae-Jin Lee (John Wiley & Sons, 2005)

## • JAPAN •

*Japanese Cooking: A Simple Art* by Shizuo Tsuji (Kodansha USA, 2012)
*Everyday Harumi: Simple Japanese Food* by Harumi Kurihara (Conran Octopus, 2009)
*Takashi's Noodle Book* by Takashi Yagihashi (Ten Speed Press, 2009)
*Sushi and Beyond: What the Japanese Know About Cooking* by Michael
Booth (Vintage Books, 2010)

## • ETHIOPIA •

*Ethiopian Cookbook: A Beginner's Guide* by Rachel Pambrun (CreateSpace, 2012)
*How to Cook Ethiopian Food: Simple Delicious and Easy Recipes*
by Lydia Solomon (CreateSpace, 2013)

## • WEST AFRICA •

*"My Cooking" West-African Cookbook* by Dokpe L. Ogunsanya
(Dupsy Enterprises, 1998)

## • MOROCCO •

*The Food of Morocco* by Paula Wolfert (Ecco, 2011)

## • CALIFORNIA •

*Bar Tartine: Techniques and Recipes* by Nicolaus Balla and Cortney Burns
(Chronicle Books, 2014)
*Chez Panisse Menu Cookbook* by Alice Waters (Random House, 1982)
*California Dish: What I Saw (and Cooked) at the American Culinary Revolution*
by Jeremiah Tower (Free Press, 2004)
*The Zuni Cafe Cookbook* by Judy Rodgers (W. W. Norton & Co., 2002)
*Mission Street Food: Recipes and Ideas from an Improbable Restaurant* by
Anthony Myint and Karen Leibowitz (McSweeney's, 2011)

## • LOUISIANA •

*The New Orleans Cookbook: Creole, Cajun and Louisiana French Recipes Past and Present*
by Rima Collin and Richard H. Collin (Alfred A. Knopf, 1987)
*The Little New Orleans Cookbook: Fifty-Seven Classic Creole Recipes* by Gwen McKee
and Joseph A. Arrigo (Quail Ridge Press, 1991)
*Mme Begue's Recipes of Old New Orleans Creole Cookery* by Elizabeth Begue
(Pelican Publishing Co., 2012)

## • MEXICO •

*Gran Cocina Latina* by Maricel E. Presilla (W. W. Norton & Co., 2012)
*Dos Caminos' Mexican Street Food* by Ivy Stark (Allworth Press, 2011)
*Tacos, Tortas and Tamales: Flavors from the Griddles, Pots and Street-Side Kitchens
of Mexico* by Roberto Santibañez ( John Wiley & Sons, 2012)
*The Essential Cuisines of Mexico* by Diana Kennedy
(Crown Publishing Group, 2009)

# • CARIBBEAN •

*Lucinda's Authentic Jamaican Kitchen* by Lucinda Scala Quinn
( John Wiley & Sons, 2006)
*Jerk from Jamaica: Barbecue Caribbean Style* by Helen Willinsky
(Ten Speed Press, 2007)

# • PERU •

*Ceviche: Peruvian Kitchen* by Martin Morales (Ten Speed Press, 2013)
*The Great Ceviche Book* by Douglas Rodriguez (Ten Speed Press, 2010)
*Gran Cocina Latina* by Maricel E. Presilla (W. W. Norton & Co., 2012)

# • BRAZIL •

*The Brazilian Table* by Yara Castro Roberts & Richard Roberts
(Gibbs M. Smith, 2009)
*Gran Cocina Latina* by Maricel E. Presilla (W. W. Norton & Co., 2012)
*D.O.M.: Rediscovering Brazilian Ingredients* by Alex Atala (Phaidon Press, 2013)

# • ARGENTINA •

*Gran Cocina Latina* by Maricel E. Presilla (W. W. Norton & Co., 2012)
*Latin Grilling: Recipes to Share, from Patagonian Asado to
Yucatecan Barbecue and More* by Lourdes Castro
(Ten Speed Press, 2011)

# CREDITS

## • RECIPES •

**Loire Valley**: Upside-Down Plum Cake © Eric Lanlard, from *Home Bake* (Mitchell Beazley, 2010). **Provence**: Tapenade © Justin Myers. **Catalonia**: Catalan Fish Stew; Hazelnut Soup with Hazelnut Crocanti and Ice Cream © Rachel McCormack. **Northern Spain**: Garlic Prawns and Asparagus © José Pizarro, from *Seasonal Spanish Food* (Kyle Cathie, 2010). **Central Spain**: Zucchini Cream; Tortilla © Javier Serrano Arribas. **Andalucía**: Gazpacho © José Pizarro, from *Seasonal Spanish Food* (Kyle Cathie, 2010); Salt Cod Fritters with Tartare Sauce © Nieves Barragán Mohacho. **Portugal**: Salt Cod Broth © Nuno Mendes. **Lazio**: Pasta and Chickpea Soup © Rachel Roddy; Fried Whole Artichokes © Jacob Kenedy, from *Bocca: Cookbook* (Bloomsbury, 2011). **Emilia-Romagna**: Tagliatelle Bolognese © Jacob Kenedy, from *The Geometry of Pasta* with Caz Hildebrand (Boxtree, 2010). **Calabria**: Scallops with N'duja; Spicy Chicken Calabrese © Francesco Mazzei. **Sicily**: Swordfish Messina-Style © Giorgio Locatelli, from *Made in Sicily* (Fourth Estate, 2011). **Eastern Europe**: Borscht © Emilia Brunicki; Bàbovka © Klara Cecmanova. **Turkey**: Beef Kofte © Rebecca Seal, from *Istanbul: Recipes from the Heart of Turkey* (Hardie Grant, 2013). **The Levant**: Mansaf © Yotam Ottolenghi. **Israel**: Hummus © Zac Frankel. **Iran**: Chicken with Barberries, Yogurt and Orange Peel; Lamb with Split Peas, Dried Lime and Eggplants, Chelow Rice © Pury Sharifi. **North India**: Rogan Josh © Anirudh Arora, from *Food of the Grand Trunk Road* with Hardeep Singh Kholi (New Holland, 2011). **South India**: Coconut Fish Curry; Oven Roasted Chicken Tikka with Mint Chutney; Banana Pancakes with Coconut and Jaggery © Meera Sodha, from *Made in India* (Fig Tree, 2014). **Vietnam**: Beef Pho © Hieu Trung Bui. **West Africa**: Ije's Hotpot © Ije Nwokerie. **Morocco**: Chicken Couscous © Paula Wolfert, from *Couscous and Other Good Food from Morocco* (HarperPerennial, 1987). **Mexico**: Fruity One-Chili Mole © Maricel E. Presilla, from *Gran Cocina Latina* (W. W. Norton & Co., 2012). **Brazil**: Black Bean Stew © Gizane Campos; Shrimp Stew; Intense Chocolate Mousse with Cacao Nibs © Samantha Aquim. **Argentina**: Grilled Skirt Steak with Chimichurri, Garlic and Tomatoes © Diego Jacquet; Dulce de Leche © Maricel E. Presilla, from *Gran Cocina Latina* (W. W. Norton & Co., 2012). All other recipes © Mina Holland.

## • TEXT •

Every effort has been made to trace copyright holders and obtain their permission for the use of copyright material. The publisher apologizes for any errors or omissions and would be grateful to be notified of any corrections that should be incorporated in future reprints or editions of this book.

# ACKNOWLEDGMENTS

FIRST UP, MASSIVE thanks most of all to my three lucky J's of publishing: Jenny Lord (a goddess among editors), Jon Elek (the raddest agent in town) and Jamie Byng (king of Canongate). Thank you all for believing in me and in this book.

To all the team at Canongate for your hard work in bringing *The World on a Plate* to life: Natasha Hodgson, Vicki Rutherford, Peter Adlington and Rafi Romaya.

Stateside, I'd like to thank my editor, John Siciliano, for buying into what was *The Edible Atlas*, and giving it its new American identity. I am thrilled with the outcome and it has been a joy to work with you, albeit remotely. Thanks to Nicholas Misani for my phenomenal cover design—I only wish I'd gotten to tuck into that pie after the shot. And many thanks to Emily Hartley, who has tirelessly and patiently worked with me—even when I've operated at a snail's pace—to bring this all together.

Further thanks should go to Christian Holthausen, Dorie Greenspan, Meg Zimbeck, and the whole Saltzberg-Strick clan for their support of my book in its American form. Love to you all.

I've spoken to some illustrious authorities on the cuisines covered in this book, all of whom have been incredibly generous with their time, knowledge and, in many cases, their recipes, too: Maria José Sevilla, José Pizarro, Rachel McCormack, Nieves Barragán Mohacho, Nuno Mendes, Jacob Kenedy, Russell Norman, Francesco Mazzei, Giorgio Locatelli, Rachel Roddy, Signe Johansen, Anissa Helou, Rebecca Seal, Yotam Ottolenghi, Pury Sharifi, Meera Sodha, Anirudh Arora, Hieu Trung Bui, Junya Yamasaki, John Devitt, Veronica Binfor, Paula Wolfert, Colman Andrews, Maricel Presilla, Martin Morales, Samantha Aquim, Herve Roy and Diego Jacquet.

Huge thanks to all their kind representatives who took the trouble to set up meetings between us: Gemma Bell, Hannah Norris, Zoe Haldane, Sarah Kemp, Clare Lattin, Lauryn Cooke, Anna Dickinson, Beau Limbrick, Rose McCullough, Kimberley Brown, Sophie Missing, Jean Egbunike, Charlotte Allen, Genevieve Sweet, Nicola Lando, Emma Daly and Caroline Craig.

To the friends who have filled a variety of roles ranging from early reader and recipe contributor/tester to eating companion and emotional crutch: Katharine Rosser, Sophie Andrews, Laura Brooke, Jessica Hopkins, Nick Carvell, Holly Jones, Petra Costandi, Ellie Davies, Gizane Campos, Harriet de Winton, Nick Taussig, Paul Van Carter, Javier Serrano Arribas, Zac Frankel, Brittany Wickes, Rebecca Gregory, Kate Willman, Sophie Mathewson, Charlotte Coats, Amy Baddeley, Katy Gault, Klara Cecmanova, Christian Holthausen, Georgia Frost, Doon Mackichan, Mary Myers, Justin Myers, Ann Boyer, Lara Boyer, Katia Boyer McDonnell, Emilia Brunicki, Deena Carter, Tony Carter, Claire Carter Scott, Meredith Sloane, Ije Nwokerie, Howard Josephs, Jonathan Harris, Laura Hirons, Jacqui Church, Kira Heuer, Janet Tarasofsky, Felicia Kozak and Lily Saltzberg. Thank you all for your encouragement and for giving me positive energy when I needed it most.

To my employers and colleagues at *Observer Food Monthly*—Allan Jenkins, Gareth Grundy and Helen Wigmore—and the whole team at the *Observer* for all your support.

To the Holland and Cozens-Hardy clans for being super relatives. Firstly, to the grandmothers to whom this book is dedicated—my "food Granny" Jane, who first awakened my love of cooking (and gluttony) and "book Granny" Mavis, who was alive long enough to see the dedication. To my brother Max for never failing to make me laugh when I needed to. To Frank for being a sounding board and needing the walkies that got me away from my computer and, most of all, to my tirelessly brilliant Mum and Dad. Just so, so much. Love to you all.

# INDEX

Recipes are in **bold**.

cabbage (cont.)
   and Eastern Europe, 121
   **Kimchi (Korea), 254**
   **Sauerkraut (Germany), 133**
   **Savoy Cabbage and Caraway Seed**
     **(Germany), 131**
Cajun cuisine (Louisiana), 304, 305
cakes:
   **Almond Cake (Portugal), 81**
   **Bàbovka (Czech Republic), 125**
   **Danish Dream Cake (Scandinavia), 140**
   and Eastern Europe, 122
   and Rhône-Alpes (France), 35
   and Scandinavia, 136
   **Upside-Down Plum Cake (Loire Valley), 31**
   and the United Kingdom, 147
Calabria (Italy), 100–4, 106
California, 4, 297–302
Calvados, 23, 24
Canton see Guangdong province
Caribbean, the 280, 319–25
Catalonia (Spain), 51–7, 69
Cây Tre (restaurant), 231
Central Spain, 63–7, 69
Ceviche (restaurant), 326
Chang, David, 3, 250n
cheese:
   **Baked Camembert (Normandy), 24**
   and France, 22, 23, 29, 34–5
   and Italy, 87–8, 95, 102n, 107
   and the Levant, 169
   and North India, 205
   and Northern Spain, 59–60
Chez Panisse (restaurant), 298n, 299
chicken:
   **Chicken Couscous (Morocco), 288**
   **Chicken Gumbo (Louisiana), 307**
   **Chicken Soup (Eastern Europe), 124**
   **Chicken with Barberries, Yogurt and Orange**
     **Peel (Iran), 189**
   and Eastern Europe, 120
   and Guangdong province (China), 241
   **Ije's Hotpot (West Africa), 280**
   **Jerk Chicken (Caribbean), 323**
   and Louisiana, 306
   and Mexico, 314
   **Oven Roasted Chicken Tikka with Mint**
     **Chutney (South India), 216**
   and Rhône-Alpes (France), 34
   **Spicy Chicken Calabrese (Calabria), 104**
chickpeas:
   **Chickpea Stew (Ethiopia), 274**

hummus, 166–7, 179
   **Hummus (Israel), 180**
   and the Levant, 169
   **Pasta and Chickpea Soup (Lazio), 90**
   and Sicily, 107
   and Spain, 64, 65, 69
Chifa cuisine (Peru), 327
Child, Julia, 22, 24
chilies, 266–9
   **Fruity One-Chili Mole (Mexico), 316**
   and Italy, 101, 102, 107n
   and Mexico, 313
   and Sichuan province (China), 245
   and South India, 213
   and Thailand, 222, 223
   and Turkey, 160
China, 222, 228–9, 230, 235–8, 257, 321; see also
     Guangdong province; Sichuan province
chocolate, 53n, 157
   and Brazil, 336
   **Intense Chocolate Mousse with Cacao Nibs**
     **(Brazil), 339**
   and Mexico, 314–15
chutney:
   **Oven Roasted Chicken Tikka with Mint**
     **Chutney (South India), 216**
   and South India, 214
cider, 22, 23, 60
Cinnamon Club (restaurant), 213–14
coconut:
   and Brazil, 335
   **Coconut Fish Curry (South India), 215**
   milk, 224
   and South India, 213
coffee (Ethiopia), 271
Colwin, Laurie, 1–2, 7, 142, 146, 147, 306
corn, 239, 310
   and Argentina, 344
   **BBQ Corn on the Cob with Jalapeño Butter**
     **(California), 301**
   **Buttermilk Corn Bread (Louisiana), 308**
   and Louisiana, 306
   *tortilla* (Mexico), 312
couscous (Morocco), 284, 285–6
   **Chicken Couscous (Morocco), 288**
Creole cuisine, 304, 305, 327
cucumber:
   **Cucumber and Mint Raita (North**
     **India), 210**
   **Pickled Cucumber Salad (Scandinavia), 139**
curry, 78, 155, 157, 200–1, 204, 206, 207, 208,
   212, 214–15

Coconut Fish Curry (South India), 215
and Japan, 258
Oven Roasted Chicken Tikka with Mint
Chutney (South India), 216
Rogan Josh (North India), 210
Thai Vegetable Curry (Thailand), 225
and Thailand, 223, 224
and the United Kingdom, 145, 147
Czech Republic, 119, 121, 122

Dagdeviren, Musa, 162
David, Elizabeth, 40, 41, 145, 221
desserts:
baklava (Turkey), 161
Banana Pancakes with Coconut and Jaggery
(South India), 218
Bread and Butter Pudding (United
Kingdom), 151
and Eastern Europe, 122
and France, 29, 35
Hazelnut Soup with Hazelnut Crocanti and
Ice Cream (Catalonia), 56
Intense Chocolate Mousse with Cacao Nibs
(Brazil), 339
knafeh (the Levant), 169
Peaches in White Wine (Sicily), 111
picarones (Peru), 329
and Portugal, 78–9
and Sicily, 107
and the United Kingdom, 147–8
Dickens, Charles, 146n, 148
dips:
Baba Ghanoush (the Levant), 173
Guacamole (Mexico), 315
Hummus, 166–7, 179
Hummus (Israel), 180
and Iran, 188
Muhammara (the Levant), 174
D.O.M. (restaurant), 333
dum cooking (North India), 206
dumplings:
bánh cuon (Vietnam), 230
dim sum (China), 241
and Eastern Europe, 131
wontons (Sichuan province), 245–6
Dunlop, Fuchsia, 241, 246

Eastern Europe, 118–26, 129
eggplants:
Baba Ghanoush (the Levant), 173
Lamb with Split Peas, Dried Lime and
Eggplants (Iran), 190

eggs:
and Portugal, 79
scotch eggs (United Kingdom), 143n
Shakshuka (Israel), 192
Tortilla (Central Spain), 67
Egypt, 179, 284
El Bulli (restaurant), 20, 136
Elkano (restaurant), 59
Emilia-Romagna (Italy), 94–9
equipment, 7–9
Escoffier, Auguste, 20
Ethiopia, 157, 260–5

fermentation, 252
Fino (restaurant), 49
fish:
and Argentina, 344
and Brazil, 336
Cantonese Steamed Fish (Guangdong
province), 242
Catalan Fish Stew, 55
Ceviche (Peru), 330
Coconut Fish Curry (South India), 215
and Eastern Europe, 121
fish and chips, 146n, 147
and France, 23–4, 29
garum, 87, 102
and Guangdong province (China), 241
and India, 207, 213, 214–15
and Italy, 101, 107–8, 114–15
and Korea, 251–2
and Mexico, 314
and Peru, 327–8
and Portugal, 78
and Scandinavia, 137
and Spain, 54, 69
sushi (Japan), 256–7
Swordfish Messina-style (Sicily), 110
and Thailand, 222, 223–4
and Turkey, 161–2
and the United Kingdom, 146–7
and West Africa, 279–80
see also anchovies; salmon; salt cod;
sardines; seafood
France, 2, 19–21, 228, 229, 230–1, 304, 305
wine, 16–17
see also Loire Valley; Normandy; Provence;
Rhône-Alpes
Frankel, Zac, 178, 180
fruit:
ackee (Jamaica), 322
Apple Tart Normande (Normandy), 25

fruit *(cont.)*
    **Banana Pancakes with Coconut and Jaggery
      (South India), 218**
    barberries (Iran), 186–7
    breadfruit (Caribbean), 322
    and Ethiopia, 271
    and France, 23, 28, 29
    **Green Papaya Salad (Vietnam), 232**
    and Italy, 87, 101–2, 106, 108
    and the Levant, 170
    and Morocco, 286–7
    **Peaches in White Wine (Sicily), 111**
    plantain, 278, 322
    and Portugal, 78
    **Preserved Lemons (Morocco), 290**
    and Scandinavia, 136
    and South India, 213, 215
    and Spain, 53, 59
    and Thailand, 222–3
    **Upside-Down Plum Cake (Loire Valley), 31**
    and the United Kingdom, 148
    *see also* apples
*fufu* (West Africa), 278, 279, 281

game (Louisiana), 305
garlic, 241, 246, 257
    **Garlic Prawns and Asparagus Salad
      (Northern Spain), 62**
Germany, 119, 120, 127–34
ginger:
    and Japan, 257
    and India, 204, 207, 213, 214
    and Thailand, 223
Goa (South India), 214, 215, 222
grape varieties, 14–18
Grigson, Jane, 146
Guangdong province (China), 227, 228, 230–3, 317

ham, 65–6, 69, 95, 143
Hanamaru (restaurant), 260
Hand and Flowers (restaurant), 144, 145
Hansen, Anna, 161
Hazan, Marcella, 84, 85
Helou, Anissa, 2, 167, 169
herbs:
    and Brazil, 336
    and Calabria (Italy), 102
    and Catalonia (Spain), 52
    and China, 241
    and Germany, 129
    and Iran, 186
    and the Levant, 168, 170

and Provence (France), 41
and Scandinavia, 137n
and Sicily, 108
and Thailand, 223
and Vietnam, 230–1
Hieu Trung Bui, 231, 233
Hungary, 119, 120

ice cream, 102–3, 342
India, 190–2, 257, 321; *see also* North India;
    South India
indigenous communities, 296
ingredients, 10–11
Iran, 170, 184–93
Israel, 161, 166, 167, 177–83, 184, 287
Italy 84–5; *see also* Calabria; Emilia-Romagna;
    Lazio; Sicily; Veneto

Jacquet, Diego, 342–3, 346
Jaffrey, Madhur, 203, 204
Jamaica, 278n, 320, 321–2
Japan, 228, 250, 256–63, 327
Jewish influences:
    and Central Spain, 64
    and Eastern Europe, 118–19, 120
    and Israel, 177, 178–80
    and Lazio (Italy), 89–90
    and North India, 209
    and Scandinavia, 136
José (restaurant), 65

Kashmir (North India), 204
Kenedy, Jacob, 84, 86, 88, 89, 96
Kerala (South India), 212, 213, 214–15, 222
Kerridge, John, 144–5
Korea, 250–5
Koya (restaurant), 259

lamb:
    **Lamb with Split Peas, Dried Lime and
      Eggplants (Iran), 190**
    **Mansaf (the Levant), 175**
    and North India, 204, 206
    **Rogan Josh (North India), 210**
L' Anima (restaurant), 84, 101, 102
Lawson, Nigella, 3, 85, 144, 223
Lazio (Italy), 54, 86–93
Lebanon, 166, 167, 170, 184, 185
lemons, 286–7
    **Preserved Lemons (Morocco), 290**
L'Enclume (restaurant), 145
Levant, the, 161, 166–76

spices (cont.)
    and China, 197, 244, 245
    *dukkah* (Egypt), 199
    and Germany, 130
    and India, 197, 198, 201–2, 209, 212–4
    and Iran, 185, 186, 197
    and Italy, 101, 114
    and Japan, 257–8
    and Louisiana, 305
    and Mexico, 314
    *pimentón*, 50, 51, 63, 64, 69
    *ras el hanout* (Morocco), 198, 286
    and Vietnam, 229
    and West Africa, 199, 279
    *za'atar* (the Levant), 168, 171, 198
    *see also* chilies; ginger
spinach: **Soused Spinach Salad**
    **(Japan), 263**
Spotted Pig (restaurant), 147
*ssam* eating (Korea), 250, 251, 252
stews:
    and Argentina, 344
    **Black Bean Stew (Brazil), 337**
    Catalan Fish Ştew, 55
    **Chicken Gumbo (Louisiana), 307**
    **Chicken with Barberries, Yogurt and**
        **Orange Peel (Iran), 189**
    **Chickpea Stew (Ethiopia), 274**
    and Eastern Europe, 118, 120, 121
    and Ethiopia, 272–3
    **Gomen Stew (Ethiopia), 275**
    **Ije's Hotpot (West Africa), 280**
    *khoresht* (Iran), 187
    **Lamb with Split Peas, Dried Lime and**
        **Eggplants (Iran), 190**
    and Louisiana, 305–6
    **Not-Quite-Cassoulet (Rhône-Alpes), 37**
    *paneladas* (Brazil), 334–5, 336
    and Portugal, 77
    **Shrimp Stew (Brazil), 338**
    and Spain, 54, 64
    and West Africa, 279
    *see also* tagines
stir-frying, 222, 236, 237
Stockpot (restaurant), 142n
sugar, 154–5, 156
    palm, 222–3
Sukiyabashi Jiro (restaurant), 257
sushi (Japan), 256–7
swordfish: **Swordfish Messina-style**
    **(Sicily), 110**
Syria, 167, 170

tagines, 284, 285, 286
    **Pumpkin "Tagine"' (Morocco), 289**
tamarind (Thailand), 222
tandoor cooking (North India), 204–5, 206·
*tava* grilling (North India), 204, 206
tea, 143, 209, 237, 240–1
Thailand, 220–7, 257
Thompson, David, 220, 222
tofu (Japan), 259
tomatoes:
    **Gazpacho (Andalucía), 71**
    pasta sauce, 84–5
    **Tomato Salsa (Mexico), 316**
    **Ultimate Tomato Sauce (Lazio), 93**
Tonks, Mitch, 146
**Tortilla (Central Spain), 67**
Trinidad, 319, 320, 321
Tunisia, 178, 179, 284, 287
Turkey, 158–65, 170, 184, 185

umami, 252
    and China, 236, 241
    and Italy, 87, 102
    and Japan, 258–9
    and Thailand, 223

vanilla, 157, 314
vegetables:
    **Bubble and Squeak (United Kingdom), 150**
    and the Caribbean, 322
    cassava, 276, 278
    and China, 241, 246
    *eshkeneh* (Iran), 187
    and Ethiopia, 271–2, 273
    **Fried Whole Artichokes (Lazio), 92**
    **Garlic Prawns and Asparagus (Northern**
        **Spain), 62**
    **Gomen Stew (Ethiopia), 275**
    and India, 208, 213, 214, 215
    and Italy, 87, 102, 108, 113–14
    and the Levant, 170
    and Louisiana, 305
    **Muhammara (the Levant), 174**
    **Padrón Peppers (Northern Spain), 61**
    **Pea Risotto (Veneto), 117**
    and Peru, 328
    **Pumpkin "Tagine" (Morocco), 289**
    **Radicchio with Bagna Cauda (Veneto), 116**
    **Soused Spinach Salad (Japan), 263**
    and Spain, 52, 53, 59, 60
    **Stir-Fried Bok Choy (Guangdong**
        **province), 243**